Bloodroot

Winner of the 1997
Appalachian Studies Award

Bloodroot

Reflections on Place
by Appalachian
Women Writers

Joyce Dyer, Editor

The University Press of Kentucky

Publication of this volume was made possible in part by grants from the
E.O. Robinson Mountain Fund and the National Endowment for the Humanities.

Scholarly publisher for the Commonwealth,
serving Bellarmine College, Berea College, Centre
College of Kentucky, Eastern Kentucky University,
The Filson Club Historical Society, Georgetown College,
Kentucky Historical Society, Kentucky State University,
Morehead State University, Murray State University,
Northern Kentucky University, Transylvania University,
University of Kentucky, University of Louisville,
and Western Kentucky University.

Editorial and Sales Offices: The University Press of Kentucky
663 South Limestone Street, Lexington, Kentucky 40508-4008

02   01   00   99   98   5   4   3   2

Library of Congress Cataloging-in-Publication Data

Bloodroot : reflections on place by Appalachian women writers / Joyce
    Dyer, editor.
            p.   cm.
        "Winner of the 1997 Appalachian studies award"—Half t.p.
        Includes bibliographical references.
        ISBN 0–8131–2059–4 (alk. paper)
        1. American literature—Appalachian Region, Southern—History and
criticism—Theory, etc.   2. Women and literature—Appalachian
Region, Southern—History—20th century.   3. American literature—
Women authors—History and criticism—Theory, etc.   4. American
literature—Southern States—History and criticism—Theory, etc.
5. Women authors, American—Appalachian Region, Southern—Biography.
6. American literature—20th century—History and criticism.
7. Women—Appalachian Region, Southern—Intellectual life.
8. Appalachian Region, Southern—In literature.   9. Women—Southern
States—Intellectual life.   10. Southern States—In literature.
11. Regionalism in literature.   I. Dyer, Joyce.
PS286.A6B57   1998
810.9'9287'0975—dc21   97–45570

Manufactured in the United States of America

Contents

Acknowledgments

It is hard to say where an interest, or a book, begins. If we could determine that, we would know who to thank and run no risk of leaving someone out. I'm afraid, however, that this book has no clear beginning. As I think back, in some form it has always been there, just waiting. So I must start by thanking all the hundreds of people who have, over the years, fed my interest in Appalachia and Appalachian studies and kept it strong. It would be impossible to name them all, so I ask that the thanks I give below to the few individuals I am able to include might come to represent my common thanks.

Jerry Williamson, editor of *Appalachian Journal,* has certainly been one of my strongest advocates and best critics. He cares about the region deeply, about both its writers and its issues. I cannot imagine doing Appalachian scholarship without having every issue of *AJ* on my shelf to the right of my desk. For twenty-five years this publication has driven and directed Appalachian studies and research. For Jerry, the *Journal* has been a labor of love since its inception in the 1970s—but *labor,* nonetheless. It was Jerry Williamson who always knew what I was working on, who always cared to ask. He even knew what books I was reading—and invited me to review them. It was Jerry Williamson who recommended to Greenwood Press that I write the bio-bibliographical essay on Jim Wayne Miller for their volume *Contemporary Poets, Dramatists, Essayists, and Novelists of the South.*

I had already begun to talk about Miller's work in Jerry's publication, but only after I wrote the piece for Greenwood did I come to fully understand that this man, Jim Wayne Miller, would remain for the rest of his days not only one of my favorite poets but also a mentor, a great resource (a deep well of knowledge), a loyal correspondent, and a friend. Although I met Jim only once, in Boone, North Carolina, he always treated me like a neighbor. His long, elaborate, single-spaced letters to me about this project on Appalachian women writers, and other projects that preceded it, fill several notebooks. At the time, the letters were invaluable resources. Now, just a short while after his untimely death due to lung cancer in August 1996, they are treasures. Often written on yellow Xerox paper, they are gold nuggets to me.

Sandra Ballard of Carson-Newman College in Knoxville deserves more thanks than I can possibly provide, even if there were unlimited space to try. Her enthusiasm and advocacy, as well as her excellent criticism, have left a permanent impression on the pages that follow.

There are many other individuals who helped me in small but important ways, helped me with details I could never have pinned down without their guidance and expertise. These people include Frank X. Walker at the Martin Luther King Cultural Center at the University of Kentucky, Mike Mullins at Hindman Settlement School, Sidney Saylor Farr at *Appalachian Heritage,* Gurney Norman at the University of Kentucky, John Lang at Emory & Henry College, Parks Lanier and Jo Ann Asbury at Radford College, Jonathan Greene at Gnomon Press, Jane Woodside of *Now and Then,* Jennifer Musgrove of the *Asheville Citizen-Times,* Liz McGeachy of Appalshop, Rebecca Blakeney at the University of South Carolina Press, Mary Gannon of *Poets & Writers,* filmmaker Andrew Garrison, and contributor Bernie Lee Sinclair (for helping with our volume's title). Writer Maggie Anderson deserves a line of her own, for without her early bold advice on the direction of this book it would have been something else entirely.

Also I am grateful to the following writers and publishers for permission to reprint some of the essays and other materials included in this volume: Nikki Giovanni's "400 Mulvaney Street," © 1971 by Nikki Giovanni, originally appeared in *Gemini* and is reprinted by permission of the author. Lisa Koger's "Writing in the Smokehouse," © 1991 by Lisa Koger, originally appeared in *The Confidence Woman: 26 Women Writers at Work,* edited by Eve Shelnutt, and is reprinted by permission of the author. George Ella Lyon's "Voiceplace" appeared in slightly different form in the *Ohio Journal of the English Language Arts* 34, no. 2 (fall 1993) and is reprinted by permission of OCTELA and the author. Jayne Anne Phillips's "Premature Burial," © 1991 by Jayne Anne Phillips, first appeared in *The Movie That Changed My Life,* edited by David Rosenberg, and is reprinted by permission of the author. "The Search for the Beulah Quintet," © 1996 by Mary Lee Settle, originally appeared in slightly different form as the introduction to *O Beulah Land* (Columbia: Univ. of South Carolina Press, 1996) and is reprinted by permission of the author. An earlier version of Lee Smith's "Terrain of the Heart," © 1993 by Lee Smith, appeared in the *News & Observer* of Raleigh, North Carolina, October 10, 1993; it is reprinted by permission of the author.

"Darling of My Heart" by Linda Prince Mathis is quoted by permission of the author. "Waiting for a Train" by Jimmie Rodgers, © 1929 by Peer International Corp. (copyright renewed, international copyright secured), is used by permission. "A Testimony to Good Living" by Bob Terrell, © 1996 by the *Asheville Citizen-Times,* first appeared in that paper October 21, 1977 and is reprinted with permission. "Catch a Falling Star," © 1957 (renewed) by Music Sales Corporation (ASCAP) and Emily Music Corp., all rights reserved, is used by permission.

I thank the National Endowment for the Humanities for two summer grants that allowed me to work with key collections, and with some of the finest human beings I have ever met, and the Ohio Arts Council for a 1997 Independent Artist Fellowship that supported the completion of this volume.

I thank Hiram College for awarding me Gerstacker-Gund Fellowships that were of great assistance. And I thank Michael Dively for his support of this project, and for his support of the writers in this volume, through the awarding of generous funds from the Michael Dively Endowment for Scholarly Publications. I also would like to thank Deans Vivian Makosky and Michael Grajek for their constant and unfailing encouragement.

The library staff of Hudson Library and Historical Society has vigorously supported my work for twenty years. And I could not have made the progress I was able to without the excellent advice and resourcefulness of Lisa Johnson (an absolute wizard), Mary Lou Selander, Pat Basu, Jeff Wanser, Rosanne Factor, and other library staff at Hiram College, as well as computer specialists Chris Haaker and Barb DeYoung. Millie Schwan, faculty administrative assistant at Hiram College, offered invaluable help with the details of this book.

Of course, it is impossible to express adequate thanks to the University Press of Kentucky for supporting the idea of this volume even before a single essay was written. The Press is, and has long been, a profoundly important advocate of Appalachian writing, and I have difficulty expressing the pride I feel in knowing that the same press that published reprints of Elizabeth Madox Roberts's *The Time of Man* and James Still's *River of Earth* is also publisher of *Bloodroot*.

I am grateful to Ronald and Nola Osborn, Richard Dyer, Dave Dyer and Janice McCormick, Edward and Prudence Dyer, and Paul and Edith Steurer for the generous ways they've supported my work. I thank Daniel Osborn Dyer, my husband. We have traveled a million roads together, including the mountain roads of my past. His sweetness and humor are boundless. And I thank Stephen Osborn Dyer, my son, who will soon write his own books, and to whom I leave the precious legacy of the Coynes and Haberkosts.

In memory, I thank my parents and my grandparents for their love and their stories and their good lives. Their memory teaches me that a book, like a life, has neither a clear beginning nor a clear end. This volume, I hope, is unfinished. More and more Appalachian women writers will emerge on the scene every day. And those writers, perhaps, will gather courage to persist from the words of the women here who light their way.

Blood Root grows throughout the United States, in shaded woods and thickets, and rich soils generally, and flowers from March to June. Although the whole plant is medicinal, the root is the part chiefly used. The fresh root is fleshy, round and from one to four inches in length, and as thick as the fingers. It presents a beautiful appearance when cut and placed under a microscope, seeming like an aggregation of minute precious stones.

—Joseph E. Meyer, *The Herbalist and Herb Doctor,* 1918

Introduction

JOYCE DYER

This is a volume of celebration. Of general celebration of the literary renaissance that is taking place in the hills of Appalachia among its sons and daughters. And of special celebration of the writing women of the Southern Highlands who are making such a profound and prolific contribution to American letters.

How is it that such light can be issuing from what we have long been told is the most dimly lit corner of America? How is it possible for us to replace the images of women on crumbling porches burned into our eyes by Walker Evans's photographs with the images of these writing women, or of the strong characters they create in poetry and fiction? How can we forget Daisy Mae from years of Al Capp's cartoon strip *Li'l Abner* or Mammy Yokum from the 1959 musical *Li'l Abner*? Can we block out the memory of our own laughter as we watched Granny on *The Beverly Hillbillies* mistake a kangaroo for a large rabbit or an ostrich for a chicken? How can we forget the powerful images of a Hollywood that even in 1996 created the character of Percy Talbott in *The Spitfire Grill*, a girl from Akron, Ohio, an outmigrant from the hills of Kentucky who was forced to have sex with her stepfather from the time she was nine years old and who murdered him with a straight-edged razor? How can we shed the common notion that Appalachian women are a homogeneous group of dependent, submissive females, small filler beads in extended families, victims of intensely patriarchal men? How can women from such a world as this write sentences the way they do?

Some of the women in this volume are well-known and famous. Their books have won or been nominated for the National Book Award, have appeared on the *New York Times* best-seller list, or have been selected by the Book-of-the-Month Club. They have won Guggenheim and Ford Foundation grants and lectured across the country and throughout the world. It cannot be said that the use of indigenous Appalachian material has necessarily been the kiss of death for a writer with an Appalachian past or present.

But many of the authors in this volume are not known beyond the hills they write about. Scholars of the region have worried about this fact for a long time. Editors Robert J. Higgs and Ambrose N. Manning suggest in their introduction to the anthology *Voices from the Hills* that the invisibility of Appalachian authors represents "a rather facile dismissal of one of the most complex and fascinating regions of America."[1] Could there still be, as writer and social historian Jim Wayne

Miller proposed, a perhaps unconscious desire by critics "to banish poor cousins to the outhouse and put out the best uncracked china for company"?[2] Have our notions about the Appalachian region influenced our response to its literature and to the very idea of its having a "culture"?

Literary history, generally, has not been kind to women who have chosen to write with a strong sense of their regions, and it has perhaps been least kind to women from Appalachia. Few groups of women writers have suffered as many literary injustices as those from the southern hills. They have had to bear injustices caused by their gender as well as by their place. Emma Bell Miles's extraordinary book *The Spirit of the Mountains* was released in 1905 but apparently not even reviewed. For seventy years after its initial publication, only a few historians, such as West Virginia University's Robert F. Munn, knew of its existence.

In his 1963 introduction to a new edition of Elizabeth Madox Roberts's *The Time of Man,* Robert Penn Warren contrasted the initial reception of this novel to its reputation in the 1960s. It was a best-seller and a Book-of-the-Month selection when first published in 1926, but, Warren said of the book's author, "The youth of today do not even know her name."[3] William H. Slavick, writing an introduction nearly twenty years later for yet another edition of this novel, recognized that "the large audience her work merits" was still missing but hoped that this would change.[4] Unfortunately, his hopeful prediction did not come true. By 1996 I could not teach *The Time of Man* because it had once again gone out of print, in spite of laudatory attempts by university presses to keep it alive.

And although perhaps more people know about the existence of Harriette Simpson Arnow's *The Dollmaker* because of Jane Fonda's decision to film it, how many have read her exquisite book *Hunter's Horn*? There are, unfortunately, numerous stories like those of Miles and Roberts and Arnow that could be told.

Sandra Ballard and Patricia Hudson, editors of a forthcoming anthology of writing by Appalachian women, have reviewed numerous recent references such as the *Oxford Companion to Women Writing in the United States* while preparing their book. Ballard explained to me, "While this 1995 reference work has an essay on Southern Women's Writing and individual entries on such writers as Harriette Arnow and Olive Tilford Dargan, it includes only *five* others from my list of 105 women writers from Appalachia." Hopeful that just a few of the names that appear in *Bloodroot* might have finally found their way into the new 1996 edition of *The Norton Anthology of Literature by Women,* I recently purchased a copy. But, as in the 1985 edition, not a single woman in this collection was named. Not one. Even though the editors announced a new policy to represent "the diversity of women's experiences, diversity of cultural heritage, racial identification, geographical background, sexual preference, religious practice and class privilege,"[5] Appalachia was once again forgotten.

Yet the simple fact remains that this region known as the Southern Highlands to some, as Appalachia to others, is ablaze with talent. Like the slag heaps near the mines in West Virginia and Kentucky, the fire has been there, smoldering, for a very long time. But in recent decades it has burst into flames, into tongues. Radio station WMMT produced a series in 1995 called *Tell It on the Mountain* that featured interviews with many Appalachian women authors. The station advertised the series this way: "In the last two decades, women writers from Appalachia have emerged as a literary force unrivaled in America for an incisiveness that transcends both cultural and regional borders."[6]

This book has, first of all, the simple ambition of naming many of Appalachia's literary women who comprise perhaps the most exciting group of writers in America today, and of letting others meet them and hear their voices. But it has another ambition as well. I wanted to know whether the region itself was fueling their art, and why and how. I wanted to know why this region, supposedly the poorest in the nation, was producing such wealth.

"What were the influences on your writing?" was the question I invited these women to talk about. I encouraged them to explore the influence that the region might have had, but only if this was appropriate. And if it was, I wanted to know not only what connection this particular place had to their writing, but also what they understood this place even to be. I wanted to know where and how the region, or any aspect of the region, figured in. I wanted to know about their childhoods. About strong men and women in their Appalachian pasts and presents who had a hand in their shaping. About the schools they attended. About whether society and class played a part. About the landscapes that met their eyes, day after day. About the bluebells, sassafras, highland cress, and bloodroot that covered the woods and hills of their pasts. About the very bloodroot of their writing lives.

In varying degrees and varying ways, every writer acknowledged that Appalachia had formed her. As different as the essays are, they all represent a return to place, a place somewhere in a particular Appalachian county, as well as the place of the imagination. This volume will not provide a conclusive answer to the complicated and intricate issue of why Appalachian women writers are flourishing and sending light across the mountains, light so visible it fills the sky. But it will begin to demonstrate, I think, how a place can fuel writing, if a writer chooses to walk—or dance—in its flames. How the very important and complex relationship these women have had with this place called Appalachia (and it has not always been an easy one, as you will read) has fed their writing—ancient fossil fuel that is their own, and no other's. How from a land often very literally associated with the devastation of fire and ash, the beautiful Phoenix can be born.

Many of the women in this collection still live in Appalachia, some in the same counties or towns where they were born. Artie Ann Bates was born in Blackey, Kentucky, and lives there with her own family now. Anne Shelby lives in the house and on the farm where her great-grandparents lived in Clay County, Kentucky. Jo Carson is a lifelong resident of Johnson City, Tennessee. Rita Sims Quillen lives in the same community in Virginia where she was born, the fifth generation to call Hiltons home. Poet doris diosa davenport studied and worked in at least fifteen states between 1969 and 1992, but returned to her hometown of Cornelia, Georgia, in 1992, and now lives in a trailer home in Sautee, just a short drive from Cornelia. Sheila Kay Adams was born in Sodom, North Carolina, and now lives on top of a mountain just thirty minutes away, still in Madison County. And Jane Stuart lives in the very house in W-Hollow in Greenup, Kentucky, where she was raised by Jesse and Naomi Stuart.

But some of the writers no longer live within the traditional geography of Appalachia. Many were raised in the region, but left. Lisa Alther, native of Kingsport, Tennessee, has lived most of her adult life in Vermont. Gail Godwin was born in Alabama and raised in Asheville, North Carolina, but now lives in Woodstock, New York, in the Catskills. Elaine Fowler Palencia grew up in Morehead, Kentucky, and Cookeville, Tennessee, but makes her home in Champaign, Illinois.

Several women born in West Virginia no longer reside there. Meredith Sue Willis, from Clarksburg, the county seat of Harrison County, currently resides in South Orange, New Jersey. Jayne Anne Phillips now lives with her family near Boston. And Mary Lee Settle, who spent her girlhood in Charleston, the daughter of a coal mine owner, now lives in Charlottesville.

Jean Ritchie, from Viper, Kentucky, has lived in New York since taking her first job there in the 1940s. But she always manages to spend several months of every year "at home" with her Kentucky family. In the late 1960s, she and her husband, New York photographer George Pickow, began looking for logs from old houses, finally finding what they wanted. Their log house, pictured on the front of Jean Ritchie's recent compact disc recording *Kentucky Christmas, Old and New,* was built on the hillside that overlooks the house in which she was born.

A few women included here came to the region later but have adopted it as their own, or been adopted by it. Bettie Sellers arrived in the Young Harris Valley in 1965 to teach at Young Harris College. Barbara Smith has a somewhat similar history at Alderson-Broaddus College in Philippi. Maggie Anderson was born in New York but raised in West Virginia. Lisa Koger was born in Elyria, Ohio, but spent her girlhood on Tanner Creek's Ellis Fork in Gilmer County, West Virginia, after her thirty-year-old mother went back to West Virginia for a visit to the home place and never returned. Llewellyn McKernan calls herself a transplanted Appalachian from Arkansas and now lives near Barboursville, West Virginia. Ellesa Clay High was born and raised in suburban Louisville but has lived her entire adult life in Appalachia. She currently resides with her son and wolf-dogs on an eighty-five-acre farm in Preston County, West Virginia. Betsy Sholl grew up on the New Jersey shore and now lives in Maine, only occasionally writing poems about the seven years she spent in Stone Gap, Virginia. Yet, the people, the landscape, the culture, and the religion she experienced during those years remain as elemental to her writing as the earth, air, water, and fire she talks about in her essay.

Appalachia, according to Clifford Grammich's recent *Appalachian Atlas,* consists of 404 counties and independent cities in thirteen states from New York to Mississippi.[7] The Southern Appalachian region, the section with a distinct culture and history that forms this book's focus, is of course geographically even more narrow, but the region's finest scholars have warned us against an exclusively geographical view. In *Who Speaks for Appalachia?* Cecille Haddix writes, "Appalachia is as much a region of the heart as of geography."[8] One of the most important new voices in the Appalachian discussion is Douglas Reichert Powell, associate editor of *Appalachia Inside Out.* "To be Appalachian is to participate, whether on location or from afar, in the acts, words, deeds, and landscapes of our ongoing debate over who are the 'Appalachians.' The region exists, securely, as long as the debate goes on."[9] David Hackett Fischer, Rodger Cunningham, and Jim Wayne Miller have also actively participated in this debate over the years, vigorously challenging narrow notions about geographical boundaries, especially urging the consideration of the multiple and complex migrations of mountain people.

When I spoke to Gurney Norman on the phone some time back, he reminded me to think carefully about Henry Louis Gates's reassessment of the Harlem Renaissance. The concept of Appalachia, he wisely told me, like the concept of the Harlem Renaissance, is no longer considered confined to a geographical region, to a neighborhood, to a decade (for Appalachia, the dominant association is, of course, with the Depression). It is, Norman said, best understood as a spirit, "a spirit that has leapt out of strict Appalachian ground." Appalachia is dynamic, as is Appalachian memory. Even mountains cannot contain it. Perhaps this is what James Still meant when he said in an interview, "I don't know where Appalachia begins, or where it ends." Or when he wrote, "Appalachia is that somewhat mythical region with no known borders."[10] These remarks, remember, came from a man who has lived in the same log house between Wolfpen Creek and Deadmare Branch at the forks of Troublesome in Knott County, Kentucky, since 1939.

All of the writers in this volume—those who came to Appalachia late, left it early, or have always remained—have been deeply affected by the spirit of the region. At first, I naively thought there might be an easy way to catch hold of this spirit and understand it. I had forgotten how elusive spirit is, how like the will-o'-the-wisp whose glow scientists still cannot explain. There is not one clear pattern or a simple shape. The writers in this book were born in different houses and traveled different roads and in many ways their stories are absolutely their own. There are many spirits that walk here, not just one.

The writers, for instance, are different ages and write of slightly different times. George Brosi, author of *The Literature of the Appalachian South,* divides Southern Appalachian writers of the twentieth century into four distinct generations.[11] Although there are no first-generation writers in this volume (those born in the first decade of the twentieth century, according to Brosi's classification), all other generations are among the contributors. Each generation brings its own political and cultural concerns, its own particular feel to the writing of its time. The second generation is represented by Lou V. P. Crabtree and Mary Lee Settle, born in the teens, and Jean Ritchie, Barbara Smith, and Wilma Dykeman, all born in the twenties. The third generation, those born in the thirties and forties, is most aggressively represented here, with such writers as Lisa Alther, Gail Godwin, Lee Smith, Meredith Sue Willis, Nikki Giovanni, Sharyn McCrumb, and Elaine Fowler Palencia. But many writers who fall within Brosi's category of "youngest generation," those born predominantly in the fifties or later, also appear within the pages of this book—Hilda Downer, Denise Giardina, Jayne Anne Phillips, Nikky Finney, Rita Sims Quillen, Lisa Koger, and Sheila Kay Adams, for example.

The women in this volume are not equally optimistic about the region. Jane Stuart talks about the peace and inspiration that greet her every morning as she looks from the kitchen window of the Jesse Stuart house. Lou V.P. Crabtree, by contrast, sees her region as both a paradise and a hell and does not shy away from talking about the offenses of circuit preachers, murder, racism and intolerance, and the abuses to the land by loggers and coal barons. The bloodroot that grew in Lou V. P. Crabtree's Price Hollow—containing medicinal and healing properties but dangerous in excess—hints at the complex nature of more than one writer's Appalachian experience.

Some women write about their Scotch-Irish, English, or German roots, the genealogies typically associated with European migration patterns to the borderlands. But doris diosa davenport and Nikky Finney talk about being Affrilachian, a term coined by Frank X. Walker at the Martin Luther King Cultural Center at the University of Kentucky to correct the definition of "Appalachian" that he found in the 1989 *Webster's Dictionary*: "the white residents of mountainous regions of the country." Marilou Awiakta and Ellesa Clay High talk about their Cherokee roots, and Bettie Sellers writes poems about the early settlers to the Young Harris Valley, the Creek and the Cherokee. Lisa Alther and Meredith Sue Willis discuss various complications to understanding identity that came with the discovery of their Melungeon, or possible Melungeon, roots. To be connected to Melungeon ancestors—a mysterious and historically misunderstood people of Mediterranean descent who settled parts of Appalachia forty years before Jamestown and intermarried with Powhatans, Pamunkeys, Creeks, Catawbas, Yuchis, and Cherokees—how does that affect a person's understanding of her Appalachian identity?

Some women, like Bettie Sellers and Lou V. P. Crabtree, are devoted to the rural. Barbara Smith, on the other hand, has gained much of her strength from the stories of miners' wives. Denise Giardina brings to life the very coalfields where she grew up in West Virginia. Nikky Finney talks about the important mix of mountain and ocean in shaping her work. And a few—Mary Lee Settle, Gail Godwin, and Lisa Alther, for example—have told stories of a more urban Appalachian South, or of the Appalachian sensibility working to be at home in other urban areas throughout the nation, throughout the world.

It is not surprising to find such differences among the women writers of Appalachia. It is a complex place in every sense. Geologically, historically, culturally, and genealogically we are only beginning to understand it. If we cannot understand these things, how can we understand something as elusive as spirit?

But as improbable as it might seem, the spirits of a particular place often reflect that place, and cannot rise from any other ground. It is not coincidental that many women in this volume, for example, feel compelled to tell Appalachia's history, though their versions are not identical. Until very recently Appalachia's historians have seen Appalachia only as a field for research, not as a home. They have not lived here, which means that they have missed much of the detail. "The sheer anonymity of my background calls out for a scribe," writes Elaine Fowler Palencia. Many other writers in this book agree.

Many women assert their role as historian. Artie Ann Bates, for example, explains that her writing is even more urgent than her work as a physician. The aging of her elderly ancestors, the irreversible loss of their memories once they are gone, has mobilized her to write. Out of love for northeast Georgia and the Gibsons, doris diosa davenport resurrects the people who lived on the Hill where she grew up, especially those who lived at 103 Soque Street. Bennie Lee Sinclair narrates some of the history of wild and lawless "Dark Corner" in Greenville County, South Carolina. Meredith Sue Willis equates her long attempt to get at the "contradictions and disjunctions" of her grandmother's life with her movement away from a simple understanding of the region made up of "after-images from childhood" and popular stereotypes. And Heather Ross Miller describes how her writing is a *natural* history, the story of the flavor and challenges and differences of three mountain ranges—the Uwharries, the Ozarks, and the Appalachians.

Part of their own history has often been connected with confronting Appalachian caricatures ("hicks" and "rednecks") and confronting, as well, the complicated emotions that these stereotypes breed. Such stereotypes persist, and the writers talk about how such perceptions affected them as they grew up, or affect them now. Rita Sims Quillen tells about her angry response as a sixth grader reading a northerner's version of the Kingsport Press strike. Artie Ann Bates deplores the role of the national media, TV shows, and movies in reinforcing our country's ignorance about eastern Kentucky. And George Ella Lyon tells about growing up in Harlan County and hearing television messages about culturally deprived mountain people. "So I thought, if I am going to write, the first thing I have to do is go somewhere and acquire a culture," she says. "I didn't know that was like cutting your throat to remedy hunger," she continues, with the wisdom of a woman, and writer, who eventually came to understand that her own cultural roots were plenty strong enough.

These writers frequently talk about the importance of the stories they heard growing up, of the oral history of their region, stories that spilled freely from the mouths of neighbors and relatives and friends. They breathed in those stories, the oxygen of their future work. The storytelling tradition, of course, is widely associated with other southern writers, but the stories these women heard were their own, stories about *their* region told in voices they would hear and mimic. Denise Giardina recalls first hearing such stories "perched upon the bony knees of old men." In numerous children's books, Anne Shelby tells the stories of McKee (population 100) in Jackson County, Kentucky, trying, she tells us, to recover the "lost world," the "small land singing world," of her girlhood there. And Sharyn McCrumb explains how her Ballad series novels are based on family stories, traditional and popular music, and her own research of the history, geology, and folklore of the mountain South.

Few have worked as hard or as long to understand their region, and its place in the country's history, as Mary Lee Settle. She spent twenty-eight years writing the Beulah Quintet, five volumes that span more than three hundred years of European and American history. And although in the process she became one of the region's most profound historians, as well as one of the few American writers to truly understand the immigrant experience, she repeatedly resists a narrow definition of "historian." In that resistance is her talent and her authority, the new history that she and other women are creating. It is a history born of humility, imagination, dreams, and an odd mixture of forgetfulness and memory. "I did not have the luxury of looking back on the years of *O Beulah Land* from the present with all the arrogance and future knowledge of a past time. That is the privilege of historians," she writes in her essay. "I had to become contemporary, think as they thought, fear what they had feared, use their own language with its yet unchanged meanings, face a blank and fearful future. I had to forget what I already knew."

Recently the world of letters witnessed the arrival of a new book, *The Future of Southern Letters,*[12] an important collection of essays that examines the current state of southern letters, also often touching on the current state of southern culture and history. It is heartening to find that three of the thirteen essays in the collection are devoted to Appalachian letters and issues. However, the voices selected to document the mountain South's history are exclusively male: Jim Wayne Miller, Rodger Cunningham, and Fred Chappell. Women writers have not yet been included among the region's true historians, but I wish they had been. Why, we might ask, was someone like Mary Lee Settle or Wilma Dykeman not invited to say just a word or two?

Appalachia's women are eager for this role. They are driven by the important and compelling and passionate mission to define Appalachia for the first time, to see it distinct from the cotton South, to understand its place in women's lives, to write its story, and to bring it up to date.

Many of the writers in this book also have in common a distinctive understanding of the relationship of art to community. They sense how their art feeds into community life and how the community feeds their art, and this knowledge seems a natural part of their inheritance as Appalachian women. Some women in this collection are quiet, deliberately isolated, and very private. But many are not and view this as a strength to their art and a necessity to their lives. They do not resist connections to others, nor do they see the conflict between serving art and serving people that many other American writers have chosen as one of their central motifs. In Wendell Berry's title piece from his book *Sex, Economy, Freedom and Community,* he defines community as many of the writers here seem to understand it: "If the word *community* is to mean or amount to anything, it must refer to a place (in its natural integrity) and its people. It must refer to a placed people."[13]

Barbara Smith has been active in social and political arenas all her life, most recently in the establishment of hospice care for a three-county area of West Virginia. During her years in Virginia, Betsy Sholl was associated with Christ Hill, a residential community that served people in need of housing and other forms of support. Hilda Downer works as a psychiatric nurse in North Carolina. Artie Ann Bates is a physician who works with abused children and moonlights in an after-hours clinic, as well as a political activist who decries the stripmining that surrounds her grandparents' log house where she now lives. Drafts of her essay to me were always typed on the back sides of old letters, memos from the Kentucky River Area Development District, and junk mail; her disks were wrapped in newspaper from the *Hazard Herald-Voice.*

For a while, Lisa Koger taught writing classes in a nursing home and edited nursing home magazines in a sixteen-county East Tennessee area. Lou V.P. Crabtree played in the Rock of Ages Band for many years and has participated in community theater throughout her life. Marilou Awiakta serves on the National Caucus Board of the Wordcraft Circle of Native Writers and Storytellers and on the Tennessee Humanities Council, and is an ongoing consultant for the Selu Conservancy at Radford University in Virginia. Kathryn Stripling Byer has worked hard to improve public schools and in 1985 received the Governor's Award for Volunteer Service in Public Schools. George Ella Lyon works with literacy students and tutors in Harlan County, and has published a collection called *Choices: Stories for Adult New Readers,* part of the series *New Books for New Readers.* And Meredith Sue Willis fights actively against resegregation in housing and the schools, bringing to her New Jersey home a lesson learned well in the hills: "At some profound level, [Appalachians] believe that everyone is related to us. Maybe we haven't seen the neighbors over the back side of the mountain for years, but we are interested in them. They exist for us."[14]

Many live dual lives as performers, bringing their art to people, moving it closer to its source in oral tradition. Sheila Kay Adams is a popular balladeer, storyteller, and banjo and guitar player; doris diosa davenport is a provocative lecturer and performance poet. Anne Shelby visits schools as a storyteller, helping to pass on the region's rich storytelling tradition to a new generation. Jo Carson creates performance pieces out of oral histories of specific communities and then performs them for those communities. Jean Ritchie, who began her career in social work, is known throughout the world for her folk songs and dulcimer playing. Maggie Anderson has participated in programs in the schools, traveling both main streets and dirt roads so that her stories might reach new ears.

It isn't surprising that many writers represented here pay tribute to people who helped them understand their region and their talent. Llewellyn McKernan's entire essay is a tribute to her Appalachian readers, a letter of deep gratitude for the courage and support her readers have shown her. Kathryn Stripling Byer talks about the poetic weaving of voices that has guided her own work, a black shawl that stretches over the hills, formed of songs and poetry and story. Maggie Anderson, Bettie Sellers, Bennie Lee Sinclair, Artie Ann Bates, and George Ella Lyon thank the literary men and women in their lives who influenced them. And Hilda Downer talks about poets being mutants who adapt to survive, becoming a part of all other poets who came before them, who live at the time they do, or who will come after.

Many women remember parents and grandmothers and other relatives dear to them. Wilma Dykeman tells the story of her father and mother and in that process describes the power of a relationship that forever shaped her writing. Marilou Awiakta talks about the way sound has always shaped her, especially the sound of her mother's voice. Jayne Anne Phillips remembers her mother's death and its lasting message for her and for her writing. Nikki Giovanni describes her grandmother Louvenia Watson, a woman who comes to represent all the strength and character and magnificence of old Knoxville. Bettie Sellers recalls a story in which her grandmother aimed a shotgun into the night and wounded a chicken-stealing parishioner from her church. Lisa Alther remembers the strength of imagination of her grandmother Hattie Elizabeth Vanover Reed. With gratitude and great humor, Gail Godwin describes her Uncle Orphy, a relative who later materialized in her fiction and began to lead her back to her ancestors. And Sidney Saylor Farr remembers the mountain women who gave her the education that was sorely lacking in the Bell County of her girlhood.

The Appalachian Writers' Workshop, founded by Albert Stewart at Hindman Settlement School in 1977, has been a profoundly significant experience for many of these authors, and they remember it. There is no question that it has had a direct and dynamic influence on emerging Appalachian writers and is in some part responsible for the literary quickening of the region. Michael Mullins, director of Hindman, talks about the workshop in an introductory statement to *A Gathering at the Forks,* the collection of Appalachian writing that celebrates fifteen years of the workshop: "One of the purposes of the Hindman Settlement School is to provide programs and activities to keep the people of this area mindful of their heritage. The Appalachian Writers' Workshop is one of these programs."[15] It supports and encourages all writers, but especially the writers of the region.

Throughout my project I personally experienced this feeling of support for and from one another. At the end of every piece of correspondence with Lee Smith, for example, she would make suggestions about other names she thought should be included. After twenty years of immersion in the contemporary Appalachian literary scene and close consultation with its scholars, I thought I knew almost every name I needed to know. In truth, my final list represents a community endeavor, a community consensus. Lee Smith recommended Kay Byer, who eagerly agreed to write. Kay Byer recommended doris diosa davenport. In turn, doris diosa davenport urged me to look hard at the work of Sheila Kay Adams. This inclusive spirit, this looking out for one another, is rather typical of the way these writers work. As I think about it, I guess this spirit of consensus, of "confluence," as Maggie Anderson might call it, quietly shaped the lines of this book from the beginning, even without my knowing it. I could have gathered up a few essays, consulted publishers about reprints, and been done with it. But I never thought to proceed in that way. The process was as crucial as the result, and the process was somehow defined for me by the spirit in which I knew these women worked and lived. Every essay included here began with a letter of invitation in 1995, moved quickly into preliminary discussions and conversations, and continued over the next two years with close correspondence about manuscripts.

Even those women who chose to reprint worked closely with me as they made selections or modifications.

The writers here speak about many other beliefs and practices that they share. For example, several articulate the importance of landscape itself, the importance of the mountains to their art. For them landscape is not just a symbol, but a fact. Even those who have left the physical boundaries of Appalachia express the hold the hills have on them. Elaine Fowler Palencia, finding herself disoriented in Illinois, discovered its cause: "I missed having hills around me, watching over me, sheltering me, cutting the horizon down to manageable size." Maggie Anderson, who directs the Wick poetry program at Kent State University in Ohio now, tells the story of the peculiar way she chose her home in Kent. She looked for the tallest house in town, with the highest elevation. And then she climbed to the top, to the attic floor, and set up shop. For these women, the land is the land. It has its own history and name. It is the hollow on Ellis Fork of Tanner Creek for Lisa Koger; it is a 135-acre old hardwood forest, with white pine and hemlock, with deer and wild turkey and the rare Oconee Bell for Bennie Lee Sinclair. It is real and vital, alive and worthy of respect. It is essential to both the quality of life these writers lead and the quality of the art they produce.

The writers will speak for themselves about other things that join them and account for the urgency of their work. Every message is distinct in this book, and yet you'll begin to hear a common melody if you listen closely. Each writer is trying to locate the very center of Appalachian experience, sounding it out way beneath the soil, way beneath the rivers and roads that define state lines. In their search, they sometimes find the spirit of Appalachia, and name it as best it can be named. As they write, they find their inheritance, underground. And claim it.

I cannot leave this essay without thanking the authors in this volume. Without thanking Appalachian writers, now deceased, who came before them. Without thanking the women of the region who are not represented on these pages. And without thanking the men of the region for their magnificent poems and stories and essays.

All of these writers have helped me find my own bloodroots over the many years that I have read their books. My family on my father's side were outmigrants from the Appalachian mines of West Virginia, all the way up the strain to Moosic and Avoca, Pennsylvania. They came to Akron, Ohio, to work in the rubber factories. My father built tires for Firestone Tire and Rubber Company for more than forty years, and we grew up under the brow of the plant where my father breathed in lampblack all those years. My great-grandfather Billie died of black lung in a veteran's hospital. My own father, thinking he had left the hazards of the mines when his family brought him to Akron as a boy, died of environment-induced lung cancer just a few years ago.

Like many of the writers here, for a long while I didn't understand my Appalachian roots or I felt embarrassed by them. As a certified brier, I would often have to endure jeers. "Hey, girl," kids from other neighborhoods would yell at me from car windows. "What's the capital of West Virginia?" I knew what the answer would be. "Akron." I hung my head and picked up steam, until I faded around the corner of Aster Avenue and bolted for home, where I always felt safe.

At college and then graduate school, I was deeply attracted, as many women in this volume have been, to southern literature. But I never once had the courage to raise my hand and ask my teachers why there were no mountains in the stories they assigned. The stories my family told all had mountains in them, and the visits to my cousins in West Virginia had been beautiful, hilly rides. The tacit lesson I so wrongly absorbed was that the mountains *had* no literature. Throughout my formal education, I never heard the name of a single Appalachian author. In 1977 I received my Ph.D., having completed a dissertation on Kate Chopin, and started a career. My major emphasis had been southern literature, but I had not read a single word about my own region.

Thanks to a series of fortunate events—including the gift of a Mary Lee Settle novel from my brother-in-law Richard Dyer, the enthusiasm of Jerry Williamson and Jim Wayne Miller for my work, attendance at a seminar about Appalachia held at Appalachian State University, and grants to study Appalachian letters—I began to read Appalachian literature with incomprehensible appetite, and to wind my way home. The books I read, hundreds and hundreds of them, were profoundly familiar to me, though I had never read a single one before. Here were mountain roads, strong women like my grandmother Coyne, storytellers like my father, histories of other outmigrants, stories about coal, words and sayings that fit my mouth.

And here, perhaps most of all, were characters who had relatively little but never gave up hope, always feeling rich in family, community, friendships, and home. My neighborhood was full of aunts and uncles, relatives galore, people very similar to the characters in the books. The men all worked for Firestone or Goodyear or Goodrich. The women who worked worked in the offices of those companies. The women who stayed at home ironed to the 12:00 *Hymn for the Day* and dreamed up new paper decorations for every holiday that Hallmark could invent for them.

My heart was full of stories I had heard in my own small brick and stucco home on Evergreen Avenue, as well as in the homes of relatives who lived on nearly every street of Firestone Park in Akron, Ohio. By the age of five, I could recite the story of my grandfather coming to Firestone Tire and Rubber Company in 1923. I knew that my grandmother had worked in a jewelry shop before her marriage and owned a small Limoges vase that the owner had given her as a wedding gift. It would mysteriously appear on her mahogany table for birthdays and holidays, filled with honeysuckle and roses in the spring and summer, colored leaves or boughs of pine in the fall and winter, and then just as mysteriously vanish into safety the rest of the days. It was the only beautiful thing she ever owned. I own it now.

I could tell about Old Billie, my grandpa's father who had worked as a blaster in Manchester, England, before coming to West Virginia, including every detail of his death at Moses Taylor Hospital. I knew about my grandpa driving mule cars and about his success as an amateur athlete at Sunday afternoon baseball games or in boxing matches. And I knew the stories about my own father at nine and ten working a tipple, taking rock dirt out of coal. I knew the difference between pea coal, walnut coal, and anthracite almost before I was old enough to say the words, and long before I had seen any.

I've never physically lived in Appalachia. I'm an outmigrant, twice removed, a brier who's learned, sometimes too well, how to behave up North. I'm an outsider. And yet the pull of that region on me, the mysterious grounding it has provided, the familiar feel of it all—these things have convinced me that somehow I've never left this place I never was. The essays here, as well as the literature by the women who write them, are part of the pull that keeps me attached. It is one very important way that I remember, and return.

What is it finally that is most at the heart of this tremendous pull? What is the *one* thing that brings me back again and again to the body of literature these Appalachian women have produced and to the place they often write about? What is it, most of all, that accounts for this excellence and power?

Wilma Dykeman, whose contribution to Appalachian letters and the Appalachian movement is without measure, gives us perhaps her most magnificent creation in the character Lydia McQueen from *The Tall Woman*. Among Lydia's many strengths and skills, she is, according to her father, "a master fire builder." Dykeman adds, "Yet it had never seemed a chore to her to build a fire—to breathe warmth and light into being against the cold and darkness and watch it grow to vivid, splendid life."[16]

And so we return to fire, where we began. The image of Lydia McQueen as a fire builder is an appropriate metaphor for Dykeman's fiction as well as for the work of most of the Appalachian authors represented in this volume. They do not often write about an indifferent and meaningless world, a world cold and dark. They do not often write without hope. They write about life, splendid life, and, like Lydia McQueen, they cast long shadows. They are often very funny women, because they believe, in spite of the tragedy they are not afraid to record, that they—and the world—will survive. After all, the mountains have been there for more than two hundred million years. Appalachian writing seldom fails to warm us into awareness of the amazing wonders of the world, wonders as textured and permanent as the mountains themselves.

I find these writers irresistible, and I hope this volume begins to show you why.

Notes

1. Robert J. Higgs and Ambrose N. Manning, eds., *Voices from the Hills: Selected Readings of Southern Appalachia* (New York: Ungar, 1975), xix-xx.

2. Jim Wayne Miller, " . . . And Ladies of the Club," *Appalachian Journal* 14, no. 1 (fall 1986): 64.

3. Robert Penn Warren, introduction to *The Time of Man,* by Elizabeth Madox Roberts (New York: Viking, 1963), vii.

4. William H. Slavick, introduction to *The Time of Man,* by Elizabeth Madox Roberts (Lexington: Univ. Press of Kentucky), vii.

5. Sandra M. Gilbert and Susan Gubar, eds., *The Norton Anthology of Literature by Women* (New York: Norton, 1996), xxix.

6. "Women Writers 'Tell It on the Mountain,'" *Appalshop Notes,* 1995-96, 7.

7. Clifford A. Grammich Jr., *Appalachian Atlas* (Knoxville, Tenn.: Commission on Religion in Appalachia, 1994), 1.

8. Cecille Haddix, *Who Speaks for Appalachia?* (New York: Washington Square Press, 1975), ix.

9. Douglas Reichert Powell, "Mapping Appalachia," *Southern Exposure* 24, no. 3 (fall 1996): 51.

10. James Still, *The Wolfpen Notebooks* (Lexington: Univ. Press of Kentucky, 1991), 27, vi.

11. George Brosi, *The Literature of the Appalachian South* (Richmond: Eastern Kentucky Univ., 1992), 12-18.

12. Jefferson Humphries and John Lowe, eds., *The Future of Southern Letters* (New York: Oxford Univ. Press, 1996).

13. Wendell Berry, *Sex, Economy, Freedom and Community* (New York: Pantheon, 1992), 168.

14. Meredith Sue Willis, "How Far I've Come—and How Close I Still Am," *Iron Mountain Review* 12 (spring 1996): 5.

15. Michael Lee Mullins, "Hindman Settlement School," in *A Gathering at the Forks,* ed. George Ella Lyon, Jim Wayne Miller, and Gurney Norman (Wise, Va.: Vision Books, 1993), v.

16. Wilma Dykeman, *The Tall Woman* (New York: Holt, Rinehart and Winston, 1962), 9, 24.

SHEILA
KAY
ADAMS

Sheila Kay Adams (b. 1953) comes from a small mountain community in western North Carolina. For seven generations her family has maintained the tradition of passing down the English, Scottish, and Irish ballads that came over with her ancestors in the late 1700s. Adams learned the ballads from her relatives, primarily from her great-aunt, Dellie Chandler Norton. She is an accomplished balladeer, storyteller, and five-string banjo player. A highly sought-after performer who travels extensively to share her heritage, she has performed at numerous folk festivals, conferences, and artist series across the nation and has been the featured performer in several documentary films. Adams was cohost and coproducer of *Over Home,* a radio show for Public Radio, and has two cassette recordings that contain both traditional and original ballads, *Loving Forward, Loving Back* (1985) and *A Spring in the Burton Cove* (1990), and a story tape, *Don't Git above Your Raising* (1992). Under the direction of Lee Smith, Adams compiled a collection of stories about her growing up years in Madison County, *Come Go Home with Me* (1995). She has three children and is passing the traditions on to them. Married to Jim Taylor, also a traditional musician and performer, she resides in the county in which she was born. Adams has kept her roots well planted in her Appalachian mountain home. As her great-aunt has said, "She may not always know where she's going but she sure knows where she comes from."

* * *

Flowering Ivy

"How do you know?" he asked one warm, early spring day.
Exhausted from the climb, I paused to catch a breath,
leaned down, and plucked a purple flower near my booted toe.
"I just do," I said.
"It's been passed down.
The words fell soft from Granny's lips,
fell like needed summer rain,
that puddled up here in my ears."

Granny said, "Mother planted flowering ivy.
She were fifteen, well, maybe not quite.
She carried that poor babe in her skinny, little girl's arms.
Wrapped hit up in her best nightgown.
Made her walk as the sun went down
on a white-hot summer's day.
Folks stood and watched.
Said now and again she would pause,
and lower her face to the bundle she clutched there at her breast.
'Ain't natural,' they muttered from behind their snuff packed lower lips.
'That babe barely formed . . .'
'But, hit were a boy-child,' someone said.
'Formed enough fer that I reckon.'
On she climbed, right up to the spine of the ridge,
dug the hole herself . . . stopping only to pick up that gown,
and rest her head into it,
with her long red hair falling wild all around.
Dark come on, still she set.
Her big thick shouldered man made the climb hisself.
Tried to talk her down.
'Come on back to the house,' he begged.
What he meant was back to his bed, his life.
'What about me?' he cried, kneeling by the raw, red scar there on the ground.
'What about you?' she asked softly.
'What about you?'
The stars rose on her still there.

He come down . . . eyes red-rimmed, big hands hanging down, empty as his
     heart.
He stood all night in the kitchen yard, looking to the ridge,
listening to the sleep-soft talk from the chickens,
roosting in the tree out next to his brand-new barn.
Toward daylight he went to the house, fetched his fiddle,
put it in an-under his chin,
and commenced to playing,
them high and lonesome tunes . . .
The warm-fingered wind picked up his song,
carried it right up the hill,
laid it gentle-like right next to her ear.
She sighed.
And then his tune found her heart.
And she threw back her small, fine-boned head.
Cried out she did.
Her cry was snatched away by the startled wind.
Was carried high where it spread out into the lightening up sky.
. . . He never heard.
She reached into the pocket of the apron that she wore,
pulled out a little sprig o' green.
Used her fingers to make a hole,
planted it there."

"Now look," I said. "It runs everywhere!
One hundred and twenty-seven years ago,
Mother sat right there.
Now look, her ivy is a laid down rug of green.
Covering up that tiny babe,
poor little Loney,
my Pap Tete,
And her."

When someone dies, Daddy says they have moved down the road and up on the
hill, meaning to one of the several graveyards there in Sodom. And they still re-
ceive visitors on a regular basis.

The young girl in the story was my great-grandmother on my mother's side.
Her name was Betty Ray Norton; everyone referred to her as Mother. She was
born in 1853, and died in 1917. I was born a hundred years after her birth, but I
know many things about her. She was 5 feet 11 inches tall. She had dark red hair

that reached almost to her knees when she brushed it out. She had dark, almost black eyes and impossibly high cheekbones. She had a wide, expressive mouth and a "damned-and-determined" chin. I know she was strong-willed, and as Mama says, she could be mean. She met my Pap Tete at a box supper and married him a year later. She asked for two promises before she agreed to marry him: That should God see fit to bless them with children he would never put his hands on them when he was mad. And that he would be faithful to her. They argued their way through many years of marriage and the birth of nine children. She only lost the one child I wrote about in "Flowering Ivy."

One night after Pap had been sneaking in late for several nights running, he eased up on the porch and took hold of the door latch. Out of the corner of his eye, he thought he saw a darker piece of the night separate off and move in his direction. He didn't even have time to take his hand from the latch, when he felt something cold attach itself right behind his left ear. He held his breath as he heard the hammer click back. It was quite a bit of relief when Mother spoke to him from the other end of the shotgun.

"Tete," she said softly.

"Lord God, Betty! Put that damned thing down. Hit's just me. What'd ye think? Hit was somebody come to harm yeer one of the younguns?" he asked.

Her answer must have chilled his heart.

"Oh no, I knowed hit was you. I been settin' out here waitin' fer ye ever since first dark."

"Why, fer God's sake?" he whispered.

"Fer goin' on three weeks now, I've laid in there in our bed, and listened to you slip in this door, fumblin' around, tryin' to be quiet, easin' in beside me and layin' real still, not darin' to so much as breathe. I'm tellin' ye right now, you have sneaked in your last time. I want to know where you've been, and who have ye been with?" and she nudged him gently with the barrel of the shotgun.

My Pap had no trouble letting Mother know that he and his cousin had been making a little liquor up on the Tater Gap. Mother hated the drinking of alcohol. But not enough to kill him for the distilling of it!

Mama says that when I was a small child, I would rock my body back and forth, and hum while folks around me talked. She thought there was something "not-right" about me. She worried about it silently for a while. Finally she mentioned it to my grandfather, the man I called Breaddaddy. She said he chewed his tobacco thoughtfully, then spat into the spit can next to his chair.

"They ain't nothin' wrong with her, 'cept she might be far too clever. She is right stubborn, and hard-headed. Wants her way far too much. You need to take care not to spoil her. But, as fer as the rockin' and hummin', Mother used to do that. She said she was rockin' to the music she heard in folks' words. I remember as a child bein' rocked to sleep in the bed as I laid next to her, listenin' to her hum. Naw, they ain't notin' wrong with my grandbaby."

I still hear the music in the voices of my home. There is a rhythm to their speech, a lilting quality that I have yet to hear in any other place. Except in Ireland. I heard it there too. A close friend of mine once said, "When I hear your family talk while sitting around the table, I catch myself trying to find the harmony in my head!"

When I sing, I hear the voices of my beloved granny, and Cas, and Inez, and Vergie, and Evelyn in my mind's ear. When I play banjo, I hear notes played by Jerry, and Tommy, and Fred, and Dwight, and Ron, and Alice. And, when I write, I hear the voices of so many strong and wonderful women—those past and present, family and friends. But the voice that whispers right next to my heart late at night, that weaves itself in and out of my writing, my soul identifies that voice as Mother's.

As I grow older, I am more and more reminded how life is a circle. I moved from my childhood home of Sodom in 1982. Oh no, not too far away, only thirty minutes or so, and still in Madison County. I have lived in five different houses during the last fourteen years. My home now is on a mountaintop. From the porch you can see Craggy Gardens and Mount Mitchell. It's a beautiful, peaceful place. I think I'll stay here.

I brought Mama to visit for the first time last week. She sat in my living room, gazing out the window. "It's a real pretty place. Don't you think?"

"Yeah, it is," I said. Then I laughed. "Never thought I'd live in this part of the county, though."

Mama looked up at me and smiled. "Let's go out to the back of the house. I want to point something out to you."

I was puzzled. Reckon what she wanted to show me?

We stood on the porch out back and she pointed off down into the woods. "If I'm not mistaken, you can take off down that ridge, and come out on the old home place."

"Old home place? Whose?" I asked, totally confused.

"Why, Mother's, honey. She was born and raised right out this ridge . . ."

LISA
ALTHER

Lisa Alther was born in 1944 in Kingsport, Tennessee, where she went to public schools. She graduated from Wellesley College with a B.A. in English in 1966. After attending the publishing procedures course at Radcliffe College and working for Atheneum Publishers in New York, she moved to Hinesburg, Vermont, where she raised her daughter. Alther currently divides her time between Hinesburg and New York City. Three of her novels, *Kinflicks* (1975), *Original Sins* (1980), and *Other Women* (1984), were featured selections of the Book-of-the-Month Club and appeared on the *New York Times* best-seller lists. These novels, along with *Bedrock* (1990) and *Five Minutes in Heaven* (1995), her most recent novel, have been included on best-seller lists world-wide and translated into fifteen languages. A novella entitled *Birdman and the Dancer* (1993), based on a series of monotypes by the French artist Françoise Gilot, has been published in Holland, Denmark, and Germany. Alther's reviews and essays have appeared in numerous magazines and newspapers, including the *New York Times, Art and Antiques*, the *Los Angeles Times*, the *Boston Globe, Natural History, New Society,* and the *Guardian*. She has done reading and lecture tours throughout North America, western Europe, Australia, New Zealand, Indonesia, and China, and her novels are studied at universities in departments of literature, women's studies, sociology, and psychology. In her attempt to portray the human reality behind various cultural stereotypes, Alther has often chosen the routes of humor and comedy.

*   *   *

Border States

When she was ninety-six, Hattie Elizabeth Vanover Reed, my paternal grandmother, would put on a stylish silk suit with a skirt to her knees, nylons and two-inch heels, costume jewelry, and full-battle makeup whenever visitors were expected at her nursing home in Kingsport, Tennessee. Right to the end, she maintained her standards for a Virginia lady.

I remember my grandmother best presiding over Sunday dinners in the night-club that she'd bought from a bootlegger and remodeled into her home. An open-air deck, where patrons had once drunk moonshine, ran the length of the living room, overlooking the slow-drifting Holston River, often frothy with waste from the Tennessee Eastman plant upriver. She dug a lily pond in the former parking lot, stocking it with goldfish that soon became bloated from the Saltines we grand-children crumbled for them. Behind the pond she planted magnolia trees. The first time I stuck my nose into one of those creamy blossoms, I refused to remove it. Seeing what was possible in the realm of scent, I didn't want to breathe ordinary air anymore, especially not the air of our town, which was sticky with fumes from the Mead paper mill.

My grandmother's Sunday dinner was a ritual as inescapable as Sunday school. But my three brothers and I often delayed it by racing to the stone wall that overlooked the valley out back to count the cars making up a train snaking past down below. The northbound trains, bulging with the trunks of primordial pop-lars, dribbled chunks of coal down the tracks, whereas the southbound trains flaunted cockscombs of shiny new-model autos.

After the caboose vanished around the bend, my grandfather sometimes teed up by the fishpond and drove his golf ball to the ninth green of the course across the river. He watched the ball climb, arc, and fall, longing to row the boat tethered by the riverbank across to the far shore to continue his game. He had been a semiprofessional left-handed baseball pitcher in his youth, and his golf scores as a senior citizen were in the low seventies.

Instead of plunging down the cliff to freedom, though, my grandfather strolled inside and sat down at the gleaming faux-Sheraton table, backed by wallpaper featuring a mural of hoop-skirted belles flouncing around the portico of a south-ern mansion. Wearing a monogrammed silk shirt, he listened in silence as my grandmother regaled my father with the fiery future that awaited those who turned their backs on the Southern Baptist Church in order to attend the Episcopal Church up the street with their misled Yankee brides. Silver platters of fried chicken, shelly beans, Parker House rolls, and molded Jello salad circulated, as my brothers and I disputed the number of tiny silver fruits on the handles of the Francis I flatware.

My grandparents grew up at the end of the nineteenth century on farms in the coalfields of southwest Virginia. Both were middle children of eight siblings. My grandmother's mother died of pneumonia when my grandmother was thirteen. My grandfather's father died of pneumonia and his mother of gallbladder disease before he was six. He was raised in his older sister's household. Like an episode from Dickens, the relative who served as executor sold off his parents' farm in 1888 and squandered the proceeds. When my grandfather was twelve, he ran away from his sister's, hiking eighty miles across the mountains into Kentucky to join an older brother.

Both my grandparents trained as teachers in Clintwood and Big Stone Gap, Virginia. Second cousins, they first met when she became his student. After their marriage she persuaded him to pursue his dream of becoming a doctor, a dream no doubt fostered by his watching helplessly as his parents died. He attended the University of Louisville, hopping southbound freight trains to see his wife. The next year he won a scholarship to the Medical College of Virginia in Richmond. My grandmother sold cosmetics in a department store, then taught at a reform school for girls, once fighting off some attacking students with her hat pin. During the summers he sold pots door-to-door and worked as a logger. His final year at school he tended Confederate veterans at the Robert E. Lee Soldiers' Home.

Returning to Clintwood, my grandfather kept a stable of six horses to convey him to patients in the remote hollows. He owned the first car in the county, until it lurched out of control and bounced down a mountainside on its hard rubber tires, crashing into a creek.

When my father was five, my grandparents moved to Kingsport, Tennessee, a new town being established in the Holston Valley to accommodate industry from the North seeking nonunionized labor. My grandfather opened the town's first hospital, while my grandmother oversaw construction of a large neo-Georgian house on the street where the Yankee plant managers were building their houses. (She later gave this house to my father upon his return from World War II with his pregnant wife and two small children, of whom I was the younger.)

One day my grandmother decided the masons were building a brick wall in the back yard incorrectly, so she took over. As she slapped mortar on a brick, a mason said, "Excuse me, m'am, but you can't build a wall like that." My grandmother looked up at him and said, "Sir, not only can I, I am."

Although my grandmother had enough drive to run several factories, such roles weren't open to women. So she was soon running the social life of Kingsport instead, attending a tea, luncheon, bridge game, or club meeting nearly every day.

Her favorite group was the Virginia Club. To belong, one had to have been born in Virginia. At their meetings, the members, whom my grandmother referred to as "those fine Colonial ladies," mused about the superiority of Virginia over Tennessee. It was not unheard of for members to cross the nearby state line when they went into labor so their infants could be born Virginians. By the time I knew her, my grandmother was not just a Virginian, she was a Tidewater Virginian whose Cavalier forebears had received land grants from James I.

Meanwhile, I was being groomed as a Virginia belle (even though I was born in Tennessee), attending cooking classes, sewing classes, and weekly sessions of Charm School at the local department store. I learned to set a table, plan a menu, arrange flowers, dress, walk, sit, and make myself up. I also learned to waltz, and when I was sixteen, I was presented as a debutante, wearing a white strapless Scarlett O'Hara gown, with kid gloves to my biceps, which bulged un-bellelike from years of football with the neighborhood boys. My boyfriend Harold and I waltzed in intricate patterns with the other Symphony Belles and their dates to "The Champagne Waltz." (Then we drove in his father's finned yellow Buick to our favorite parking spot and struggled like the Laocoön to free me from my hoops.)

All my life I have longed to belong to some group, so as to escape the lonely task of self-definition. The closest I ever came was in high school when the Queen Teens invited me to join. Finally I knew who I was: I was a Q.T. We were said to be more trashy than the Sub Debs or the Devilish Debs and to give better parties.

This hard-won self-knowledge evaporated, however, when I arrived at college near Boston during the civil rights years. No one up there had ever heard of the Queen Teens, and when they did, they laughed. I was summoned to the Wellesley gym, stripped down to my underwear, and photographed in profile like a police lineup. Fortunately, the carriage I had learned by strutting around the Kingsport department store with textbooks on my head got me exempted from Remedial Posture. I was conscripted into Fundamentals of Movement, however, in which I learned how to sit down in an MG without flashing too much thigh. I was also given a speech test. Thanks to my Yankee mother's childhood coaching on how to pronounce "cow" in one syllable, I passed. Nevertheless, at dinner one night a hallmate observed, "It's so amusing to hear you say something intelligent in that southern accent of yours." After the murder of the three civil rights workers in Mississippi, a woman from across the hall barged into my room to announce, "You southerners make me sick!"

I was astonished because, until then, I'd rarely thought of myself as a southerner. To the contrary, I'd always been teased on the playground because my mother was a Yankee and my pronunciation of "cow" was so weird. And I had assumed that every young woman in America was forced to waltz in hoop skirts. Since East Tennessee is mountainous, it had hosted few plantations or slaves. And when Tennessee seceded from the Union, East Tennessee tried to secede from Tennessee. My father's great-grandfather was a sergeant in the Union army. My grandmother's great-uncle lost an arm fighting for the Union at the battle of Cranesnest River. Several forebears moved from southwest Virginia to Kentucky to avoid fighting for the Confederacy. To say nothing of my mother's ancestors in New York or of her lullabies, which included a Union battle hymn called "Sherman's Dashing Yankee Boys."

But it was also true that other forebears fought for the Confederacy, one dying of measles shortly after enlisting in the Virginia Infantry. And Sullivan County, where I lived, had been prepared to secede from East Tennessee if East Tennessee seceded from the Union. As children, my brothers, neighbors, and I played War between the States, giving each other transfusions with lengths of string from bottles of water dyed red with food coloring. Most of us owned gray cardboard Confederate Army caps, and no one wanted to be a Yankee, so this fate usually befell the youngest children.

In sum, I was one baffled college freshman, accepted because my Appalachian origins (of which I was unaware) appealed to the missionary instincts of the admissions committee but now expected to transform myself into something called "The Wellesley Girl." After a bout of mononucleosis that allowed me to sulk in the infirmary for a month, I decided to sort out my confusion by writing a short story. Little did I know that this in itself marked me as a southerner. As Flannery O'Connor once wrote, "The Southerner knows he can do more justice to reality by telling a story than he can by discussing problems or proposing abstractions. . . . It's actually his way of reasoning and dealing with experience." But when I had one of my characters say, "Law, honey, where'd you get that hat at?" my writing professor informed me that real people didn't talk that way. This was the first time I'd ever realized that the people I'd grown up among weren't real.

It takes a long time to figure out who you are, and it often takes leaving a place behind to recognize how it has shaped you. As Sarah Orne Jewett wrote Willa Cather, "One must know the world *so well* before one can know the parish." After college I moved to Vermont and wrote my first novel, *Kinflicks*. Predictably, it concerns a young woman who grows up in Tennessee, goes to college near Boston, and moves to Vermont. And during the funk that for me always follows publication, I started wondering why, if my grandmother loved Virginia so much, she'd moved to Tennessee, why she rarely went back, why we hardly ever met our Virginia relatives.

I asked my father. He explained that once when he was visiting kin near

Clintwood, his uncle Cas invited him to go fishing. "Fishing" consisted of sitting on a creek bank all afternoon drinking white lightning. When it was time to go home, Cas lit some sticks of dynamite and tossed them into the water, then collected the fish that landed onshore. When my father told him that was against the law, he said, "Son, over here I am the law." My father also described my grandfather's being chased on horseback by an armed thug for defending a cousin during a knife fight. He packed a .38 Special for several years afterwards. My father speculated that his parents had left southwest Virginia as much to escape the alcoholism and violence as to try their luck in a new boomtown.

The next time I was home, I went to see my grandmother's aunt, Ura Grizzle, who at 103 seemed close to death. She lay in her bed at her daughter's house, eyes closed, face copper against the white pillow, hair pulled back to reveal a broad forehead and high cheekbones, looking like the Cherokee she used to say she was. Discovering it was unfashionable to be Indian, she later denied it. I, however, was from a generation for whom ethnicity of any sort seemed exotic, so I asked about her Cherokee forebears. Even though her daughter assured me she was awake, her eyes and lips remained shut.

Next I went to southwest Virginia on my own (driving in two hours a distance that used to take my grandparents twelve). I could tell this trip upset my grandmother, but she said nothing. She felt well-bred people should communicate like bats, via ultrasonic squeaks. I was eating lunch at a cafeteria in Clintwood when the participants in a trial at the nearby courthouse came in. The waitress told me that a couple had had a son who was a high school football star. He ran into a goalpost, broke his neck, and was buried in the local churchyard. Now his parents were divorcing, and his mother was moving fifty miles away. Wanting to take her son along, she was suing for custody. As I buttered my cornbread, I first understood the origins of the black humor that had recently made *Kinflicks* successful. It was a regional trait, I realized, based on the assumption that human behavior is so bizarre that the only recourse is to laugh.

Later I returned to East Tennessee to research an article on snake handling for the *New York Times.* My doctor father used to tell us at the dinner table about snake handlers who turned up in the emergency room. Some died and some didn't. What I found in the backwoods frame churches were farmers, truck drivers, car mechanics—people for whom the fondling of copperheads was their only excitement. The famous mountain feuds, over such issues as who left the gate open so the hogs got out, had entertained their forebears similarly. Might it have also been rural monotony that propelled my grandparents out of southwest Virginia? I wondered.

At this point my Appalachian relatives began to become real to me, despite my writing professor's assurances that they weren't. Because I had grown up in an industrial town in a river valley surrounded by amiable carpetbaggers rather than in a mountain cove, I had failed to grasp the fact that I, too, was Appalachian. For the first time, I began to ponder the caricatures in the funny papers and on television—*L'il Abner, Snuffy Smith, Hee Haw, The Beverly Hillbillies, The Waltons. The Waltons* evoked nostalgia, the others, contemptuous amusement. Yet, beneath surface differences, the Appalachians I knew were similar to the Bostonians and Vermonters I'd kept company with since leaving home. The language of the heart, it seemed to me, was universal. At least that had always been the guiding impulse behind my writing.

Still reflecting upon why the rest of the nation would need to view Appalachians as quaint or venal hillbillies, I moved to England. The Vietnam War was just ending, and many of my British friends were leftists, so I received frequent lectures on American imperialism, for which I was apparently a running dog. I was bewildered because I had never thought of myself as an American. I was just getting used to myself as a southerner and an Appalachian.

As usual, I plunged into a novel as a way to organize my confusion. The question I posed was why, if you have several people coming of age in the same environment, do some leave and others stay? Why did certain fish decide to crawl out on dry land? Why, in other words, did my grandparents leave Virginia? And why did I leave the Tennessee river valley they bequeathed me? The resulting novel, *Original Sins*, features five characters growing up in a small East Tennessee town. Three leave and two stay. After 592 pages, I came to the banal conclusion that the ones who left did so because they didn't fit in.

Applying to my story the Marxist analysis I'd absorbed from my left-wing British friends, I further understood that other Americans needed to see Appalachians as ignorant hillbillies in order not to feel guilty for having plundered our timber and coal, wrecked our environment, and exploited our labor. Victors always portray the vanquished in unflattering terms in order to rationalize their own brutality. At the same time, it occurred to me that perhaps their guilt wasn't really necessary, since the forebears of most Appalachians stole their land from the Cherokees, the Cherokees having stolen it from the Copena, the Copena from the Hopewells, the Hopewells from the Mound Builders, and so on back to the dawn of our greedy species.

Tired of being attacked in London for being an American when I was attacked in Boston for not being one, I returned to Vermont to lick my ethnic wounds and write my third novel. *Other Women* concerns the interaction between a therapist and her client, a lesbian mother and nurse who is trying to comprehend the violence in the world. Since therapy was nearly as popular as polio when I was growing up in Tennessee, I suspected after publication that I had now disqualified myself as both a southerner and an Appalachian. To make matters worse, southern and Appalachian women were known for standing by their men, single-handedly harvesting crops and raising children, sewing dresses from flour sacks and planting petunias in diesel tires, even as their men drank, caroused, and knocked them senseless. I had seen the "accidents" resulting from this ethos several times while working at the hospital as a candy striper during high school. By writing about a woman who preferred to stand by another woman, one who treated her with tenderness, it was likely that I had now doubly disqualified myself from my natal groups.

During my subsequent creative drought, I first began to suspect that in my northward flight toward freedom, I hadn't really left home. The Vermont house I was living in was a brick Georgian identical to the one my grandmother had constructed in Kingsport in 1926, except that mine was built in 1803. The foothills around me were similar to those I had roamed as a child. Vermonters, although more reticent than East Tennesseeans, had the same droll affability. Some had the same unfortunate tendency to assault their women when they were having a bad day. The accent was different but the grammar "mistakes" were the same. I could just as easily hear "I ain't never seen nobody like you" in Vermont as in Tennessee.

Vermont, I realized, was merely the northern end of the Appalachians, which was why I felt so much at home. The entire mountain range had been settled by Anglo-Saxons and Celts. The ballads, clogging, speech patterns, black humor, and Calvinism were nearly identical all along its length, apart from local variations based on contributions from different ethnic groups, particularly the Cherokees in the south and the French Canadians in Vermont. Modern civilization had disrupted this mountain culture in the mid-Atlantic states, but it still existed at either extremity. To paraphrase Pogo, I had met the enemy, and they were us.

In the grip of this insight, I wrote my fourth novel, *Bedrock,* which features a Vermont village full of eccentrics, composites of people and situations I had known in both Tennessee and Vermont. And although I had lived in Vermont for twenty-five years by then and had several eighteenth-century ancestors buried in the Rockingham, Vermont, churchyard, a Boston reviewer maintained I had no right to satirize Vermonters since I was a southerner.

Having finally recognized, accepted, and stitched the Appalachian patch into the crazy quilt of myself, imagine my dismay as I was reading a book by a self-professed Melungeon, Brent Kennedy, and realized that he was a third cousin I'd never met. The Melungeons are a group of some twenty thousand people living in the region where East Tennessee, southwest Virginia, southeastern Kentucky, and northwestern North Carolina join. Several hundred thousand people outside this area are thought to have Melungeon ancestry without knowing it. The first Anglo-Saxon settlers to arrive, in the last half of the eighteenth century, found the olive-skinned ancestors of present-day Melungeons already living there, in European-style houses.

When I was a child, babysitters used to threaten us with abduction by six-fingered Melungeons who reputedly lived in trees on the ridges ringing town. Although Melungeons always maintained that they were Portuguese, researchers claimed they were "tri-racial isolates," resulting from intermarriage among Native Americans, escaped slaves, and mountain whites. Considered "free persons of color," they were pushed off their land, denied the vote, and prohibited from marrying whites or attending their schools.

Recent genetic, cross-cultural, linguistic, historical, and medical evidence reported in my newfound cousin's book suggests that they may, in fact, be partly Portuguese and Turkish. Some historians maintain that their progenitors were explorers, missionaries, colonists, and soldiers from several Spanish towns and forts known to have existed in the southeast in the late sixteenth century, in addition to several hundred Turkish sailors believed to have been dumped on the Carolina coast after a failed attempt to establish a colony in Cuba. The thinking is that these groups may have merged with each other and with Native American tribes over several generations, gradually being forced onto inaccessible mountain ridges by the Anglo-Saxon settlers, who were intolerant of their darker skins and covetous of their rich bottomland.

If my cousin's calculations are valid, each of my grandparents would have been about a quarter Melungeon. Was this the missing link, I wondered? Whether "tri-racial isolates" or Portuguese-Turkish–Native American hybrids, might my grandparents have left Virginia because they were targets for discrimination? Did they want a fresh start among people who didn't know them? Could this be why my grandmother was so uncommunicative about her relatives?

These new speculations sent me into a frenzy of family research, which I won't detail since people's genealogies are almost as tedious as their vacation slides. Suffice it to say that I was succumbing to a family obsession. My mother's grandmother was the national genealogist for the D.A.R. and documented eleven lines of her family that came to America before 1650. Another Virginia cousin has published a book trailing one branch of my grandmother's family, the Vanovers, back to seventeenth-century Holland.

I would be inclined now to agree with the adage, "Ignorance is bliss." I soon discovered that both sides of my family have been in this country for twelve generations, the Cherokees and perhaps the Melungeons for longer. Yet I had studied Buddhism, and all I wanted was to be here now. What was I to do with all these snarled roots? It seemed I was English, Scottish, Irish, Scots-Irish, French, Alsatian, German, Dutch, and Cherokee. If my Melungeon cousin was correct about our shared ancestors, I was also whatever mix that that entailed. My ancestors' faiths had been Primitive Baptist, Huguenot, Dunkard, Church of England, Congregational, Puritan, Dutch Reformed, Jewish. The men had been soldiers, sailors, privateers, carpenters, paupers, coopers, weavers, syphilitics, millers, preachers, drug addicts, tavern keepers, suicides, farmers, doctors, debtors, coal miners, lawyers, draft dodgers, teachers. Except for a couple of suffragists, a midwife, and a breeder of championship chickens, the women died leaving no trace but their children. Despite my heroic efforts at self-definition, I now knew that my genes constituted their own private Balkans. I felt deep nostalgia for the days when I had been a Queen Teen and identity had seemed a simple issue of not being a Sub Deb or a Devilish Deb.

My fifth novel, *Five Minutes in Heaven,* became an attempt to unite these scattered beads of mercury—urban and rural, northern and southern and Appalachian, American and European. My main character grows up in East Tennessee, lives in New York City as a young woman, then moves to Paris. Experiencing these cultural differences, she comes to understand that love in its highest sense is the only force that can override the conflicts and violence that such surface variations incite. A couple of reviewers demanded to know why an American would want to write about France.

At the moment I am in the process of establishing my United Nations within. As my model, I have selected that early Appalachian existentialist, Hattie Elizabeth Vanover Reed. Almost everything I know about creating fiction is a legacy from her. Faced with the void, or with a reality too grim or too complicated to endure, she simply decided that she was a Tidewater lady and then turned herself into one. After she finished the brick wall behind her Georgian house (a wall still intact after seventy-five years), the architect stopped by to admire it. She replied, "Why, thank you, sir. I know that my wall will stand, because I have studied Thomas Jefferson's walls at the University of Virginia."

MAGGIE
ANDERSON

Maggie Anderson was born in New York City in 1948 and moved to West Virginia when she was thirteen years old. Her family is from Preston County. She is the author of four books of poetry including *Years That Answer* (1980), *Cold Comfort* (1986), and *A Space Filled with Moving* (1992). She is also the editor of *Hill Daughter: New and Selected Poems* (1991) by former West Virginia poet laureate Louise McNeill (1911–1993), and coeditor of *A Gathering of Poets* (1992). Anderson, associate professor and director of the Wick Poetry Program at Kent State University in Ohio, edits a chapbook poetry series and a first book series through the Kent State University Press. She worked for ten years (1978–88) in West Virginia communities through the Artists-in-the-Schools-and-Communities Program and was poet-in-residence in Marshall, Mercer, and Jackson counties, as well as in the West Virginia Penitentiary at Moundsville.

* * *

The Mountains Dark and Close around Me

> After I left the farm, I often felt as I had when I used to plumb the depth of water as a child. In summer, after every big rainstorm, a flood would come, and our tiny cow-spring trickle would become a roaring stream that flowed foamy and green over the grasses. I would go out barefoot in the early morning with a long, straight pole; and with my dress tied up above my knees I would wade along the shallows to measure the deep holes. I felt my way out into the current and walked slowly upstream, my feet and legs stinging with the cold. As I walked on and on up through the wild morning, I would become John Ridd of *Lorna Doone* with his trident, walking up the spate of Doone Valley. Then the mountains would come dark and close around. I walked until I could feel the black danger and death in it. As I am walking still. For you walk to death, don't you? Because you cannot ride.
>
> —Louise McNeill, *The Milkweed Ladies*

I don't like the term "influence." The large shaky hand of Harold Bloom's anxiety hovers over it; and for women writers, "influence" has too often been used as a way of establishing our partriarchal lineage and our lack of originality. When I think of who and what have had lasting effects on my work, I prefer to think of "confluence," coming together with intent. "Influence" hierarchizes. The landscapes I have known, the writers who are essential to me (those I have known in person, and those I have known only through their books), the words and songs and trees I search out, all form confluences that make my work possible. These confluences make me stronger and allow me to flow toward and beside others.

I wrote the weather report in my journal this morning because as Thoreau noted, "In a journal it is important in a few words to describe the weather, or character of the day, as it affects our feelings." Also, my uncle Homer, who kept a daily journal for most of his life, documented weather and temperature every day. After he retired, he wrote the temperature three times a day, checking it on the big round thermometer outside his back door. My uncle Homer didn't document much—a few drives he took, some deaths, and the dates he had his car serviced—but he was one of the first people I knew who wrote regularly and I have followed his example of chronicling my life.

This morning the weather was rainy, temperatures in the forties, a gray fall day. I am sitting in my house in Kent, Ohio—the tallest house I could find to live in—and I am in my studio on the third floor. Out the west window, I can see almost to Akron, which from this height is an optical illusion of a far line of hills. A far line of hills always reminds me of West Virginia, which always makes me feel at home.

The image of an unremitting line of hills that defines any mountain land-scape affects me more deeply than any other. Sometimes, when I have lived out of West Virginia for long periods of time, I have dreamed the deep swayback of Laurel Mountain where it joins Cannon Hill outside my aunt Nita's kitchen win-dow in Rowlesburg; the wide sweep of the Potomac Highlands that beckoned from my high school classroom windows in Keyser; or the gentle slope of the farmland in Marshall County near Cameron and Hundred. I lived five years in Charleston, West Virginia, where the steep hills pull tight and dark around the chemical valley drawing beautiful, bloody sunsets out of the miles of fiery lights along the Kanawha. And when I think of the hills from my perch here in Ohio, I think of my friend poet Irene McKinney's family farm in Barbour County, the far range of the Blue Ridge into western Virginia, the winding roads through the foothills, and the dirt paths rutted up and down the farm itself, from barn to field to salt lick to stream.

I know, of course, that the mountains can narrow our horizons, lower our ceilings, and hold us in, both literally and metaphorically. But I must also admit that these hills comfort me. Perhaps because of their great age (the range of mountains that makes up the Appalachian region from Georgia to Maine is two hundred million years old), the hills provide a sense of history and, therefore, of implicit continu-ance. The fact of their long past suggests the possibility of a long future, and those who live in the mountains stand at the confluence of what Louise McNeill named "a place called solid":

> We could sense, just beyond our broken-down line fences, the great reach of the American continent flowing outward. Because we stood so long in one place, our rocky old farm and the abundant earth of the continent were linked together in the long tides of the past. Because the land kept us, never budging from its rock-hold, we held to our pioneer ways the longest, the strongest; we saw the passing of time from a place called solid, from our own slow, archean, and peculiar stance. [*The Milkweed Ladies*, p. 8]

What moves in the mountains is water: the fast, unnavigable rivers, the fresh-ets and little creeks, the waterfalls, and the man-made lakes, stippled with motorboats and skiers. The Appalachian region is a geography of earth and water, and these converge awkwardly, paradoxically. The rivers have always been a mode of transport, carrying out the lumber, the coal, the steel, barge by barge, and now carrying in the tourists on white-water rafts. The waters are beautiful when they are quiet, lit by sunlight and the froth of the backwash, but they are also the means of "danger and death," the fast rising we cannot outrun.

On the big desk in my attic studio are the outward signs of various confluences: containers for the things I gather, pencil boxes, flowers, little notes to myself of things to do, and books. There are piles of books on my desk in tidy rows organized to complete this or that project, and there are volunteers, books that come in the mail or books from friends. The titles of my books reflect an agitated mind, or an interestingly enthused one: *Ladies of the Rachmaninoff Eyes,* a novel by my friend Henry Van Dyke; three novels by Ronald Firbank; and the exhibition catalogue for last year's Florine Stettheimer show at the Guggenheim. I always have a copy of Muriel Rukeyser's *The Life of Poetry* near me, and now I have the new edition from Paris Press with a foreword by Jane Cooper. Almost any line from this book, read closely, stays with me for days:

> In time of crisis, we summon up our strength.
>   Then, if we are lucky, we are able to call every resource, every forgotten image that can leap to our quickening, every memory that can make us know our power. And this luck is more than it seems to be: it depends on the long preparation of the self to be used. [p. 1]

Or:

> All the poems of our lives are not yet made. [p. 214]

Also on my desk are Louise McNeill's *Hill Daughter* and *The Milkweed Ladies;* the Jargon Society edition of the Appalachian photographs of Doris Ulmann opened to the woman who looks like Jim Wayne Miller, Mrs. Teams of Pine Log, North Carolina; Patricia Hampl's *Spillville,* a fictionalized account of Dvořák's stay in Iowa in 1893, with engravings by Steven Sorman accompanying the text; and *Two Journals,* words and drawings by James Schuyler and Darragh Park. Often, things converge to make little subplots: the porcelain bowl I bought in Budapest, filled with shiny Ohio buckeyes I gathered on my walks in September when I was reading Mark Doty's book of poems, *Atlantis,* and his memoir, *Heaven's Coast;* the notecard on which I typed these lines from Doty's "Grosse Fuge":

> I bring home, from each walk to town, pockets
> full of chestnuts, and fill a porcelain

bowl with their ruddy, seducing music
—something like cellos, something that banks deep
inside the body. The chestnuts seem lit
from within, almost as if by lamplight,
and burnished to warm leather, the color
of old harnesses . . . [*Atlantis*, p. 23]

Below these, handwritten, "Dear Mark, me too."

Buried under a stack of books, some photographs: the Blackwater Canyon in Randolph County, West Virginia; Irene beside her cousin Bert's barn, me on a rusty old tractor outside Irene's house, and both of us together at the Hindman Settlement School in Kentucky standing on the bridge where Mike Mullins killed the big copperhead after the reading.

And one new book: *Sally Arnold,* a picture book by my friend Cheryl Ryan, in which a little girl makes friends with an old "witchy" woman named Sally Arnold who lives on Sally's Backbone, up above Lynn Camp. The illustrations by Bill Farnsworth are warm and evocative. I can locate the topographical source of this story along the road through Glen Easton that Anna and I used to drive to visit Cheryl and her husband, poet Marc Harshman, on Bowman Ridge nearly twenty years ago. Sometimes we took a long walk before supper, or maybe one of their neighbors from Lynn Camp or Saint Josephs would stop by. It was the 1970s, and we were different then, of course, both slower and younger. But this was another important confluence: a brief time when we came together in Marshall County, West Virginia, in the random talk of dailiness and work, shared meals, and a friendship built slowly over time.

With West Virginia poet Louise McNeill, I think I had what might properly be called a "literary friendship." We never shared much of the casual, leisurely talk I associate with friendship. We rarely spoke about our own lives apart from the writing, and we never ate dinner out or went shopping or to a movie. What we did together was work. On two extended visits I made to Louise, we forged what Tillie Olsen calls "the strong bonds of shared labor," as we put together the manuscripts of Louise's memoir *The Milkweed Ladies* and her new and selected poems, *Hill Daughter*. Because of the condition of Louise's health during those two visits, we were also forced to navigate an intimacy that neither of us would have approached had Louise been less physically frail. She was, however, never mentally frail, nor was she particularly easy to get along with (what intelligent, complicated person is?). She remained, in all the time I knew her—nearly thirty years at her death in 1993—the same formidable and determined person I had first met when I was in high school. I have told this story before:

Louise McNeill was the first poet I heard give a poetry reading. In 1964, I was sixteen years old and McNeill came to read at the junior college in Keyser, West Virginia, where I lived. I had read very little poetry and, except for the few poems by Emily Dickinson in my school anthology, I had read no poems by women. I knew nothing of the literature of my region and so, although I had decided by that time that I wanted to be a poet, it would never have occurred to me to write about my place, about West Virginia, or about anything that I really knew and believed. When I first heard Louise McNeill read her poems, I felt the strength of affirmation for what I did not even know I had been denied.

Of that evening, I remember most clearly McNeill's stature. I thought she was, possibly, the tallest woman I had ever seen, though perhaps the resonance of her voice made her seem taller than she really was. I remember she wore a blue dress and a hat, and when she stood to read, she walked out from behind the lectern and did not read, but recited. . . . Her voice was strong and musical, and she had an unmistakable mountain accent, deep and nasal, twanging at the heart. [*Hill Daughter*, p. xiii]

I have one other very clear memory of Louise. In 1979 I was poet-in-residence in Marshall County, West Virginia, and had invited Louise to give some readings. The morning I drove her to Wheeling so she could get the bus back to Lewisburg, we were both in good spirits. The readings had gone well; she had impressed a whole new generation of young people during several school visits; and her good friends Larry Groce and Devon McNamara had come to town for the party the night before. She announced to the driver and the assembled passengers that she was going—they all were going—"over the mountain." As she turned to climb onto the bus she admonished me, "Maggie, don't ever wear red sandals." Louise had been insisting to me (much of her own life to the contrary notwithstanding) that it was possible to be a successful poet without leaving West Virginia. I heard about these red sandals often as I spent more time with Louise in later years. They were her metaphor for the showy things one might pay a lot of money for and put on, or more precisely, change into, in order to chase after literary success and honor in some "foreign" place. This was all unnecessary, Louise maintained. Just stay at home, close to the sources that feed your deepest poems, and with your own people. "Look at Robert Frost," she told me. "He never went anywhere."

In the summer of 1987, I traveled to South Windsor, Connecticut, where Louise and her husband, Roger Pease, had moved into an apartment attached to their son Douglas's home. Both Louise and Roger required live-in home help, and so when I arrived to work with Louise on the manuscript of *The Milkweed Ladies,* there was also a Polish woman there who spoke almost no English and who cared for Louise as a nurse and housekeeper. Roger had gone to a nearby nursing home for the ten days

I was to be there, so that, Louise said, "we can work undisturbed." The three of us—Louise, Jean (the Polish housekeeper), and I—made up an odd little household in an expensive condominium, surrounded by other similar condominiums owned by young professional couples, in South Windsor, Connecticut, on Morgan Farms Drive, a street named for what had been destroyed to build it. And every day we worked on Louise's memoir of "The Farm" on Swago Creek in West Virginia.

For two weeks, we three women lived together. The work with Louise and Jean's silent tending of our needs seem to me now equally important confluences in my life and work. Louise and I were up and at work by eight o'clock every morning. We managed to do about thirty pages a day of what turned out to be arduous negotiating for both of us. Not only did Louise tire easily but I was also asking her to cut large sections of the manuscript, which, since it was a memoir, must have seemed like chipping away large sections of her life. We were respectful of each other and our differences, but we also, inevitably, got on each other's nerves. Sometimes, when we had been impatient with each other, we made up for it the next day with an exaggerated professionalism that was almost decorous. And Jean took care of us, in the way countless male writers have been tended—all our basic needs were met. Odd that I learned, in Louise McNeill's home, of the concentration and productivity that can come when the mind is freed from all daily concerns. Louise and I drank coffee, smoked cigarettes, and talked about the mountains back home and about her work. Jean cleaned and cooked. Louise napped in the afternoon. I typed (on the Smith Corona electric typewriter with no correction tape they had rented for me to use). We ate supper at five o'clock every evening so Louise and I could work a little more before she went to bed at eight o'clock. I stayed up until midnight or later typing the day's revisions.

Occasionally, Jean and I sat outside on the lawn chairs after Louise had gone to bed and watched as the sprinkler system watered the flowers. Once or twice, with a dictionary, we tried conversation. I learned that in Poland there were trees, "not like here," Jean's arm extended to encompass Morgan Farms Road, the state of Connecticut, and all of America. "In West Virginia, too, there are trees," I said. I named the Polish writers I had read: Czeslaw Milosz and Zbigniew Herbert. We could not discuss their work, of course, but Jean took my hands in hers and held them to her lips and kissed them. "Love, love," she said.

I was often surprised by how few of the Appalachian writers who were her contemporaries Louise had read. She read widely but mostly history, books on plants and animals, and later, scientific books, often on nuclear physics and on the political and scientific significance of the atom bomb. Some of Louise's most passionate and eloquent poems are those she called her "atomic poems," and the final chapter of *The Milkweed Ladies,* "Night at the Commodore," is a classic of antinuclear literature. Louise's formal education was, primarily, in history. She earned a doctorate in history from West Virginia University and taught both English and history courses for most of her life. She had never heard of James Still. She had heard of, but had not read, Mary Lee Settle and Elizabeth Madox Roberts. She had read Jesse Stuart and knew him personally, but she had never read Harriette Arnow or Emma Bell Miles or Mildred Haun. My own information on these writers of our region came after a long journey and another confluence with another writer.

In the summer of 1977, I traveled from Morgantown, West Virginia, to San Francisco on a Greyhound bus. I wanted to cross the country, which probably seemed to me, at twenty-nine, a thing writers must do. My destination was a women writers' workshop in Santa Cruz where Tillie Olsen was to be one of the speakers. Irene McKinney (who had donned her "red sandals" and gone west that winter) was teaching in this program too and knowing that she would be there gave me the courage to set off on my own.

I met Tillie Olsen that summer and spent quite a bit of time with her. Although I had admired her work for some years, it turned out she had much to teach me that I didn't even know I needed to learn. Tillie introduced me to the writers of my own region: Rebecca Harding Davis, Harriette Arnow, Elizabeth Madox Roberts, Edith Summers Kelley, James Still, and many, many others; she sent me off with detailed reading lists. My years of education in West Virginia had not taught me the literature of my people. I had to learn it, far from home, and not from Louise McNeill but from Tillie Olsen—Nebraska-born Californian writer of the working class. Tillie later wrote a jacket blurb for *The Milkweed Ladies:* "Oh, what a treasure of weathered beauty and wisdom this book is; what a magical evocation, not only of seventy-five years of deepest living in this our time, but also informed with a poet's memoried sense of nine generations of her people."

It's been raining all weekend and I've been in my high studio wandering through books and papers trying to map my confluences. I've piled up a few more volumes on my desk in this process, so that now the tiny winding path that is still desk has come to resemble the multiple crossings of Paint Creek between Charleston and Beckley on the West Virginia Turnpike. I have added *Report from Part Two* by Gwendolyn Brooks, Jane Cooper's *Green Notebook, Winter Road,* and manuscripts from my now fifteen-year-old Pittsburgh writing group—Patricia Dobler, Lynn Emanuel, and Judith Vollmer. This random assemblage reminds me of the fortunate accidents art requires, and how much a matter of luck it is when we find what we need when we need it. I have been lucky in the sources for my work that have appeared when I needed them, and I have been very lucky in my friends.

Often, my friendships have been literary confluences that have deeply affected my work. In my long friendship with Irene McKinney, I always hear the familiar voices of my people in unself-conscious accent or in the meandering turns our conversations take: the long-winded anecdotal humor, the "archean and peculiar stance" we share as women writers from West Virginia. "I'm a hillbilly, a woman, and a poet," Irene says, "and I understood early on that nobody was going to listen to anything I had to say anyway, so I might as well just say what I want to." And in that self-mocking yet prideful defiance lie several generations of struggle. Irene's statement is, in some ways, a contemporary counterpart to Louise's lesson of the red sandals, and both carry the implicit understanding that there is an Outside and an Inside in the worlds of money, art, and power. If you are a woman poet from West Virginia, there can be little doubt as to which side you are on.

I like to think that as Appalachian women writers, we have now come far enough in our work and in our lives that we can manage to dress in whatever costumery we need to—or choose to—and still not "get above our raisin'." I don't know. I do know that I love the West Virginia landscape and grieve for its maimed reconfiguration and destruction in the name of money and progress. I know that I love my people, but we sometimes share an awkward affection. Occasionally, I have to stomp away from the dark, close mountains of home, swearing this will be the very last time. Always, I have to come back.

Marilou
Awiakta

Marilou Awiakta (b. 1936), whose family has lived in Southern Appalachia for more than seven generations, grew up in Oak Ridge, Tennessee. Raised on America's atomic frontier, she has pioneered the unique fusion of three traditions: Cherokee, Appalachian, and the high-tech world. Currently a resident of Memphis, Awiakta received both the Distinguished Tennessee Writer Award in 1989 and the award for Outstanding Contribution to Appalachian Literature in 1991, and has been featured in nationally distributed programs sponsored by Kentucky Educational Television and Appalshop. She is the author of *Abiding Appalachia: Where Mountain and Atom Meet* (1978; 8th ed., 1995), *Rising Fawn and the Fire Mystery* (1983), and the widely acclaimed *Selu: Seeking the Corn-Mother's Wisdom* (1993), a work praised by Gloria Steinem, Paula Gunn Allen, Wilma Mankiller (Principal Chief of the Cherokee Nation), Alice Walker, and Jane Caputi. An audiotape of *Selu*, read by Awiakta and with music by Joy Harjo, was nominated for a Grammy in 1996, and the book was a Quality Paperback Book Club selection in 1994. Lines from *Selu* were recently engraved in the granite River Wall of the Bicentennial Capitol Mall in Nashville, and a poem, "Motheroot," is lined in the marble border in the walkway of the new Fine Arts Mall at the University of California, Riverside. In the fall of 1997, *Poèsie Première*, a French literary journal published in Paris, featured Awiakta and her work, with translation and interpretive essay by Alice-Catherine Carls.

*　*　*

Sound

In mid-May 1996, I stepped before a university audience in Ohio to give a presentation from my recent book, *Selu: Seeking the Corn-Mother's Wisdom*. The people were warm and responsive. Feeling good, I announced the first poem, "Song of the Grandmothers," and opened the book.

The pages were white—blank! Without warning, my near vision was gone, my far vision blurred. Fortunately, I'm a sayer—a sounder—and know most of my poems and stories by heart. Also, generations of grandmothers were whispering in my ear, "Don't be puny, honey. Get the job done." So I did. But I could not do as the grandmothers' song says, "walk without fear." I spent the summer sitting quietly in a wrought-iron chair in my backyard, staring into the hazy branches of a great ash tree and replaying in my mind the eye specialist's words: "In an ischemic event of this kind, the worst scenario is that you'll remain certifiably blind—able to see hand motion only. The only treatment is to rest, take a little medicine—which probably won't do any good—and pray. Pray a lot."

I did what he advised and tried to cope with the idea that my life as I'd always known it might be over. Out of the long silence came this thought, "Sound has shaped me." Dwelling on that keynote, I began to hear this poem, then the essay. Months later, when my sight returned, I translated them onto paper:

> Like most mountain people,
> I'm a natural-born listener
> and sounder
> Sound has shaped me:
> mountains sending thoughts
> elders telling stories
> memory running in my blood
> or crying out from ground
> where blood was spilled.
> Everything I see/smell/hear/taste/feel
> converts to ultrasound—
> silent waves
> I translate to words on the page,
> sheet music of the song.

*   *   *

During my childhood, I heard my inner song clearly and spoke or sang it simultaneously. It was easy. Gradually, other sounds, some of them violent discords, mixed into mine. Reweaving my harmony seemed impossible until one snow-stilled afternoon in January 1976. I heard my own song clearly again. With a more experienced and trained ear, I translated it directly into the poem "An Indian Walks In Me"—my credo. From it grew my first book, *Abiding Appalachia: Where Mountain and Atom Meet,* the center from which my other work has webbed out. Most important, the primary sounds—the influences—that have shaped me converge in this poem. It's my bell tone, my inner tuning fork. Bringing myself and my writing into harmony with it has been my life's work.

> An Indian walks in me.
> She steps so firmly in my mind
> that when I stand against the pine
> I know we share the inner light
> of the star that shines on me.
> She taught me this, my Cherokee,
> when I was a spindly child.
> And rustling in dry forest leaves
> I heard her say, "These speak."
> She said the same of sighing wind,
> of hawk descending on the hare
> and Mother's care
> to draw the cover snug around me,
> of copperhead coiled on the stone
> and blackberries warming in the sun—
> "These speak."
> I listened . . .
> Long before I learned
> the universal turn of atoms, I heard
> the Spirit's song that binds us
> all as one. And no more
> will I follow any rule
> that splits my soul.
> My Cherokee left me no sign
> except in hair and cheek
> and this firm step of mind
> that seeks the whole
> in strength and peace.

I was born and brought up in the centuries-old Appalachian mountain tradition of listening and sounding (translating). "Listening" means using all the senses to commune with the cycle of sound: from audibles, to waves of energy that precede them, to the ultimate silent song—the spirit or energy—at the core. As they have done for generations of other people, the mountains themselves taught me to "lift up my eyes" and listen. From elders who translated what they heard into words, spoken or sung, I slowly and naturally absorbed what literature calls "the oral tradition."

Mountain speech carries the sound of the land where it's spoken. That's a primary reason I say "sound has shaped me." It's also why one of the most intricate aspects of my work is translating what I hear into print, translating from the oral to the written form. Inevitably something is lost . . . until the words are sounded, because as the elders say, "Sound is what moves the heart."

My heart is what moves me to set the sound-cycle in motion: say poems and stories for people, then listen to what they say (or commune) to me. Sometimes my rowdy streak takes over and we "rustle" in jokes or songs for the sheer fun of it. From childhood, however, I've usually listened quietly to the elders. As my maternal grandfather, Papa, told me, "If you don't pay attention, you don't learn anything. If you pay attention you do." From my earliest memory, I've listened carefully to this:

On my birthday—January 24—my mother, Wilma, always sings me a song and tells the story, "I Remember the Night You Were Born." Same song. Same story. For decades now via telephone. At set intervals, I put in my two cents (sometimes four cents), which vary, depending on how I feel at the time. If I've gotten off-center during the year, the sound of the story restores my balance. It is the sturdy, humorous *tone* in Mother's voice that carries the meaning, including the cultural belief, common to most people in Appalachia, that you're born with the nature God's given you. And you're not likely to change much.

This year (1997), I answer the phone, and Mother swings into a jaunty tune from the 1930s called "Marilou" (my first name) and ends with "Happy birthday to you. Happy birthday to you. Happy birthday Marilou Awiak-TAH . . . (middle name)! Happy birthday to you!"

"Hey, Mama!" (laughter, greetings) I feel her black eyes twinkling.

"I remember the night you were born . . . twenty minutes after midnight. You weren't due 'til late February, so I'd come back home alone to Knoxville to visit Mama and Papa for a while. In the fall, your daddy and I had moved to Nashville. It was during the Depression (1936). Everybody had to go where they could find work and there was talk of war coming in Europe. It was bitter cold in Knoxville . . . a big snowstorm brewing. That's when you set your mind on being born."

"I must've heard the 'call of the mountains' and decided to come home too."

"I wouldn't doubt it. Well, my water broke at the dinner table . . . water flying every which way. Bill (her teenage brother) got real excited. Papa said, 'Calm down. I've been through this five times birthing my own children. Everything will be all right!' And Mama got me a towel. (chuckle) Isn't that the way! Papa and Bill rushed to get the car started and drove me to Fort Sanders Hospital. Isn't that just like you to get everybody swirling and working!"

"To the life. I just can't help it." (laughter)

"You were breech, so I had a long labor. But you had your own way of doing things even then. All at once, you put your head to your feet and backed out. It's a good thing you only weighed four pounds, six ounces—or you'd have split me in two! Quick . . . you've always been quick. And you write the same way . . . moving along . . .

"You had a head full of blue-black hair and were yellow as corn. Most prematures are. I thought you were beautiful, of course, but Papa teased that you 'looked like a little possum.' When he saw my feelings were hurt, he said what he really thought: 'She has a lusty cry. She likes her dinner (the breast). And she has *a good head of hair*,' three prime signs of good stock, especially the hair—like a thick, glossy coat. Strong life-force. Papa was a fine judge of stock. He said you would 'thrive and do well.'

"By that time the snow was really deep, biggest snow East Tennessee had seen in years. Your daddy rode all the way from Nashville in the bus to see you, two hundred miles over those treacherous mountains in the snow. We were all real proud, you being the first grandchild on both sides. We named you 'Marilou,' after Mama."

(We pause, honoring my grandmother's memory. Missing her.)

"Now, tell me about Mrs. Shackleford (in Nashville)."

"We took you home to our little upstairs apartment in her house. She was an older woman. Very spiritual. She had 'the sight.' And she was a Shakespeare scholar too. She'd rock you and quote Shakespeare to you by the hour. You'd make cooing sounds, like you understood. I can see Mrs. Shackleford now, going to the window, holding you up to the light, and saying, 'This baby is a special baby. This baby will be a poet or a musician.' And even so. Now, how are Paul and the children?"

One advantage of the written word is that it provides the opportunity to *see* content. I've always *heard* the influences in this story and perceived them in my life and work. (My credo poem has essentially the same themes, for example.) But I've never realized until now just how deep the influences are or how much heritage and cultural values are conveyed in the precise, invariable details. Obviously, the story affirms me and my "voice." It also roots me in my homeland, in my family and in their stoic way of coping with the wider web of historical events, like the Depression. Among the subtler aspects the story conveys is that I come from sturdy stock and am not expected to be "puny" and "whiny." Furthermore, I'm to maintain the strength and humor of my maternal line: "We named you after Mama." And my mother is her mother's daughter. But enough of writing and analyzing. It's December again, and I'm already looking forward to answering the phone on January 24, when I'll hear Mother sing the song and tell the story. I'm also wondering if I've told our children—Aleex, Drey, and Andrew—enough of "I remember when *you* were born."

Sound has shaped me. When this revelation first came to me, I was thirty years old and sitting on a flat tombstone in northern France. The small, walled cemetery belonged to the nearby village of Couvron. I often came here to think and write and keep quiet company with the folks I'd gotten to know through reading their tombstones—like we did back home in Tennessee where visiting the cemetery was a family outing, often with a picnic, or at least a Big Orange (soda) and a Moon Pie. It's a comfortable feeling to weave yourself into the cycles of your ancestors and your country's history.

Beyond the old stone walls of the cemetery, spring wheat strewn with poppies rippled in the sun. The breeze carried the scent of newly plowed earth, fertilized with raw manure. Near the cemetery was an overgrown bunker from World War II. Across the field at my back was Laon Air Force Base, where my husband was stationed and I worked as an interpreter and liaison. It was 1966. President de Gaulle was demanding that all NATO forces withdraw from France and anti-American sentiment was running high, which made my job stressful. From our base, two reconnaissance jets thundered into the blue sky, probably on the way to film suspicious troop movements on the Russian border or in East Berlin. All of us "dependents," including our two small daughters, had evacuation cards—just in case. When I felt "puny," I ran my fingers through my hair as a reminder.

The base and the cemetery were situated on either side of a narrow, black-topped road, part of the classic northern invasion route; foreign armies have marched it eighty-seven times since the days of Julius Caesar. The French call this region "les champs aux puces"—the flea fields—because of the continual destruction.

Memories of spilled blood still cried out from the ground. Listening to them, and thinking of the cycles of war, I remembered that sound had brought me to France . . .

. . . In 1951, on the first day of my sophomore year at Oak Ridge High School, I was walking down the hall behind a senior boy and a woman I knew must be the renowned, vibrant, and redoubtable "Madame Zizi." (Actually, she only allowed her second-year French students to call her that. Everyone else had to say "Madame" or "Mrs. Zimmerman.") She and the boy were speaking French. The beautiful sound was so spellbinding that I followed them upstairs to the door of the French class, where her rule was "Listen . . . speak." No English allowed.

Then and there, I set my mind on taking French, learning to speak it fluently and, one day, going to France. To qualify, I first had to slog through Latin II and Caesar's Gallic Wars, a drudgery made bearable only because Mrs. Zimmerman was the teacher. After that, for six years—two in high school and four at the University of Tennessee, Knoxville—I studied French for two hours every night in my dormitory, which was on Fort Sanders hill. Most of my other study time was spent on English literature and writing. My ear was also increasingly tuned to a certain man's rich resonant voice. In time Paul and I were "harmonizin'"—and he didn't laugh when I told him my dream of sitting at a writing table near French doors flung wide, with gauze curtains floating outward toward a rose garden. I would write amazing poems and stories . . .

. . . the bone-hard tombstone brought me back to reality. A very resonant reality. I realized that my three years in France marked the watershed of my life. That I was, in fact, sitting on the spine of that watershed—my thirtieth year. According to the French, the age of thirty is when one leaves girlhood and its illusions behind and comes into full bloom as a woman, understanding what is possible in life and how to make the most of it. My illusions *were* gone, but I saw no sign yet of "the bloom," and as much as I loved France, I'd become increasingly lonesome for the sound of my own language and for the memories that vibrate in my homeland. Even the tombstones, with their French names and epitaphs, told me that these were not my folks and I could not weave myself into the cycles of their history. I stood up and said aloud to myself, "I'm American. I'm a Cherokee/ Appalachian poet and I'm going to sing the songs of home—at home." A foreign context really brings out the power in the blood—sets the DNA to singing.

During the next decade of work, which led to the writing of "An Indian Walks In Me" and *Abiding Appalachia,* I gradually realized how much the sounds of France—of the land and the language—had influenced my perceptions. I became consciously aware that, as poets have always said and science now affirms, people and events discharge their energies into the land, and these residual energies signify their presence in silent waves or vibrations. My ear became more finely tuned to this frequency.

Living and working in a foreign language had also sharpened my ear to nuances of tone and meaning in words, especially spoken words. Translating from one language to another, like translating from the oral to the written form, is an intricate process. An imprecise choice of word or tone can alter meaning, sometimes disastrously. When I came back to Appalachia, I heard beauties in our mountain speech that I'd never noticed before, because when I was growing up it was "just the way we talked." I also listened more acutely to the heritage singing in my blood and to the meaning of stories and songs the elders had told me.

My gratitude for the elders and others who kept the heritage going grew deeper because, for the first time, I was aware of a great gap of silence in my formal literary education: There had been no voices from Appalachia in the texts or reading lists. Because the sounds of mountain culture were all around me at that time, I hadn't noticed the silence. At the University of Tennessee, my advisers had been English professors who were from Appalachia: Mr. Charles Webb and Dr. Bain Stewart. From the first essay I wrote, they understood my song. What a blessing it was to have had their guidance in listening—and translating what I heard to the page. I could recall many of our conversations verbatim.

And I was sure that wherever I lived in the future, the sounds of the mountains would abide with me. My mind was set on "singing" them. But who would listen?

It's said that writers continually sound—measure the depths of—their childhood and youth, although it may not be evident in all their mature work that they are doing so. I know this is true for me.

There is an element in my birth story that I alone see as foreshadowing some violent discords in my life, as well as my yearning to resolve them. In the still of the night, I was born on the site of the battle of Fort Sanders, one of the bloodiest battles of the Civil War. By morning, snow had blanketed the hill with a thick, peaceful comforter and a feeling of serene joy. But I wonder if, deep in the earth, reverberations from boots marching in Germany were disturbing the old blood soaked so long ago into the hill. And if the blood was already crying a faint warning. Being a natural-born listener and ultra-sounder, I may have unconsciously picked up the silent vibrations.

It's certain I did so early in my life. Although the family kept me snugly wrapped in love and stories and songs (we are a musical family), the elders increasingly spoke in grave tones, especially when they gathered around the radio to listen to the news from Europe—news that sometimes carried the voice of a German leader who ranted pure, unmistakable hatred. "HIT-ler." His very name had the force of a blow.

Mother says that even babies sense what's happening around them because they're listening to sounds and vibrations, not words. She told me, "Usually you were happy and playful. But one day when you were about three and a half (in 1939), something happened that let me know you were feeling the grownups' anxieties. I was walking past neighborhood stores with you skipping and chattering beside me. Above us, a monarch butterfly died in the air and grazed your shoulder as it fell to the sidewalk. You stopped and bent over, looking at it intently. Then you picked it up by the wings and said to it:

Oh, Little Butterfly,
how I wish you weren't dead.

So you could fly
with other butterflies instead.

Then you put it carefully on a window ledge. 'To keep it safe,' you said."

I would have forgotten this moment, if Mother hadn't recalled it to me as I was growing up. I understand now that this poem was my first expression of my theme song. Everything I've written since is a variation on "Oh, Little Butterfly."

What I do remember of my preschool days are: Sunshine. Cornbread. Swinging. Running. Blackberries. Digging deep holes to smell the earth. Playing with my cats and a big white hare named Buck Rogers. ("No dolls, please. Too cold.") Homemade fudge and milk. And stories, a constant, murmuring stream of stories—told or read aloud. Stories about Cherokee and Scotch-Irish relatives, past and present. About friends and neighbors. Folk stories. Readings of classic fairy tales, myths, Bible stories—which were not simplified versions for children because my parents believed the originals "trained the ear."

In the summer of 1941, the Japanese government sent a Friendship Doll to every state capital, including Nashville. My kindergarten class borrowed the doll from the state museum. The summer emphasis was "our friends the Japanese." I was intrigued with them and with the name for their country, "Land of the Rising Sun." I had a special love for the sunrise and would often slip out of bed in the dark before dawn and sit on the back steps to wait for the sun.

On a Sunday morning in December I was lying on my stomach "reading" the funny paper, while my father sat nearby, really reading the paper. Back in the kitchen, Mother was cooking breakfast and singing along with the radio, a soft, pleasant sound in the background.

Suddenly, Mother ran into the room, crying and stammering, "My God, Bill . . . the Japanese have bombed Pearl Harbor . . . our boys . . . our boys!"

"When?" Daddy jumped up to put his arm around Mother as we all hurried toward the radio.

"At dawn. They came out of the rising sun. Our boys didn't have a chance. Not a chance."

We stood with our arms around each other, listening to stunned reporters describe ships burning . . . sinking . . . men dying, wounded . . . smoke . . . confusion. President Roosevelt read the Declaration of War.

Pearl Harbor was an earthquake shaking the whole country. The aftershocks went on and on. Within days, government officials were going from door to door in Nashville, asking how many refugees each family could take if the West Coast had to be evacuated because of invasion by the Japanese. Mother's brothers joined the Navy. Writing these words today, I feel again the shock waves of grief, confusion, outrage, and fear as my country mobilized for war. I also hear the screams of a burning man that made Mother and me run to the front porch later that winter.

Across the street in the parking lot of the dry cleaner's, a man in flames ran round and round. (A spark from the cleaner's furnace had ignited his fluid-soaked clothes.) Another man chased him with a garden hose turned on full force, shouting, "Stop! Stop!" The burning man stumbled and sank to his knees, clawing the air, trying to climb out of his pain. When water hit his arms, flesh fell off in fiery chunks. As the flames went out, his cries ceased. He collapsed slowly into a charred and steaming heap.

Silence. Burned flesh. Water trickling into the gutter.

Our boys . . . our boys . . . they didn't have a chance.

Hooked in the mouth, part of my soul sounded—dove for the bottom. It would not work free of pain until a winter afternoon more than three decades later, when the words "seek the whole in strength and peace" surfaced in my mind. The rest of my credo poem emerged soon after.

As with many other children in my generation, what held me in balance during the war—and restored joy in my life—was family. Seeing them rally, I rallied. The Cherokee/Appalachian people are survivors. History has made us that way. Only a strong spirit keeps you going. My birth story alone told me that; at this point life was already amplifying and deepening its influence.

Daddy's job at the National Youth Administration was phased out, and after my sister, Adele, was born in 1942, we moved back to Knoxville. Word was that the government was building a secret installation a few miles from there, creating more jobs. Daddy had found a small apartment—a feat, for housing was scarce. I wrote my version of the housing shortage in my first story, "Mr. and Mrs. Honeybee Find a Home," which I illustrated with smiling bees. I was smiling more then too, because listening to my parents at home—and President Roosevelt and Winston Churchill on the radio—I felt they had gotten a hold on the crisis. Such is the innocence of children. I often thought of the Cherokee story of Little Deer, the small white chief of the deer, who sees to it that the hunters show proper respect for the deer. I didn't analyze it. I just felt that he should be on the scene. Here, from *Abiding Appalachia,* is my memory of how I sounded-out the situation at the time. It's called "Genesis."

> . . . the mountains abided, steeped in mist.
> But in the deep was a quickening of light, a freshening of wind.
> And in 1942, as fall leaves embered down toward winter,
> new ground was turned near Black Oak Ridge.
> The natives pricked their ears.
> These descendants of old pioneers

lifted their heads to scent the wind.
    A frontier was a-borning.
Many had to pack up hearth and home and go.
Others joined the energy that flowed to Black Oak Ridge
as to a great magnetic power:
    Thousands of people streamed in.
    Bulldozers scraped and moved the earth.
    Factories rose in valleys like Bear Creek
    and houses in droves sprang up among the trees
    and strung out in the lees of ridges.
A great city soon lay concealed among the hills.
    Why it had come no one knew.
    But its energy was a strong and constant hum,
    a new vibration, changing rhythms everywhere.

It charged the air in Knoxville, where we lived
and when I saw my parents lift their heads,
I lifted my head too, for even at seven
I knew something was stirring in our blood,
something that for years had drawn the family along frontiers
from Virginia to West Virginia, on to Kentucky and Tennessee.
Now, a few miles away, we had a new frontier.
Daddy went first, in '43—leaving at dawn, coming home at dark
and saying nothing of his work except,
"It's at Y-12, in Bear Creek Valley."
The mystery deepened.
The hum grew stronger.
I longed to go.
Oak Ridge had a magic sound—
They said bulldozers would take down a hill before your eyes
and houses sized by alphabet came precut and boxed, like blocks,
so builders could put up hundreds at a time.
They made walks of boards and streets of dirt (mud if it rained)
and a chain-link fence around it all to keep the secret.

But the woods sounded best to me.
My mind went to them right away . . .
    to wade in creeks and rest in cool deep shadows,
    watching light sift through the trees
    and hoping Little Deer might come.
    In the Smokies I'd often felt him near
    and I knew he'd roam the foothills too.

Woods were best. And if the frontier grew too strange
   my mountains would abide unchanged,
     old and wise and comforting.

So I kept listening to the hum, and longing . . .
Mother said we'd go someday, in the fullness of time.
And when I was nine the fullness came,
exploding in a mushroom cloud that shook the earth.

Sound has shaped me.

Two days after Christmas 1945, we moved to the hill in Oak Ridge—a federal reservation for atoms, not Indians—where I would grow up. Our home was a "B"—a small, cemesto (a type of masonite) cabin, with a chimney and a front porch. I loved it and the surrounding woods, where I roamed as I'd imagined I would do. This was the land of my ancestors—the Cherokee and the Scotch-Irish. Their spirits were there, blended with the silent song of the land. I listened to them constantly, trying to make sense of the screams of burning people at Pearl Harbor, at Hiroshima, at Dachau. I was also trying to cope with the Cold War between Russia and America, a war that made the nuclear center at Oak Ridge a prime target and the disaster drill siren at school a familiar and dreaded sound. *Our boys . . . our boys.* It could happen again. I was listening in the deepest part of me, in the part of my soul that had sounded to the bottom. The only trace that this was so is in a picture of my face at that age, a smiling hopeful face, except for a faint shadow in the eyes.

When I'd say to Mother, "I want to be a poet when I grow up," she'd reply, "That's good. And what will you do for the people?" What I most wanted to do was seek peace—for myself and for others. But how to go about it?

I kept listening to the sounds that were shaping me.

One of them was the atom's powerful, ultrasonic hum, an energy that seemed alien to our mountains and our ways. The elders said it would take at least four generations for people to understand the atom and use it respectfully. With these words resonating in my mind, I followed the mysterious hum as it spiraled deep into the invisible. On a snowy winter afternoon many years later, I would reach the place "where mountain and atom meet," a quiet place where I would be still . . . and hear my song again.

ARTIE
ANN
BATES

Born in 1953 in Blackey, Kentucky, where she currently lives with her husband and son, Artie Ann Bates is both a medical doctor and a writer. Her children's book, *Ragsale* (1995), tells the story of a favorite Saturday event from her own childhood—ragsalin'. Bates has published essays and poems in journals such as *Appalachian Heritage*. Vitally committed to her community and to prominent social issues in eastern Kentucky, she frequently writes political and environmental commentary for local newspapers and the *Lexington Herald-Leader* and medical consumer items for both radio and print. She is trained in health sciences but has always carefully complemented this training with literature and writing classes. She studied with Harry Caudill and Gurney Norman and has participated in nine workshops at the Appalachian Writers' Workshop at Hindman Settlement School in Knott County, Kentucky. Bates is currently writing historical fiction for adolescents about eastern Kentucky and completing a child psychiatry residency in Louisville, Kentucky.

* * *

Root Hog, or Die

Unlike the big cities, where survival depends on the delivery of goods and services, Appalachia is a place where many still root a living out of the land. For my ancestors of five generations, the creed of survivors was "root hog, or die."

My past started in eastern Kentucky long before I was born. David and Nancy Back, my great-grandparents, bought the farm in the head of Elk Creek in 1907, about thirty-five years after it was built by her brother. Their youngest daughter, Artie, my grandmother, was married in the living room of that farmhouse in 1913.

Her oldest daughter, Eunice, and Eunice's husband, Bill—my parents—bought the farm in 1955. At the time of the purchase, I was two years old. We still lived at the mouth of Elk Creek in the house where I was born. I was the fifth of six children in my family. Daddy was an underground coal miner and Mommy an elementary school teacher.

Daddy worked for twenty-two years in the mines and never finished high school. He was real educated, though, in the field of poor people. There was always one or two staying at our home, coughing, picking sores on their faces, rolling Prince Albert cigarettes. He thought you should always help people because, as the Bible says, you never know when one of them might be the Lord.

Most of the people I associated with, until age eighteen, were grandparents, aunts, uncles, cousins, and neighbors. They had also lived in Letcher County for four or five generations, descendants of the first white settlers to the area. I rarely saw anyone that I did not know, except for the train engineers who waved as they passed each day. Occasionally an insurance agent or vacuum cleaner salesman would knock on the door, and Mommy would turn off the pressure cooker or washing machine to listen, as we stared at his crisp white shirt.

Even then I had some clues that the outside world had its own view of Appalachian Kentucky. We had always watched *The Beverly Hillbillies,* and *The Andy Griffith Show,* where the country folks had to set things straight for the more materialistic city folk. At that time I was not offended by those shows. The hillbillies were the wise ones, and there was a lot of truth in that. Of course the mountain people I knew did not always seem so wise, for they were just regular people to me.

The four houses we lived in from my birth to age eighteen were within a three-mile radius. One of them, the David Back house, I live in now. By the time I came along as a late-in-life baby, my parents were tired, so they no longer traveled. My only links to the world beyond the mountains were television and visitors from off. Some of those visitors were from places like Boston, California, England, and China, touring the mountains in the 1960s out of curiosity generated by media publicity. Others worked as Volunteers in Service to America or as missionaries. Now and then, one or two of them stayed with us, and then my mother had extra cooking and washing to do.

My first experience living among strangers occurred when I began college at the University of Kentucky in the summer of 1971. These strangers thought *I* was the stranger. If I said, "I'm hotter'n far," people looked at me. Often I had to repeat words to be understood. Those turns of speech I had heard and used for eighteen years were not spoken except by me and one other Letcher County girl on the upper dorm floor. The same was true in the fall semester, in a different dormitory. That semester, the only other person in the dorm like me was a girl from Harlan County. We clung together.

The unfamiliar ways of city people were the norm and my ways were the abnorm. For instance, I could not understand how those people could stay away from their families until Thanksgiving, while I went home every weekend. How could they move into the dorm and continue their regular habits when I felt like my whole life had been put on hold? Why was my early life so different from theirs; where had I been; why did I feel that I was the one who had to change? Spring semester I came back home to Hazard Community College. I was too homesick to stay any longer.

It took only one spring semester back home to realize I had to leave again. I had seen the world beyond the mountains, and it was different from anything I had known. I wanted more than a degree from going to college: I wanted an education in how to live in that other world. Next fall semester I found myself back at the University of Kentucky in Lexington, homesick but determined to root out a life in the city. It would be fifteen years before I could return home to stay.

I was still very much under the influence of my raising for a long while. That meant I was quiet, passive, and had been indelibly imprinted by the message that I was never to purposely hurt anyone's feelings. When someone in Lexington made an eastern Kentucky slur, I said nothing. It stung, but I had been taught never to give comebacks to strangers, only to my pesky brothers. One of my toughest challenges was learning to defend the background that had produced me.

Another challenge was choosing a career. My bachelor's degree from Kentucky in 1976 was in nursing, but as a child I had wanted to be a doctor. I always bravely looked at cuts and bruises. When anyone needed a Band-Aid applied, I was the one who ran for it. The doctor who delivered me at home was my family doctor until I left Elk Creek. I was fascinated with Doctor Adams. On his office desk sat a big jar of multicolored pills like jelly beans. I went to him every time I had a sore throat, a headache, or a wart on my thumb. We talked about medicine, and he told me that Granny Combs could take off warts better than he could if her patients believed in her. She used a corncob and a stolen dishrag.

I do not recall ever telling anyone I wanted to be a doctor, because I was too shy. Medical school seemed like it was just for rich kids from the city. My silence allowed few to encourage me, not even my dad, who also liked cuts and cysts. He was often a lay-doctor and once removed a sebaceous cyst from a friend's face using whiskey as an anesthetic and needle and thread for suturing. The place healed as if done professionally. Some of his nerve passed down to me.

Eventually this nerve, along with the realization that people are not born with medical knowledge but can learn it, gave me the courage to think seriously about medical school. In 1980, after three years of nursing, I left work to start undergraduate and graduate courses that would prepare me for a profession I once had thought out of reach. I also had an alternate plan in mind if I were rejected by medical schools. I would pursue a master's in literature. I was accepted into medical school, but my joy was tempered by the sudden thought that this might mean I would never study literature. As a last chance, I enrolled in two classes at Kentucky I had always wanted to take. They changed my life.

The first of those was Harry Caudill's Appalachian history class. It catapulted me into vocalizing. His analyses filled in the blanks that I had carried for my whole life. New questions arose: why had I never before learned the economic history of eastern Kentucky from school or family; why had I never been able to get through *Night Comes to the Cumberlands;* why had some people in Letcher County disdained Harry for the book; why had the slavery of miners been downplayed; what could I fix?

For these discoveries, and more, I credit Harry Caudill. He helped me to understand why I talked the way I did. Like the northern Europeans who settled the Appalachians, I spoke the words of my ancestors. Nestled in the Appalachians, they spoke with accents that never left, at least not very fast. Under Professor Caudill's guidance, I began to trace the words my parents had spoken over and over, "You have to come back home, you are needed here." Though returning was still a long way off, I regained some of the joy of my early years in the mountains through Harry Caudill, of feeling pure lucky to grow up there.

The second class was creative writing, with Gurney Norman. A student from Inez lent me his copy of *Kinfolks*. I found my family in the short stories. The class assignments were open for any stories and essays, but when I put my pen to the paper, what came out were stories of home. I wrote about Elk Creek, hog killings, Mamaw, grandmother Ma Cornett, Daddy, Mommy, and stripmining. I began to wonder if I could ever write for a living.

With the newly discovered spark of creative writing, I embarked on medical school in Louisville. At this excellent school, the course work was more interesting than

I had expected, but it was not everything I wanted. I wanted to write, but most of the writing I did was on patients' histories and physicals. The standard form for H and P's seemed unnatural to me, so I tried reorganizing it. My instructor said I could do it my way but warned that nobody else would, so I changed. On the hospital wards I regurgitated facts during the day, and at night kept a journal of free associations. In the medical school world, most of the free associators were on the psychiatric ward, on thorazine.

While those two forces battled each other, my husband, John, and I had a baby boy. Davy made medical school taste like stale crackers. He was the best pediatric learning lab nature could provide, and the University of Louisville School of Medicine granted me a leave of absence to stay home for a year. My journal filled with every brilliant word and skill Davy learned. My heart overflowed with the magic of John and of my son. I lived in the present.

During that time I audited an evening creative writing class taught by Lee Pennington. He took up where Gurney left off and pushed publishing. He said I should set goals for my writing, and that one of my stories "could have been by one of the great writers." I had a poem accepted for publication, a literary first for me. I also had numerous essays, poems, and stories rejected by magazines. Like a pioneer clearing wilderness just to see how the land can be used, I had no idea what lay beyond this drive to write. It was clear, however, that I had to finish medical school, so I returned.

The diaries I kept were my salvation through that world of men's values by day and nurturing a toddler at night. Caring for burned babies on the surgery ward and for adult cancer patients, and sharing an on-call room with male classmates were not easy. In the diaries I kept during those difficult years, recording events of my workdays did not feel like a creative act. It was just a way to reduce stress so I could sleep.

In one journal entry written as a student I record an episode in which I held retractors to pull the skin away from the surgical site. The surgeon cut into a bleeder and the blood spattered onto our scrub gowns. The spatters, I wrote, looked like a brown-speckled banana. Writing similes did not get me a better grade on my surgery rotation, but it helped me endure it. It also gave me grist for a novel about a young woman in medical school, with a baby, and a husband like John, willing to quit his job and stay home with a child.

Benefits of an internship back in Lexington included one week of vacation. The chairman of the department allowed me to take my vacation after just one month of work so that I could attend the Appalachian Writers' Workshop at Hindman, Kentucky. Here I met Barbara Smith and George Ella Lyon and about forty other writers. Inspired, I wrote several poems that I nervously read at the participant reading. Jim Wayne Miller said they were "fine." The energy of that first workshop kept me up nights for a month, pouring out more of my rich past from the mountains.

During the internship year, 140 miles from home, I was painfully reminded of the culture gap between America and Appalachia. A good portion of my colleagues that year were not from anywhere near Appalachia, and their opinions were formed from the telescope of media. They maintained their ignorant theories about the region based on the poor who were turfed from the mountains onto the big teaching hospital.

I was often caught off guard by their slurs about my region. I overheard medical trainees telling incest jokes in the halls. There was the one about the eastern Kentucky bride who was returned to her family by a disgruntled groom when he realized she was still a virgin. As the punch line goes, "If she ain't good enough for her own kin, she ain't good enough for me." Again I had that feeling that if I did not root hard enough, I would die of humiliation. I decided that this humiliation must be why so many of the medical students from the mountains were quiet.

Other times the prejudice came in simple statements of "fact." "Well, Artie, you know even *Psychology Today* has an article about higher rates of violence in eastern Kentucky." I didn't know. To answer the question about violence in Appalachia I asked an anthropologist who had done research in eastern Kentucky. She said there were higher rates of death by murder in all of the southeastern United States but lower rates of lesser crimes such as rape and robbery. Knowing what I knew from my own upbringing, I interpreted that to mean that mountain people will leave you alone if you leave them alone, but if you keep pushing you may get shot! I also took security in that, figuring that if I minded my own business when I moved back home, others would leave me alone. With that understanding I did not fear my people, nor did I see them as hopeless. I would get my chance to find out.

Returning home in 1987 was like running through the ribbon at the finish line. It was as if a cheering crowd welcomed me back, and nothing could go wrong. I knew the rules here and everything would fall into its natural place.

For the first two or three years I found many causes to champion. The threat of a dam on Linefork to supply upstream water for Lexington lawns sent me writing essays to the newspaper and organizing meetings. My son started public school and I joined the PTA, working for it to be as strong as possible. I had forgotten, though, how much the fifteen years of city life had changed me. I no longer fit in like I once had, and my acquired confrontational style, a must for city life and surviving the medical world, was offensive to people here. Eventually I realized I had insulted; I was too pushy. I had obviously lived away.

One of my first goals was to get my accent back and to remember how I spoke. The writer in me reveled in local dialect. The backs of my prescription pads became mini-notepads filled with sayings, both wise and silly, from my patients.

"These young miners don't appreciate what the old miners have done for them."
"I don't need a pap smear cause I don't smear with Pap no more anyhow." Once a
man came in complaining of a sore place inside his mouth. I asked if the place
hurt when he chewed, and he said, "I don't chew." Like a bee wallowing in honey,
I absorbed the talk.

My final move was with John and Davy into the David Back log house. It was
the childhood home that I longed for while away. Moving turned out to be a
mixed blessing. Family stories seemed to jump out of the newspapered log walls,
but there was also heartache. The head of the holler has been strip-mined for the
last thirty years.

I had been furious with those who maligned the mountain people, but I was
even more furious to live in the belly of the stripmining. The log house sits in a
three-sided valley that has been stripped on all three tops. The head of the holler
is a moonscape that will not grow weeds. Before the companies came, it was as
God made it for millions of years, and as Great-grandpap Dave had loved it. My
son will never walk it that way.

The stripping of Elk Creek started during my high school years, before I left
for college. I hated it but did not fully realize stripmining's deadliness until I lived
under it. I wager that those who orchestrate it would do differently if they too
lived under it, but most do not.

At times the pain of seeing the holler changed was unbearable. With the house
shaking from blasting, and trucks rattling twenty-fours hours, day and night, I wondered when I might lose control and run up the hill shooting, or move away. John,
Davy, and I decided, however, we would root out a living on Grandpap Dave's
farm. The dream to live on Elk Creek had sustained us through the tough years of
medical school. We could not leave just because the mountain had been spoiled.

Our house is the last one in the head of the holler, and naturally I thought
that I would no longer hear slurs about eastern Kentucky. This idea was shattered
by the national media, which is an everyday part of life in Appalachia. Recently, in
August 1996, I watched a short segment of a show on the TV station Comedy
Central. The show was called *Dream On,* and the young man on the program was
strongly attracted to his beautiful cousin whom he had not seen since they were
children. At one point their restraint waned and they began to guiltily tear at each
other's clothes. All the while they were saying things like "we shouldn't" and "at
least we're not having sex" and "at least we're not having children." To this last
statement the young man replied, "At least if we were having children we would
be accepted in some Appalachian cultures."

When I ranted about this injustice in front of my twelve-year-old niece, she
quietly told me about the movie *Clueless,* which I have not seen. She described a
scene in which Cher, a sixteen-year-old, discovers that she loves a young man,

who is also her stepbrother, and the wedding scene that immediately follows this discovery. Seeing only the backs of the bride and groom at first, viewers think that Cher is a teenage bride marrying her stepbrother. Then, in a voice-over, Cher corrects the viewers' error. "This is California, not Kentucky," she says.

Would my niece have told me this had I not been fuming about the TV program? She obviously noticed the slur. The dangerous part is that because she is young, she most likely blended it into her self-worth unconsciously. I wondered how many other Kentucky kids saw the movie and the TV show and had no one to editorialize for them. How many other movies and TV shows use script lines like this without concern? On a national level, Kentuckians must root for the survival of our identity.

Now that I've resided in the mountains for ten years, the culture is mine again, but there are many changes. The way of life here is affected by television, like everywhere else in America. With the passing of my parents' generation will pass the last ones who remember the way life was here before electricity, cars, and white bread. Losing their memories by not recording them will be irreversible. The very thought mobilizes the writer in me to act. There is urgency in writing the stories of my elderly ancestors while they are still able to tell them.

With the passage of time, and the aging of local historians, I have to write now. For the last three years I have practiced medicine part-time to allow more hours for writing and family. Medicine used to be what I had to do and writing, what I got to, but that's changed. Medical work can be done later, but these stories may not. There is urgency for writing mountain stories, for my son, my nieces, and other local children are quickly growing up. They must know their Appalachian past.

Our vegetable garden is a connection to my ancestors' stories. Our garden is a fraction of the ones that Great-grandpap Dave or even my parents tended, but it has been productive of beans, corn, tomatoes, and pumpkins. The final harvests seem less exciting than the storytelling that comes along with raising it.

Around here, gardens are the talk, and seeds are the words of conversation. Those seeds, kept in fruit jars in basements, in plastic cups in freezers, and in boxes on shelves, are the history of the area. Seeds are the memory of this place, the reason that rooting hog led to life.

Mamaw Bates passed on to Daddy the Little Berthie bean seeds from her sister-in-law's sister Berthie Back. Daddy and Mommy keep a white pole bean seed, called Thelma beans, that Thelma Croucher gave them. They have a similar bean, called Mary Jane beans, given by Aunt Mary Jane, Daddy's oldest sister, now deceased. My neighbor gave me a bucketful of a pole bean with brown beans inside that he called goose beans. They are so flavorful that we saved seed for next year, like the ancestors.

Out of curiosity, I asked my dad about the oldest bean seed he had on his shelf. He traced a half-runner seed back three generations. Passed on to him by a wife of his cousin, who had received it from a sister-in-law, it came originally from her mother-in-law, Aunt Peggy Whitaker. The surprise of this tracing is that those seeds came from Aunt Peggy, whose husband built the log house later bought by Great-grandpap Dave. In short, the seeds on Daddy's shelf could have come from the garden below our house in the late 1800s and early 1900s.

Thinking of those seeds, I had to think of the difference in Aunt Peggy's life compared to mine. She had to root hog, or die with regard to food and clothing. I have to root hog, or die with regard to a career and paying bills. The seeds also join us. I live in the house she lived in from 1875 until 1907. We share a garden spot, sweep cobwebs off the same logs, and chink the same drafty windows. No doubt we share prayers about husbands, children, and what to make for supper.

Taking tiny seeds and growing bushels of beans, making a living out of seemingly nothing, is the essence of root hog, or die, and of Appalachia. We take a little rocky piece of land and tend a garden to raise a family. We take strip-mined property and plant trees. We go as a group of hillbillies to city council meetings in Lexington to oppose dams on Linefork Creek. We write stories like those in *Kinfolks* that speak to families everywhere.

Appalachia has taught me to survive wherever I land, especially on a little piece of rocky ground. It has given me a conscience to write some of its history, one of making do. The reward of root hog, or die, is life.

JOHN NEWMAN

KATHRYN STRIPLING BYER

Kathryn Stripling Byer (b. 1944) is currently poet-in-residence at Western Carolina University, in Cullowhee, North Carolina. She was born in southwest Georgia and raised on a farm surrounded by cornfields and numerous cousins. Byer was fascinated by the mountains from an early age, always deeply influenced by her paternal grandmother's unrealized desire to one day return to the Blue Ridge Mountains, the place of her birth. She graduated from Wesleyan College in Macon, Georgia, and took an M.F.A. from UNC–Greensboro, where she studied with Allen Tate, Fred Chappell, and Robert Watson. While there she won the Academy of American Poets Student Prize for the UNC system. Her first volume of poetry, *The Girl in the Midst of the Harvest* (1986), was published in the Associated Writing Programs Award Series, and her second, *Wildwood Flower* (1992), received the Lamont Prize for the best second book by an American poet from the Academy of American Poets. Her most recent collection, forthcoming in 1998, is *Black Shawl.* Her poems have also appeared in *Georgia Review, Hudson Review, Southern Review, and Nimrod,* among others, as well as in numerous anthologies.

* * *

Deep Water

TUCKASEGEE

Wherever I walk in this house
I hear water. Or time,
which is water, the same

Tuckasegee that runs past my window.
What matter that some days I weary
of it like the songs I sing
over and over again in the kitchen,
pretending I cannot hear water departing
though I so plainly hear it,
if only from habit? A sequence

of bones rots beneath where I walk
on the trail that unwinds down the hill
to our yard where the leaves also rot.

Every morning I braid what is left
of my hair so that I may unbraid it to braid
it again. So we harvest our gardens

that winter will lay waste.
We mend seams that pull apart
slowly and scrub sweat from what
we have sewn. With the same hands

we knead bread and gather the crumbs
as they fall, put away
what we take out and take stock
of what we have left. It is all the same

work. It has always been
done, this undoing,
ongoing, no matter who
paces the rooms of the houses

alongside the banks,
whether praising
or cursing whatever is living
or dying within them. Until

it runs out like the river,
our time is the music
the water makes, leaving
who's left of us listening.

"Solitude," said Emma Bell Miles in *The Spirit of the Mountains,* "is deep water, and small boats do not ride well in it." No one who has lived for long in these mountains can doubt the power of that solitude. It can cause a woman to sink into its depths and never rise again. It can drive her crazy trying to break its hold on her, all the while drawing her closer and closer to the edge of some jump-off, the distance rising up before her like a vision of freedom.

The worst thing that icy blue water can do to a woman is to render her silent. Resigned to its hold, she becomes mute when she ought to be singing. A singer knows how to navigate deep water, setting the ripples spreading, sailing the song on its way. A singing woman knows how to travel, how to hang on for dear life and ride on the wave of her own voice.

To the women living in these mountains years ago, singing must have seemed the only way they could travel. Though their men might hightail it to Texas or spend weeks away on hunting forays, though the circuit rider might come and go, waving his Bible and shouting his message, they remained. They knew their place. They knew its jump-offs, its laurel hells, its little graves grown over with honeysuckle and blackberry briars. They knew the lay of cloud shadows rolling down one ridge and up another. And their place knew them. Out of that reciprocal knowing, they were able to sing their way through their solitude and into a larger web of voices, voices that I have come to see as connective tissue stretching across these hills. Or, to draw on an image that has haunted me for a long time, like a black shawl that gathers up all of these voices into its complicated, endlessly evolving pattern.

When I came to the western North Carolina mountains at the end of the sixties, I was leaving a place where my people had already lost their old songs. As hard as I try to remember my kinswomen singing, I have to confess that all the while I was growing up in rural south Georgia, I rarely heard them sing, except in church, and as far as I was concerned, that didn't count. Church singing as I knew it was singing under duress. I do recall my mother singing Hoagy Carmichael songs by heart to me or singing along to the lyrics of "Begin the Beguine" or "Stars Fell on Alabama" as she listened to the radio. When I was a teenager I loved crooning back to my record player every hit song by The Platters. But the people who sang as if their everyday lives depended on it were the black women who cleaned our homes, often cooked our meals, and soothed our stubbed toes and yellow-jacket bites—and their men who drove their tractors up and down the dusty furrows, singing the blues as I've never heard them sung since.

If I brought with me no firsthand experience of an ancient singing tradition, what I did bring to my new home was an intuitive understanding of the fierce rootedness to place that my neighbors shared. I, too, had grown up in a traditional extended family, whose emotional center was the land upon which its menfolk farmed and its women bore children, scrubbed generations of garments clean, and stood for hours over kettles of mayhaws, waiting for the juice to spin a red thread. Back then, to wander far from home was unheard of. Children were supposed to stay close to home, and land was supposed to be handed down and down, as were clothing, stories, memories. My mother's brothers and sisters settled within a few miles of my grandparents' farm, and the lone daughter who dared to marry an outsider from nearby Sylvester, a mere thirty miles away, never failed to be overcome with emotion when it came time for her to leave after her weekly visit. She and my grandmother would fight back tears as they said goodbye. The figure of my grandmother growing smaller in the rearview mirror, the dust cloud diminishing as her daughter disappeared over the cattle-gap, those images of separation cut to the quick of my young girl's heart. Now in middle age, I find them no less affecting. "It is cruel how the power of time is a power only to separate," mother and daughter echo during their deathbed vigil in Fred Chappell's *Farewell, I'm Bound to Leave You*. I could feel that separation edging closer with each family gathering and its inevitable farewells.

Perhaps because we were isolated, we could feel the power of time and its silences more readily than those who lived in the world that lay beyond us, a world that, before television, drew closer at night, when through the static on the radio, I could hear the sound of its voice singing across the airwaves, pulling at me with its blues and country music all the way from Nashville and Cincinnati.

Sometimes its voice was a train whistle across the fields, sounding like a high-pitched woman's wailing, a sound that I later came to know as "high lonesome," its song reaching out to the distance as if from a bottomless chasm of lament and longing.

No wonder I would go at sunset to the farthest field on my father's farm, the one that ran alongside the highway where the freight trucks thundered past on their way to Atlanta and beyond. There I could sing as loud as I wanted and nobody could hear me but the cows. I knew nothing of the old ballads then, but, as it must have been for the mountain women crooning "Fair and Tender Ladies" while they sat at their looms, singing was for me a kind of dreaming forward, and backward, in time. I could look beyond the border of oak trees and imagine that the blue massing clouds were mountains, the Blue Ridge, where my father's mother had wanted to be when she died. Mountains: the word itself enthralled me. In the heat and mosquito-ridden flats of south Georgia, I longed for them. The place my grandmother had once called home.

Now she was silence itself, a face in the photographs that never spoke, a mouth that never moved. She had been born in the north Georgia mountains, in a gold-mining town named Dahlonega, where her father, an Irish miner, had brought his family after several years of mining life in the Black Hills of the Dakotas. Her mother, a painter and schoolmarm turned, in later years, Pentecostal preacher, was a woman about whom family legend told that she was the first white child into the Black Hills, carried there by her German immigrant parents. While my grandmother was still a small child, the family moved back to the Black Hills. Growing up in mining camps, she must have fancied herself a frontierswoman, and photographs of her from that time show a tall, handsome girl, wearing boots and a jaunty hat, looking confidently into the camera.

By the time my grandmother was a young woman, the family had returned for good to Dahlonega. She set about receiving her college education, after which she came to south Georgia to teach Latin. She married, had one son, became a widow, and when she remarried, her second husband refused to go back with her to the Blue Ridge Mountains she loved. So she stayed. She became a successful businesswoman, she supported an extended family through the Depression, and after a series of illnesses, she became a morphine addict, thanks to the indiscriminate prescriptions of her physician. She starved to death, weak and hungry, and not even my father's deathbed promise to carry her back to the mountains when she recovered could save her.

I was ten years old when she died. She had already become a stranger to me; for a long time my brother and I had been forbidden to visit her because of her physical condition. She left me little more than a few photographs and a book-shelf of volumes on magic, palmistry, prophecy. The black arts.

As for memories, I have only the image of her hands in her lap, picking fleas from her Persian cats. The extravagant Easter baskets she lavished upon my brother and me on Easter morning. Her face in the casket that lay in our living room during the two days before her funeral, her mouth tightly shut.

She left me nothing of her voice. What she did leave me were questions, imaginings. What had she thought as she lay on her bed during the months leading up to her death? Had she tried to sing her way out of her solitude and back home? Sometimes I think that all of the poems I have written since I came to the mountains have been an attempt to find a song that would sail her away, out of the sad story in which she had become trapped, back to the mountains where she belonged and longed to be.

"Solitude is deep water . . . "

The water swirling around her bed is deeper than I can imagine. In my family mythology, she has become one of those "small boats" that Emma Bell Miles does not credit with much sense of navigation. But who among us is not at some time in our lives such a boat, at the mercy of currents we seem powerless to control? Even Emma Bell Miles succumbed to the same depths, dying in destitution and disappointment. "There is so much death," as Czeslaw Milosz reminds us in his poem "Counsels," "and that is why affection / for pig-tails, bright-colored skirts in the wind, / for paper boats no more durable than we are . . . "

If the Deep South is a dusty plain haunted by childhood, these mountains have become a crazy quilt of trails haunted by women's voices. Not long after I arrived in Cullowhee to teach English at Western Carolina University, I found my imagination being stirred by those trails, the leaf mold and dirt of them, their shifting light, their windy sounds, their atmosphere of mystery and solitude. As I hiked them with my husband, himself a native of the East Tennessee hills, voices seemed to rise right up out of the leaf mold.

What those voices were saying grew out of the stories and songs I was already learning from women who had lived in these mountains all of their lives. No sooner had I moved into the basement apartment I rented on Tilley Creek than my neighbor, Mrs. Alma Pressley, appeared with a potted plant, a jar of honey, and an invitation to come with her to a gospel-singing. In the afternoon while I sat grading freshman essays, I could hear her as she walked the road between her house and her children's homes in the cove, singing, always singing.

"What is that song?" a friend from New York asked once over tea. "It sounds so quaint."

I didn't know. It sounded like nothing I'd ever heard. It floated in and out, stopping while she bent to pull weeds or pick up beer cans thrown along the road, starting up again as she resumed her walk. It did not sound at all quaint to me. It sounded as stubborn and tireless as the creek that ran through my backyard.

Less than a mile down the road lived Miss Alma's kinfolk, among them a woman who was to become like another grandmother to me, Willa Mae Pressley, a quilter whose mother, Delphia, had taught her the art of stitchery and pattern. Delphia Potts had been a woman whose love of books drove her to teach the children in Cullowhee Valley to read, stitching words together as surely as she stitched her calicoes. She taught her daughters, Willa Mae and Annie Lee, well; the two of them were as generous with their craft and their words as their mother had been. For all of one semester, they accompanied me to Asheville where, in the employ of the WCU Extension Department, we taught our skills at the Asheville Mall. Lap-quilting. Cornshuck dolls. Poetry.

While we journeyed, Willa Mae told me about her life. She told me of Christmases when her parents would walk the six miles into Sylva on Christmas Eve, returning after dark with bags of oranges and peppermint sticks. She told me about the Easter morning when she sat in the church built upon the ruins of the home place where she had been raised. "I didn't hear a word that preacher was saying," she declared. "I was out running on the hills again."

Her stories became woven into the poems I had begun to write, and they joined there with another voice, that of a woman raised on the far side of the valley, Linda Mathis, who grew up learning the old songs from her daddy, a fiddler and singer from Caney Fork. When Linda first called me on the phone years ago, after having seen an article in the local paper about a chapbook I had published, her voice was shaking. She had written some poems, she confided, and she asked if I would hear them out. On the telephone? I was hesitant. What if they were awful? What would I say? I can still remember the silence on the line before Linda began to read her first poem. I listened hard and what I heard coming across the distance was a woman's voice informed by the old songs that had helped her ancestors survive. Over the next few years, as I read her poems and she read mine, we shared voices. All one has to do is look at the work we were writing during that time to see the commingling of voice. When one night Linda brought to my poetry workshop the following poem, I felt a surge of recognition stronger than I had felt in many of my literature classes in college.

Darling of My Heart

Much water has passed over the small
    pebbles since that day long ago
I strolled across the bridge singing
    Shady Grove.

And you lingered in the shadows
    tall and handsome in your white
        shirt and dark vest.

How long I would have sung of the
    darling of my heart—I would not know—
        for your horse called out to me.

You stood there with your damp curls on
    your forehead looking at me.
I went to you and you came to me.
        We crushed the wildflowers under our feet.

Under a gazebo of green laurel we touched,
　　　as quietly as grass blades brushing
　　　　　in the wind.

I am alone now, and I remember quiet-like
　　　and smile.
Yet again my memories are as strong as the wind,
　　　and I am left weak and hungry.

　　Here was a voice that sounded like a sister to the unfolding voice of a woman I was just beginning to know through my own poems and whose name I had not yet discovered, a woman solitary and abandoned, strong yet susceptible to the shiftings of season and memory. This woman spoke with the authority of one living within what Emma Bell Miles has called "the rift that is set between the sexes at birth and widens with the passage of the years." As I began to listen to her, she became the evocation of those female spirits that haunt these mountains still. She became also, in some personal, ancestral sense, my lost grandmother's voice, yearning for the high places, all too familiar with the low.

　　This mingling of voice that I shared with Linda Mathis and Willa Mae Pressley was only the beginning of a poetic weaving together of voices that has continued up till the present. Over the years needed to write the book *Wildwood Flower* and the poems that kept coming after its completion and which now comprise my new collection, *Black Shawl*, I was guided by two other voices, those of Emma Bell Miles and Lee Smith. Along the way, these authors gave me priceless clues to the identity of this solitary woman whose voice I could not get out of my head. When her first poems began to speak to me, I had no idea who was saying them, only that they had somehow originated on a hike up the Kanati Fork trail in the Great Smoky Mountains. Halfway up the trail, I happened upon a deserted home-site hidden away in the darkness of vines and brush. What sort of woman could live up here, I wondered. How could she stand it? Something of her presence followed me the rest of the hike, and by the time I had come back down the mountain, "Wildwood Flower" had written itself out in my head. Whoever this voice was, I knew she had been waiting a long time to speak.

　　And speak she did. Many of the poems to follow flowed out in the same urgent way, taking the imagery of my own life, the trails, the ice on windowpanes, the clothes blowing on the line, and using them as windows into the life of another woman in an earlier time. But who was she? As I read Emma Bell Miles's *The Spirit of the Mountains,* I began to understand who she was, the world she moved within. From Miles's description of a mountain homestead, I knew the puncheon floor of her cabin, the "cat-holes" in the walls where the chinking had fallen out, the cast-iron spider on her stove, the porch on which stood her loom, where on good days she would sit, singing "over the thump of the batten," an old song from Scotland or Ireland, *Oh the cuckoo is a pretty bird* . . . , changing nary a word, for the song was, as Miles puts it, "too anciently received."

Soon I discovered that the name of this woman was Alma, combining both the generosity of a real woman, Mrs. Alma Pressley, who had welcomed me to these mountains, and the metaphor of soul that could encompass a woman's spiritual journey as well as her literal one.

How well I remember those winter mornings as I worked to complete the manuscript of *Wildwood Flower,* pages of rough drafts strewn around me, and *The Spirit of the Mountains* and *Oral History* at the ready. I knew that when the going got rough, when Alma turned contrary and taciturn, I had those old prophetesses that Miles celebrates in "Grandmothers and Sons" and Smith's irrepressible Granny Younger to help me out.

One poem in particular kept eluding me, the piece that later became "Weep-Willow." I had begun the poem years before as part of my book of south Georgia poems entitled *The Girl in the Midst of the Harvest.* On the porch sat my grandmother, surrounded by flies, dust, and drought, trying to sing a song that I could never get to sound quite right. So now in the last stages of writing Alma's story, I pulled out this old poem, knowing that if I could relocate its deep southern voice into the North Carolina mountains, I could rescue the poem and make it sing as it should.

And who better to help me in my task than Granny Younger? For what seemed like the hundredth time, I opened *Oral History* and began to read aloud, "From his cabin door, Almarine Cantrell owns all the land he sees." Now, there is nothing taciturn about Granny, and I was happy to follow her yet again through the nooks and crannies of her story, wallowing in the vitality of her language that, in its flow, sounded so much like singing. I was looking for a clue, for a glimmer, for one compelling *word,* if nothing else, and on this particular morning these were the lines that turned my poem around: "Sometimes I know the future in my breast. Sometimes I see the future coming out like a picture show, acrost the trail ahead. But that night I never seed nothing atall. If I had it would of been graves and dying. It would of been blood on the moon. And I never saw a blessed thing in the night but them lightning bugs a rising from the sally grass along by Grassy Creek."

The sally grass, the lightning bugs rising from it, and the creek bubbling through it—these images began to work on my imagination, and when I returned to my poem, I found it transformed by the music of Granny's mountain dialect, so much so that in the process of moving its "place" from south Georgia to Appalachia, I began to realize that the singer in the poem was not my own grandmother but Alma's, singing her endless ballads to the darkness, one of those "keepers of the ballads" who have kept the old songs alive, a woman who could sing "Fair and Tender Ladies" so hard and clear that the hair would rise up on the nape of your neck.

When I sent the finished version of "Weep-Willow" to Lee, she wrote back in her breathless way, "This poem is exactly what my new novel is about. Except that my character doesn't sing to get through the night, she writes letters." Would I, she asked, let her use the poem at the beginning of her next book? Who could say no to such a request? As far as I was concerned, "Weep-Willow" was, and always will be, Lee's poem. And Granny Younger's.

Later I learned that what had been happening over the time I was completing *Wildwood Flower* and Lee was finishing *Fair and Tender Ladies* was nothing less than a long-distance collaboration. While I was reading *Oral History,* she was reading an earlier manuscript of Alma's poems that I had sent her, so that for a little while that winter Alma, Granny, and Ivy Rowe spent some time visiting with each other in our separate, yet connected, imaginations. Neither Lee nor I really knew how we were helping each other, nor did we know that we were engaged in a meeting of voices, but that made no difference, for voices have a way of doing what they will. They have a life of their own. They will take over and carry you right along with them.

Where those voices have carried me is home, harking me back to grandmothers and great-grandmothers lost, yet found again in the voice of Alma and the several voices in my new manuscript, *Black Shawl,* voices who have been able to say for me what it was like to walk particular traces, stand in particular shadows, singing the old ballads and waiting for something to happen.

Writing poetry has shown me how to wait, how to make the silence at the heart of that deep water Emma Bell Miles calls solitude *listen.* Poetry has taught me how to stir the depths, how to set the ripples spreading.

I look out at that blue silence lapping over hill and hollow and begin to sing, each poem like a small boat on the current. Sometimes the words wobble, sometimes they spin.

Sail away, Ladies, Sail away!
Who knows how far they will carry me!

Jo
Carson

Jo Carson (b. 1946) is a well-known writer and performer from Johnson City, Tennessee, who explores a wide range of literary genres, including poems, essays, plays, short stories, children's work, reviews, advertising, and speeches. She is the author of numerous award-winning plays: *Daytrips* (1989; Kesselring Award), *Preacher with a Horse to Ride* (Roger L. Stevens Award from the Fund for New American Plays, 1993), and *The Bear Facts* (NEA Playwright's Fellowship, 1993–94). A new play, *Whispering to Horses,* had its premiere performance at Seven Stages in Atlanta during the 1996–97 season and won a 1996 AT&T Onstage: New Plays for the 90s Award. A series of monologues and dialogues, *Stories I Ain't Told Nobody Yet* (1989), made Editor's Choice on *Booklist* and the American Library Association's recommended list in 1990, and was brought out in paperback by Theatre Communications Group in 1991. This series has served as performance material for Carson for several years in a variety of venues here and abroad. She also has published picture books for children—*Pulling My Leg* (1990), *You Hold Me and I'll Hold You* (1992), and *The Great Shaking* (1994)—as well as a short story collection called *The Last of the "Waltz Across Texas" and Other Stories* (1993). She has created performance pieces out of oral histories of specific communities, performed by and for those communities, including Colquitt, Georgia, and Jonesboro, Tennessee, and she is fiction editor for *Southern Exposure* magazine. Carson, who was honored at the Sixteenth Annual Literary Festival at Emory & Henry College in the fall of 1997, is also a companion to a medium-sized dog, a source of apples for a couple of horses, a successful grower of peppers for garlic pickles, and the black peg half of a cribbage tournament that has gone on for several years.

* * *

Good Questions

In 1994, I was one of thirty playwrights in the country invited to apply for a major award. I did not win the award. It went to a man who was dying of AIDS, and it allowed him the wherewithal to die at home. The award was for a body of work, a sort of achievement award, as opposed to being project-specific as most grants are. Most grants ask that you describe the project you want funded, submit a budget for it, and at the end, assuming you get the money, write a final report. This one offered a substantial check to the winner with no strings attached. The application asked some really hard questions about how I see myself and my work and then gave a very limited space (mostly one-half of a standard page, single-spaced) in which to answer them. Limited space means you don't get to spend much time or language getting to what you have to say. In movie parlance, you have to cut to the chase. It took about two weeks' work to write and cut my verbiage sufficiently to be in the chase.

I am glad I answered the questions even if I didn't win the money. I found the exercise more useful than I imagined it might be when I first started filling in the blanks, because it made me think about what I've done and what I want and what I am trying to do. So, when the request for this essay came in 1995, I thought I'd pass the good questions along. I'd much rather pass along just the questions, especially since I didn't win the award, but the essay doesn't make much sense that way, so I'm including my answers and some comments on them.

Just to say it, lots of backup stuff like a biography and work samples were included in the application that are not included here.

So, the good questions:

1. Give a brief description of your work.

    Comment: I am a writer/performer with more than twenty years' work behind me, and I am all over the map of literary genres—poems, essays, plays, short stories, children's work, reviews, advertising, speeches—just about everything but novels, and I'm thinking of trying that next. So I wanted to find some way to speak of some of the range of things I do without just sounding scattered.

    Answer: All my work fits in my mouth. By that I mean it is written to be spoken aloud, even the essays and short stories and poems. I have a gut feeling that if work doesn't fit in my mouth, it won't fit in a reader's head, so I am the noisiest writer I know. Everything is spoken aloud in process. This eccentricity has pushed my work in some very specific directions: I write performance material no matter what else the pieces get called, and whether they are for my voice or other characters' voices, like the plays, they are first to be spoken aloud. With the performances I do of my work, I am often called a storyteller and I like the old sense of the word, but in current usage, it is not an accurate description. I don't "do" Jack Tales. I don't really have a description for what I do as a writer/performer. I do have a tradition. I come from a nest of raconteurs who are not afraid of hard stories or the extremes of the human condition. I just take the process one step further: I write stuff down.

2.   What are your primary artistic concerns?

Comment: There is an obvious answer that applies honestly and earnestly to everybody who ever tries to write. We want to be good at it. We want to be very good. We want to be published. We want to be read. We want the Pulitzer or equivalent recognition of heat and heart and work. Don't these folks know this? Well, yes, they do. So say something new. And best make it true as well.

Answer: I am obliged to try to write, I am miserable if I am not working/ writing on something, so my real, gut-level, honest-to-God, primary artistic concern is to do it. I spent years with pickup jobs I didn't like, writing on lunch breaks and weekends. I did it because I needed the money, but my focus was always the writing, not the job. I did not endear myself to many employers. I am haunted by a recurring question from those years: "Why don't you quit messing around and do something constructive?" What people (particularly my family) meant was a regular job that made a contribution to a community, like teaching or real estate. Sometimes I think about real estate; why aren't I in real estate? People I know in real estate have respectable positions in this community, and they are not suspect in the way I still am, several years and books and plays later. Art is not valuable to my neighbors and real estate is. So what am I trying to do? The pursuit of art, any art, is not always a choice; it is a quest, another version of the shaman's journey, in which the calling is to look into the void, or the newspaper and your neighbor's windows, or, for that matter, your own heart and report back what you see. It is the messenger's job and I worry about that. The joke is "shoot the messenger," which makes for fine dramatic action, but the truth is that the messenger is mostly just dismissed. I do not want to be so easily dismissed. No wonder I think of real estate.

My private journey is to learn to make this squirrelly language say what I really mean.

3.   How has your work changed in the last five years?

Answer: I spent eight years of the 1980s as a caregiver, with my father, for an Alzheimer's victim, my mother. I wrote a play out of the experience. The play is about duty and madness. It was hard as hell to write because it was so personal and I felt so exposed. In it, the character who is me thinks a lot about murder. Try saying this out loud: my real duty is to murder my mother. I didn't do it. She is now a vegetable in a nursing home, and death would be a gift. (*Comment:* Since I wrote this, my mother died, in January 1995.) I don't want to spend time in jail for giving that gift, so I don't. I tell this story because the experience taught me several things that I've been living with for the five years since the play, *Daytrips,* was first produced. These two are the most important to my writing: (1) If I am not scared in some way of what I am writing, I am not yet close enough to the bone, and I need to dig deeper. Nothing I can imagine is outside the realm of the human condition. I just have to have the courage to say it. (2) Comedy is about surviving human flaws and frailties, tragedy is about dying of them. Comedy is often the more difficult to live with and to write, but the tough, honest, ironic vision I love is the closest I can come to an accurate reflection of what I see. And I am convinced there are circumstances in which we laugh or we die, and comedy itself is the stuff of redemption.

4.   What are your artistic goals: short-term, long-term, "big dream"?

Answer: I have come to love the process of work better than the product of it. I enjoy having books people can read or plays to produce, but by the time a piece gets to print or production, I am usually quite done with it. It has to be able to fly on its own. Because of this, my big goals are almost all oriented to process. I am continually drawn to study things that change how I see the world. I did master's work in geography—geography these days is the study of spatial relationships of almost anything you care to name. I read history because it is a fourth dimension in a place. (I write some out of history.) I am currently working at Chaos theory (the work available for mathematical idiots) because, again, it changes and enriches my perceptions. Out of Chaos, synchronicity, and out of synchronicity, Jung, and out of Jung, Christian mythology. This list is serpentine and (I hope) lifelong, and it all feeds the writing. No, more than that, it is essential to the writing.

The play I am currently working on is about my father and me, but the structure is a fractal, a pattern in nature produced by Chaos. A tree has a fractal pattern, but so do our lives if you look through time. And stories are, by their nature, fractals. I'm playing with it, I'm obsessed with the idea of stories as fractals. My long-term artistic goal is to stay obsessed, if not by Chaos, then by some set of ideas that continue to change how I see the world, and the big dream is that the products of these obsessions (my work) will keep producing sufficient money that I can live comfortably and pursue whatever comes next. I am well aware of the privilege of all this.

5.   What kind of responsibility do you think an artist has to society?

Comment: I choose to answer this question in a political context, which may or may not have been smart, you never know. This is the stuff of a whole essay—if not books—in itself and gets brushed by fast and glibly in this answer. On the other hand, the observations about conscience are very much in keeping with how I try to work. Writing is predatory. I am either chewing on myself, i.e., using my own experience, or what I can observe or presume to understand, but make no mistake, I am a consumer with a large and hungry tooth for the human condition, and everything I see or know or hear about could be fair game.

Answer: I believe art and science are similar creative pursuits—some even suggest that art often leads science—but science climbed off a moral hook back during the Age of Reason and art still has coattails caught on it. Jesse Helms does not try to censor science; it is the pursuit of a purer knowledge, and the secrets of the double helix are far enough removed that he is not threatened, though, in this day and time, some are. He does not understand that art is also the pursuit of knowledge, but it is mostly stuff of the human heart, always murky and sometimes uncomfortable, and when he sees something that frightens him, he feels free to be offended. I am offended by Mr. Helms, but I am caught by this moral hook that comes with art. For me, it means I will apply a conscience, my own—not his—to the work I do. It does not mean I will censor what I feel is true to make it pleasing for him or anybody else. *Conscience* is from Latin, *consciens,* which means to know well. (*Science,* from *sciens,* means to know.) I write out of what I can—from the Latin meaning—presume to know something about, including a place, people, a community, a religious and social tradition, and my own experience. This is not an exclusive list. I write out of what I feel—in current usage of the word *conscience*—is important to say out loud, out of what I can make live in words, and I holler as loud as this messenger knows how about the things that hurt.

6.   How does this understanding of social responsibility reveal itself in your life and work?

Comment: Rereading this, I gave a very odd answer. Rethinking it, it is an accurate answer for me; I just didn't tie in very well what such grounding has to do with social responsibility. It would be another whole essay about—again—the older functions of a storyteller in a community.

Answer: I am of and from a place like very few people are these days. I live in the place I grew up (I've come back here) and I write out of it. This is the geography that fits my imagination or that my imagination has been shaped to fit. I am here by choice, and if a person can love a landscape, I do. These old mountains feed my soul. It is a place with strong negative stereotypes I am obliged to address for no better reason than my address. It is a place where economics are hard, and the economics of art are close to impossible, a place where my sex is still told, in the fundamentalist churches, that her job is to obey her husband, a place where, if you are murdered it is much more likely to be by family than by strangers. It is also a place where Faulkner's old verities still have value, and neighbors tell one another stories over the back fence. I do not know how to write without this grounding. I would not know where to begin. So my work has a region, and for it, an accent. It has a specific rhythm and some diphthongs to it; it also has a tradition of narrative and play with words so it adapts well to literary endeavors. It belongs to a place I am part of, and if my work has any lasting value, it is because I make it as true as I can to this place.

7.   List your five most important and vital professional achievements (this question gave a full page for the answer).

Comment: This was the hardest of the questions for me to answer. It is not something I think about. I'm inclined to be flippant and name all five as getting whatever project is due at the moment out by the deadline. (Or very shortly thereafter.) I worry and cuss a lot about deadlines; I think about deadlines. And I've been asked most of the previous six questions before, in some fashion, usually on my feet, usually by taking questions after I've done a performance or a reading, so I already had someplace to begin with them. There was no such comfort with this one. I surprised myself with this list. Was this really what I thought was most important? How very odd. In retrospect, it reflects the grounding and community I speak of in question six, and if I had to make up the list again tomorrow, having thought about it twice now—once for answering the questions the first time, the second for this essay—it would not change much at all. What is missing (and is probably best done with graphics) is a personal delineation of the different levels of a sort of energy/food chain in the making of art, i.e., who feeds me, who I feed, and so on. One way to talk about it is levels of community, but I think the energy chain image is actually more accurate. Anyway, it is an interesting approach to reading this answer and a real comment on what I see as important.

Answer: (A) I have gotten good reviews for books and plays, and I have won awards for plays: a 1989 Kesselring Award for *Daytrips,* a 1993 Roger L. Stevens Award from the Fund for New American Plays for *Preacher with a Horse to Ride,* and an NEA Playwright's Fellowship for 1993–94 with *The Bear Facts* as the script that went through the peer review process. I have also been produced a fair amount. I value these things immensely, not just for the money, though—make no mistake—when money comes, it makes my life more comfortable. The achievement, as I see it, is that people who are knowledgeable in my field find worth in my work.

(B) I make about half my living doing reading/performances. I am something of an exotic as a performer, but Appalachia has been fashionable lately, so I have been a useful exotic to hire. That was pure good luck. The achievement is this: I work almost exclusively by word of mouth, other people's recommendations, no advertising beyond a business card with my name and address on it, and I have for years, around here, other places in this country, and abroad. In these gigs, I do readings of my work with a performer's sensibility, no more, no less, and I do ten to fifteen of them, sometimes more, a year.

(C) I do little readings here, too. I always use some of whatever is new on the computer, and I have a following of people, a few in any given audience, who have come to hear the new work. There are a hundred or so total in this group. If that seems small, remember Johnson City is not a big town, and this is the place where one county high school English/drama teacher I knew only ever went to see plays she'd seen before and already knew she liked. I love what happens with this audience. They are very much part of my process with new work—it gets kinks worked out of it aloud—they know that and make a point to participate.

(D) Grade school, high school, and college teachers in the region and out of it are using my work in the classroom, often in the context of Appalachian studies, but not exclusively. This is another real-life, in place, validation of work that says I hit something square on the nose, and I am pleased, honored, and encouraged by the use.

(E) I wrote a play (*comment:* actually four, so far, 1992–95) out of oral histories for the town of Colquitt, Georgia, in an ongoing project called Swamp Gravy, and after a rough start in which I was very suspect because I was not from there, I am told now by several people, women particularly, black and white, that I changed their lives for the better with what I did. All I did was hand their stories back to them revisioned toward their performance of them, and I say that, but what we did, director Richard Geer and everyone else who worked on the project, was honor (as in "give dignity to") a community's stories by telling them. I am moved by the process and the power of these stories, and the project feeds my soul because I get to see the changes in how people see themselves. And that change in vision is the stuff that changes lives. This is the power of art made visible, and I don't get to see it, much less participate, nearly as often as I'd like.

8. List other things you'd like us to know about you (this question also allowed a full page for the answer).

Comment: Rereading this, I am surprised by my choices here, too. Three out of the four sections are about support, and the fourth is old dreams. Wonder why I thought this stuff was useful. I'd choose different things now. I'd talk more about the oral history work I am doing, about my new play, about projects I want to do in the future, generally things that imply I have a future and I'm not going to fold up shop like some clam if I am awarded enough money to live on for a while. It does, in retrospect, seem politic to say something about the future. Twenty-twenty hindsight, worth what you pay for it. I might include the (D) section of this answer even now, the old dreams, mostly because I find it funny how driven I still am by old dreams.

Answer: (A) I was one of the organizers of the founding meeting of Alternate ROOTS (Regional Organization of Theaters, South), which is ongoing with close to twenty years of service and support to performers and theaters trying to be about community in the South. After attending her first ROOTS meeting, writer Linda Burnham said she'd found heaven—and in a way it is. It is also one of very few organizations where issues of race and sexual otherness are addressed directly, and a social conscience is there for the making if you don't already come with one. It has been the source of much of my education about racism, and it has been an extended and very supportive critical family in which to try out new work.

(B) I worked for several years with a theater called The Road Company, based here in Johnson City, that produced plays out of the community, one of the little 1970s ventures that managed to survive. It was, for the most part, collaborative work, and I cut my teeth as a playwright on a series of new plays we did. The company toured them for several years, mostly in the South. I also worked occasionally as a member of the acting ensemble. Acting was never a position I was comfortable in; I'm too inclined to rewrite in the moment, which is fine for me but hard for other actors. I've maintained a good relationship with The Road Company ever since I left the ensemble. They've done staged readings or productions of all my new plays. Every playwright needs this sort of relationship. I am fortunate enough to have it.

(C) My father gave me the house I live in. It isn't the least bit fancy—some day I'll add a bathtub to the shower—but it is decent shelter, and I am grateful. It was rental property he had. After the years of caregiving for my mother, I had run myself out of resources, he knew it, and he gave me the house. He said, "You'd have bought something if you hadn't helped me," and he was probably right. If I had bought, I'd have a bathtub, but I'd still be paying on a mortgage and I'm not. So the house has become a sort of safety net, a level of economic permission to take chances with my work and try things that may or may not be marketable but seem important to try. It is the best way I know to honor the gift. I sometimes work specifically for markets, like with children's books and essays, but the risky stuff I do is the real work, and the house makes the risk taking possible.

(D) This is silly, but I don't know many people who can say it: I have achieved two of my big childhood dreams. The first is professional. There is a novelist Josephine Carson (Josephine is my given name), and I used to look with envy at her cards in the card catalogue at the library and imagine how I would feel if they were mine. I am now in the card catalogue (better said, the computer) several times over, and I feel pretty much like I thought I might about it. Ecstatic. The second is a great joy in my life and yet another way to keep changing my perceptions. I keep a horse. If Miss Kate is not quite Walter Farley's Black Stallion, she is close enough for a woman in her middle years, and I ride her miles and amazing days in these old mountains.

So ends the list of good questions and my assorted answers. There was a revelation for me in this endeavor. It comes with question four and the first line of my answer about having come to like the process of work better than the product. It is true now, but it used to be the other way around. I liked having products better than I liked making them, and I suffered through the making for the reward of a poem (or the like) in my pocket. Or my notebook. Or whatever journal. As little as ten years ago, I still had to tie myself down to get work done, and I felt like a difficult child with homework I didn't want to do. (I spent a lot of my childhood inside that feeling; at least it was familiar.) I don't know exactly when or why the change happened, but I am grateful it did. Maybe I was just a long time growing up, but I like to think of it another way. Maybe I finally came onto a voice I could use—the change happened about the time I realized I could and should use my place and my experience. I've heard freedom described as moving easy in harness. Maybe what I found was a harness that fit well enough I could move easy in it.

LOU
V.P.
CRABTREE

Lou V.P. Crabtree was born in 1913 in the hills of Appalachia, where she has spent most of her life. She now lives in Abingdon, Virginia. Crabtree graduated from Radford University and studied at the American Academy of Dramatic Arts and the Faegin School of Drama. She taught for thirty-five years, served as regional auditioner for the American Academy (New York and Pasadena, California, branches), played in the Rock of Ages Band, and participated in school and community drama throughout much of her life. Currently, she lectures on astronomy and writes space poetry. Her stories, poems, and historical essays have appeared in publications such as the *Laurel Review, Shenandoah, American Way,* and *Sow's Ear. Sweet Hollow,* published in 1984 and now in its fifth printing, consists of seven stories about the lives of Appalachians fifty years ago, stories that are both stark and mystic. Her play *Calling on Lou* was performed in 1984 at the Barter Theater, the state theater of Virginia in Abingdon, and toured in 1985. Crabtree has completed several novels and short story collections that have never been offered for publication, including *The Village, Portions, Time in Place,* and *Nine Christmas Stories.*

*   *   *

Paradise in Price Hollow

Paradise in Price Hollow was partly Adam's paradise *before* the apple got caught in his throat.

Was I a spirit set down in that paradise for sixteen years, to find out what it is to be human? Or was I a human set there to absorb the spirit that would last eighty years and plant something in the heart of me? That something would save me—help me to stand apart, isolated, all the while observing the diversity of life's systems, circles, patterns. That something would give me roots to write from.

Price Hollow is a small hollow between hills and ridges, so deep that when you look up, crosses from a winter's sun break through the naked trees. It is in Hogoheegee, Washington County, Virginia, a wide area that the Great Spirit gave to Indians to hunt and fish. But perhaps Price Hollow could be any one of the thousands of hollows in the great Appalachian chain extending from Maine to Georgia. Perhaps readers could name it Snake Hollow, Hant Hollow, or Tin Can Hollow and see it as their own.

Even winter had its wonders in Price Hollow. Long shadows from that sun, like the arms of night, arrived early in winter to give sweet rest to man and animal. Red berries of the hawthorn bush became black "haws" over the cold days and made good springtime chews.

In Price Hollow, faith taught one to wait out the winter, to smell the odor of peppermint on the cow's breath, or the odor of freshly laundered clothes hung on the line like Dutchman's britches—a flower. Faith took you from the softness of the mole's ear to the softness on the belly of a leaf. Contained in that same softness, one learned years later the answer to the question—what is faith? Part of faith is wait. In the wintertime, one learns to wait.

Forbearance was in every soft breeze.

Mistletoe caught in tops of highest oak trees. Holly and bittersweet climbed upwards over cliffs. Holly and mistletoe brought the Christmas season dear to writers. In Price Hollow, Christmas was one orange, holly tied with a red ribbon, a native tree with paper chains.

Christmas gave me nine stories—never published, but blessings still. "Next year Baker would be gone from Christmas Island," I wrote. "Tomorrow he would look where the Saints rode off on a whale's back toward a plume of smoke, fifty, perhaps a hundred miles, from Christmas Island." In "Noel" the birth, again, mysteriously signals a journey. "This was the night of departure. Many years ago members of the Huron tribe began making the trip to Mackinac at Christmas time. It was forgotten how long ago."

In spring, there was honey in the bank and honey in the tree.

When Old Mother Goose picked her geese or turned over in her featherbed, spring snowflakes settled down and never thawed or melted.

The service tree bloomed, its flowering the first sign of spring.

In Price Hollow, imagination ran from "apples in the hole," buried for greater preservation, to the moon wrung out in lifeblood—observed in simple flowers, the bloodroot. Enchantments of the heart—bees buzzing, bluebells ringing chimes, pears, peaches, plums warming the inside of the mouth—were everyplace. A child's delight was the pot pies made from a million berries—strawberry, blueberry, blackberry, raspberry.

So many wonders were in Price Hollow. Pristine wild wonders. Who planted them there? Surely, bird, wind, and animal carried seeds about. No doubt, human inhabitants, long lost and forgotten, did the same.

The redbud, or Judas tree, retained its purplish, rosy flowers displaying Judas's betrayal and remorse when he hanged himself.

There was the dogwood with Jesus' crown of thorns and bloodstains on four petals, like the cross. There was every nut to delight animal and child: walnuts—both black and white—hickory nuts, chinquapins, acorns, chestnuts that my brother Bud raced to get after a storm.

There were pears, plums, wild cherries, and Indian peaches with red juices and red-painted Indian skins. Hill apples, winter apples, rusty coats, early and Virginia beauties. I claimed the red Indian peach trees and laughing said Bud could have the rusty coat apple tree.

The great oak was mine too—my home perched high on great limbs among great branches. Here Bud and I played games like claiming trees and writing letters to the animals. Bud said he got an answer once. I wondered if he did. In this same world, shared by all, lived a mother vixen, her grey fox mate and their cubs, in a den among the great roots, spreading, protruding, from the ground. The four cubs, grey with white-tipped backs, chased their tails round and round the great oak until they fell dizzy over one another. With her long ears, the mother listened, hearing a mouse yards away. She would find the sound, leap and pounce, and carry dinner home to her cubs.

In Price Hollow there were herbs for sickness: mountain tea, sassafras, willow bark, catnip, burdock root. There were the castor oil plant and heartweed. Sage was for cooking, as were wild onion, watercress, highland cress, mushrooms, wild parsnips, Indian turnip, wild ginger, cinnamon, lemon flower, and rhubarb—all used by good cooks.

In the heavens were stars. My space poetry started from the star rising on top of the ridge in Price Hollow.

Closer overhead, where butterflies lazed, were birds, bees, crows, buzzards, ducks, geese; in trees were frogs, skippers, snake doctors, and dragonflies. Underground were ants, snails, moles, groundhogs, skunks, polecats, digger wasps. In woods were deer, panthers, bobcats, wildcats, and foxfire. At home were horse, cow, mule, hog, pig, dog, cats, and kittens.

Indians went down the hollow to fish at the river. An old Indian had a canoe. If he liked you, he would row you across. If not, you had to wade. Pests, like Bud and me, waded.

Little Indian children stood and eyed me from the opposite hillside. Bud had Crow Boy as a hunting and fishing friend. The time came for the Indians to depart downriver; Bud ran away with Crow Boy. When Old Black Fish brought Bud home and my father said he would whip Bud, Old Black Fish grunted and left without speaking. Indians do not whip children.

The spring seeds of my writing were childhood stories such as these. Indians and Indian scenes would return to me for the rest of my life. Because of my poems, I was adopted by a Cherokee tribe and given the name Grandmother Wolf Woman (Lisi/wa-ga/A-ge-ye). I was given presents: tobacco—with smoke blown north, east, south, west—and the privilege of attending council meetings. And my poetry was given new form from such attachments.

> I will boil rose bushes
> gathered in the country
> and wash the doorsill
>   of your hogan
>   with rose water. [from "Burial"]

Jacks-in-the-pulpit returned in the spring like circuit preachers to preach near creeks flanked by a field of daisies, yellow and white.

And so did real preachers once more find their way to Price Hollow. They walked on foot the paths up to doors, being satisfied with eating chicken dinners or exiting quickly when all they got to eat was poke salad greens cut with a scythe and boiled in the washing kettle.

A fascination with words developed from a visit by one of those traveling preachers. My father made me recite a chapter from *Les Misérables* for this preacher man. After my performance was over, the preacher looked at me hard and said, "She is going to become a tragedienne." How ever in the world did an old hill preacher know that word? I never forgot the word, years later bringing it back in writing. Words are the writer's tools, as paint is to the artist.

* * *

But Paradise in Price Hollow was also partly Adam's paradise *after* the apple got caught in his throat.

The yellow adder—a flower with a long black tongue—was like the snake in Adam's paradise. Adam's real snake, with two holes on top of his mouth and forked darting tongue, picking up scent molecules and taking them to the roof of his mouth, became a metaphor in my writing when life's dark and physical side entered through the two holes in my own nose.

A drink of water called for by Lazarus, in hell, bubbled up in unpolluted springs under cliffs and coal seams.

Yes, the devil was there. Just as he was in Adam's paradise. Just as he is everywhere. "Maw has baked the devil in the pie," I had a character say in *Sweet Hollow.*

There was a seamy side of life in Price Hollow, and I always knew this.

The same preachers who taught me words had sex along the roads—even in the pumpkin patch. I write about this in *The Village.* Fairleanah enticed Preacher-Man. He then wanted to save her soul by baptizing her in the river, but he accidentally drowned her instead.

Murder was in Price Hollow too. An old deserted house with dark vacant eyes stood where the last man who was hanged in Virginia murdered his unfaithful lover.

Do witches belong to the devil? Old Angie, the witch, put a spell on cows to keep their milk from churning butter.

"Come like Jesus," said the unmarried mother in *Sweet Hollow* when she was asked who the father of her son was. She attempted to excuse herself, calling on the virgin birth, for in the hollows no one would forgive or forget her adultery. Forever after her words were uttered, the boy was laughingly called "little Jesus," or "woods colt," or "bastard." He went away and did not come back. Those who mistreated him looked and wished for his return, as those in the Scriptures had. A sentence deleted from a shortened original publication of the story about Little Jesus I keep in my heart as my best: "Come back, Little Jesus, and I will give to you my golden catalpa and my red flame maple and all the Judas trees, high on the persimmon ridges, above the red-gashed sand gullies."

There were dark caves where bats hung upside down. The same caves where ancestors hid in the Civil War, then called the pigs to hide their tracks. Characters for stories hid in the caves for a Civil War novel I called *Time in Place.* I did not plan on Old Sook being the heroine of this book, but she took over. Black she was, the wife of Old Tom, a slave carried uphill to be buried outside the white graveyard. Old Sook was not permitted to go uphill when they buried her husband, so she sat on the woodbox in her kitchen and wept in her apron. The child narrator of the story, the "I," had legs too small to climb the hill, so she was left with Old

Sook in the kitchen. The image of Old Sook crying, prohibited from attending her own husband's burial, stayed with the narrator the rest of her life and extended into her writing.

Intolerance was in Price Hollow too. Is one ever too young to learn tolerance for other races when all must eat, breathe, drink, and bleed red blood?

And where does tolerance begin and end? Should we tolerate the slugs who come out of the ground to eat with the cats? Then the whole family appears, with babies, one-fourth-inch babies, to drink the cat's milk? Should we step on them, squash them underfoot and out of nature's plan?

Can one go back? No. I did return with NBC and American Airlines once in a four-wheel drive into gullies, straight up hills, around fallen trees, across rocks. "I feel like I am on an American safari," said the cameraman as a cow poked her head into the van.

But I cannot really ever return to the place I knew as a child. Those sixteen years ended and gave way to twenty years of meager living, years not unlike those after the Civil War when the slaves left and cornfields lay vacant and liquor stills were idle from no corn to feed them. Price Hollow, where one was never hungry or naked, never lonely or alone, had disappeared.

One can never go back. Loggers came, trees fell, and the soils of hill land wore down. The coal seams were ravaged, hunters killed the animals, and in the flat places, tobacco and marijuana were planted. A garbage disposal at the head of the creek polluted the water and destroyed fish downriver.

Forbearance. No, there was none. Only greed, ignorance, money, power.

But I took the memory of Price Hollow into my writing, all my writing days.

I sit on my porch and they come. Abingdon, Virginia, where I now live, is a writers' town where many people come to write. They come to my porch from Roanoke, Virginia, and Knoxville, Tennessee, from South Carolina and West Virginia. At Price Hollow I sat on old women's porches. I write about their stories in *The Village*. A piece of this hooked to a piece of that and a new creation surfaced in the sequence. The world has become one great paradise from which to gather locale, special wording, characters, and plot. And writing has become the way to keep so much alive. I kept Bud alive, who died at thirty in Hitler's war. I kept him alive as he learned about life walking around "The Jake Pond" (*Sweet Hollow*, pp. 69–73).

And now young writers come to sit on *my* porch. "Keep a journal," I say. Remember Anne Frank, the Jewish girl who hid during the Holocaust. Keep a journal. I have said it a million times. Later one will be surprised. There you will find the special word you need, the phrase, the character, the action, the plot.

They come. I sit on the porch as I sat with those old women in Price Hollow.

Keep a journal, I tell them. You think you will remember, but you won't.

They come. Could they be new characters out of the real world? Keep a journal, I tell them. Your seed to remember.

There was a bright side and a dark side to Price Hollow. Both cows and snakes roamed those hills. But writers must deal with all of life, and this was perhaps the most important message Price Hollow taught me.

"Holy Spirit" (*Sweet Hollow,* pp. 59–68) is in some ways a very dark and troubling story, but one critic placed it in the realm of sacred literature. It tells the tale of Old Rellar, a poor woman who is badly treated by an ornery and abusive husband and has as her only pleasure the naming of the fourteen miscarriages she buries atop a hill. But Old Rellar still knew what love was. She loved the cow and the snake and was even more generous and more humble than Rose of Sharon at the end of Steinbeck's *Grapes of Wrath.* Not wishing to waste the milk that has built up in her breasts in anticipation of each birth, Old Rellar allowed piglets to suckle at her breast. And her last act before death was to patch the clothes of her husband.

Nobody knows what the holy spirit is. But surely part of the holy spirit is love beyond understanding.

Only a place that confronts such contradictions and questions as this can speak to me about death. Old, in pain, palsied, troubled—I turn to memories of Price Hollow, where wonder and brutality crossed and met each day. Memory arises again, shapes a poem called "Dying in Price Hollow," and takes me where heaven lay.

> Death residing in his palace
> comes to all in Price Hollow
> drawing a curtain
> dimming inner dimensions
> until the same curtain parting
> exposes peppermint in the spring
> the sweet juices of wild summer grapes
> the flowering chickasaw plum
> the eyes of opossums among persimmons.

DANI NIEVES

DORIS
DIOSA
DAVENPORT

Born in 1949 in Gainesville, Georgia, with a "caul," according to her great-aunt, doris diosa davenport sees with the aesthetic/politicized eyes of a working-class, lesbian-feminist, Affrilachian (Southern Appalachian African American) visionary. She is a performance poet, educator, and writer with a B.A. in English from Paine College in Augusta, an M.A. from SUNY/Buffalo, and a Ph.D. from the University of Southern California in Los Angeles. She has published an eclectic range of articles, book reviews, essays, and four books of poetry: *it's like this* (1980), *eat thunder and drink rain* (1982), *voodoo chile/slight return* (1991), and *Soque Street Poems* (1995). Writing grants have been awarded to davenport by the Kentucky Foundation for Women, the North Carolina Arts Council, the Syvenna Foundation for Women, and the Georgia Council for the Arts. She is a member of Alternate Roots, a consortium of artist-activists in Atlanta, and is available for poetry performances or lectures via SPEAK OUT!, a speakers' bureau for social change.

*   *   *

All This, and Honeysuckles Too

Once, in an aerobics class, the instructor told us to check our pulses. I checked, then told her I didn't have one, so she showed me how to find it. In a similar way, external sources taught me how to find my heart: northeast Georgia. While living here, from age five to fifteen, I was aware that I enjoyed the scenery and the seasons. Other geographical areas, between age sixteen and forty-five, provided conscious acknowledgment of and an aching need for "my" Appalachia. But even as a girl I already "had an I," defined by people, experiences, and landscapes of northeast Georgia. Like summer breeds insects, these southern mountains spawn eccentric people and behavior. Recently I received a postcard with my name and "Lesbian-feminist Anarchist Affrilachian" written under it. Some of all that, and educator-writer-performance poet, was already in place by age twelve.

I have written extensively about my Affrilachian experiences. Some aspect of the people or the place appears in everything, prose and poetry, as anecdotes, allusions, single poems, and entire manuscripts (*Soque Street Poems*, 1995). Northeast Georgia determined my worldview, behavior, and value system. I still prefer a live(ly) conversation or a good story to anything on the electronic highway. One of my favorite meals is greens and cornbread. In January 1996 I finished another book of poetry, *Kudzu,* written about my being home. So when I first considered this essay, I thought I had nothing else to say. But there is more. As much more as there are mountains and hollows and endless hidden highways and people.

A frequent question from outsiders (foreigners) is "What's it near?" Out of laziness, we will say "eighty miles north of Atlanta," but that is still inaccurate. Northeast Georgia is an area of small towns in about a fifty- to seventy-mile radius, an area of red dirt, hills, rivers, lakes, forests, with twisting roads and two-lane highways. Some of the towns are Cornelia, Clarkesville, Hollywood, Tallulah Falls, Helen, Sautee, Clayton, Mt. Airy, Toccoa, Cleveland, and Dahlonega. The towns that defined my growing-up world were in Habersham, Hall, White, and Stephens Counties. In the nineteenth century, northeast Georgia was a popular resort area to some people; to us, in the twentieth century, it was just home.

The inhabitants that I knew then were mostly working-class, connected by orneriness, inaccessibility, and blood ties. And, although most of the Cherokee were forcibly removed from this area, many of us do have Native American blood. Still, until recently most of us were multigenerational, generic Affrilachians or Eurolachians. Some were "drifters" who became permanent residents; others were wealthy "summer people" and retirees. In the past fifteen years, happily, fairly large populations of Asians and Mexicans have moved into the area. Anyway, I was born in Gainesville but really lived and grew up in Cornelia. I attended Cornelia Regional Colored High School, one "magnet" school, which included grades one through twelve and all the African-American children from five adjoining counties (bused in, daily).

This is an area of exquisite beauty with people living off in the woods along tricky, circuitous highways. Most of the people own their land with modest working-class homes (and trailers) and maintain a way of life that seems, despite heavy traffic (cars and drugs) and increasing deforestation and pollution, unchanged in its basics. *Basically,* we keep to ourselves and mind our business—and everyone else's. Very specific directions are needed to find us. For us African Americans, we give directions, then sometimes meet you and lead you in the rest of the way. I like it like that.

For me, home is a place where at least two things have to have happened: a minimal nurturing love and one positive experience that holds you in memory. For me, there is my mother and the community of the Hill, and this locale—the essential environment of the Southern Appalachian foothills, the Chattahoochee National Forest, the original Cherokee Homelands. This area was and is my sanctuary, my sacred place of mental, physical, spiritual, and psychic renewal. I have been disappointed by many events and people in my life; this land never disappoints or lets me down. Even when not fully conscious of the geographical environment, I was acutely conscious of the human environment: 103 Soque Street and the Gibsons and "the Hill," the African-American community of Cornelia.

At one time, there were twenty of us living in my maternal grandparents' four-room house. That's what I say, sometimes, because I'm addicted to exaggeration (and telling lies), but probably there were only fifteen (Momma, Mevie, Daddy John, Sara, Gladys, Kookie, Harvey, Philip, Kitty; Dolores, Sandra, Tanya, Maggie, Audrey, and me). Cousins, friends, and visiting relatives could easily push it to twenty-five. Our lives were profoundly affected by how and what we were to each other.

Back then, I had a rock-solid definition. I was one of John and Evie Gibson's twenty-odd grandchildren; Ethel Mae's oldest. By age ten, I was the oldest of six girls, and my mother, a single parent, worked as a maid for fifteen dollars a week. My grandmother also was a maid; my grandfather was a low-paid car mechanic. We were poor, yet rich, in each other. As one of my great-aunts said, the good Lord tried to make up for it with how we looked. Like, "Y'all gone always be poor, but here: you can look at each other and git happy, at least." And we do. All the Gibsons—I said, *all* the Gibsons—are good-looking. Some of us look better than others, but I swear (and you can ask anybody) none of us is unattractive. We come in all sizes and shapes, and a range of browns and blacks, but all looking good. (In fact, there were no ugly people in this family until one or two dramatic accidents, about twenty-one years ago, but that's another story.) Plus, you could look at one of us and see the others. (I used to respond to my aunts' names, Gladys or Kitty, or just "one of John's, and Evie's, ain't you?")

When I went to college, at sixteen, I had an identity partly based in provincialism, poverty, defiance, and ignorance (of the outside world) but a healthy ego that said I was just fine and it might even be a desirable thing (for others) to be who and what I was, which included being female, African American, and rural southern too. Plus, it was a while before I realized that most folk were *not* like the folks I'd grown up with. I saw, and still see, my selves as natural, never "pathological," deviant, marginal, minority, and other late-twentieth-century dismissive euphemisms. As Ntozake Shange said in an interview in *Poets & Writers,* "If I am the center of my own universe, then how can I be marginal?"

My universe also revolved around natural beauty and the supernatural. Spring put a spell on me then, as it does now. Opinions and obstacles to the contrary, I still believe that (some) people can fly. There really are alternate realities, although I have yet to find one I can comfortably live in. Because just as there was not then, there is not yet a place (or even the concept, for most people) for little African-American girls who are born mystics/philosophers/intellectuals. I had no choice but try to live in what has been called the "real" world, one that has ever been, mostly, unreal to me—except in northeast Georgia.

One of my first memories is being a baby, in my crib, near a window. A huge grinning wasp flew up at me and said, "I'm coming to get you." In first grade, *Alice in Wonderland* made me concentrate on alternate realities, on the other side of any mirror (if I could just figure out how to get there). The movie *Peter Pan* (with Mary Martin) had me convinced by age eight that I could fly. (No, they didn't really register as "whitefolks only" movies because I already knew lots of black folk, like my daddy, Claude Davenport, who did miraculous, unusual, eccentric, or bizarre things.) Soon after that, I was just as convinced that fairies and vampires were real. Then too, I'd gotten a fifty-power microscope and meticulously analyzed and dissected stuff, a skill that I'm sure led to a Ph.D. in English. All this was connected to me; the ghost at 103 Soque was as real as what I saw under the microscope. Back then, however, my chosen profession was a scientist or a nun.

Nuns fascinated me and I was deeply religious from age ten to thirteen. In our heavily Protestant environment, I have no idea where I could have seen or heard of them, but I liked their style: long, flowing robes—and crosses, to keep off vampires. More important, they lived reclusive, solitary lives, in convents. I thought that if I was a nun, I wouldn't have to have babies, or men. That infatuation with nuns probably influenced my own reclusiveness. Well, that and living in four rooms with twenty-five people—the cause of my lifelong need for both quality interactions with lots of people *and* a desire for meditative, creative solitude.

By first grade I had discovered an internal sanctuary in reading. In fact, I believe I was born reading (through my caul) like others are born crying. It is a voracious, lifelong habit. Because of it, reading Zora Neale's *Their Eyes Were Watching God* in 1972 and, later, Morrison's *Sula* were major events in my life. I absolutely knew that the Hill was like Hurston's community, minus the black mayor; the first paragraph of Morrison's *Sula* haunted me until I finished *Soque Street Poems.* When I read and reread Marquez's *One Hundred Years of Solitude,* I feel like so much of it, the "magical realism," applies directly to my experiences in northeast Georgia. In fact, I have a deep appreciation for works of fantasy, horror, science fiction, and murder mysteries, for they come closest to the magical/surreal/bizarre surprises and pleasures of my growing up in northeast Georgia.

A friend of mine visited Ghana; when she saw its red dirt, she said she finally understood my attachment to the red dirt of northeast Georgia.

But, this "problem" of place.

For Africans and all other people of color, including Native Americans, this place called the U.S.A. has always been made to be unnecessarily problematical (by Euro-Americans). For us, "place" has been politicized, and frequently considered an oxymoron or a non sequitur. Consequently the collective imagination of generic "Americans" is still rather neurotically limited when it contemplates the existence of black folk, ignoring or denying the fact that many of us in rural areas have a passionate personal and collective attachment to "our" land. Why not and how else? Our African ancestors were *passionately* attached to their homelands (which is why some of them flew back home from Ibo's Landing on St. Simon's Island). The African holistic worldview, like that of many Native Americans, included the living, the land, the ancestors, and the Deities. I believe that, even now, some of that affects southern African Americans profoundly. Not only are we here in northeast Georgia, we have *been* here, as tenaciously as some of these giant pine trees, as steadily and pervasively as the kudzu.

While growing up here, I had no chance to thoroughly explore these hills. The first time I saw the Soque River, three years ago, it was a small sign just before a little creek, and before that I knew only that "Soque" was a Cherokee word and the name of our street. From childhood to young adulthood, I went, regularly and religiously, up to The Tower, down to Russell Lake, and out to George Washington Carver Park (the colored people's park). And at least once a year, to admire Tallulah Gorge. I was always aware of the mountains surrounding us but am only now enjoying a slow discovery of the area and its history.

I don't yet know how my family got here. I don't know, not back past three or four generations. (My daddy's folks came from Atlanta.) I do know my maternal ancestors have always been here, and that has "fixed" me. At least since about 1830 there have been some of us in these hills.

Still, the hard-core researchable facts can wait a while longer. Right now, I am dealing with the ongoing mystical-sensual experience of me in these mountains again. This experience is a main preoccupation with me, as seen in the following journal excerpts:

(12/94) There was a moon, growing toward fullness, like this winter. Phases. After yesterday's overcast rainy day, steady nonstop rain and drizzle, saturation of cold, wetness like real wintertime, this morning is clear, bright, joyous, and on the way to being dry.

Sunshine woke me up, smiling. I hear the mountains sing each morning and am pulled by their song to get up, to *be* with them, awake and conscious. These hills and mountains are always "doing something" and the ripples of that infinitesimal motion run through these valleys, run through me. And everything becomes one—over and over and over each day the connections renewed in the air, the dirt, the trees; the sky and earth, and all between, living and dead: *one*. I am bound into these hills in a timeless, absolute fact of being. Beingness. A humming like the Original Electricity speaks to me in wordless whispered conversations. I feel and I know all of this every minute and I still can't describe this morning's sunlight.

An awareness. Not that clinical detachment presupposed, years ago, when those well-meaning white girls at Smith College asked, "What's it mean to you, being black?" After I recovered from the shock of such a weird question, I said, since they obviously expected a response, "It just is, like having two arms." That remains true. Being African is a matter-of-fact joy and something I cherish. But, it is so much a part of me until I can't "see" it, that much. That's how it is with these hills, mountains, valleys. How it is with being "Appalachian." I am so much a part of all this, it so much a part of me, all I know is the "is-ness" and when I'm asked what it means, frequently my only response is a smile.

(12/94) I remember how I got depression at Paine College in Augusta in 1964. The dirt was not red, there were no mountains. While flunking physics, I used the textbook as a sketch pad for a precise drawing of Tower Mountain. In 1971 I asked the dean at West Virginia State College if they had mountains there, and when he laughed and said yes, I took the job he offered me. In Camarillo, California, "Jo Ann's Mountain" in the back of her house made me ecstatic. The distant mountains at Venice Beach meant daily, constant joy. The mountains and valleys of St. Croix, of the Italian Alps, the village of Introd, where repeatedly I said, "No wonder I loved Introd so much." *This*—my Appalachia—is an "Introd." My great-aunt Fannie Mae said uncle Jess did love these mountains, but Daddy John "could just eat 'em," he loved them so. These mountains in my blood, calling. Calling.

(3/95) Still (Re)Defining Affrilachian. An affinity for "place." A barely conscious, ever-present connection; blood-tied, to these hills and valleys. (Or else, an absolute *dis*connection like my aunt Sarah, which is a whole other thing. Still, always vehemently aware of what they deny, disconnect from.) All of rural Appalachia is another country, another world, and some parts more so than others. Most of us share(d) a physical and psychological isolation from the rest of the world.

So that, African Appalachians, *within* this isolation, develop an overly specific connection to the place and to each other. Until two years ago and Frank X. Walker, I hadn't placed me or northeast Georgia in a context of Appalachia. (Frank invented "Affrilachian" to define being both Appalachian and African.) I have never felt "American," but rather, culturally and politically disconnected from and disenfranchised by this entity called the U.S.A. ("Babylon," as Bob Marley calls it). Because of its rampant disregard for my well-being, the U.S.A. flag is the same as the Confederate flag as the Nazi flag to me. Yet, northeast Georgia and the Hill are, and always have been, my beloved home.

It's as if I, and we, existed in and for our communities, so much so that these places were extracted *out* of the U.S.A.: southern, maybe; American—maybe not. I feel nothing for the political entity called the U.S.A., yet I love northeast Georgia. I deplore the politics of the U.S.A., yet ignore those of northeast Georgia. I pity other southerners (excluding natives of New Orleans and the coastal areas) without this context: hills and valleys, eccentric peoples, our African-derived communities and cultural habits.

However we came here, whatever our ancestors and kin did, it had the long-term effect of *binding* us here, heart and soul. And in these isolated pockets of Appalachia, we remain(ed) "African," within an insularity that protected and nurtured; an inwardness that needed no outside interference or corroboration.

(a letter to some long-distance friends, 8/95) The beginning of this was soft, soft, and foggy, in an overcast late summer morning. The heat has been one hundred degrees holding steady for days and before that, in the high 80s and 90s. Intense, brutal, humid heat from morning to midnight; each day, as the sun rose, the heat did too. Even here, in this valley with the mountains on all sides, the heat prevailed and controlled everything. Then this morning's softness. Sweet. A reprieve. And somewhere in there is the promise of autumn's softness.

Each morning in this valley has a promise.

This is what I want you all to know: just being here takes up most of the conversation space in my head. Involved in a continuous dialogue with the mountains, I just don't have a whole lot to say. Enclosed in this most satisfactory form of daily magic, it's all I *can* say, or there is nothing else to say. If you could come here and see it; if you could see it—northeast Georgia—maybe then, you'd know. This is what I know, and that's the most important knowledge (and activity) I have here lately. (And this is also what I am "doing.")

(9/95) The rising sun. The sprinkled sun, through the trees and leaves, and through my lace curtains onto the bed, onto me. I rise as the morning calls, caresses me (and I, it) as I sit, naked on the bed facing the sunrise over the mountains, in gratitude. The sun's golden light, the clear morning air; deep green of the pine trees; dark brown tree trunks, and my naked golden-brown skin; my black and red dreds covering my back and waist, a little morning mist over the mountains. All one.

(12/95) Mystical. Magical. Supernatural. Ensorcelled. Enchanted. Hexed. Conjured. Voodooed. Bewitched. Captivated. There must be at least a thousand words, even in *this* inadequate language, to describe what *it* is. *It.* What I have longed for, looked for, hoped for, and needed all my life. The most basic essence of what I have found here in these hills and valleys. I watch me, daily, being totally turned out, turned in to this natural and miraculous Beauty. Listening, and watching in awe, to the slightest nuance. Very rarely, in the moment of its occurrence, would anyone (probably) know to say, "After *this* I won't be the same." But for the past year, caught up in transformative moments, I have known it. Each day, each minute, in this intensely present Beauty, I have been involved in the Miraculous.

(from poetry notebook, 3/95) Still defining what it's about for those of you who still doubt these mountains in me. Me and my mountains (like Momma said the other day, she thinks it's in my genes; even if she'd left with us, I would have returned).

And now, this Sautee Valley surrounded drenched before space in time before there was a Sautee these mountains sat around and around and wrapped around each other and what was caught stayed inside them in a lilting loping walk; in a rhythm how they talk in loops and spirals, resonant hollows. My momma's peoples came out of Hollywood and Rabun County long before I was born the mountains saw me coming to Cornelia, to Sautee.

What was unconscious is not now submerged memory surfacing and every time someone asks what these mountains are to me more of this comes: Can't you see? See, we lived on a hill in a part of a mountain. If you go up to Tower Mountain, you could see if you look out at Farlinger Street from that spot behind the community house too but for a view—and I know you don't have that much time I know—just sit on the steps of Shady Grove Baptist Church (and look out there) at the top of Soque. We walked up a sloping mountain to get to church and down to walk to school. To get home every day from work, we curved our way around and around our little piece of mountain, the hill, here before we got here, waiting in space and time, and whatever is here, is. These mountains raised me. At the top of Soque, there was a house, a small wooden house with no bathroom inside or out (mountain madness runs in my family) but still. (The words to the songs "Exodus" and "This Is My Country" meant this *land* is *mine.*)

Was on a little bitty mountaintop. And I wanted to play piano and compose a song about my hill but I was six, then eight, and lessons were not free, though almost, at Shady Grove. Sit there on the steps and see us baptized back in time at the "baptizing pool," baptized in the pool across the street coming up sanctified in these mountain waters hallelujah I wanted to play that tune on a piano out of reach these mountains leaning toward me: no piano. Try speech. Miz Cook could tell you, by fifth grade, I sure could talk. And long before that, had learned to walk in ritual with everybody else around and around this hill, our mountain— oh, well, you say but we not, in, exactly, the mountains. *Look.* Oh, look. In the distance there they are in the front part of my brain, dancing, dictating, singing (this song) me out, out, out and back, again.

Mountain stories sustained me and called me home again you can ask anybody on the hill every chance I got, I came home. To see Miz Zelma, go to Sally's or Fred's Tavern and out I went to Buffalo, New York, and San Francisco, and Los Angeles, and Oklahoma, and everywhere I went, these mountains went.

These mountains coming out. out. as a teacher. out. a lesbian feminist. out, poet. out. writer, activist. out, anarchist. out, performance poet and always what I ever was all that I can or will ever be in these soft green mountains surrounding me, saying, yes. To everything I ever could be (Oh, say you *do* see). My folks came out these mountains. These hills and valleys and forests were my birth. Whatever was here, is. And this is where I *be.*

The preceding entries might sound like I live a hermitic life of total idyllic (idiotic?) meditation. That is not totally true, since my life here consists of intense, sometimes frenzied activity as well as restorative solitude. The "descriptive entries" above were written while I continued with lectures, poetry performances, and activities at the Sautee-Nacoochee Community Center (SNCA) and elsewhere. (I "discovered" SNCA in the fall of 1993 and soon became active there both onstage and off. Last summer [1995] I was in a dance performance there, a great thrill, and another dream actualized.) I wrote the last section about "these mountains" on Sweetwater Coffeehouse's porch, here in Sautee, finally realizing why I'm compelled to that porch. Because everything started on the Hill on the big porch of 103 Soque where we mostly lived until it got too cold. I would sit there and write and read (James Baldwin's *Another Country* and Bram Stoker's

Dracula at age twelve) and keep track of who came and went, in and out, up and down the street. I wrote on the little porch at 121 Soque, two houses up from 103 Soque, stories and diary entries (the five-year kind with the tiny little lock and key).

The mountains were always there. Sometimes hazy and distant, sometimes clear and up close, they moved and shifted in different weather, but back then I didn't even know that *that* mountain was only twenty miles away. Mt. Yonah, about four thousand feet high, the tallest in northeast Georgia. I liked the mountains around me and liked having them in the distance, like dreams. Recently, my uncle Paul said that as a boy he too was fascinated by these mountains. Once, at the back door of their house in Clarkesville, he asked his mother (my grandmother), "What's that?" And she replied, "Mt. Yonah."

So now, in July 1996, the world is coming to Atlanta, as they say—and to northeast Georgia—in the form of the Olympic Games. For better or for worse, the Olympics is a major event for us, for all of Georgia. Yet, for me, there was recently an equally significant Major Event: the Gibsons' reunion at 103 Soque Street. Each visit, each reunion, involves a Ritual of Return with endless discussions of logistics (especially rides from the Atlanta airport) and timetables. Each time, I feel the same aggravation and excitement. We come, like huge living puzzle pieces; as each one arrives, each of us is more complete (even if some of us don't know that).

As the mountains were an ever-present background, the Gibsons—my momma's family, some one hundred of us when I was growing up—were always the foreground. I don't recall a time, after age eleven or so, when I was not a writer. I don't remember clearly when my obsession to write about the Hill started (maybe in my first college literature class). But, in the late seventies, a deep longing began. A longing for the actual physical presence and reality of my family in my mountains. A need to be immersed in us as we once were, at 103 Soque Street. So, I repopulated the Hill and that house, in *Soque Street Poems,* even while my mother was slowly renovating the house itself. These people, these mountains, are why I am a writer. As long as some of us are alive, as long as I have access to these mountains and to some of us, I will be a writer.

In 1992 I returned to Cornelia with a grant specifically to finish writing *Soque Street Poems.* I came to the *real* setting of my poems, of my peoples, I came in daily contact with the people of the poetry, and I wrote. Sometimes they asked, "How's the book coming?" And when I read to them from the completed book in January 1994, I felt like one of my life's purposes was fulfilled. I finished *Soque* in Cornelia, and in October 1994 performed it at the Sautee-Nacoochee Community Center. In November 1994, through a series of accidents and miracles and the kindness of two wonderful people (Richard and Jimmie Tinius), I moved to

Sautee, into a trailer across the highway from Mt. Yonah. In September 1995, SNCA published *Soque Street Poems,* and the responses to that book, from relatives to total strangers, have been amazingly gratifying.

Overall, my life has been a constant, excruciating financial struggle since my return home, but I am not yet ready or willing to leave again. I live with a deep sense of satisfaction. I have done what many writers only dream of. I am always gratefully aware of my people, particularly my communities in both Cornelia and Sautee; of the spiritual-mystical essence of these Appalachian foothills, all of which I claim, with humility and pride, as *my* home.

HILDA
DOWNER

Hilda Downer (b. 1956) spent her earlier years in Bandana, North Carolina. Currently, she lives outside of Boone, North Carolina, with her husband, Shelburne Wilson, who is a physician and Galloway Beltie cattle breeder, and her two sons, Branch and Meade. She works as a psychiatric nurse and part-time English instructor at Appalachian State University. Recently, she received an M.F.A. from Vermont College. Her first book of poetry was *Bandana Creek,* published in 1979. She has published in numerous journals and anthologies as well. Downer volunteers at her son's school to promote art projects and poetry writing by students. She enjoys painting, sewing costumes for her children, and making folk dolls.

*   *   *

Mutant in Bandana

I was supposed to have been a ballet dancer. However, there were no dance classes anywhere near Bandana, the small Appalachian town I grew up in. I practiced leaps and singing in this place named for the red bandana Clinchfield Railroad tied to a laurel branch to denote an imaginary train station. That train, often rattling baggage in my sleep and offering a prediction of snow for the next morning by the strange way its whistle sounded, never tunneled through my door with ballet slippers, but there was paper and pen.

Since the roots of poetry for me dig into the place I come from, I cannot separate my love of writing from my love of Bandana. *Bandana*—I love the very word. When I write, my thoughts travel from the Sink Hole Mine to the varied blue of distant mountain ranges. In these mines next to my grandfather's house, I collected pretty rocks—the ones I have always known the names of as though I had named them myself: garnet, mica, feldspar, aquamarine, burle. I could sing as loudly as I wanted. I could write poetry there. Even now, I must write from that spiritual spot of feldspar purity and complete freedom. Those cataracts and creeks, the banks glinting mica in Morse code, are the physical wording of my poetry and spirit.

I am so often called back to Bandana soil. The minerals in the vegetables and spring water match those in my body. Almost a physical need prompts my return to Bandana to eat potatoes and beans grown there, and to stop by Granny Ann's spring for a drink from the dipper where wild spearmint smells mixed with the water's deeper clean. Like ocean salmon returning to the birthplace, I am called to Bandana out of necessity. Just as it is a survival technique to lay eggs in freshwater, for only the fittest to survive, I return to a place where a plowed garden offers a joy in its openness—even in its rich waft of dirt and death. Bandana has taught me all about survival.

I have been in such harmony with Bandana smells sometimes that the mine shafts and dugout cellars may as well be my nostrils. I could kick a pebble in the road ahead and compose the next line of a poem before stopping to retrieve the pebble in an iambic measure of distance. I could drive with my eyes closed the road that curves with the familiarity of my own hips. The path up to the mines crooked like an arm, one side mossy and smooth as the antecubital space, while the other side, graveled by water runoff, wrinkled as an elbow. A spring sheltered with fern eased down one of the path's legs, pale from feldspar, down to Bandana

Creek, down to the white strands of the waterfall sifting like hair, down to the tumbling sound of Toe River's attentiveness to every single rock as though sound were using a magnifying glass. The path worn down to red clay smiles the same thin red line of my C-section scar, pleased with itself at what my body has done. The scar, almost invisible like the shadow of a scar, convinces me that my babies did not come from me, but from the souls bursting out of Bandana rocks hammered apart by rock hounds searching for emeralds.

I didn't know I loved Bandana then. And I was only beginning to understand how its lessons in survival would be my greatest source of strength.

I hated it there most of the time when I was a girl. I could not wait to get out of Bandana. There was no sky more oppressive than the sky above Bandana. The redundant walls of my jail cell were on one end the Black Brother mountain range and on the other, the Roan Mountain. Trapped by these bookends, even if there had been ballet classes closer than Asheville, I couldn't have gotten there because my family was too stereotypically poor to send me. We did have electricity, a bathroom, and a TV set. We had no car, no radio, no newspapers. I know that hunger and feeling ignorant are the fangs of poverty. I was the first person in my family to graduate from the sixth grade. The people I come from were prejudiced and superstitious so that a lot that I learned from the Christians I went to church with, from the way some teachers taught, and from the way my mother treated her children was how not to be.

I plotted my escape with my best friend, Reba, who is also a poet, so we wrote songs to become famous singers. We facetiously called ourselves Bandana Creek, after a band that we admired, Goose Creek Symphony. Though we practiced while walking or doing dishes, dancing with plates and singing into butter knives, there was that stumbling block called shyness. Plan B was to write ourselves out of the mountains. We continue to do this today—to write ourselves out, which we know now is inadvertently writing ourselves in. Still, we write for the same reason we did even as girls—for survival.

That poetry can be used for the soul to travel beyond mundane sadness is my point in referring to events that happened in Bandana. When outsiders came in buying up land cheaply, nailing up No Trespassing signs, and building what they called "mountain chalets," they would sometimes stop and ask us what that huge illuminated building was perched on one of Bandana's ridges. They were referring to Glen Buchanan's chicken house lit up to warm chicks at night—what we called Bandana Hotel. We would make up stories, providing them with descriptions of the fanciness of a stay there. We encouraged them to at least try a meal—the best omelettes and fried chicken anywhere. We survived such terrible intrusions this way.

We called ourselves the lost generation because we wanted to continue the old ways of quilting bees, community cakewalks, chair caning, dyeing willow oak baskets with pokeweed—but even our own mothers had abandoned many of the traditions, decorating their homes with gaudy plastic butterflies and gold ducks flying across the paneled walls. By the time we were in junior high school, our grandmothers had relinquished calico and gingham for polyester and fake satin for quilting. Beds flashing these bizarre quilts foreshadowed the lining of coffins and were just about useless for anything else, slipping off too easily at night to provide warmth.

The women we grew up among collected at Reba's house to talk about their last remembered shock treatment or how much Librium or Valium they were on. They thought we were crazy. On Saturdays, they permed or rolled hair, and cooked or canned. One of our blue-haired relatives would alarm the others in the kitchen as we passed through: "She's not wearing a bra!" I would hold my arms up, under arrest, and we would rub our backs along the wall, kicking our legs out, rising and falling just to prove their point that we were, indeed, crazy. Once, as we started to enter the kitchen, someone literally screamed like a mountain lion (which, in turn, sounds like a woman screaming), warning us not to come in if we were "on the rag." We told them we didn't believe in that stuff about ruining their pickles being canned. We walked right in. The kitchen fluttered in wooden spoons, buckets, and Mason jars as we outran them to Reba's family car. Locking the doors to inner quiet, we laughed over the fact that we really didn't have our menses. Then, we described the scenery as we traversed the expansive West, driving in place.

We were making the best of a bad situation, taking a trip without leaving the farm. We were not only surviving but surviving with a joy. I believe poetry itself is a survival technique no less evolutionary than the first fish that grew legs and did so in order to survive, and if it is beautiful, as Reba is a beautiful woman, then it is like an orchid that is specialized and beautiful in order to survive. Perhaps this is why men I brought to visit from college were always amazed that all my cousins and friends were beautiful. To survive there or get out, they had to be.

I, on the other hand, did not look like them. I was the only one in my high school with the reputation for writing poetry. I could not have survived there otherwise. Without poetry, my soul would not fit into this body. My body would not fit into place. Without a notebook in hand, I couldn't survive waiting on doctors or dentists or movies. More recently, writing poems was my way of praying when my baby nearly died. I need food, water, shelter, and poetry.

In retrospect, the women that influenced me so much may not have been real. The place that is so intertwined with my soul may not even be real. It may be as imaginary as the train station represented by a bandana restless in the wind. I refer to women specifically because men just weren't around much. My father left when I was a baby. Some of the men had to go off for work and returned on the weekends to go hunting or fishing. There was always a dichotomy—at family suppers where the men ate first, then the children, and finally the women, or at church where men stood out on the front porch before service while the women congregated and whispered inside. The roles of women and men were strong. Recently, a friend was amazed that I do not know how to build a fence even though I grew up with cows all around. Men were the only ones I ever observed building a fence.

Perhaps for the reason that I did not fit in with all my pretty relatives, I must have subconsciously decided to mutate. I must have needed something more to me to justify my existence. Being a little different was my talent. I honed the skill of being odd by writing poetry. Eventually, it became my survival tool because what made me an outsider also provided me a place in this world.

I'm thankful to my mother for my oddness. As I get older, I do look more like her. Yet, I never resembled her in her youth. She was beautiful, with dark hair and eyes, while I am light. When I was working on a local newspaper, a man I interviewed told me that my mother had the prettiest legs in three counties. She was famous for her white and perfect teeth. Once, in music class in grade school, my teacher took me aside and asked me if she was really my mother. With tears in his eyes, he said she had been so talented he didn't know what to do with her. I heard the same words about myself from my creative writing teacher in college, John Foster West. Secretly, I have criticized her for not having used her talent. She could sing and play any instrument by ear that she picked up. Once, someone she grew up with related that my mother had written Liberace, who did not answer, of course, to ask him if he could help her become a pianist. I understood her frustration as my own. I didn't even know of anyone to write to help me become a writer because Thomas Wolfe was already dead.

Liberace and Thomas Wolfe were names that were taught to us. I discovered Flannery O'Connor on my own. I didn't come across many female poets until I gleaned the books in my college library. My first encounter with a real-live female poet was when I met Charleen Swansea after she had accepted my first book of poems for publication. John Foster West drove me to Charlotte to her house. Her architecturally designed cinder-block house looked huge but sedate on the outside and that is probably why we opened the car doors so gently. "Bang," the door to the house slammed open. A disheveled woman ran out shaking a dust mop at West, shouting, "Hello, you horny bastard." She pulled his bald head down to her lips. Because we were not as brazen in Bandana, she was not at all how I pictured a poet. She wasn't at all shy like me. She was wild with ribald stories featuring things like a drunken poet talking about entropy on top of a refrigerator and herself with a breast hanging out. When I met Charleen, I knew there was more to life, somehow.

Yet, Charleen never encouraged me to be like her. Instead, she urged me to write about what *I* knew. I supposed that was writing about "that something more to life" that keeps us alive. Language suggests that there is always more out there, like the mountains in the distance. Charleen was the physical proof of that for me. She was giving herself to her art. Poetry is the higher ground for the strategic survivalist.

I admire ants, bees, and spiders because they all have skills. Ants can form bridges out of their bodies. Bees know a mellifluous sign language. Nothing is more like the writer than the writing spider that repairs its web sometimes with letters of the alphabet. Truly, they live the life of a poet. With all these creatures, too, there is always more to discover about their natures, always something more.

In Bandana, a use of poetry for me was to get away from myself. Sometimes, some psychiatric patients become overwhelmed with this concept, "I can't get away from me." T.S. Eliot said, "[Poetry] is not the expression of personality, but an escape from personality." I like to think I can escape both inner and outer landscapes and that I am living in the mountains on my own terms. I nearly stopped writing for almost ten years, and the word "bottle" usually surfaced in the occasional poem written during that time. Again, I was trying to escape through my poems. Until I returned to writing, there was no way out.

Writers don't write because they're depressed, but in spite of it. I probably don't write because I grew up in poverty in the Appalachians, but in spite of it. Still, West used to ponder over what other writers had to say if they didn't come from the mountains. Writing, nevertheless, is a good coping mechanism, a way to survive in a world that doesn't make sense or even seem real. If someone thinks writers are crazy when they're writing, he or she should see them when they're not.

I have never felt that I am quite safe when I'm away from home. I returned home, having spent three months at MacDowell Colony in 1979, to find my seventeen-year-old brother in jail. His court appearance was scheduled for the next day. The lawyer I saw that evening confessed he didn't have time to prepare and the best thing I could do was to defend my brother myself since I "knew the story." In fact, I did know the story, had always known the story, since the story (not those pink ballet slippers) was my birthright. When I brought the story to the courtroom, Judge Braswell interrupted me, asking me a question that I have never liked, "Are you a poet?" I didn't know how to answer this question since I didn't know what it made me responsible for. I was only twenty-one and I had little proof. For the first time in my life, I felt being a poet might matter, so thinking I would go to hell for perjury, I said, "Yes." He called a fifteen-minute recess. Back in his chambers, he told me that he had read my book that had just come out, and he ushered two pages of his poems onto the table asking for critique. I had little experience with workshopping, but I pointed out the unique imagery and offered some helpful hints. Judge Braswell issued my brother's custody to me instead of sending him to prison. Since then, my brother has done very well with his own tile-setting company and a wonderful family. In effect, my own poetry has not only saved my life but my brother's as well.

What being a poet means to me goes beyond just being an Appalachian poet. It is being a part of the poets who came before me, that exist now, and will come after me. The poets are a race that connect and transcend all races. They are mutants well adapted to survive. With pen as survivalist's tool, the writing provides a deeper meaning, a joy to life that makes survival worth it. The poet could live as poet without the poetry but had to invent poetry to offer the will to live. Through the power of language, the life you save may be your own.

WILMA
DYKEMAN

Born in 1920 in Asheville, North Carolina, Wilma Dykeman now lives in both North Carolina and Tennessee. In seventeen books of fiction, history, biography, social commentary, and essays, Dykeman explores the world of nature and conditions that limit human potential. Her first novel, *The Tall Woman* (1962), set in the mountains during the Civil War, has never gone out of print and is now in its thirty-ninth printing. Other novels include *The Far Family* (1966), a sequel to *The Tall Woman,* and *Return the Innocent Earth* (1973), praised in its most recent edition by Reynolds Price and Wendell Berry. Her non-fiction career began with *The French Broad* (1955), in Holt Rinehart's Rivers of America Series. It, too, has never gone out of print. *Neither Black Nor White* (1957), winner of the Hillman Award for the best book of the year on world peace or race relations, *Seeds of Southern Change* (1962), and a Time-Life volume, *The Border States* (1970), were written with husband James Stokely. Text for a photographic study, *The Appalachian Mountains* (1980), was written with son Dykeman Stokely, and son Jim Stokely was coauthor of *At Home in the Smokies: A History Handbook for Great Smoky Mountains National Park* (1984). An adjunct professor of English at the University of Tennessee for twenty years, she has conducted writing workshops in numerous states and was the first woman elected to the board of trustees of Berea College in Kentucky. Dykeman's awards and honors include a Guggenheim Fellowship, a Senior Fellowship of the National Endowment for the Humanities, Honorary Phi Beta Kappa, three honorary doctorates, the North Carolina gold medal for contribution to the arts, and Distinguished Writer of the Year at the Southern Festival of Books. Her articles have appeared in many of the nation's leading magazines and anthologies. A popular lecturer on a variety of subjects, her twenty-five to thirty engagements a year take her from coast to coast. Travel across the United States and on five continents has enriched her vision of the uniqueness and universality of all our lives.

*   *   *

"The Past Is Never Dead.
It's Not Even Past"

In the beginning there were the two of them.

Then there was the place: the woods and wild azalea and rhododendron thickets, the spirited creek, the moss-backed boulders, where they made their nest, which was as personal and sturdy as any nest built by thrush or eagle.

It was the relationship between my mother and father and the ways in which they related to the world around them that shaped, in varying degrees, everything I have written.

Two major differences challenged my parents, or rather I should say challenged their acquaintances. When I was born my father was sixty years old and my mother was twenty-four. He was from the North—a small town forty miles from New York City—and she was of the South, the mountains of western North Carolina. By age and region they were indeed separated.

How did these opposites meet? Willard Dykeman was a widower with two grown children when he came to Asheville for his daughter's health and to satisfy his own curiosity about a part of the country described in *Harper's* and *Atlantic* magazine articles he'd read and Horace Kephart's book *Our Southern Highlanders*. (From the beginning, printed words were decisive in our history.) He met one of those Highlanders, Bonnie Cole, whose brown eyes were bright as a chinquapin and alert to details of the world around her, especially a tall, slender, grey-eyed stranger who spoke in crisp accents and was also alert to the new acquaintance he had just made.

Second in a family of seven, she was obviously the peacemaker between brothers and sisters, the daughter who liked a tidy house and apples in the bin, hams in the smokehouse, and rows of canned vegetables and fruits glowing like jewels (dark ruby beets, golden peaches, pale creamy corn, beans of many hues of green) on long shelves when winter came. Obviously, too, she was a child of the outdoors, reveling in the seasons that changed the mountains embracing her little valley from spring's tender green and dogwood white to autumn's rich tapestry of the hardwoods' leaves and at last the noble stands of evergreens under winter's wind and snow. Sounds, smells, tastes—she relished variety of the senses almost as readily as she seized any book that came to hand. (She read *Pilgrim's Progress* at age ten and said all she remembered was being very tired when she and Pilgrim had finished the journey.) She laughed easily, like her lumberman father who was a master storyteller and had a winning way with people. It was her mother, who had been a schoolteacher at age seventeen, who gave her a love of reading.

When Willard took his daughter back to New York he sent Bonnie a copy of Thoreau's *Walden*. After a little while he came back to the mountains, alone this time, and to the consternation of friends and both their families, the elderly Yankee and the Appalachian mountain girl were married. (It reads like a bad local-color novel.)

The learning experience that began that March day continued for seventeen years for both of them—and even longer for their only child. Not formal learning in any intentional, programmed way, but the important learning by example, in daily revelations and small epiphanies.

The central, most enduring lesson I absorbed (that "knowledge carried to the heart" described by poet Allen Tate in "Ode to the Confederate Dead") was that every person was special and unique. No human being could be stereotyped by sex, race, class, religion, age, nationality—all the ways we separate ourselves from each other without at the same time honoring our variety. I learned that no corner of the world was without wonder, that every living creature or plant or drop of water holds miracles if we would look, listen, think, relate.

Their contrast in ages suggested the most apparent gulf that should have separated my parents. In reality it was the least significant of differences. Next to their physical attraction for each other, evident in ways small and large, their strongest bond was surely a love of work and place and, paradoxically, of the books that carried them away from that work and place to a larger universe.

Of course, my father had retired from the farms he had in New York, and so he was bound by no daily schedules of work except those imposed by his own wish to grow things—garden, grapes and apples, two small Jersey cows for delicious cream and butter b.c. (before cholesterol)—and his need to make things, in a workshop built for the woodworking he had always wanted to try and was now inspired to follow by the richly grained black walnut of our mountains.

One of the delights of my childhood was to perch in that big room with its pungent blend of many woods, gather the shavings that curled from his knife onto the floor, and watch a plain piece of wood take shape, become something special to itself. Carefully but with certainty he worked, often pausing to see, I think, if the wood and he followed the same purpose. I loved to watch his deep-set eyes and strong, bony, gentle hands examine his handiwork. (I have wondered if my efforts at shaping sentences and paragraphs were inspired by witnessing his care in his workshop.)

As for my mother, her vigor was a perfect complement to my father's energy. Her hands knew the feel of earth puddled around new plants in the garden, of the paddle pressing butter in its half-pound mold with the daisy design, of caring for furniture, china, linens, all the memorabilia he had brought south to this new home. Inside and outside she laid claim to her fifteen acres and the cottage-type dwelling my father had suggested, simple and honest in keeping with its setting.

Her footsteps often found the path to three special treasures. Because the place was on the north side of the mountains where snow fell deepest and lingered longest, three cold, pure springs bubbled from hidden sources in the earth. The largest, nestled in a narrow ravine behind our house, was a steadfast source of water for our home regardless of flood or drought. Another, beneath a rock ledge, provided for animals on our place. And the third fed a shallow, moss-fringed pond where tadpoles became frogs and clouds floated upside down in its reflection. Runoff from these springs spilled into the stream plunging toward a distant river. The voice of the water was an ever-present theme song for our days and nights.

She always spoke of it as The Place. (Once, enduring heat and thirst on a drive across arid miles in Spain, she loudly protested her faithlessness to an abundance that was hers: "I can taste that water pouring out of our spring. Why did I ever leave The Place?") After my father's death, for more than a half-century she preserved and shaped and created it with no less care than a painter setting forth a vision on canvas or a composer bringing forth music only he had heard.

Their joy in work and place stamped itself indelibly on my life.

And always, there were the books.

There were the books they read to me and the books I read for myself. Frances Hodgson Burnett's *The Secret Garden* sent me into a delirium of Christmas joy. A child's abridged Charles Dickens overwhelmed me with pain. I borrowed my father's sharpest pencil and obliterated the names of Mr. and Miss Murdock from the pages of *David Copperfield* and Bill Sikes from the story of *Oliver Twist,* thinking, I suppose, that their cruelty would be somehow avenged, or at least forever expunged, if their names were lost.

The sharpest memories, however, are of those times when my parents read to each other. How delicious it was in the early darkness of a winter evening to see them pulling two great oak-and-leather Stickley chairs up to the fireplace where hickory logs blazed on andirons wrought by a descendant of Daniel Boone, and watch as my mother opened a novel, a biography, a travel adventure, or a heavy red anthology of a thousand-and-one poems printed on elegant, tissue-thin paper. She was usually the one who read aloud, sometimes interrupted by my father who added his own footnotes to history or quoted a line from a familiar poem or commended the brilliant deductions of Sherlock Holmes. Their reading was as varied as their other friendships.

I usually understood little about this adult reading. What I did understand was that books connected us to the world. From this little mountain cove we could reach out across space and time to know strange people and places and the intertwined evil and good that awaited our innocence and our choices.

While they read I rocked my doll in the little chair they said was a hundred years old, a time that seemed as distant to me as the era of George Washington or Thomas Jefferson. Or I drew and colored pictures with a horde of brilliant pencils and paints sent to me by the half brother who lived in distant exotic places. (When a craze for collecting postmarks swept my class at school, envelopes from his travels won me blissful popularity.)

Most of the time, however, I simply lay on the thick Navajo rugs that were my mother's pride and joy and studied their black and grey and white and red designs and wondered about the woman whose fingers had woven these patterns that made our floor look like a beautiful wall. The smell of wool still clung to the newer ones, a reminder of that immense mountainous and desert West we visited when I was seven years old. And my mother's reading lulled like the rhythm of the train that had carried us into that wondrous West I have returned to throughout my life. Sometimes I did listen to the words, captured by a dramatic encounter, a vivid description, a line of verse leaping like music.

Above all, there was the *National Geographic* magazine. Dependable as dawn and shining like sunlight with its golden cover, it arrived in our mailbox each month, bringing glimpses of life I could hardly imagine. Gradually the thought grew, as it must have done in millions of young minds through generations, how satisfying it would be to travel to unfamiliar corners of the world—and write about the journey! (I knew I needn't aspire to photography. My minimal ability with anything more mechanical than a fountain pen was confirmed when the first wristwatch I was given promptly broke a spring under my enthusiastic winding.) Writing, real writing—not the nameless valentines and little verses I scribbled to galax leaves and a luna moth at my window—gradually began to seem more full of promise, drawing upon the possibility of another pleasure my parents shared: travel.

What I did not realize was that one of the exotic destinations at that moment for "local color" travel writers and folklorists was the very place where I lived. Southern Appalachia had been discovered as "the land that time forgot," the habitat of wild moonshiners and feudists, of natural beauty and winsome girls courted by gangling, illiterate bear hunters. Though its wealth of forest and mineral resources had long since been exploited, now the magnificent scenery that survived was being embraced into national parks and parkways, natural treasures for future generations. And, paradoxically, perfect settings for promoting the stereotype of a primitive people and culture.

Thus, when my mother went North to visit her husband's family she carried the burden of more than her own virtues or shortcomings to be weighed and accepted. (Her stepdaughter's prior assurance to all friends and kinfolk, based on an affection growing from that first acquaintance in Asheville, was dismissed as a predictable effort to make the situation pleasant for her father.) The image of all the Southern Appalachians rode with my mother on that long journey.

As she would do so many times in the future when I could observe, she overwhelmed the stereotypes by ignoring them. I can imagine her at that first dinner with her curious, nonstorytelling, courteous, and possibly suspicious in-laws, always being herself, perhaps a bit nervous but watching every move and gesture, observing every idiosyncrasy, hearing every nuance of words and dialect to mimic later to my father's delight, and ready with laughter, supported by some important inner source of dignity and self-worth.

Little wonder that efforts to discover and understand people's differences, the need to claim certain places as one's own, are themes woven into much of my writing. How fortunate that my parents' relationship to people and place was confirmed and enlarged by the man I married.

That is another story, but it is necessary to mention here James Stokely's passion for knowledge—that available in books and that waiting in the great world of nature all around us—and his courageous celebration of human diversity everywhere, especially in the South he knew so well and in the country he wanted to make more just.

James once asked me about my father's and mother's attitude toward my first attempts at writing. As I thought about an answer I realized that their response to my scribbled efforts prepared me in some ways for later responses from editors, who had a very practical interest in my ability, and from readers who invested their time and money in my books. When I brought my parents a poem, a story, the first three pages of a novel, my efforts were neither dismissed as child's play nor greeted with pronouncements that I was the most gifted of beginners. They read, remarked on anything they discovered that seemed worthy of mention, and encouraged me to keep working with words. Just as my mother couldn't always be sure that the yeast would rise as she wished in the wonderful bread she made, just as my father sometimes couldn't find the shape he needed in the finely grained board under his hands, I learned that I might have to try several efforts before I produced the story or book I wanted.

Honest, they were. And the past they left me isn't even past.

SIDNEY SAYLOR FARR

Editor of *Appalachian Heritage* and assistant to the Special Collections librarian at Hutchins Library at Berea College, Sidney Saylor Farr (b. 1932) is a poet, short story writer, and essayist. Farr is the author of five books that represent a wide and rich range of genres. Two of her books, *More Than Moonshine: Appalachian Recipes and Recollections* (1983; reprinted for the fifth time in 1995) and *Table Talk: Appalachian Meals and Memories* (1995), are unusual recipe books that feature, among other things, prose recollections. Interspersed among recipes for such items as baked groundhog with sweet potatoes and cracklin' bread are poignant and crafted reminiscences that tell the story of Farr's life growing up in the mountains of Kentucky on Stoney Fork near Pine Mountain in the 1940s. Farr made an important contribution to Appalachian scholarship with the publication of *Appalachian Women: An Annotated Bibliography* (1981). In 1993 *What Tom Sawyer Learned from Dying* was published, the story of a man in Rochester, New York, who had a near-death experience. A poetry collection, *Headwaters,* was released in 1995. Farr has directed workshops and delivered lectures on Appalachian and literary topics across the nation, from Anchorage, Alaska, to the communities of her home state.

*   *   *

Women Born to Be Strong

I am the oldest of ten children. My family lived about as far back as it was possible to go in Bell County, Kentucky. Father worked in the timber woods and at a sawmill, when there was employment to be found, and when there was no work he made and sold moonshine. We ate what we grew on the place or could glean from the hillsides. Just about everything was made by hand. We had little contact with people outside the region.

I married shortly after I turned fifteen; it seemed there was little else to do. I wanted to go to school, but Father said no. There was no money for me to go to the Red Bird Mission School or the Pine Mountain Settlement School as a boarding student, and the nearest high school was fifteen miles away, with no school buses at that time.

It may seem strange for me to say, but even though growing up in the mountains of southeastern Kentucky prevented me from having a formal education, there was no lack of stimulation and opportunities to learn. No one ever told us we were Appalachians and therefore poor benighted people, so we did not have that in our consciousness.

We shared with our neighbors and kin. When Father planned to butcher a hog, he would send word to neighbors up and down the creek that they should come by the next day for a mess of meat. They did, and he would take meat to older or infirm people, and there would be feasting everywhere as families cooked the fresh pork. When neighbors butchered, the same process was usually followed. These mountain people shared everything. They were my teachers, especially the mountain women. Some of the women were in our extended family, while others were neighbors and friends. I didn't know it at the time, but what they gave me was exactly what I would need one day to write.

Some were storytellers. We lived near Granny Brock, my father's grandmother, from the time I was five until I was twelve years old. It was told in the family that Granny Brock had had seven husbands, some still living, others long gone. Her first child, Father's mother, was illegitimate. It was said of both Granny Brock and Grandma Saylor that they were two of the prettiest women in Bell County. In my opinion, however, Grandma Saylor was a pale candle in Granny Brock's dark radiance.

Granny had weathered incredible storms during her lifetime, but she laughed a lot and told me stories of pioneer days and how, when she was young, a blizzard hit and a bear tried to get into their log house, going around and around outside, snuffling and growling. She told how her mother sat up all night to protect the children. She spoke of old folk tales and superstitions. She told of times when her children were hungry for meat, and she took a rifle into the woods to kill squirrels or quails. She told about husbands who came and went, and about her children who stayed and had to be fed. "Especially Little Mike. I did the best that I could," she said.

"Mike was my little crippled boy," she told us. She often talked about the night when he was born, a night when the snowfall came down and came down until even the fenceposts were buried in the snow. The Granny Woman had a hard time getting to her, and Mike had a hard time getting born into this world. When he did come, his little feet and legs were all twisted. Granny Brock said she cried that whole night through, and many other times, too. Since Mike couldn't run and play, she said, he invented games and made up little songs to amuse himself. Granny shared his songs with us, one, especially, about planting corn in the springtime. "'*When the whippoorwills call, it's corn planting time, when the whippoorwills call, it's corn planting time.*'" I asked Granny many times to talk about Little Mike, and I would sit near her, loving the story and loving her.

"Little Mike lived to be eight years old," she would say, moving toward the end of her tale. "Then the Good Lord just took him home. It was on a night almost as bad as the night he was born. It snowed and the wind kept blowing and the cold creeped in." Granny Brock had tried to keep Little Mike as warm as she could. But she reckoned an angel came down on that snowfall and carried him away. Granny would tell me sad stories like this, and we would sit and not say another word for a long time. Then she would brighten up and tell me something funny or risqué, tell me stories about some of the older folk who lived up and down the creeks, stories that horrified my mother and taught me to hold my tongue.

Some of my happiest memories are when Father and Granny Brock went fishing in the evenings and Mother allowed me to go with them. I loved to listen to the stories they told, Granny doing most of the talking.

"Now, Wilburn," she would say, "do you remember Old Willie Simpson? Now there was a slick, sharp man. They wasn't nothing he wouldn't connive at doing."

"Yeah," Father would chuckle. "Remember the time he told Uncle Joe that he could steal one of his sheep, walk by the house and tell about it, and Uncle Joe would never recognize it?"

Granny Brock chimed in, "And one dark rainy day, Willie walked by carrying a heavy sack on his shoulders."

"Old Man Willie called out to Uncle Joe, 'Come and go home with me, Joe,'" Father took up the story.

"'No, can't, Willie. Why don't you come in and stay awhile?'"

"'No, I've got to be getting home. The wether's dark and heavy.'"

"Joe thought he was referring to the dark rainy day," Granny chuckled. "He done what he said he'd do. He stole one of Uncle Joe's sheep, a wether, and told him about it. He did it in a slick way and Uncle Joe never caught on. Later on, when Joe found out the truth he just laughed. 'A man that smart ought to get away with stealing a sheep,' was all he said."

Father and Granny chuckled together, then fished awhile in silence until one of them remembered another story or an anecdote. I sat and listened to them until the moon was high in the sky.

I started writing stories and poems two decades later, and it seemed natural when I began to hear Granny's voice in my head. She "spoke" through many of my poems.

And there were other storytellers in those mountains, with tales even more stark and painful than Granny Brock's. Hettie Howard was an elderly woman in the neighborhood whom everyone called "Aunt" Hettie as a title of respect. I greatly admired Aunt Hettie. She lived with her nephew, Jeff Hoskins, and his wife, Minnie. Lora, Jeff's younger sister, was one of my best friends. She and I often visited Aunt Hettie and sat with her to listen to old tales about when she was a girl.

Aunt Hettie had a trunk that she allowed Lora to open one time to show me what was inside; I was both attracted and repelled. Aside from a few keepsakes, the contents were a memorial to Aunt Hettie's only daughter, Julia, who had been married to Sam Nunn, a jealous and possessive man, with whom she had several children. One day he shot and killed Julia, rode into Pineville, the county seat, and turned himself in.

Among the contents of the trunk were the clothes Julia Nunn had been wearing at the moment of her death and a picture of her taken shortly before her murder. Her photo showed a pretty brown-haired woman with a shy smile and big dark eyes looking directly into the camera. She had on a little brown hat trimmed with a green feather. The underclothes in the trunk were stained reddish brown with her blood, as was her dress and her very small shoes.

I was fascinated and asked to see the contents time and time again. Lora and Aunt Hettie told me over and over every detail of what had happened that day. As I listened I was filling in the rest of the story, although I did not know it at the time. I was amazed how Aunt Hettie could speak so clearly of her long-dead daughter. I decided she had to be one of the strongest women I knew. I wanted to be like her, strong and able to talk about painful events. My talk, however, would take the shape of writing.

Aunt Dellie, married to Father's brother, Otis, acquainted me with the stories in books. She was a reader. A young woman with black hair, brown eyes, and the whitest teeth I ever saw, Aunt Dellie was probably part Cherokee, as were many southeastern Kentucky people. Her father and mother lived near Pineville, and sometimes they could get discarded books from the town library for Aunt Dellie. She read every one and then gave each book to me. One book I will never forget was the book of the Mormon faith. It confused and frightened me. When I asked Aunt Dellie what it meant, she confessed that she did not understand what it was all about. It did not seem a bit odd to either of us that we had read every word of that book in spite of our confusion, for we both loved the printed word. It was through Aunt Dellie that I read *Little Women, Heidi, Pilgrim's Progress, Lorna Doone, Gone with the Wind,* and other classics.

Aunt Betty and Aunt Laura, my father's sisters, taught me about nature and the imagination, two lessons that I'm not sure you can ever really learn inside the walls of a classroom. Aunt Betty was thirteen years older than I, but we were friends, stealing as much time together away from our unending chores as we could. She was a big, strong woman who cut down trees and sawed them into logs for firewood, repaired fences and roofs, and performed other jobs ordinarily considered to be men's work. I knew she would rather be outdoors any day of the week instead of indoors doing housework. Aunt Betty liked boys but was too shy to flirt with them, and they acted shy and distant with her. She did not get married until her late forties.

Aunt Betty was a loner, never desiring to go out much where there were crowds of people. She was happiest at home or in the woods. She taught me to recognize varieties of trees and the kind of mast they produced. She taught me how to know ginseng. We dug roots and gathered wild herbs that she dried to sell in late autumn for cash. Aunt Betty often talked about people and events surrounding them in terms of nature. We gathered wild greens in early spring, bringing home tiny spears of poke, which was the first green thing up in April. I guess you could say she taught me metaphor.

Eight or ten years ago Aunt Betty decided she would learn how to make baskets patterned after the old willow baskets mountain women used to make, only using honeysuckle vines instead of willow. Willow trees were scarce on Stoney Fork, and she was the first to use honeysuckle vines instead of willow wands to weave her baskets. She made hundreds, of all shapes and sizes, and for different functions. As her confidence grew she began to sell them, and other people on Stoney Fork began to imitate her work. I became one of them, though poems, not baskets, would be the product of my weaving.

Aunt Laura, my father's youngest sister, was reckless and wildly imaginative. One weekend she fell through the barn loft. We were in Grandpa's barn playing in the hay. She rolled down the side of a pile of hay and fell through an open place in the floor. I started to cry for fear she had been killed. The lower part of the barn was open on either end, and Grandpa's big shoat had wandered in to sleep in the shade. Aunt Laura landed on the pig's back. "Well shit, Pig," she said. "I have done killed you!" I laughed so hard I nearly fell after her.

Her imagination was as wild as her physical recklessness. We romped in the woods and went to the "hospital" at Gum Spring around the hillside on Peach Orchard. Two tall trees grew near the spring, and these were "doctor" and "nurse" in our fantasy, while the smaller bushes were patients. Aunt Laura was the voice for doctor, nurse, and patients and diagnosed dreadful diseases for both of us. Her voices were so real to me that sometimes I looked to be sure the doctor, nurse, and patients had not come alive. The doctor prescribed a gallon a day of Grandma Saylor's bitters. (Grandma Saylor brewed roots and herbs together in a concoction she called her bitters. She insisted that everyone drink a cup each wintry day. I always cried when it was my turn because it tasted so bitter.)

From Aunt Laura I learned to be reckless about physical safety while climbing trees, rooftops, high rocks. I learned to be creative by listening to the imaginary people and situations she introduced me to in playhouses and woods and wild games.

My mother was another creative force in my life, but her brand of creativity was somehow a little different from Aunt Laura's. I always saw it coupled with frugality and hard work, and I came to understand that imagination lived side by side with both these things.

My mother had a big family to care for and no time or energy to create pretty things. But she found a way to satisfy her creative yearnings by the patterns she chose to use, in the colors of her materials, and with the tiny stitches in her quilting.

She planted flowers in cans and boxes and filled our yard and front porch with colorful blooms. Certainly my mother had a green thumb. She could make anything flourish and grow. After I married and left home, many times she would visit, taking home with her slips and cuttings of my plants. Months or years later, my original plant long gone, I would go to her house to get cuttings, and start all over again while hers would live on and on. Nothing ever died under her care.

I have no memory of my mother ever having idle moments. Father always butchered two or three hogs in the late fall and early winter. Mother rendered all of the fat and scrap pieces trimmed from the meat down into lard, which she used for cooking.

Soap-making took place on a clear day when Mother had no other major job to do. I remember how she would clean the hog intestines by slitting each strand open and washing it in the little creek running near our house. She draped the long pieces of gut over a rail or pole and let them dry. When ready to make soap, she cut the dried guts into short lengths and put them into her big black kettle along with fat trimmed from the organs and the residue from the rendered fat.

After pouring water into the kettle, she mixed in the appropriate amount of lye and then boiled the mixture into soap.

I never liked to be around when she made soap. I did not like the smell, and I was afraid of the lye she used. My younger sister and I were given the task of keeping the pile of wood replenished in the backyard where a fire was burning under her black washpot. Mother would stand, stirring the foul-smelling liquid, warning us not to walk up too close to it for fear we might be splashed. She repeatedly told us how dangerous lye was and how we were never to play with it or get near it. I did not like for her to work with such a substance.

I used to dream of having a whole washtub full of pretty, nice-smelling soap. "When I grow up and have my own home," I said to her one time, "I will never make lye soap. I will buy pretty soap that smells good." She smiled at me and said, "If you have enough money to buy things like that, why then I reckon you won't ever have to make your own soap."

But my mother always knew more than she ever said. To any product there is a dangerous substance, something you have to know about but learn how to control. I would make poems instead of soap in much of my adult life, but the lesson of my mother I took with me.

I felt restless, sometimes, when I was young. I was always the rebel, never quite believing as others did that our task was to live the best life we could in "this vale of tears," knowing our reward would be in heaven. I yearned to know what was beyond the boundaries. Sometimes when I stood on a cliff or lay in a green meadow warm with sunshine, I felt such harmony and peace that I questioned the dark teachings about delayed happiness and rewards.

I dreamed of seeing cities, towns, lakes, and oceans, which I read about in books. And when missionaries from the Evangelical United Brethren Church at Red Bird, in Beverly, Kentucky, came to Stoney Fork to start a community center and build a church, I was happy. This was my first experience with people from outside the region, and I thought they were perfect.

I began to feel ashamed of my mountain past in the presence of the missionaries, ashamed of our poverty and lifestyles so different from theirs. I worked hard to talk like them and grew obsessed with being worthy. I found out about the American School in Chicago where students could take all high school courses by mail. I enrolled and began working toward a high school diploma, graduating in five years.

My husband decided we would move to Indianapolis in 1960, and this brought me the first experience of working in an office. I managed to fit in very well and began learning firsthand about things I had only read about before—such as traffic lights, city buses, taxicabs, and policemen. But my husband could only find work in a paper mill, and he grew to hate the place, longing to go back home.

We compromised and moved to Berea in 1962, where I got a job as associate editor of *Mountain Life & Work,* a quarterly publication of the Council of the Southern Mountains, and where I eventually received my college degree. In Berea, where the foothills of the Cumberland Mountains begin, I was brought face-to-face with my people and Appalachia again. In 1964 the council became very involved with the War on Poverty, and activists, social workers, and educators came in on a wave of money from Washington, D.C., and streamed out into the mountain communities to live and work. And they streamed into their home base at Berea and into the magazine offices. I heard their secondhand opinions and solutions, and I did not like what they said. I knew then that this was where I belonged, because I understood this place.

The mountain women of my past were calling me back and forcing me to remember them again. As I thought about them on a more conscious level, I realized that they had never really left me, nor I them. I often had found myself thinking their words when I had a decision to make. I was dreadfully homesick for the mountains while I was gone, remembering the way they looked when light played over the landscape at different hours of the day and night. I remembered sunsets, sunrises, early morning mist, and white fog after hard rains. I began putting the mountains and the people down on paper in the shape of poems.

It should not have surprised me that one of my first poems was about Granny Brock.

GRANNY BROCK

"Granny, is it gonna snow a lot?"

"The woolly worms done give us their opinion,
and crickets are singing their lonesome winter song.
The corn shucks are thick and stiff this year,
and moss is growing on the north side of trees.
That's a sure sign of a bad winter," she says.

"Granny, is it going to rain?"

"My bees worked in the clover early and late,
and the moon had a ring around it these past few nights.
There were red clouds in the sky this morning,
the wind turned tree leaves underside over,
and red birds called 'wet, wet, wet' all day long.
That's a sure sign of rain," she says.

"Granny, why do bad times come?"
"The east wind of trouble travels far and near,
and bad times come but they do go away.
Once I was younger in older times,
when a good day's work brought a good day's pay.
Back then was the day burst,
now it's coming down dusky,
but it's not yet plumb dark in our land—
that's a sure sign," she says.

The richness of my life, of the women in my life, makes amends for the lack of educational opportunities in my growing years, when I should have been in high school and college preparing for a career. The lessons of all the mountain women I knew on Stoney Fork were the important ones. I know that now. I guess, really, I've always known.

NIKKY FINNEY

Nikky Finney was born in 1957 in Conway, South Carolina, at the edge of the Atlantic Ocean. She was raised in several different towns across the state. Choosing to remain in her beloved southland, she attended Talladega College in Talladega, Alabama. Her first book of poems, *On Wings Made of Gauze,* was published in 1985. She has been published in the anthologies *In Search of Color Everywhere* (1994) and *I Hear a Symphony* (1994). After eight years of California life, currently she works and writes in Lexington, Kentucky, where she is a founding member of a community-based writing collective, The Affrilachian Poets, and assistant professor of creative writing at the University of Kentucky. She was the scriptwriter for the PBS documentary *For Posterity's Sake: The Story of Morgan and Marvin Smith* (1995). Her second volume of poetry, *Rice,* was published in August 1995. Each year she reads her work and directs writing workshops at dozens of different colleges and art festivals around the country. She has been writing for as long as she has had memory.

*   *   *

Salt-Water Geechee Mounds

Long before Frank X. Walker, a local artist in Lexington, Kentucky, read in a 1989 edition of *Webster's Dictionary* that Appalachian meant "the white residents of mountainous regions of the country"; long before he took his pen and carving tools and grafted the word "Affrilachian" out of his need to be recognized and to bring recognition to the African presence in Appalachia; long before I moved to Kentucky and began reading about the thousands of black folk who had lived and raised families all along the hills of the Blue Ridge and Great Smoky Mountains for generations; years before a black woman ever stood up at one of my readings and questioned the accuracy of my being invited to read my work at a conference for Appalachian writers, because, as she put it, "I was obviously more salt water than I was mountain"; before any of this, I was a girl from South Carolina who grew up knowing that the sea didn't resemble the mountains but they were family just the same.

In these Kentucky days, even when I am nowhere near the sea, seawater is still near. The childhood waters of the warm Atlantic return to me in my sleep and cover me from way over yonder. There are spiritually inhabited areas underneath this old family water where doors and windows have been left open. Here, the old ones welcome and bid that I, a brown mermaid with lobster hair, move on through with pencil and paper, on yet another family treasure hunt.

My eyes are always stitched open when I move in this particular water because I know I am searching for the faces of family. I am afraid to blink because I don't want to miss even one of the sixty million and more who jumped off the slave ships rather than be a member of the landing party. Those who started or finished a fight and were thrown overboard because the word "obey" did not mean the same in their language. And those who in the oldest way of human travel, simply took flight, got tired, and had to go down in a watery eternal rest. I tell you, I cannot look at the Atlantic Ocean, cannot touch her and not feel my greatest-grandmother's trembling, fearful heart or see her chalky, steady eyes asking me, "What story do you wish to hear today?"

In these Kentucky days, when I am traveling too fast or standing too far away to see the family hills, there is still something mercurial rising and falling in me, remembering me back to the folding high red earth that is just south of here and most sacred to me as well. I require any landlocked places that I currently inhabit to at least come with mountain horizons, so that I may keep my eye on something beyond the easily explained breakable city. I am partial to Sunday walks through the up-down earth not for exercise or fresh air but for hearing. I am out listening for the words, for the breath of my ancestors who I was told always fled to the highest ground to escape the slaughter going on below. I go into the hills as often as I can to listen out for the marooning voices that I know are there, living still.

These two pulpit places are where I know the old Geechees will come and talk to me. This returning to old water and old ground that I do is how I get to myself and to their words. Their words are not supposed to reach out for me. This is utter respect I feel. I am supposed to travel to them and with my whole self extend all that I know and feel. This work is about diving into two hundred years of historical wrecks for which hardly anyone wanted to go down. This kind of work has to be done at the site and not from somewhere far away. I return to the sea to listen and then sometimes to the hills to talk.

I was born inches away from the sea at the bottom of a fiercely Confederate state, in the small coastal town of Conway, South Carolina, on August 26, 1957. The backyard of our first family house was all sand and seashells. Hundred-year-old oak trees with their canopies of Spanish moss dotted the entire street of tiny wooden houses. The lilting Gullah voices of the children of pure Africans was the first air I ever breathed and the first stories I heard. There were postcards sold near the beach that spoke of the legend of the live oaks and the Spanish moss that blanketed them. These cards told a story that the moss of the live oak was the hair of a southern maiden who had lost her rebel sweetheart and hung it there hoping for his return. But there were others of us whose great fathers had fought against the Confederacy and believed the moss to be the braided hair of all the Africans who had run away and been caught and hanged there. To us the live oaks were said to house the spirits of the slave dead. I learned there were indeed two sides to every story. And I knew I wanted to be one of those telling and passing on the infinite dark sweet side.

For me, the dark sweet side of the story began with the Africans in low-country South Carolina, the community, the food, the songs, the tragedy, the generosity, the language, the sand, the mosquitoes, the heat, the sea that we had traveled across. This original culture fed me in a thousand invisible ways. It gave me the power of humbleness and the notion of my tiny replaceable place within the universe. The hurricanes and tornadoes that barreled through each season laying flat man-made wooden dreams were early lessons in man's arrogance and unwillingness to listen more often to nature than to human beings. It was a lesson that I quickly took to heart. I was never ashamed to talk to the sea as if she could hear me. I said prayers and made up my best stories as I walked beside her as a youth. In respect for the dead, in honor of whose listening, and in gratitude to all who crossed over so that I might come through, I take flowers to her waters now as a woman.

The dark sweet side of the story also has to do with the rich family farmland at the very top of the state, bought after slavery by my great-grandfather and his brother, who swore to each other to never again work for another white man. This was the up-high ground of my mother's people. There were generous lessons and influences for me all around in the wind, the lightning, the endless fields of table crops grown in soil that I too had sprouted in as a child alongside the soybeans, silver queen corn, cotton, and peanuts. I remember the many rides on my grandfather's horse-drawn wagon, and how his actions in the field told me that he believed as I believed, that it was never a question of really owning the land but how the land in fact owned you.

I witnessed how valuable the land was to our everyday eating as well as to my grandmother's livelihood. I remember not being amazed that the only thing they would buy in town was coffee and sugar, that everything else needed was either made or grown or bartered for. I remember not marveling at how cruel the cycles of mother earth could be, but that it just was. I remember how we always planted a seedling for anything important in the family: births, deaths, and weddings. I remember never considering that this country way of life would ever change and yet it did. And what was never simple but unembellished and real has always stayed with me and in these ordinary days rises again to life in certain phrases, lines, and ways of saying. From both my seawater culture and my red hills community I learned to honor and respect the presence of things I could not necessarily see with my eyes but could absolutely feel with my own whole body. This lesson in taking my head out of the pages of a book and into life and living was invaluable as I began to dream about writing books of my own one day.

I grew up the quiet and reflective only girl-child of a close-knit black family. My mother and father met in 1952 while attending neighboring historically black colleges in South Carolina. Both were the children of farmers and both had begun their lives organically connected to hundreds of riverlike acres of self-sustaining family land. Both my mother's home in South Carolina and my father's birthplace in Virginia shared this particular human association to land and place. As a result of this strong geographical legacy and my own affinity for words and books, I have never had the luxury of taking for granted sea, soil, life, or the presence of alphabets that might help illuminate that life to the world at large.

My mother's birthplace, and my second home, was a place thick with the spirits of the first Americans, the Indians. The Cherokee and the Santee nations were names that were often called, but this part of rural South Carolina has hundreds of Indian words and names thick within its soul. This place where the red hills and mountains were the natural jewelry of the land. On clear days in Newberry County, at the top of my grandparents' farmhouse or from the hayloft or from the roof of the milking barn, I could see the tips of the Great Smoky Mountains way off in the distance like some great mysterious land always kept at bay. I stared deep at these great slopes whenever they appeared into the frame of my life, creating stories about how they got there and who it was that lived deep inside their folds. Little did I know that years later I would relocate to the Kentucky River basin to live, listen, teach, and write side by side children of mountain people and recognize the curves and mounds in my own saltwater soul.

I remember my earliest spirit to be that of a child moving through the world more at home on the outside than the in. I relished the solitude of the open cow pasture or the blackberry patch or the creek that slithered through the woods filled with deer or the swampy tadpole ponds where I fished alongside my grandmother who used the solitude to always teach me something that she had a feeling I would never read in any book.

As an adolescent girl, I remember taking pictures of things with my eyes and then filing them away for some reason. But my grandmother remembers back even farther. She remembers how quiet I was when she pushed me up the dirt road in the stroller to her garden. For hours I would sit there while she worked, never crying, she tells me. She says I was content to watch and listen. She says whatever was there was enough for me as I stared at the trees and the hills and the wind moving by. I often wonder if this was my young spirit preparing myself to be the observer, the one who would question and wonder and, like those before me, never readily obey.

I've always trusted my eyes. I believe my writing life began as a result of a heightened ability to see something terribly wrong and my inability to turn away from it. I believe my writing life began as a result of seeing something so right somewhere and not being able to forget its beauty. I was never terribly good at accepting others' definitions of things. So at some moment early in my life, when I could no longer bear to sit and witness something that tore through me with such force as to bring actual pain to my insides or cause tears and steal away all words, I began to dissect the moment on paper. I began picking up a pencil and working through to my own understandings. Writing was my way of fighting fiercely and privately. Nothing before or since has ever given me the symbiotic feeling of waging war and declaring for myself great peace of mind.

Both my parents were intimately involved in the ongoing national movement for equality and justice that was raging in the South during the sixties. The violence and unfairness we bitterly received, via our racial and economic differences, caught me off guard as a child. I could not make sense of it alone. Our parents and grandparents tried to keep it away from the younger ones as much as possible. But it touched every aspect of our lives in the sixties. The scenes of all the marches, the talk of all the murders, the laughing white faces in kangaroo courts, the water hoses, the Black Panthers, the buses, the fear on the faces, the missing sons, the bombs and fire and beatings, seemed attached to the hem of our clothing by some invisible cord that followed us wherever we went. The vicious words they tried but could not keep out of our young ears.

As I grew older and continued to notice the raging differences and injustices that American culture was teaching me everywhere I turned, I realized I had to fight back in some way that was real for me and not just somebody else's way of fighting. For me, the first visual snapshots that would eventually push my hands down into the barrel of my own particular words were the fierce, outspoken voices of family and neighbor alike.

Writing became not just a way for me to understand but, for me, then a girl of fifteen, a way to also help battle against what I felt was the pure corruption of what I had been taught all my life: the only leg we humans ever have to stand on is truth. Early in my life I felt accountable to more than just my life. Early, I felt things being passed on to me for reasons I did not fully understand until now. Now, in part, I believe they were passed because of the impact of my human community and the powerful physical environments that helped shape my spirit and mind. I believe I have been given some insight into things because of my connection to the hills and the land and because of my affinity for the sea. These places had helped set my independent spirit in stone. These places had also helped make me highly visually oriented. The stillness of the hills and the constant motion of the water. There was always something deeply stimulating about them for me. I was enamored with not just the existence and connection of the land and sea but also its aesthetic form and shape. As a writer I wanted to be able to see what I was talking about without looking at the words but by simply listening. I wanted anyone else who might ever hear my words to see them just as clearly.

In 1975, while trying to decide which historically black and academically swift college I would attend, my father and I made our last college tour stop one Sunday afternoon. We entered Savery Library at Talladega College in Talladega, Alabama. As I walked into the marble foyer, my eyes caught sight of a striking panoramic mural above me. It had the most palpable tension and jewel-like colors of any pendant I had ever seen. The first image I noticed was that of a fierce battle. I had seen other historical pictures of men fighting, but none had ever instantly meant so much to me. These were the faces and bodies of black men aboard a ship, wielding machetes, fighting for their lives with every ounce of strength, and, in a rare artistic depiction of black folks, winning.

I moved farther into the room. My feet were moving, but I was unable to look down and leave the story above me, not for one blinking moment. Like some ticking human clock, I turned slowly, eventually to see the room in whole wide view. Stretched the entire length of both the east and west walls, at least ten feet high and thirty feet long, were six murals that instantly took my breath away. They were as real as photographs to me. What I saw in each stroke of the artist's hand struck like lightning. I was from that moment on physically and spiritually altered.

My eyes jumped from one panel to the next. I stood twirling in the middle of the floor, pulled up swiftly into each painted frame of story, turning my whole body from one to the other as if they were the giant pages of a book sitting above me. I remember the librarian touching my arm and cautioning me not to step on the sacred ship that I had not noticed painted within a beautiful circle that sat in the middle of the floor. I would later learn how that ship had something to do with the murals and from that moment on, everything to do with me.

On the west wall was one-half the story: fifty-four Africans stolen from their home and sold into slavery in 1839; Africans who mutinied and took control of the *La Amistad* during the three-month journey; Africans who were later tried in New England, their legal counsel the former president of the United States, John Quincy Adams; Africans who three years later were found not guilty of mutiny or murder and were finally repatriated to Sierra Leone.

On the east wall was the other half of the story. Here was the founding of Talladega College. On the last three panels were the faces of slaves heading through the mountains to Ohio and freedom on the Underground Railroad. There was another frame depicting the opening day of school for Talladega College in 1867. In the last wall plate was the building of the brand-new school's first library, Savery Hall, the very building I was standing in a century later. There I stood with my eyes and heart sewn to these pictures that I knew in some way had entered and made some profound difference in me. Then and there I knew that this would be where I would attend college. I knew I wanted to write as clearly, as meaningfully, as precisely as the artist of these murals.

These six panels with the most beautiful Blue Ridge peaks rising out of one, with the Atlantic Ocean spread out toward forever in another, would essentially anchor and sail the vessel of who and whose I was in the world for the next twenty years. They would touch everything that I would eventually push out from between my writing fingers. Little did I know that these six panels would influence me so deeply. The individual stories in the separate panels as well as the one collective story told by them all became a beacon of understanding for me. I came to understand a great deal about myself as a black woman and a writer because of the images on those walls, set in oil paint by the knowing stroke and brilliance of the African-American artist Hale Woodruff. Here somehow was my own life's commitment illuminated frame by frame. The images of black people engaged in a high-seas battle for their right to be free, refusing the corruption of greed and evil, dropping to their knees in total reverence once returned to the land of their birth, and then the crafting and building of sanctuaries for black minds and knowledge. These were some of the most precious themes for me, themes that I wanted to explore in my own writing one day. These were things I knew people in my community had urged me to remember as I got older and stretched farther away from home. These were the things the land, the high ground, and the sea had fed to me over the years and would continue to feed me.

Later I walked outside. I found and stood in a deep grassy bowl that sat in the middle of the campus. My eyes looked out over beautiful land that rose up from the tiny valley where the college had sat since 1867. I glanced first one way, then another in a 360-degree circle, and all I could see in every direction were the oceanic peaks and valleys of the Blue Ridge Mountains. It looked like someone had poured water into a blue mold in the open sky. I had no idea how truly divined a moment it was. It would be twenty years later before I would hear the geographical evolutionary theory stating how at one point in time all the land masses on the face of the earth were linked as one. And if you were to test that theory by pulling all the countries of the world in together across their individual oceans and seas, you would notice something phenomenal—especially if you are an Affrilachian poet—and that is the Appalachian mountain range melding perfectly into the long green valleys of Africa like one single sacred ground.

For the next four years as I studied and grew into my writing shoes, I often walked through the indigo hills of the Cheaha mountain range, sometimes camping out but mostly just listening out and always talking to the old ones. Here indeed was where the same voices that had started out whispering to me against the backdrop of the sea began to loudly call and echo out the same things that had to be cared for and written out correctly. Black and brown voices speaking directly to me and to my hands, urging me not to play with the words, saying there was much too much at stake. Such voices would continue to reach me for the next four years, there in the folds of the hills as well as underneath many a hundred-year-old Talladega oak tree. The place itself and the people would implore me to do my work and use everything I had seen from the sea to the red hills to tell it right.

In these Kentucky days even when I am nowhere near the sea, I am still reaching to tell the dark sweet side of the story. In these Kentucky days surrounded by land that rolls on all sides, the Talladega-Woodruff murals remain center stage in my vision as the newest poems and stories that quilt my heart move from muscle to manuscript. I am still drawn to write of those who resist corruption of their culture, who value a handshake more than an unreadable fancy signature, who attach no dollar sign or bulldozer to the word "progress." The water in my life has taught me to honor the earth in my life. The steady earth has taught me to treasure the moving restless sea. They both move with great utility through my writer's heart. I know no matter what, I cannot be bought or sold. I am forever searching for family, and my watery blue mountain heart tells me I will never find them all.

DENISE GIARDINA

Denise Giardina was born in 1951 in Bluefield, West Virginia, and grew up in a coal camp. She is a graduate of West Virginia Wesleyan College and Virginia Theological Seminary. Her first novel, *Good King Harry* (1984), was compared to Dickens by the *New York Times*. Author of *Storming Heaven* (1987) and *The Unquiet Earth* (1992), two novels that cover sixty years of coalfield history in fictional Blackberry Creek, West Virginia, Giardina tells the unwritten story of a time now vanished, a story that American history has long neglected. Both novels have been highly praised by the national media, as well as by writers such as George Garrett, Annie Dillard, Carolyn Chute, Barbara Kingsolver, and Clyde Edgerton. Giardina is currently living in Charleston, West Virginia, and is writer-in-residence at West Virginia State College.

* * *

No Scapin the Booger Man

I learned to read and write in standard English at Thorpe Elementary School, but before the teachers enticed me with the clean preciseness of spelling and grammar, mine was a different language. I was no prodigy who reads at age two or three and goes bored and superior to first grade. I stared with some curiosity at the tiny black squiggles that were supposed to be words, but I did not read until I was urged to it. I saw no need to hurry. I had the stories.

I heard the stories first while perched upon the bony knees of old men. My papaw sang the violent, pure tales of the mountains. Back and forth his knee would sway, and me upon it, back and forth.

Froggy wint a courtin and he did ride, mm hmm.

Papaw's voice ud leap up at the end of a line like hes surprised at somethin.

Uncle Brigham talked out his stories. He wudnt really my uncle, jus lived nex door, a good hearted coal miner who drank too much likker an hit his wife. He allays told his stories in the summer dusk with the frogs a peepin an the litnin bugs hoverin like the Lords gardan angels. Uncle Brigham ud sit in the front porch swing an tell bout the strange feller buried in the tater patch an the poor fool who dug up his big toe an took it home an wouldnt you know he et it an here come the booger man to git it back.

Don't tell me no more Uncle Brigham cause I dont want to know.

Im on the firs step. Im on the second step.

I WANT MY BIG TOE.

They never was no scapin the booger man.

After while I was makin my own stories an lettin um run round inside my head. One a my favorites was bout the people at lived in a ole partment buildin in Welch. Welch was the county seat an it was jus glamrus as any city with its neon Falls City beer sign an so many buildins you couldnt never go in em all. Strange thangs must go on in such buildins, an stranges of all in at partment buildin, cause it had balconies. People at lived in partment buildins with balconies, ey wouldnt be like the rest of us. Eyd be from forrin countries whur theyd been princesses and dukes, only now they was in exile. Eyd have their jewls in the closet an therd be little statues an vases that was made a red an green glass an theyd be lots of flairs, specially roses. Them princesses ud be lookin to go back to their homes some day.

Like lots of my stories, this un didnt have no end.

I learned about endings later, when I was taught quotation marks and spelling. Learning to spell ended any illusions I may have had that we are totally free and independent creatures. No, there was a higher authority that molded us all to its will and ordered our lives for us, an authority as inexorable in its own way as the booger man. Spelling and grammar are benevolent dictators perhaps, subjugating one raw culture that a broader one may be experienced. Coal companies are not so benevolent, and even as I lost my own Appalachian innocence, I lived through the destruction of my community.

Home then was Black Wolf, West Virginia. Ten houses, little boxes once painted white but now grey with coal dust. A hulk of a company store (with a poor creature, half man, half monster, named John the Con, held captive in its basement, but that was only another of my stories). A rusting tipple around the bend. Red dog where grass should have been. Owned by Nassau Coal Company, bought out by Page, bought out by Pocy Fuel, bought out by Consol, surface acreage held in fief to Pocahontas Land, owned by N&W, which ran its screeching black trains through the coal camp for the sole purpose of frightening children at play.

In Black Wolf I grew so intimate with death and decay that even now they feel like home to me. Andy Wyatt fell on a conveyor belt in the mine and was crushed, Douglas Finley was shot by his daddy, the jobs were gone, the children's teeth rotted black in their gums, Uncle Brigham moved to Richmond and drank himself to death, we left Black Wolf and the houses were torn down behind us. The school is gone as well, being only the handmaiden of power and not the wielder of it.

The remainder of my life has been a searching for home, a search complicated by the fear that I would despise it if I found it. I first became aware of my predicament during a conflict in Kanawha County, West Virginia, over English textbooks. I was fresh out of college and serving as a substitute teacher in the eastern end of the county. I shared the anger of a powerless people at the erosion of traditional mountain values, yet I could not join in the protest against multicultural school textbooks. I still lived up a holler, but I fled each Sunday to a local Episcopal church to worship with people who disdained the ways of "crickers." The innocence I had lost when I obtained my education was irretrievable, and I had become as alien as the mythical Hapsburgs in my Welch apartment building. On the other hand, I felt equally estranged from mainstream America. Who the hell was I?

I have bounced all over the place while trying to answer that question. I have lived in a radical Christian community in Washington, D.C., a Jesuit community in rural West Virginia, and a Kentucky coal camp named David. Before that I attended an Episcopal seminary, and researched absentee landownership in southern

West Virginia. I have been an operating room clerk, a hospital chaplain, and a clerk in a bookstore in Durham, North Carolina. Now I am back in West Virginia—probably to stay. But I am in Charleston, not the coalfields. And I have no plans at this time to write another coalfield novel. I am moving on in both my life and my writing.

I have achieved a measure of contentment through conjuring lost places and writing about them—medieval England and the coal towns of southern West Virginia, both vanished worlds. Perhaps it takes a hybrid to help create a body of writing where once there was only oral tradition. This time the stories have endings, generally sad but hopeful ones. As Uncle Brigham would say, they never was no scapin the booger man. But in the mountains we keep trying.

NIKKI
GIOVANNI

Born in 1943 in Knoxville, Tennessee, Nikki Giovanni has recently published an illustrated "love poem" entitled *Knoxville, Tennessee* (1994), for her grandmother Louvenia Watson. Giovanni was graduated from Fisk University in Nashville, Tennessee, and is professor of English at Virginia Tech. Her most recent publications include *The Selected Poems of Nikki Giovanni* (1996) and *The Love Poems of Nikki Giovanni* (1997). Her most recent illustrated children's books are *The Genie in the Jar* (1996), with Chris Raschka, and *The Sun Is So Quiet* (1996), with Ashley Bryan. The selected papers of Nikki Giovanni are held at Mugar Memorial Library of Boston University.

* * *

400 Mulvaney Street

I was going to Knoxville, Tennessee, to speak. I was going other places first but mostly to me I was going home. And I, running late as usual, hurried to the airport just in time.

The runway is like an aircraft carrier—sticking out in the bay—and you always get the feeling of drunken flyboys in green airplane hats chomping wads and wads of gum going "Whooooopie!" as they bring the 747 in from Hackensack to La Guardia. It had been snowing for two days in New York and the runway was frozen. They never say to you that the runway is frozen and therefore dangerous to take off from, and in fact you'd never notice it because all the New York airports have tremendous backups—even on clear days. So sitting there waiting was not unusual but I did notice this tendency to slide to the side with every strong wind, and I peeked out my window and noticed we were in the tracks of the previous jet and I thought: death has to eat too. And I went to sleep.

The whole thing about going to Knoxville appealed to my vanity. I had gotten a call from Harvey Glover about coming down and had said yes and had thought no more of it. Mostly, as you probably notice, artists very rarely have the chance to go back home and say, "I think I've done you proud." People are so insecure and in some cases jealous and in some cases think so little of themselves in general that they seldom think you'd be really honored to speak in your hometown or at your old high school. And other people are sometimes so contemptuous of home that they in fact don't want to come back. This has set up a negative equation between the artist and home.

I was excited about going to Knoxville but I didn't want to get my hopes up. What if it fell through? What if they didn't like me? Oh, my God! What if nobody came to hear me? Maybe we'd better forget about it. And I did. I flew on out to Cleveland to make enough money to be able to go to Knoxville. And Cleveland was beautiful. A girl named Pat and her policeman friend couldn't have been any nicer. And he was an intelligent cop. I got the feeling I was going to have a good weekend. Then my mother met me at the Cincinnati airport, where I had to change over, and had coffee with me and had liked my last television appearance. Then they called my flight, and on to Knoxville.

When we were growing up Knoxville didn't have television, let alone an airport. It finally got TV but the airport is in Alcoa. And is now called Tyson Field.

Right? Small towns are funny. Knoxville even has a zip code and seven-digit phone numbers. All of which seems strange to me since I mostly remember Mrs. Flora Ford's white cake with white icing and Miss Delaney's blue furs and Armetine Picket's being the sharpest woman in town—she attended our church—and Miss Brooks wearing tight sweaters and Carter-Roberts Drug Store sending out Modern Jazz Quartet sounds of *Fontessa* and my introduction to Nina Simone by David Cherry, dropping a nickel in the jukebox and *Porgy* coming out. I mostly remember Vine Street, which I was not allowed to walk to get to school, though Grandmother didn't want me to take Paine Street either because Jay Manning lived on it and he was home from the army and very beautiful with his Black face and two dimples. Not that I was going to do anything, because I didn't do anything enough even to think in terms of not doing anything, but according to small-town logic "It looks bad."

The Gem Theatre was on the corner of Vine and a street that runs parallel to the creek, and for ten cents you could sit all day and see a double feature, five cartoons, and two serials plus previews for the next two weeks. And I remember Frankie Lennon would come in with her gang and sit behind me and I wanted to say, "Hi. Can I sit with you?" but thought they were too snooty, and they, I found out later, thought I was too northern and stuck-up. All of that is gone now. Something called progress killed my grandmother.

Mulvaney Street looked like a camel's back with both humps bulging—up and down—and we lived in the down part. At the top of the left hill a lady made ice balls and would mix the flavors for you for just a nickel. Across the street from her was the Negro center, where the guys played indoor basketball and the little kids went for stories and nap time. Down in the valley part were the tennis courts, the creek, the bulk of the park, and the beginning of the right hill. To enter or leave the street you went either up or down. I used to think of it as a fort, especially when it snowed, and the enemy would always try to sneak through the underbrush nurtured by the creek and through the park trees, but we always spotted strangers and dealt. As you came down the left hill the houses were up on its side; then people got regular flat front yards; then the right hill started and ran all the way into Vine and Mulvaney was gone and the big apartment building didn't have a yard at all.

Grandmother and Grandpapa had lived at 400 since they'd left Georgia. And Mommy had been a baby there and Anto and Aunt Agnes were born there. And dated there and sat on the swing on the front porch and fussed there, and our good and our bad were recorded there. That little frame house duplicated twice more which overlooked the soft-voiced people passing by with "Evening, 'Fessor Watson, Miz Watson," and the grass wouldn't grow between our house and Edith and Clarence White's house. It was said that he had something to do with numbers. When the man tried to get between the two houses and the cinder crunched a warning to us, both houses lit up and the man was caught between Mr. White's shotgun and Grandfather's revolver, trying to explain he was lost. Grandpapa would never pull a gun unless he intended to shoot and would only shoot to kill. I think when he reached Knoxville he was just tired of running. I brought his gun to New York with me after he died but the forces that be don't want anyone to keep her history, even if it's just a clogged twenty-two that no one in her right mind would even load.

Mr. and Mrs. Ector's rounded the trio of houses off. He always wore a stocking cap till he got tied back and would emerge very dapper. He was in love with the various automobiles he owned and had been seen by Grandmother and me on more than one occasion sweeping the snow from in front of his garage before he would back the car into the street. All summer he parked his car at the bottom of the hill and polished it twice a day and delighted in it. Grandmother would call across the porches to him, "Ector, you a fool 'bout that car, ain't cha?" And he would smile back. "Yes, ma'am." We were always polite with the Ectors because they had neither children nor grandchildren so there were no grounds for familiarity. I never knew Nellie Ector very well at all. It was rumored that she was a divorcée who had latched on to him, and to me she became all the tragic heroines I had read about, like the *Forever Amber* or *All This and Heaven Too* chicks, and I was awed but kept my distance. He was laughs, though. I don't know when it happened to the Ectors but Mr. White was the first to die. I considered myself a hotshot canasta player and I would play three-hand with Grandmother and Mrs. White and beat them. But I would drag the game on and on because it seemed so lonely next door when I could look through my bedroom window and see Mrs. White dressing for bed and not having to pull the shade anymore.

You always think the ones you love will always be there to love you. I went on to my grandfather's alma mater and got kicked out and would have disgraced the family but I had enough style for it not to be considered disgraceful. I could not/ did not adjust to the Fisk social life and it could not/did not adjust to my intellect, so Thanksgiving I rushed home to Grandmother's without the bitchy dean of women's permission and that dean put me on social probation. Which would have worked but I was very much in love and not about to consider her punishment as anything real I should deal with. And the funny thing about that Thanksgiving was that I knew everything would go down just as it did. But I still wouldn't have changed it because Grandmother and Grandpapa would have had dinner alone and I would have had dinner alone and the next Thanksgiving we wouldn't even have him and Grandmother and I would both be alone by ourselves, and the only change would have been that Fisk considered me an ideal student, which means little on a life scale. My grandparents were surprised to see me in my brown slacks and beige sweater nervously chain-smoking and being so glad to touch base again. And she, who knew everything, never once asked me about school. And he was old so I lied to him. And I went to Mount Zion Baptist with them that Sunday and saw he was going to die. He just had to. And I didn't want that. Because I didn't know what to do about Louvenia, who had never been alone in her life.

I left Sunday night and saw the dean Monday morning. She asked where I had been. I said home. She asked if I had permission. I said I didn't need her permission to go home. She said, "Miss Giovanni," in a way I've been hearing all my life, in a way I've heard so long I know I'm on the right track when I hear it, and shook her head. I was "released from the school" February 1 because my "attitudes did not fit those of a Fisk woman." Grandpapa died in April and I was glad it was warm because he hated the cold so badly. Mommy and I drove to Knoxville to the funeral with Chris—Gary's, my sister's, son—and I was brave and didn't cry and made decisions. And finally the time came and Anto left and Aunt Agnes left. And Mommy and Chris and I stayed on till finally Mommy had to go back to work. And Grandmother never once asked me about Fisk. We got up early Saturday morning and Grandmother made fried chicken for us. Nobody said we were leaving but we were. And we all walked down the hill to the car. And kissed. And I looked at her standing there so bravely trying not to think what I was trying not to feel. And I got in on the driver's side and looked at her standing there with her plaid apron and her hair in a bun, her feet hanging loosely out of her mules, sixty-three years old, waving good-bye to us, and for the first time having to go into 400 Mulvaney without John Brown Watson. I felt like an impotent dog. If I couldn't protect this magnificent woman, my grandmother, from loneliness, what could I ever do? I have always hated death. It is unacceptable to kill the young and distasteful to watch the old expire. And those in between our link commit the little murders all the time. There must be a better way. So Knoxville decided to become a model city and a new mall was built to replace the old marketplace and they were talking about convention centers and expressways. And Mulvaney Street was a part of it all. The progress.

And I looked out from a drugged sleep and saw the Smoky Mountains looming ahead. The Smokies are so called because the clouds hang low. We used to camp in them. And the bears would come into camp but if you didn't feed them they would go away. It's still a fact. And we prepared for the landing and I closed my eyes as I always do because landings and takeoffs are the most vulnerable times for a plane, and if I'm going to die I don't have to watch it coming. It is very hard to give up your body completely. But the older I get the more dependent I am on other people for my safety, so I closed my eyes and placed myself in harmony with the plane.

Tyson Field turned out to be Alcoa. Progress again. And the Alcoa Highway had been widened because the new governor was a football fan and had gotten stuck on the old highway while trying to make a University of Tennessee football game and had missed the kickoff. The next day they began widening the road. We were going to the University of Tennessee for the first speaking of the day. I would have preferred Knoxville College, which had graduated three Watsons and two Watson progeny. It was too funny being at UT speaking of Blackness because I remember when Joe Mack and I integrated the theater here to see *Li'l Abner*. And here an Afro Liberation Society was set up. Suddenly my body remembered we hadn't eaten in a couple of days and Harvey got me a quart of milk and the speaking went on. Then we left UT and headed for Black Knoxville.

Gay Street is to Knoxville what Fifth Avenue is to New York. Something special, yes? And it looked the same. But Vine Street, where I would sneak to the drugstore to buy *Screen Stories* and watch the men drink wine and play pool—all gone. A wide, clean military-looking highway has taken its place. Austin Homes is cordoned off. It looked like a big prison. The Gem Theatre is now some sort of nightclub and Mulvaney Street is gone. Completely wiped out. Assassinated along with the old people who made it live. I looked over and saw that the lady who used to cry "Hot fish! Good hot fish!" no longer had a Cal Johnson Park to come to and set up her stove in. Grandmother would not say, "Edith White! I think I'll send Gary for a sandwich. You want one?" Mrs. Abrum and her reverend husband from rural Tennessee wouldn't bring us any more goose eggs from across the street. And Leroy wouldn't chase his mother's boyfriend on Saturday night down the back alley anymore. All gone, not even to a major highway but to a cutoff of a cutoff. All the old people who died from lack of adjustment died for a cutoff of a cutoff.

And I remember our finding Grandmother the house on Linden Avenue and constantly reminding her it was every bit as good as if not better than the little ole house. A bigger backyard and no steps to climb. But I knew what Grandmother knew, what we all knew. There was no familiar smell in that house. No coal ashes from the fireplaces. Nowhere that you could touch and say, "Yolande threw her doll against this wall" or "Agnes fell down these steps." No smell or taste of biscuits Grandpapa had eaten with the Alaga syrup he loved so much. No Sunday chicken. No sound of "Lord, you children don't care a thing 'bout me after all I done for you," because Grandmother always had the need to feel mistreated. No spot in the back hall weighted down with lodge books and no corner where the old record player sat playing Billy Eckstine crooning "What's My Name?" till Grandmother said, "Lord! Any fool know his name!" No breeze on dreamy nights when Mommy would listen over and over again to "I Don't See Me in Your Eyes Anymore." No pain in my knuckles where Grandmother had rapped them because she was determined I would play the piano, and when that absolutely failed, no effort on Linden for us to learn the flowers. No echo of me being the only person in the history of the family to curse Grandmother out and no Grandpapa saying, "Oh, my," which was serious from him, "we can't have this." Linden Avenue was pretty but it had no life.

And I took Grandmother one summer to Lookout Mountain in Chattanooga and she would say I was the only grandchild who would take her riding. And that was the summer I noticed her left leg was shriveling. And she said I didn't have to hold her hand and I said I liked to. And I made ice cream the way Grandpapa used to do almost every Sunday. And I churned butter in the hand churner. And I knew and she knew that there was nothing I could do. "I just want to see you graduate," she said, and I didn't know she meant it. I graduated February 4. She died March 8.

And I went to Knoxville looking for Frankie and the Gem and Carter-Roberts or something and they were all gone. And 400 Mulvaney Street, like a majestic king dethroned, put naked in the streets to beg, stood there just a mere skeleton of itself. The cellar that had been so mysterious was now exposed. The fireplaces stood. And I saw the kitchen light hanging and the peach butter put up on the back porch and I wondered why they were still there. She was dead. And I heard the daily soap operas from the radio we had given her one birthday and saw the string beans cooking in the deep well and thought how odd, since there was no stove, and I wanted to ask how Babbi was doing since I hadn't heard or seen *Brighter Day* in so long but no one would show himself. The roses in the front yard were blooming and it seemed a disgrace. Probably the tomatoes came up that year. She always had fantastic luck with tomatoes. But I was just too tired to walk up the front steps to see. Edith White had died. Mr. Ector had died, I heard. Grandmother had died. The park was not yet gone but the trees looked naked and scared. The wind sang to them but they wouldn't smile. The playground where I had swung. The courts where I played my first game of tennis. The creek where our balls were lost. "Hot fish! Good hot fish!" The hill where the car speeding down almost hit me. Walking barefoot up the hill to the center to hear stories and my feet burning. All gone. Because progress is so necessary. General Electric says, "Our most important product." And I thought Ronald Reagan was cute.

I was sick throughout the funeral. I left Cincinnati driving Mommy, Gary, and Chris to Knoxville. From the moment my father had called my apartment I had been sick because I knew before they told me that she was dead. And she had promised to visit me on the tenth. Chris and I were going to drive down to get her since she didn't feel she could fly. And here it was the eighth. I had a letter from her at my house when I got back reaffirming our plans for her visit. I had a cold. And I ran the heat the entire trip despite the sun coming directly down on us. I couldn't get warm. And we stopped in Kentucky for country ham and I remembered how she used to hoard it from us and I couldn't eat. And I drove on. Gary was supposed to relieve me but she was crying too much. And the car was too hot and it was all so unnecessary. She died because she didn't know where she was and didn't like it. And there was no one there to give a touch or smell or feel and I think I should have been there. And at her funeral they said, "It is well," and I knew she knew it was. And it was so peaceful in Mount Zion Baptist Church that afternoon. And I hope when I die that it can be said of me all is well with my soul.

So they took me up what would have been Vine Street past what would have been Mulvaney, and I thought there may be a reason we lack a collective historical memory. And I was taken out to the beautiful homes on Brooks Road where we considered the folks "so swell, don't cha know." And I was exhausted but feeling quite high from being once again in a place where no matter what I belong. And Knoxville belongs to me. I was born there in Old Knoxville General and I am buried there with Louvenia. And as the time neared for me to speak I had no idea where I would start. I was nervous and afraid because I just wanted to quote Gwen Brooks and say, "This is the urgency—Live!" And they gave me a standing ovation and I wanted to say, "Thank you," but that was hardly sufficient. Mommy's old bridge club, Les Pas Si Bêtes, gave me beads, and that's the kind of thing that happens in small towns where people aren't afraid to be warm. And I looked out and saw Miss Delaney in her blue furs. And was reminded life continues. And I saw the young brothers and sisters who never even knew me or my family and I saw my grandmother's friends who shouldn't even have been out that late at night. And they had come to say *welcome home.* And I thought Tommy, my son, must know about this. He must know we come from somewhere. That we belong.

JERRY BAUER

GAIL
GODWIN

Gail Godwin (b. 1937) is a native North Carolinian on both her mother's and her father's side and was raised in Asheville. She claims Alabama as well, because her mother was visiting Krahenbuhl cousins in Birmingham when Gail was born. She is the author of nine novels and two collections of stories. *The Odd Woman* (1974), *Violet Clay* (1976), and *A Mother and Two Daughters* (1982) were nominated for National Book Awards; *A Southern Family* (1987), eleven weeks on the *New York Times* best-seller list, won the Janet Heidiger Kafka Award, presented by the University of Rochester, and the Thomas Wolfe Award, presented by the Lipinsky Foundation, Asheville, North Carolina. *Father Melancholy's Daughter* (1991), also a *New York Times* best-seller, was a Book-of-the-Month Club main selection and won the 1991 Alabama Librarians Award. She is a Guggenheim Fellow and received an Award in Literature from the American Academy of Arts and Letters. Godwin is an alumna of Peace College in Raleigh, North Carolina, and the University of North Carolina at Chapel Hill (B.A. in journalism); she holds a doctorate in modern letters from the University of Iowa and has taught at the Iowa Writers' Workshop as well as at Vassar and Columbia University. Her books have been translated into eleven languages. Her most recent novel was *The Good Husband* (1994), and she is completing a sequel to *Father Melancholy's Daughter,* which is titled *An Evening Gone.*

* * *

Uncle Orphy

Every few weeks, my widowed grandmother would sigh wistfully and say to my mother and me, "I feel like going out to see Uncle."

"Uncle" was her older brother, Orpha Rogers. She'd had a younger brother, Furman, but he was killed by a train when he was twenty-five. I called Uncle "Uncle Orphy." My mother, who liked to concoct naughty names for those close to her, called him "Uncle Orful," not to his face, of course.

"Out," where Uncle Orphy lived, was about as far as you could get from Asheville without being somewhere else altogether—or so it seemed then. Actually it was only about a thirty-minute drive. During this drive, my grandmother would elaborate on the fallen fortunes of herself and her sister Ida and her brother Orphy due to the fact that their widowed father, Frank Rogers, had married again and had a second set of children, to whom he left everything in his will. My grandmother called these children "the steps." In the mid-1800s the Rogerses had been tobacco planters and owned a great deal of land, but now even the family homestead had been sold off by Frank's grasping widow and been turned into a horrible, sprawling, tacky development. Ida had married and divorced, done fancy needlework for the Vanderbilts in Biltmore for a while, then taken her youngest daughter and gone to live in Florida; Edna, my grandmother, had married Thomas Krahenbuhl, a second-generation Swiss whose job as general foreman on the Southern Railway took her out of the mountains for much of their married life; Orpha was the only one who had stuck at home in Buncombe County, where Rogerses had always lived as far back as we could trace, which was to Orpha and Edna's great-grandfather Robert Rogers, who was born at the end of the eighteenth century.

After a prolonged drive, the mountain roads narrowing from pavement to gravel to dirt, the craggy pastures on either side tilting so alarmingly skyward that I couldn't understand how the poor cows kept their balance while they ate, there we would be at the bottom of Uncle's steps.

There were so many steps that you couldn't even see the log house at the top, where behind the screen door Aunt Fanny's long, skull-thin face would already have materialized at the first sound of our car. Since I was the only one who didn't have to stop on all those stairs for breath, I was always the first to see this rather spectral welcome floating at us from behind the screen door.

Inside was cool and somewhat dark; in winter, there would be a fire in the woodstove. There was a framed picture I liked over the sofa, some old magazine illustration: I think it was of a pretty young woman in a thin white dress climbing down (or up) a steep cliff in the moonlight, but maybe it wasn't. The house smelled of roasting meats and stewed fruits and beans and cornbread if we were there for a meal, and of freshly baked cake and biscuits if we could only stay for tea. Fanny made fresh biscuits three times a day, my grandmother said, because Orpha never could stand eating a cold biscuit. I knew I must "sit still" for some family gossip and answer a few questions about myself; then, until summoned to Fanny's groaning table, I would be released to the outdoors where I could climb the chinaberry tree with branches low enough for me, or go and sit in the outhouse, which fascinated me with its two holes in the long wooden seat and its stack of magazines and the dank, woodsy smell overpowered by the strong odor of Pine-Sol.

Uncle sat in his chair, waiting for us. He had a fleshless face like his wife and a long, arched, bony nose exactly like my grandmother's. One of his blue eyes had no pupil ("A nail flew up and put it out," he told me matter-of-factly), and I tried not to stare at its blank pale center. In earlier years, he always stood up and allowed his sister and niece to hug and kiss him, then bent down and, with a long-suffering, good-humored, "*Ohhhh,* me," hugged his grandniece. He smelled at various times of fertilizer, leather, wet animal pelts, fresh milk, starch, and Octagon soap. In later years he remained seated, his knobbly hand resting patriarchally on top of his hickory cane, and, uttering the same "*Ohhhh,* me," allowed us each in turn to bend down and plant kisses in his sparse white hair.

He referred to himself always as O.M. Rogers and signed his letters to us that way: "Hope I see you again sometime. Buy you a remembrance with this little green paper. your uncle, OMR."

He wrote this to me inside a "Hello There!" greeting card when he was ninety-three and I was in my thirties. The date was March 23, 1975; he would live three more years. It wasn't my birthday; perhaps I had been to see him on a recent visit to Asheville and he had enjoyed me. I used to make him laugh, not always intentionally. Once I entered his house and he took one look at me, said "*Ohhhh,* me," and began to chuckle til he held his sides. It was my new haircut, which, I realize in retrospect, must have made me resemble a frizzled mushroom. In one of my "serious" phases, he leaned forward in his chair and inquired anxiously, "Do you ever let *little things* bother you?" Surprised and rather pleased by what I thought for him was a personal question, I confided at once, "I'm afraid I do, Uncle Orphy."

"Then . . . ," he paused for effect, "don't ever sleep in the same room with a mosquito." He doubled over in soundless laughter.

On one of my last visits to him—now I, too, had to pause and catch my breath halfway up those Himalayan steps—I got up the nerve to ask him what the "M" in his name stood for. Nobody knew or would tell me.

"Montraville," he said, shaking his head. "Isn't that awful? I never tell people. I think it was something my mother found in a book."

He eschewed alcohol and tobacco. "After Mother and Fanny died," my mother writes in her unfinished autobiography, "I kept up my visits to Uncle and took him my Christmas tree cookies (which I'm sure he would not have touched if he had known the icing was made with rum or brandy); at Easter I took him flowers and he always said I shouldn't have spent my money on him."

But in a lengthy newspaper tribute written about him on his ninety-sixth birthday ("A Testimony to Good Living"), he contradicts his daughter Helen, who has just told *Asheville Citizen* columnist Bob Terrell that her daddy never smoked or drank.

"Yes, I did. I smoked once. I rolled a cigar out of tobacco leaf and smoked it. There was a wagon sitting there and first thing I knew, that wagon started going round and round. I dove under it and when I sobered up I come out. I drank one time, too. When beer come out, I got two bottles and put 'em in the icebox. When they got cold, I opened one up, took two sups, and thought I'd never tasted anything that bad. I poured the rest of it out and gave the other bottle away."

There were other stories in the tribute, stories I vaguely remembered, or had forgotten parts of, from his own telling. Bob Terrell had been a sharp listener, and I was grateful to him for keeping the language the way my great-uncle would have spoken it; Terrell also caught the deadpan quality of my uncle's narratives, and it was like hearing Uncle Orphy speak when I was at last old enough to pay full attention.

There was his story of Asheville's Great Flood of 1916, which washed away his store at the east end of Craggy Bridge.

"That flood was something! I was sitting here on my front porch and a man came by from [Craggy Bridge]. I asked him, 'How's the river over there?' and he said, 'Pretty bad. Rogers Store just washed away.' I said, 'I better go see.' Sure enough, it was gone. People told me it just washed loose and floated away. Down the river a ways it hit a tree and turned upside down and all the goods come out of it and floated away. There was a lot of goods in that store."

A young man Orpha and Fanny had raised like a son waded into the water and got into the upside down store and managed to get the papers and deeds out of the safe. "That was a huge safe. We found it later buried in the sand down the river bottom. We poked around with a steel rod till we found it, but when I hooked a team of mules to it and tried to pull it out, they pulled the knob off and ruined it."

He loved to ride horses, and when I was a little girl, he put me astride an enormous pig and let me ride it. In the Terrell piece there was also the story about the one time he rode a motorcycle. He was so exhilarated by the experience, he zipped by his house and told Fanny to hop on. "We headed up this dirt road and it was pretty bumpy. I had to pay attention to where I was going, and when I looked back, Mother wasn't there. I turned around and went back down the road and found her. She'd bounced off, but luckily wasn't hurt."

He served as a deputy under three sheriffs. One day the sheriff called and told him two escaped prisoners were headed his way toward the bridge. One of these was one-armed and had a coat hanging over that shoulder. Orpha got to the bridge just in time to see two strange men coming from the other side, and one of them had a coat hanging off his shoulder.

"I slapped him on that side and he didn't have an arm, so I told them they were under arrest. The other one grabbed my pistol and took off, but I held onto the one-armed man and took him in. I heard later that the other one went to New York, got with another partner, and went to rob a post office. They tied up the clerk and laid my pistol on a shelf while they gathered up what they wanted. The clerk worked his way loose, got my pistol, and killed both of 'em. Took me three months to get my pistol back."

Orpha and Fanny, like true mountain people, were a hospitable couple. Anyone who showed up close to mealtime, even a stranger, was invited to stay for a meal. Their daughter Helen told my mother that during Fanny's last days in the nursing home, she hallucinated that her house was full of people and said to Helen they must hurry and get enough food prepared for all these people and make up beds for them.

At Fanny's funeral, my mother writes in the autobiography she didn't live to finish, Orpha's half-niece, daughter of one of the "steps," a beautician who always insisted she was "really more of a Rogers than the other side," grabbed his arm ahead of his own daughters and walked him up the aisle. Mother reports, "I heard him say to her what I thought at the time was 'Don't leave me,' but it wasn't that at all, I later learned. It was 'Don't *lead* me.' After the funeral, I took [the half-niece] back to the beauty shop and went on home. She called me from time to time and I would call her. Once she said she had a new bathing suit and it was prettier than any dress she had ever had. 'I want to be buried in that bathing suit,' she told me. But she wasn't."

Over the decades of my writing life, I have made emanations of people close to me, many of whose blood I share, rather like a sorcerer making phantoms out of pieces of hair and dust and spit and incantations—and the sorcerer's own needs of the moment.

A mere wisp of Uncle Orphy's spirit blew through *The Odd Woman* in affectionate cameo references to Edith's strong country brother, "Iz."

He materializes for several significant appearances as "Uncle Osgood" in *A*

Mother and Two Daughters. He's the family member from the country who, by revealing a painful secret about himself, convinces Leonard Strickland to stick to his duties at home in the mountains rather than go to Spain to fight in the Civil War. He's the old uncle from the country who embarrasses Leonard's daughter Lydia at the crafts fair with his quaint hillbilly way of talking and his disfigured nose. (I took the nose from an old man I once saw carving birds on Okracoke Island; something about his unruffled just-*thereness* must have reminded me of Uncle Orphy.) Uncle Osgood is the one who later sends Leonard's older daughter, Cate, a carved turtle when she's at a low point in her middle age, and it is to Cate that he leaves his little house on the top of an "impossible" hill deep in the Carolina mountains when she reaches the age where she needs a place to call her own. "Do you ever let *little things* bother you?" he once asks Cate, and when she walks into the trap he replies, "Then don't sleep in the same room with a mosquito," and doubles over with his joke.

Writing about Uncle Osgood and remembering Uncle Orphy marked the beginning of my slow climb back into the steep hills of the spiritual terrain of my ancestors, a country where fate and hardship are spoken of matter-of-factly, if not with humor, and passed on to others not only for edification but to entertain them with a good story. Osgood-land is a state of mind in which you make do with what you have and don't take more than you need (I was shocked to learn from the Terrell article that Uncle Orphy's tiny house sat in the middle of thirty-six acres!), and strangers are always welcome to put their feet under your table and share what you have. Osgood-and-Orphy-land is a place of independence ("Don't lead me"), but it's also a place where you never take yourself too seriously, even when you're alone in the room with a mosquito.

The real man with his unusual name sticks with me, and I'm slowly growing into his legacy. I think of him when my Heavenly Blues bloom, still only a few a day, in late summer. His tumbled in astonishing profusion over a single sunny lamppost in the backyard: a summer after summer miracle from a little packet of seeds hardly larger than grains of pepper. Yet until a few years ago, I never could spare the time to buy the packet or plant the seeds.

I have not been able to find the source of the name Orpha—though there's a female Or*pah* in the Book of Ruth who, interestingly enough, submits to her mother-in-law Naomi's wishes and remains in her homeland, while the other daughter-in-law, Ruth, insists on leaving Moab with Naomi. If Orpha *is* named for Orpah, how prescient of his mother to know at his birth he'd be the one to stick at home. I have yet to find any reference, fictional or otherwise, to a Montraville, but shall continue to look.

ELLESA
CLAY
HIGH

Ellesa Clay High was born in 1948 and raised on the suburban edge of Louisville, Kentucky, but has lived her adult life in Appalachia. She received her Ph.D. from Ohio University in 1981 and has since taught creative writing, Appalachian literature, and American Indian literature in the English Department at West Virginia University. High's fiction, nonfiction, poetry, and scholarly work have appeared in many magazines and anthologies over the years, and she has received numerous awards, including an Andrew W. Mellon Foundation Award and a James Still Fellowship in Appalachian Studies. Her best-known work, *Past Titan Rock* (1984), provides a unique portrait of mountain life in the Red River Gorge of Kentucky and received the Appalachian Award in 1983. Today High has "hunkered down" on an old farm in Preston County, West Virginia, with her son and wolfdogs. For the last several years, she has been listening to, collecting, and writing her own material about the Eastern Woodland tribes of Appalachia. The essay included in this volume is part of an ongoing writing project she has tentatively titled *Wolf Trail Spring*.

* * *

The Standing People

Appalachia

Direction:	West
element:	water
color:	black
animal:	black bear
medicine:	roots
knowledge:	what can be learned in the Cave
strengths:	perseverance, sacrifice, humility; honoring of tradition and ceremony; respect for elders; realizing the importance of dreams; ability to dream alone; facing the unknown, especially the Darkness within; reflection, as in pools; accessing the power of silence; closeness to the female energy of earth and water; respect for the struggle of others; commitment to and defense of a higher order of right and wrong than may be dictated by outside forces; love for the Creator; understanding of death; groundedness
weaknesses:	the same, imbalanced

I live in a place of sacred white deer and slag heaps. My son and I drink from a spring pure and forthcoming as dawn, which downhill joins the Cheat River, one of the ten most endangered streams in the nation. A wolf spirit guided me here, and together we protect a spot I call Wolf Trail Spring. Who I am, what has influenced me, and where I'm going might best be understood by a walk around this farm. Here, I'll unlock the gate.

Of course, we might just define this place as the tax assessor and real estate agent have:

85+ acres, with chestnut stumps marking boundaries (100 acres computer estimate), near Parker's Run, Pleasant District, Preston County, West Virginia. Mineral rights—negligible. No gas found. House, built circa 1880, empty for 30 years. No running water or central heat. Electricity and telephone service available. Unusable except for hunter's camp. Barn more valuable, though it too is falling down. Several other outbuildings, including cut-stone milk house built circa 1785–1825. Salvage value only. Mature timber, ready for harvest. High level field in back—potential air strip. Needs work.

This type of appraisal, though, illustrates why much of West Virginia, and Appalachia in general, remains unknown, lost, unacknowledged, misinterpreted—the wellsprings of its meaning secret.

So let's you and I roam around for a while, that is if you don't mind the soft female rain that can last for days here—something we share with Seattle and other places. There, ocean moisture hitting the mountains over time created a northern rain forest, the old-growth giants of the Pacific Northwest. Similarly, America's prevailing winds again "picked up steam" crossing the Great Plains, then dumped their load on the Appalachians, conditions that fostered the greatest hardwood forest on earth. This shimmering green blanket stretched from Maine to Georgia, encompassed West Virginia, and supported untold diversity of plants and animals as well as uncounted tribes of indigenous peoples. By the 1920s, most had been clear-cut away.

Then these mountains cleansed themselves with fire and water. The left-behind tree bones tindered and ignited themselves with the sparks plentifully found around stream-driven logging equipment. Much of the ten million acres timbered in West Virginia burned, and the rising smoke was prayer made visible from the earth. God's answer was flood. With nothing to hold it to the ridges, the soil created by trees over thousands of years eroded away in a few seasons, choking the streams with silt and industrial pollutants from logging and mining. At the turn of the century, the Cheat and its tributaries were "dead." The river spirits had buried themselves, for nothing could live in the tangerine mire flowing over them. The mighty land animals left too or were destroyed. My brother, the wolf, was last seen in West Virginia in 1903, when Randolf County hunters shot the only one they could find.

The biggest tree recorded in West Virginia was felled in 1913 not far from here, down close to Lead Mine in Tucker County. That single white oak was so strong, it had to be split apart with dynamite, and its body filled an entire train. To me, this farm really begins with that big oak over there I call the Wolf Tree. See it? It's only a third the size of the famous Lead Mine tree, but it's still impressive—twelve feet in circumference and four feet in diameter at the level of our shoulders. Beyond it, distance bends and wavers in strange ways. Can you feel how time thickens and thins around its trunk? Sit here in the mist for a while and you will never get to the house.

The Cherokee, named "mountaineers of the South" by James Mooney in 1900, tell how sin and disease originated in the world. In the beginning, all things lived in harmony and could speak to one another. But as they multiplied, the humans especially began crowding the others, stealing territory and making weapons to kill those in their way. Finally, the animals had had enough. Led by the bears, they met in council and in retaliation sent so many diseases to attack the people that no one would survive. The plants, though, had been nourished and befriended by humans. They could not stop the diseases the animals were sending, but they could supply cures for them. Thus, every plant provides a remedy for us, or a lesson, if only we can discover it.

And I see in your eyes you are thinking, "That's all fine and good, but what does this have to do with writing?" Sit back under the shelter of this Wolf Tree and I'll tell you another story.

Although I've lived my adult life in Appalachia, I was born and raised almost fifty years ago on the gnawing, suburban edge of Louisville, Kentucky. It was a good place for a while—mostly farmland and forest. And I was doubly blessed by having parents who treasured family above all else, and who understood that a child needs time alone in the woods with the extended companionship of animals and plants. I can still say today that my father was the best man I've ever known. My mother was a teacher and a poet, who grew verse as abundantly as the beans she raised in her garden and fed us with in summer, and whose canned tomatoes lasted through the winter. Even today in her eighties, almost blind, and paralyzed in a nursing home, she lives a writer's life—pulling poetry from herself past my father's death, past the pain for which there seems no cure, past the loss of her physical strength. Certainly I've been privileged to learn from many writers from many ages. But today I think that as great as my human teachers have been, what I know best about writing I learned early and from teachers without words as we think of them.

As a child, I had four great "Standing People" for teachers. A weatherworn osage tree with a fox den at its base provided its own kind of day-care center—its bent down branches framed hideouts, its roots made cradles and cubbyholes, and its jagged sticks proved excellent as war clubs, particularly against my brothers. Our two horses loved to munch its bitter green fruit, which we lobbed into their pasture like crinkly hardballs. How my pony could transform osage oranges and poison ivy into tasty snacks has remained a mystery to me. Grandmother Osage gave me a place where my imagination could play and grow in safety, and for this I thank her.

Two teachers used water for instruction. A hemlock by the creek pooled silence for me. I called it a "luxury place," and indeed it was. This tree brought water and wind together, sunlight and whispers, gleaming conversations of minnows and crawdads at its feet, hawk and crow sometimes peering from its top. One gusty day I finally climbed it. Swaying for hours, I too became green-needled and barked. For this, Brother Hemlock, I thank you, for you helped me understand metaphor and the importance of what is not said.

A sycamore, on the other hand, played music with the stream, its roots like harp strings drawn from bank to bank, water falling into lullabies with the sun, marches and overtures with the rain. In winter, its melody turned solid with ice, building tiny, trickled mansions there, still mossed and rainbow-pillared in the January thaw. I would sit and listen until my body numbed away, as I learned of rhythm, line, and song from the sycamore, its white speckled body hymned sky-ward, lightning trunked from creek to cloud—its seedballs many worlds orbiting around it. A Kentucky Odin might have hung upside down from its branches, discerning runes in the creeks' drifts and eddies.

Then an elm, a stern uncle I now see, crashed me back to earth when I was eight, preaching parables in gravity and falling from grace. My brothers and I had built a crude tree house in its branches. The first time we climbed up, we dangled a rope to the ground, and sat for a moment, staring after it. Then both my broth-ers turned and dared me to go down it first. I did, and fell fifteen feet head first into blackness. So I learned of hands too weak to hold on, of grieving parents and sirens of pain, of ruptured spleen and concussion. I learned that hours may clot but they will not turn back, that actions have consequences which grow in rings. Today I thank the elm. He taught me a lasting lesson about abstraction I've since used in writing—if you wish to take your readers to ethereal thematic heights, you'd better ground them first in the concrete details of the world.

The elm also forced me through a doorway to a place of spirit. I remember coma as a gray peace, a floating continent of contentment. Distant voices some-times mumbled at the corners, reminding me of something I'd forgotten, but not for long. After a few days, somehow I came back, and that was fine too, I would later believe. But after months in and out of the hospital, I seemed different from the children around me, few who were friendly anymore. I thought about why that was, and about the goodness of Death I'd glimpsed, and about why God had returned me.

I began trying my hand at writing, mostly poetry whose metaphors might capture the visions and waking dreams, the unseen messengers and spirit travel, nature shape-shifting all about me—the simple glory of just being alive. It was then the powerful animal guides of my life began coming, most of which I rarely, if ever, discuss. One, though, has helped me directly with writing, and I'll share him with you.

I had forgotten how one summer when I was twelve, a raven flew into our yard and stayed with us for four days, gobbling fruit in the Queen Anne cherry tree next to the house. Each morning he croaked and called until I walked out-side, and then he followed me from porch to garden, from patio to stable, down across the fields and back—floating close above me and crying in a language I could almost understand. Listening and smiling, my mother guessed that he'd been the pet of some farmer, who'd split his tongue and tried to teach him to talk. But why was he shadowing me? To that question, she didn't even speculate. One silent morning he was gone, and over time my memory of him also faded into the recesses of childhood.

Until 1990, three decades later. In a writers' workshop, I was asked to close my eyes and visualize my creative self, and from out of nowhere he flapped, carbuncular and cawing, definitely worse for the wear. He landed on my shoulder and this time I understood him, as he pecked at my ear and chuckled, "I'm your creative spirit, and I will never leave you."

And I opened my eyes and cried hard minutes in front of twenty people. My marriage was failing, I had written nothing for months, and deep inside I felt like a worthless rubble of a woman. Now I knew that was wrong. And I wept—not only for joy but also in shame at not recognizing, having faith in, or taking full responsibility for the gifts I'd been given in this world.

About the same time the raven first sailed into my life, my mother handed me a strand of beads, smooth and variously colored as maize, and said, "These were my baby beads, and my mother's, and her mother's, and probably her mother's—they're older than memory. I want you to have them." Then nothing more was spoken and their significance was lost, again for almost thirty years, when the Cherokee roots of our family tree were acknowledged with the European ones. I already was teaching American Indian literature at the university when my godmother told me, the last time I saw her before she died, of our native bloodline. The beads had been this ancestor's, whose family had moved from northern Georgia around the time of the Trail of Tears and had settled in southern Indiana. The hills there were much like home, and these Cherokee found a haven around Corydon, which later, I've been told, became a stop for runaway slaves on the Underground Railroad. When I asked my mother why she had never told us about this part of our heritage, she merely said she hadn't found it "interesting" and thus not worth mentioning. But for me, something deeply felt from childhood, yet not understood, had been named.

Long before that, the Standing People of my youth were gone. In the late 1950s, the "developers" had come, and I had watched my teachers and sacred friends bulldozed down without thought, much less prayer or even enough respect to make something useful from their bodies. Evidently, such concepts as "ecology" and "environmental awareness" had not yet penetrated the general consciousness. I remember walking around one night as a child, seeing the wrecked trees burning in great heaps, their wisdom and light flickering in the dark, embers releasing themselves to the stars.

You see how I love to talk! We're not far from the gate, and it's still almost a half mile to the house. Over there are twenty-five acres of trees called the Coal Bank Woods because of the shallow vein of coal that chunks out of the ground. But it is lack of such minerals that has kept this farm from being stripped, as is often the case here. And with the timber market booming again, the trees all around are coming down—some afternoons this valley sounds like a big dentist's office, drills whining, saws echoing, setting my teeth on edge. Few seem to recall the slash-and-burn destruction that happened here less than one hundred years ago, the smoky evidence of which could have been viewed from outer space. Once again, multinational corporations are setting up shop, pulp mill camps are being built, and local people remain hungry. And I have to ask, what lessons from the past will be put to use now? Will we look seven generations ahead, as eastern woodlands cultures have for thousands of years?

At Wolf Trail Spring, a community of Standing People remains—red oak and white, tulip poplar, sassafras, wild cherry, black walnut and hickory, elm and hemlock and service. That line of sugar maples gathers and sweetens one of the many springs blessing this place, and for as long as I'm here, there'll be no Trail of Tears for these friends or the great clans of plants they shelter. We need each other, and they are teaching me still.

You'll have to come again and stay much longer. Then I'll show you the white pines that protect the house and purify the air. We'll visit some of the great medicine helpers, *Atalikuli* or ginseng, yellow root, and *U"le Ukilti* or Indian Physic. You can meet Issac (a.k.a. Eagle Boy) the chestnut pony, Kiva and Shaman the wolfdogs, the cats and cattle. *Awi Usdi* or Little Deer, the Cherokee Deer Spirit, protects his kinsmen in these northern hollows, and wild turkeys, ascetic and wizened as church deacons, stroll processionals through the morning fog. The happiest water in the world is here, friends tell me. And the Wind Hole and the Warrior's Path. And perhaps now you see that since we came through the gate, we've talked of nothing but writing as I've come to understand it.

In *Past Titan Rock,* my book on the Red River Gorge of Kentucky, I asked, "Why did I feel I knew this place when I first arrived? What ties me here now? Why does most truth worth knowing always seem just beyond reach?" And a man whom I pictured as a kind of "Spirit of the Gorge," replied, "Because of the way you think and see." Then he showed me a mountain, white with the past.

I now know that from the beginning of my life, my Cherokee heritage was somehow mysteriously guiding me, and what it taught me through the Standing People of my childhood took me to the Red River Gorge. And what I learned from staying there and writing about that place brought me to Wolf Trail Spring, one of the great, ongoing adventures of my life. But that is for another day and another story.

Just remember that the Lenape or Delaware people called these mountains *Allickewany* or Allegheny—"the place of the footprint" in eternal snow or "he is leaving and may never return." Then you'll be on your way back here.

LISA
KOGER

Lisa Koger was born in 1953 in Elyria, Ohio, and raised in Gilmer County, West Virginia. A former newspaper reporter, she received a B.S.W. from West Virginia University, a master's degree in journalism from the University of Tennessee, and an M.F.A. from the Iowa Writers' Workshop at the University of Iowa. She is the recipient of an Iowa Teaching/Writing Fellowship, a National Writer's Voice Project residency, two Kentucky Arts Council Professional Assistance Awards, a Kentucky Foundation for Women Writing Grant, and the 1989 James Michener Award. She has taught creative writing at the University of Iowa, the Graduate Studies Center in Rock Island, Illinois, Mississippi State University, and at various summer workshops. Her first nationally published story, "The June Woman," appeared in *Seventeen* magazine as a summer novelette in June 1985. Her first collection of short stories, *Farlanburg Stories,* was published in 1990 by W.W. Norton. Koger has published work in *Ploughshares, New York Times Book Review, Atlanta Journal/Constitution, American Voice, Chattahoochee Review, Highlights,* and other newspapers, magazines, and anthologies. She currently lives in Somerset, Kentucky, with her husband and two children and is working on a novel.

*   *   *

Writing in the Smokehouse

When I was a young girl growing up on Ellis Fork of Tanner Creek in Gilmer County, West Virginia, our hills were alive not with the sound of music but, literally, with multiflora rose. The shrub had been touted by farm magazines and county agents as modern agriculture's answer to the worrisome cost of maintaining fences. "Horse High, Hog Tight, Bull Strong!" advertisements had said, and soil conservation representatives had promised that a landowner who situated the plant next to an existing fence would be able to spend an extra day fishing instead of replacing rotten posts.

What no one had known—or what they'd neglected to mention—was multiflora rose's propensity to spread. Plant it, and in no time at all you have yourself a fence. Two years later, you have nothing *but* a fence. Go for a stroll, lose your direction, and you wind up wandering for years in a thirty-acre jungle that used to be prime pasture.

There is a similarity, I think, between the spread of multiflora rose and the effect of writing on a life. What at first seems an innocent enough undertaking and one easily confined to a designated plot, turns out to be invasive, no respecter of boundaries. That first sketch loosens the soil for a weak story, which propagates, producing other weak stories, which slyly meander and thicken into less weak stories, which grow stronger and longer and tangly like novels. The slightest word of encouragement—from anyone—is as potent as a year's supply of Miracle-Gro, and before you can say "bush hog," you're ensnared.

I never wanted to "be a writer," but as far back as I can remember, I've liked to write. Thieves don't set out to be thieves, either. They acquire that title because they like to steal. At one brief point I thought I wanted to be an interior decorator. The notion blossomed in April during my senior year in high school but was short-lived, lasting only two weeks. My interest in interior decorating was a sign of senior panic brought on by the fact that all my classmates had definite plans. Some were headed for careers as teachers, accountants, and veterinarians; others were headed down the aisle. Even those who had distinguished themselves during the preceding twelve years by breaking noses or ripping commodes from the walls in the school bathrooms had found a home with The Few, The Proud, The Brave. They beat their chests in the lunchroom, crushed their milk cartons, and counted (as best they could) the days until they could officially call themselves Marines.

Not wanting to appear immature or directionless, I leafed through a career-choice booklet in the library and selected a future for myself. I've never regretted that my selection did not pan out. "That's good," says my mother. "Judging by the decor of the dumps you've lived in since you've been an adult, rare is the decorating school that would've had you."

Recently, I wrote a short essay for my mother's high school alumni newsletter. Some years back, when I was a freshman in college, her alumni association generously awarded me a partial scholarship, and I have felt indebted to them since. After I submitted the essay, the alumni president called my mother and said they wanted to give me a little something as a token of their appreciation for my most recent efforts. I was afraid it was going to be another scholarship. "We'd like to give her something useful," the woman said. "Perhaps something for her apartment." When she inquired about my decorating scheme and furniture—Early American? Queen Anne? French Provincial?—my mother thought a moment and said, "None of those. I'd say it's more like Early Grapes of Wrath."

In short, my career as an interior decorator ended before it started. These days, I earn what little money I make from teaching and writing. But I feel happier, better grounded, knowing that I am really a circuit-riding preacher's great-granddaughter turned loose on the world and a temporarily unemployed newspaper reporter who gains an inordinate and heathenish amount of satisfaction from making up stories or, as my great-grandfather would have put it, telling lies. As for the teaching and writing, I tell myself daily (and have for the past ten years) that I won't be in either business long. I am just an honest woman trying to earn a living until I can make it big as a waitress at some swanky place like Holiday Inn.

Nor am I especially comfortable talking about writing. I have come to think of the process of writing as being analogous to the cartoons in which Wile E. Coyote, pursuing Road Runner, dashes over the edge of a cliff, then hovers for a few seconds in midair. As long as the coyote is unaware of his predicament, he's safe. It's looking down that gets him into trouble. I think the same can be said of too much talking about the hows and whys of one's own work.

Also, it seems to me that by talking about writing, I'm being dishonest, implying that I know something when I really do not. I have a friend who has an undergraduate degree in sociology who would swear I feel that way because of my blue-collar background. "As a product of your early environment, you are simply unable to admit you are capable of knowing anything," he would say. He is intrigued by dwarfs, polio survivors, and people from blue-collar backgrounds, and he makes an effort to invite specimens from all three categories to his parties whenever he can.

I have another friend, a fellow journalist, who had an unhappy childhood— a discovery she made while working on a master's in psychology. She would tell me that my reluctance to talk about writing has its roots in the fact that I'm female and have spent too many years in the male-dominated, rural semi-South. I have been robbed of any feelings of self-confidence, she would say, reared by adults who themselves were brought up to believe in M&M for women (M&M standing for Meekness and Modesty), rural America's version of S&M.

Both theories are interesting, but I suspect my reluctance is not nearly so complicated. I think it's hard for me to talk about writing simply because the more I write, the more difficult and inexplicable writing is. Which is not to say that, through reading and spending an unhealthy amount of time on university campuses, I haven't acquired a certain familiarity with the elements of fiction (character, plot, point of view, setting, dialogue, etc.) and gained a passable understanding of how those elements work together in a short story or novel. Any diligent dog can be taught such tricks. But I have no magic formula that will guarantee success or make the work any easier, and some part of me thinks that with as much money as I've forked over for tuition and as much time as I've spent taking literature and writing classes, I ought to.

Yet, my experience with writing has taught me just the opposite: there are no formulas, magic or otherwise, no literary shortcuts through the woods to Grandma's house. Understanding a little about the elements of fiction—the difference between round and flat characters, the distinction between a series of unrelated events and a plot—is important, but with good writing the whole is always more than the sum of the parts. And I have learned that trying to be a better writer by only reading essays about writing is a little like trying to be a good cook by saving recipes from *Southern Living*. After a while, there's no substitute for tucking your hair behind your ears and heading for the kitchen. A little dab of this. A pinch or two of that.

So why write about writing at all? I am only one voice, one opinion, but I'd like to think that by agreeing to write this essay, I'm not only sharing a part of my life but taking a stand on issues that are important to me.

I'd like to think I'm writing for those who write for only one reason—because there are few acts on earth that feel as if they matter as much. I'm convinced that writing has nothing to do with dressing a certain way, living in a certain place, or trying to cultivate the "right" friends. I'm writing for those who already know that what's imagined is important but in the long run never quite as important as what is real—a sick cow, a colicky baby, a troubled friend.

I'm writing *not* for those who want to "be writers" so they can be rich and famous and loved, but for those who might be confused about which fork to use if they were rich, for those who are content to let movie stars be famous, and for those who already know (because their grandma or mother or husband or child told them) that they are loved. It's not a matter of saying that one set of motivations is more legitimate or worthy than another but more a matter of knowing my own heart.

Finally, I'd like to think I'm writing for those who know that all essays about writing are, to some extent, irrelevant. What ultimately matters is not the writer or his background—only his work. At the same time, I suspect that trying to separate a writer's work from his background is a little like trying to separate a turtle from its shell. I know that's true in my case. Home—the people and the place—has been extremely important to, and to some extent responsible for, my work. Remove home and its influence from my back, and I will have lost not just shelter but an essential part of me.

I grew up in a community where people had meat on their bones, physically and spiritually. As a reader I like fiction with heft and heart rather than fiction that is fashionably thin. I like "necessary" fiction, stories that feel as if they were born because they had to be born, to give life to a character who had begun to kick and thrash about because he knew when his incubation period was up. I am put off by stories that are born to showcase "style"—perfectly crafted, soulless stories that when held up by the heels and smacked, will breathe but, other than that, have nothing in common with the living. Knowing what I like as a reader is one thing; writing that way is another.

I also like a strong sense of place in fiction. I want to know where people live. I want to feel that a character's personality, his behavior, and the choices he makes are, to some extent, the result of where he finds himself geographically and of where he has been. In my own life I'm drawn to people who feel strongly about place. It doesn't matter whether that place is as large as Philadelphia or as small as Scooba, Mississippi. It's the size of the feeling for place that counts.

I grew up in a family that valued place. We valued it so much that we could not bear to take vacations that would necessitate traveling more than fifteen miles from home. We didn't choose that distance arbitrarily. Fifteen miles was the maximum distance we figured we could walk in a single day in case homesickness struck, our car broke down, and we craved to spend the night under handsewn quilts in our own cozy rooms.

We valued place so much that our babies held off being born and our old ones refused to die unless they had assurance, in writing, that they were doing it on family-owned land. I left that land a long time ago, I'm told, but I have no recollection of leaving. Like a magician, I have performed a clever trick; my physical absence has fooled them. Some part of me has been there all along, a disembodied spirit, invisible and content amongst them. That contented side of me, the side that needs to be home to feel grounded, has enabled the rambunctious rest of me to go off and explore other places. Florida, Georgia, Tennessee, Indiana, Alabama, Kentucky, Iowa, Mississippi. I have lived in all those states, but I've only had one home.

I spent the first twenty years of my life in a remote section of West Virginia, a state many newspapers and magazines refer to as "educationally disadvantaged" and "economically deprived." Like most kids, I didn't think of my corner of the world in terms of advantages or disadvantages. Home was a neutral place, a neither this nor that place. Home felt good because it was home, the only place I'd ever been. It took several years of college and a few thousand dollars in tuition to alert me to the fact that I should've grown up feeling defective and defeated. I have tried on numerous occasions to dredge up such depressing feelings but to no avail.

My father worked as a welder on an assembly line for General Motors in Cleveland, Ohio. He was a first-rate welder and took pride in what he did. My mother was a teacher-turned-housewife; she was complex, college educated, well traveled. She had grown up on a farm that had been in her family for generations, and her life was shaped by the fact that there was only one place on earth she wanted to live. She was thirty years old, married, and pretending to be happy in Ohio when she was struck by an overwhelming urge to return to her home place and the house where her mother still lived. My father took her back to West Virginia for a weekend visit. That visit has lasted almost forty years.

My parents' arrangement was not especially unusual. Many men in our community worked away from home and drove long distances to be with their families on weekends. Local jobs were scarce. I have been told that fathers don't figure much in my stories, which may be a little like being told there's a fly on the back of my head. The fly may be there, but I can't see it, and as long as it doesn't turn into a hornet and start to sting me, I don't plan to worry it to death.

The women I knew during my early years were strong—not necessarily in a physical sense or even psychologically, but strong in a steady, rhythmical, scythe-swinging way. They cut brush, herded cows, milked those cows, fed chickens, gathered eggs, slopped pigs, tended yards and gardens, and in their spare time took care of rowdy kids. The women's movement of the sixties and seventies was something Chet Huntley and David Brinkley talked about on the six o'clock news, and such goings on were about as relevant to farm women's lives as a pair of go-go boots. "Burn your bra if you want," these women said, "but all it'll get you is the cost of a new one."

Those few who may have felt occasional twinges of dissatisfaction attributed those feelings to the time of month, the weather, or too many kids. There were only three children in our family, but I went to school with a family that had nineteen. Some women seemed to have babies because they *could* have them. Others had them because they hadn't figured out how to prevent it. In any case, having a family was practical. Kids could gather eggs, pull weeds, help during haying season. Treat them right when they were little, and when you grew frail and toothless, they'd be around to take good care of you.

Appalachian people, particularly mountain people, are peculiar, I think, in the sense that they take pride in their geographic isolation. The characters in my stories seldom live in towns. My ancestors on my mother's side migrated into the narrow, brushy hollows and traveled as far back as they could in one of those hollows before they found the right spot to build their house. In cities, happiness is often having good neighbors. In our family, happiness is, and always has been, having no neighbors in sight. My mother's people found their happiness on Ellis Fork of Tanner Creek, but during the years twenty-six families eventually joined them. By the time I came along, most of those families had opted for "the good life" in Indiana, Michigan, or Ohio, and the number of households left on our hollow had dwindled to two.

Sumac and blackberry briars grew where log houses once stood. Copperheads and blacksnakes sunned themselves on crumbling cellar rocks. The couple of dwellings left standing were used to store hay in winter, and during summers, lovers loved there, kids played there, and those too young for one activity but too old for the other vented their frustration by writing cuss words on the walls. I spent many afternoons in those houses with my brother and sister, making hay tunnels, listening for ghosts, savoring the familiar smells of decay. I was proud that we were one of the two families that had remained on the hollow. In those days, I thought tenacity meant strength.

I knew no writers when I was growing up, unless you count John-Boy, as in Walton, as in Thursday evenings on CBS from eight to nine o'clock. Even then, I believed more in Will Geer, who played the grandfather. He seemed more real, less like an actor. Men like Will Geer lived and died in half the homes up and down Tanner Creek.

We had a television antenna rigged up in a pasture, high on a hill about half a mile from our house. Wires ran down the hill, zigzagging around maple, hickory, and birch, which meant that every time the wind blew or a branch fell our TV screen went blank. I grew up with a warped sense of plot, thinking that all stories ended precisely at the moment of greatest suspense.

My father had mounted our antenna on a section of two-inch, rusted water pipe. Cows and calves with itchy backs rubbed against the pipe and knocked it down at least once a week. Even when the antenna stood, we picked up only two channels. "Signal's just too weak," my mother used to say. I knew nothing about television signals or how they traveled. As I got older, I interpreted my mother's words and our poor reception as a sign that we might be living in the "wrong" place, just far enough from civilization to be able to see what it offered but, for all practical purposes, out of reach. I had no idea where the "right" place was, but I used to stand on top of our antenna hill and gaze south, thinking that if I stared hard enough, I'd be able to see the state capitol, ninety miles away, in Charleston. The governor lived there, I knew, and I felt sure that good TV reception was just one of the many perks available to a man in such an important political position.

In addition to our two TV channels, we also received a local newspaper. The largest town in our county was Glenville, the county seat, population somewhat less than two thousand, unless you extended the city limits down the Kanawha River a mile or so to take in all the Grogg babies. The town boasted a weekly, *The Democrat,* but it was filled mostly with birth announcements and obituaries, as though nothing of real consequence happened during the years between. Like most small-town papers, ours was heavy with advertisements dedicated to the proposition that no selling technique works as well as unrestrained exuberance: "Whole Fryers!!!!! Now 39 Cents a Pound!!!! Hurry!!!! While Supplies Last!!!!" Whole fryers were usually thirty-nine cents a pound when I was growing up, and the fact that most people raised their own but still rushed to town to buy their share is reason to think we were all either greedy or starved for event.

Our newspaper was edited by a personable and intelligent man. The paper was mostly a one-man operation and, according to rumor, not especially profitable, so I thought of the editor as more of a businessman-turned-martyr than a writer. I did have a great-aunt, a former schoolteacher and perfectionist, who supposedly kept a journal. Family history had it that after she retired from teaching, she abandoned her journal writing and channeled her energy into correcting the grammar and spelling in letters written to her by her brother, who eventually stopped speaking and writing to her altogether. So much for family feuds and local literary role models.

Most of the writers we read in high school English classes suffered from the most serious and irreversible forms of writer's block, having been dead for more than three hundred years. Dutiful adolescent that I was, I read what I was supposed to read, memorized what I was supposed to memorize, then stuck my finger down my throat and regurgitated enough to get A's on the tests. I secretly believed the real reason people read literature was not for edification and enjoyment but to make sure they didn't embarrass themselves by going off to college convinced that Beowulf was the football coach's dog.

Occasionally, I saw writers interviewed on television, but more often than not those writers were men. They had bags under their eyes, they smoked too much, and they didn't talk like anyone I knew. Real writers were already in the grave or living in New York City, I concluded. Judging by appearances, one place bordered the other, and the wall between was appreciably thin.

During this time, I had another life that sustained me, a life that had nothing to do with television or newspapers or tests. Living in the hollows of Gilmer County and along the banks of Tanner Creek were people who had begun to interest me far more than the characters in any book. Ours was an old community made up of families who had lived on their hilly farms for years. We knew one another's secrets. We were great-grandparents, grandparents, mothers, fathers, babies, several generations living in the same house. We were fox chasers, sheep herders, turtle hunters, snuff rubbers, tale tellers, and whiskered wizards and witches in the eyes of little kids. We scared those kids by telling stories about Yahooty, a fictitious man who roamed the back roads cutting off ears and tossing them into a bloody burlap sack. In those days, life seemed deliciously uncertain, and the air was filled with magic and horrendous possibilities.

But we were a crafty bunch, we chasers, herders, and hunters, and in some instances as stingy as dead people with our information. I learned early that being an adult meant having access to certain kinds of information. I longed to be a member of the club. The kind of information I was interested in was frequently exchanged during social visits. Those visits didn't involve any conscious planning, the way it's often done in cities. No one said, "Let's get together and do lunch." Instead, we visited when there was a birth or a death in a neighbor's family, or when we had company that had overstayed their welcome and we were weary of trying to entertain them by ourselves.

The women congregated in the kitchen or, in warm weather, sat in rocking chairs on the shady porches. The few men present squatted and talked in the yard or sat on a porch on the opposite side of the house. The children were given cake and coffee, depending on the leniency of the mother, then were shooed away to roam the hills or to play in the yard. The trick was to figure out a way to hang around without being conspicuous. Pretending to be sick or sleepy often worked, though if you overdid it you could wind up at home with Vick's salve up your nose or a musterole pack on your chest. Personally, I always found feigning illness more than a little tricky. Sneaking under the porch with the dogs is the method I employed and would recommend.

The conversations ranged from the exquisitely juicy to the mundane, and the older people often told the same stories time after time. But I never tired of listening. I heard things as a fourteen-year-old that I hadn't known to listen for when I was nine. And I sensed necessity in the telling. It was as though certain people had been assigned the task of making sense of or explaining a particular past event, and the only way they knew to complete their task was through verbal repetition. They didn't just talk about a happening—they *re-created* it. Like good carpenters, they built a solid foundation and worked their way up. They were masters at nailing a character with a single hammer stroke. They knew how to get a job done, pick up their tools, and get out. I matured under their moldy porches, a willing apprentice, a secret sharer in their lives. Painlessly, I learned to think in terms of beginning, middle, and end.

Looking back on those times, I think of the porch conversations as recording sessions, where tracks were laid down, one over the other, so that the end product was multilayered and more than it was at any one time. And if I listen closely, I can split those voices into days and years, can hear myself grow up in a single voice singing a progressively clearer song.

I wrote my first short story during the spring of my junior year in high school. I didn't write it because I *had* to write it in the sense that I clutched my breast, suffered, and put pen to paper as a way of satisfying burgeoning artistic impulses. My motives were simpler and more practical: I wrote that story because I wanted a decent grade in the class.

My story was about an elderly woman who killed people for their money, then threw their bodies into a well. My character received punishment from God by being trapped in her attic and eaten by rats. It is often said that writers are too close to their own work to see it clearly, but clearly I see a stinker of a story—the result of too much Poe and the inevitable Baptist influences. I also recognize in that first story bits and pieces of ghost stories I'd heard the old people tell late at night at Halloween parties or molasses boilings.

Gory thing that it was, my story went over well at school. I received a top grade, and my teacher read what I'd written to several classes. I remember a brief period of elation that seemed inappropriate, wildly out of proportion given the rinky-dinkiness of the situation. That feeling had less to do with a good grade or with class reaction than with a new awareness of the potency of words carefully chosen and affixed to paper. For some time, I had been telling ghost stories to my brother and sister each morning as we walked a mile through the fog down our hollow to the bus house. Now and then, they'd request a specific story, and if it varied the slightest bit from the original, they'd sulk and scuff along and say, "That's not the way you told it the first time." There was something to be said, I had to admit, for the semipermanence of paper.

I grew enormously fond of the characters in my stories—despite their criminal leanings. I never felt that I was *creating* characters so much as *releasing* them. And I sensed there were many more where those had come from, wandering inside me like restless sheep, checking for holes in the fences, waiting for the day when I'd grow lax and forget to shut the gate.

Years later, in beginning writing classes, I'd listen to instructors talk about the sense of power writing can give by allowing authors to create characters who are totally under their control. My characters are not so polite or compliant, so I've never experienced that sense of power. When I write, I invariably feel that I'm the one being bossed. So it was with that very first story I wrote when I was a junior in high school. Writing gave me a defenseless, uncomfortable feeling, like riding a rickety ferris wheel or walking a log across a flood-swollen creek. I didn't write another story for the next four years.

By the time I finished college, I had started to write again—secretly, clumsily, with the skill of an adolescent robbing a 7-Eleven store. I wrote poetry mostly. Awful stuff. I had attended college on scholarships, had participated in work/ study programs, and had graduated with a bachelor's degree in social work from West Virginia University in December 1974. I majored in social work to learn how to save the world. By the summer of 1975, I had decided that saving the world was a bigger task than I'd originally thought. I had married, gone to Florida to be a migrant worker and pick oranges, and worked for a newspaper in Elberton, Georgia, all in a period of less than a year. Suddenly, I found myself in Knoxville, Tennessee, where my husband had accepted an engineering job. For the first time it occurred to me that I couldn't walk home.

Embarrassed that I had a college degree but had never read *Don Quixote* or *David Copperfield* or anything by someone named Marcel Proust, I started taking English classes at the University of Tennessee. At night, I waitressed and served fish in a restaurant so dirty it should have had a "B" for botulism engraved on the forks and spoons. That fall, at UT, I enrolled in my first fiction writing class. The professor was Dr. Robert Drake, a Yale graduate and an extremely formal and terrifying man. He was an excellent teacher. He was the first person I knew who admitted that he took writing seriously, and though it sounds trite to say it, his class changed my life.

We used Cleanth Brooks and Robert Penn Warren's *Understanding Fiction* as our text. I had never read a book *about* writing, and I learned to read in an entirely new way. Flannery O'Connor, Eudora Welty, Ring Lardner, Caroline Gordon, Carson McCullers, Katherine Mansfield, Truman Capote. I heard many of those names and read their work for the very first time. From them I learned that a thing can be both ordinary and exotic if you train your eyes to see it. I wanted to develop that kind of dual vision.

The stories I wrote that semester were bad; I knew nothing about craft. I don't say that from hindsight—I had enough sense to know it at the time. But I tried to write about characters and situations that mattered to me, and I was determined to write better. Dr. Drake repeatedly pointed out what worked and what didn't, and I took what he said as fact.

During the next couple of years, I continued to write fiction, none of it good enough, I thought, for publication. A couple of my stories were accepted by the college literary magazine, and I entered a short story contest at UT and won that. But all I had to do was reread one story from the Brooks and Warren book to know that my work wasn't half as good as I wanted it to be. In March 1979, I completed a master's degree in communications at UT and sold my first nonfiction piece to the *Knoxville Journal*. I had opted for a graduate degree in journalism instead of English because I wanted to write, not just talk about writing. I enjoyed nonfiction; it felt safe. I did my research, completed the interviews, wrote the piece, and that was that. I didn't have to worry about holes in fences or shutting any gates.

That same year, as a result of my master's thesis, I received a grant from the Tennessee Commission on Aging to teach a writing class in a nursing home and to edit nursing home magazines in a sixteen-county East Tennessee area. Thrilled that I had found a job that would allow me to combine social work and journalism, I spent my days teaching, editing, and delivering camera-ready magazines to printers. Fiction became something I did in my spare time.

My first child was born in August 1980, and there was even less time for writing. By then, we were living in West Lafayette, Indiana, where my husband was trying to finish a graduate degree at Purdue. I had never spent much time around babies until I had my own, and I remember little about that first year except holding my wailing son under one arm, holding a baby-care book in the other, and trying to figure out what a "good mother" was supposed to do.

I once read in Virginia Spencer Carr's biography of Carson McCullers, *The Lonely Hunter,* a comment McCullers supposedly made concerning children: "Ah diddun want any. Ah always felt they would innafere with my woik." She was right. They do. But so does living: eating, sleeping, bathing, not to mention taking a walk in the woods, reading a good book, spending a day with a friend, all the things that make a life more pleasant, a little more worthwhile. Choosing whether or not to have children is a personal decision, and I can only speak for me. Though I've often had to wait to write until after 8:00 P.M. and work until midnight, then get up at 5:00 A.M. to get writing time in, I have never once regretted my decision. I have two kids now, and I must say that the second one takes just as much time as the first. But my kids have enriched my life and, I hope, made me a less selfish, more patient person. I like to think I'm even a little less wicked in my treatment of some of my fictional characters.

In 1983 I turned thirty, and it seemed that overnight my writing changed. "In what way?" a younger writer recently asked me, and I couldn't tell her except to say that I was able to see new connections between events and to view those events as part of a whole.

The following summer, I attended a weeklong writing conference in New England where I met a medical doctor, a fellow student. Bright, ambitious, a couple of years younger than I, this doctor wanted to write more than anyone I've ever met. "If I haven't published a story in a nationally circulated magazine by the time I'm thirty, I'll kill myself," she said to me one night, her eyes filling with tears. She was obviously sincere, at least at that moment, and her statement caught me off guard.

I don't remember what I said to her, but whatever I said was probably the wrong thing. I listened to her talk for a couple of hours, and when she went to her room, I continued to think about what she'd said. I didn't feel or even understand her sense of urgency concerning publication, and I took that as a sign I wasn't serious about writing. I wanted to publish, but I wanted to publish work I could be proud of, and if it took me sixty years to produce that kind of work, so be it. I was thirty years old and writing in an abandoned smokehouse in Kentucky at the time. My mother-in-law had once cured meat in this smokehouse, and hooks still hung from the ceilings and protruded from the walls.

My husband and I had made the difficult decision to leave the city and academic life and give our children a rural childhood, at least for a while. We were living and working on a farm in Monticello, Kentucky, where my husband had grown up. I was freelancing and selling some nonfiction but concentrating more and more on fiction, writing and rewriting each story until I knew the pages by heart. Mud daubers shared my smokehouse, and now and then, when I'd written a sentence I thought was decent, I'd get brave and read what I'd written to them. By this time, I had sent a few stories out to magazines, and they'd been rejected, as they should have been. But until that night at the writing conference in New England, I'd never really thought of publication as being the ultimate goal, nor had I thought of writing as being connected to any sort of timetable. One wrote, I thought, the way cows chewed their cuds—leisurely, languorously, eyes closed, concentrating wholly on the task.

I never saw the doctor again after that week, but I hope she published a story. And if she didn't I hope she grew stubborn on the last night of her twenty-ninth year, gritted her teeth, and swore on her great-grandmother's grave that she'd write the best story she could even if she finished it at the age of 105.

Seventeen magazine accepted a story of mine that same year and published it as their summer novelette. A familiar voice inside my head told me that the only reason they'd accepted my story was that their regular writers had gone on vacation or had died. When the story came out in June 1985, I received some complimentary copies, but I went to the drugstore and bought a copy just for the thrill. I found a quiet place in a local park and opened the magazine. As I read, I mentally flogged myself about certain word choices. I'd worked on the story, off and on, during a period of three years. That same familiar voice inside my head reminded me that a *real* writer could have written a better story. But I also heard a new voice, barely a whisper, acknowledging my story's imperfections and quoting something I'd once read about stories and poems never being finished—just abandoned.

* * *

In late spring 1987, I was accepted as an M.F.A. candidate at the Iowa Writers' Workshop. I'm lucky to have a husband and family who have always encouraged and believed (more than I have) in my work.

Suddenly, too soon, it is several years later. I've graduated, have had the opportunity to teach fiction writing at the university level, and have had the chance to work with and learn from several writers whose work I respect and admire. My first collection of short stories, *Farlanburg Stories,* was published by W.W. Norton in July 1990. I have mixed feelings about publishing, though I don't want to seem ungrateful. On the one hand, I am always delighted that someone identifies with or likes my characters enough to offer them a home. On the other hand, I am sad that I won't be able to work on those stories anymore to try to make them better. I have come to think of my stories as relatives I'm especially fond of, and I worry now that they may be, if not terminally, at least permanently ill.

I have no regrets about my long, slow path to publication. Ted Solotaroff, in his article "Writing in the Cold," said that graduate writing programs are "mostly wasted on the young." I'm convinced that I would not have benefited as much from a workshop experience before the age of thirty.

Solotaroff goes on to say that writing programs can serve as a kind of greenhouse, enabling talent to bloom, but that those same programs can make "the next stage—being out there by oneself in the cold—particularly chilling." With that in mind, I unpack my long johns and head east then south, taking with me what I have learned. I leave this stage, this midwestern literary mecca, and sally forth again to write in the cold, nose to the ground, searching out my own scent, following it all the way home.

GEORGE
ELLA
LYON

Born in 1949 and raised in Harlan, Kentucky, George Ella Lyon was educated at Centre College, the University of Arkansas, and Indiana University, where she studied with poet Ruth Stone. She began submitting book manuscripts in 1972; her first book, *Mountain,* was published in 1983. Since then Lyon has published a second collection of poetry (*Catalpa,* 1993), thirteen picture books (including *Come a Tide* [1990], featured on Reading Rainbow; *Who Came Down That Road?* [1992], a *Publisher's Weekly* Best Book of the Year; and *Basket* [1990], winner of the Kentucky Bluegrass Award), three novels for young readers (including *Borrowed Children* [1988], winner of the Golden Kite Award), an autobiography (*A Wordful Child,* 1996), and *Choices* (1989), a book of stories for adult new readers. Her most recent books are *Ada's Pal* (1996) and *With a Hammer for My Heart* (1997). Lyon recently collaborated with Jim Wayne Miller and Gurney Norman in the editing of *A Gathering at the Forks* (1993), an anthology that celebrates fifteen years of the Hindman Settlement School Appalachian Writers' Workshop. She was also the executive director of the Appalachian Poetry Project, a 1980 pilot project designed to support poets and poetry in the Central Appalachian region. Lyon lives in Lexington with her husband, musician Steve Lyon, and her two sons, Benn and Joey. She makes her living as a freelance writer and teacher.

* * *

Voiceplace

Early in "Song of Myself," Walt Whitman declares that he is "one of the Nation of many nations, the smallest the same and the largest the same" and then gives us fourteen long lines of places and ways of life, from the "Kentuckian walking the vale of the Elkhorn" to the fishermen "off Newfoundland, / at home in the fleet of iceboats." He concludes the catalogue by saying: "I resist any thing better than my own diversity, / Breathe the air but leave plenty after me, / And am not stuck up, and am in my place."

Whitman knew that democracy did not require and should not produce sameness—even within the individual ("Do I contradict myself?" he asks. "Very well then I contradict myself"), that in fact our strength and vitality spring from our variety. No melting pot for Whitman, no stew even, but many pots aromatically bubbling with everything from grits to borscht to fricasseed buffalo. What has happened to our taste for differences?

"I hungered for the burr of Appalachian r's," writes West Virginia poet Mary Joan Coleman in "D.C. Working Girl Lonesome." Living in the city, she longed not only for the place but for the *voice* of home. She grew up where the ruggedness of landscape and life shaped the language, where metaphors outnumbered even kinfolks. Having moved to a place where her accent was ridiculed, she realized her loss. For the history and spirit of a place are in its voices; to accept the denigration of the speech you were born into is to sever one of the threads of ongoing life.

It is also to foster the false impression that culture happens somewhere else, New York or Los Angeles, Chicago or Boston, and has to trickle down to the rest of us, that culture is a commodity that we buy or travel far to see rather than something that comes *from* us and speaks *to* us. It implies that stories—and therefore the people who tell and hear them—are more important in the metropolis than in the mountains or the Midwest.

It took me a long time to recognize the vital connection between voice and place in my own life and work. I grew up in Harlan County, Kentucky, in the coalfields, and was in high school during the War on Poverty. I remember the TV stereotypes—not just on *The Beverly Hillbillies* but on the news—of mountain people both materially and culturally deprived. So I thought, if I am going to write, the first thing I have to do is go somewhere and acquire a culture. During that process I would learn to sound like I was from somewhere else. I didn't know that was like cutting your throat to remedy hunger.

In college I wrote poetry primarily, and my subjects were medieval music, Dutch painters, and love. The language was that of a person born in a book and majoring in men's studies. We called it English. But I kept a journal, too, where I set down things that interested me. One was a sentence I'd seen printed in crayon on a young child's paper at Pine Mountain Settlement School: "I hope how soon Spring comes." I loved the way the rising sap of spring, hope itself, lifted the words into a new order. Not standard but rare, expressive. "How I hope Spring comes soon" is tired by comparison.

Another thing I took notes on was how my grandmother talked. "I feel like a stewed witch," she'd say. Or "I ain't seed you in a month of Sundays." I wrote down names of relatives she remembered: Honey-eating Richard, Pie-belly Miracle. I wrote down a story she told me of Old Aunt Martha Money who could cure the summer complaint. I didn't put this into poems. I just collected it. Poems, as far as I knew, didn't have stuff like that in them. But I valued the live language and elemental nature of her stories. Let not thy left brain know what thy right brain is doing.

After graduating from Centre College and the University of Arkansas, I studied with Samuel Yellen and Ruth Stone at Indiana University. It was exactly what I needed. Not just the workshop, but the community of writers that it fostered. Among those friends the most immediately important to me was Michael Allen, an Ohio poet who wrote about Sunday dinner at his grandmother's, about growing corn, about everyday things that he knew as well as his face. I was astonished. Could I do that? Why not? Ruth's class added to this realization the fact that it was not only possible but crucial to write out of my experience as a woman. Suddenly I had a wealth of material. In the twenty years since then, I've been trying to figure out how to be true to it.

Where you're from is not who you are, but it's an important ingredient. I believe you must trust your first voice—the one tuned by the people and place that made you—before you can speak your deepest truths. Irish poet Seamus Heaney, recent winner of the Nobel Prize, confirms this, saying in a radio interview, "I think for words to have any kind of independent energy, in some way they have to be animated by the first place in ourselves. Until that happens, words don't have that freedom and conviction that you need to write poems." We see, then, that if a person's experience of the written voice confirms her "first voice"— both in what she reads and in how she is taught to write—then her growing literacy will be fed by strong cultural roots.

As an Appalachian, my education to this possibility was continued by discovering Jeff Daniel Marion's literary magazine *The Small Farm* in 1975 and *Appalachian Journal* the year after. Danny and I began corresponding, and I found out there was a whole passel of people out there writing down how their grandmother talked and why she talked like that and why her farm was taken away from her. I found out there was an entire tradition of Appalachian writing; furthermore, some of the songs my daddy had sung to me were Child ballads. In short (though it wasn't short—it took years) I found out I had a culture. I'd been to college and graduate school, London and Paris, the Smithsonian and the New York Public Library, and now I needed to go home. For while I found all sorts of necessary and wonderful things in those places, I couldn't find my voice.

I don't mean I went home literally—I'd been going back for holidays and summer visits all along—I mean I went home inside; I began to pay attention to all those voices, to the language and people I grew up with. In doing so, I abandoned the larger culture's belief that such voices had no place in art, had, in fact, nothing to say.

Kurt Vonnegut says that he finally realized he had to sound like a person from Indianapolis because that's what he was. No construct, no posture could give him as convincing a voice. This doesn't mean, of course, that he had to write about Indianapolis; it doesn't even mean that someone picking up *Slaughterhouse Five* would know he's from Indianapolis. It means Vonnegut did a countercultural thing: he took that voice seriously enough to believe it could speak to us all. Never mind that it's not from a designated cultural area. It's an ordinary voice. An ordinary voice given to visions.

I was aided in this homecoming by poet Lee Howard, whom I met early in 1980 right before her book, *The Last Unmined Vein,* was published. Lee didn't just write about life in Clay County, Kentucky, she wrote in voices of people who lived there. The first section of her book, "Motherlode," is a seam of the voices that nurtured hers. I was thrilled by the sound of these poems: "Lord gal, you have no idea / what meeting meant to me," Aunt Neva starts out in "The Meeting"; and Uncle Orville gets our attention with "Now it's neither here nor there / to most folks / but then I've never figured myself / to be like many / much less most." Lee's work, eloquent with everyday voices and concerns, gave me courage and a new direction. Ultimately this led me into fiction and playwriting; most immediately it gave me access to experiences, to strength and wisdom I could not claim on my own.

The first voice poem I wrote was called "Her Words." The speaker is a combination of two women I knew growing up. Some of it is direct quotation:

> You gotta strap it on
> she would say to me
> there comes this hardship
> and you gotta get on up the creek
> —there's others besides you—

so you strap it on
Oh, you give St. Jude what he'll take
hand it over like persimmons
with the frost on
it ain't nothin
there's more stones in that river
than you've stepped on
or are about to
Once your hands
can get around sumac
once your feet
know the lash of a snake
you'll strap it on
that's what a good neck
and shoulders are for

In winter
at the settlement school
our wet hair would freeze
on the sleepin porch
and we'd wake up
vain younguns that we were
under blankets of real snow
Come Christmas
we'd walk sixteen miles
home to Red Bird mission
only once gettin
lost in the woods
snowed over
down the wrong ridge

Nobody's askin
for what ain't been done—
build against cold
and death scalds the dark—
you strap it on
there's strength in the bindin'
I scrubbed on a board
I know what it's about

    As this poem illustrates, place is not just location, geography; place is history, family, the shape and context of daily life. How can I separate the mountains from my grandparents, who seemed for a long time as large and absolute as anything else against the horizon? Their importance is evident in the fact that four of my picture books are connected to them. How can I distinguish between where we stayed—my mother was the one of six surviving children who remained in Harlan alongside her parents—and the stories of those who left? Each place exists in context and in contrast with others and I grew up not only in Harlan, but in not-Lexington, not-Dayton, not-Orlando. I grew up where the Greyhound bus did not go through but turned around and went back. It was not because, as jokes would have it, we were so bad that nobody wanted to go farther; it was because the road through to Virginia was a cross between a washboard and a roller coaster.

I didn't grow up *in* Harlan either, but four miles south, in a neighborhood bounded on two sides by the Cumberland River, one side by the railroad, all sides by mountains, and called Rio Vista. I'd like to know how that sudden Spanish got there. Certainly my parents got a great river view as the Cumberland rolled through the living room in 1977. This and the flood of '63 were the source for *Come a Tide.*

I think being rooted nourishes a person. It limits you, too, the way all actuality limits possibility. But it gives you a context, a tapestry of conditions and stories into which your story will be woven and from which you can follow the thread of others. My metaphor for writing is listening—perhaps in part because I had visual problems as a child—but I couldn't do it if I didn't have a choir, a cacophony, a family reunion of voices in my head. Totally fictional voices speak out, too. Part of my work is extending the invitation.

Just as I know we are all mortal, all bound to drop out of that reunion one by one, I also know that the spirit survives. This is my experience. It came to me naturally in childhood, before I could read or write, but it's taken me many years as a writer, as an adult, to find my way back to it. I cannot give you any doctrine, only testimony. Places have spirits; they haunt us as they are haunted by the lives that have been lived in their shelter, on their ground.

Let me give you an example by tracing the origin of *Who Came Down That Road?* In the fall of 1990, driving home from a day spent in two schools, I decided to treat myself to a stop at Blue Licks State Park. It's the site of the last battle of the Revolution, fought after the war had ended. The news hadn't made it to Kentucky yet.

It was a perfect October day, trees in full color, air so clear as to be almost clairvoyant. I stopped first at the monument and was struck to learn that the battle took place on my husband's birthday, August 19. Then I noticed the evocative names of Kentuckians who fought there: Stern, Farrier, Jolly; Black, Green, Brown; Rose, Corn, Price, Boone; Joseph Oldfield. Elemental names. Walking around the monument, I found that, except for the commander, the opponents were listed only by tribal or national name: Shawnee, Delaware, Wyandot, Mingo, Ottawa, Canadian. I took notes. Something said, "Pay attention."

In the little museum, where I went next, I found that the battle was a rela-tively recent event in Blue Licks's history. The park is situated on a buffalo trace that runs down from the Ohio River to the salt lick. White settlers had followed Indians down the trace, just as Indians had followed buffalo, buffalo had followed mastodons, and so on, back and back in the past. The museum had a few artifacts from the Fort Ancient people who settled nearby and quite a few mastodon re-mains, including a twenty-five-pound tooth, extracted from local ground.

When I came out I saw a historical marker pointing to a part of the buffalo trace you can still walk on, so I set off into the woods. No one was around but me, and soon I was far enough away from the museum at one end and the highway at the other to really enter the place. The dry grass and crimson leaves were shining. It was hard to tell wind from light. And I had the strangest sense that someone else was there. I kept turning to look behind me or stopping to listen. Nothing. Fi-nally I realized it wasn't anything *visible* I was sensing, but a spirit-trace the travel-ers had left, like the path they'd worn into the ground. And I began to imagine, almost to hear, a child asking, "Who came down that road?"

I've learned about the hazards of writing while driving, so I just let the possi-bility cook till I got home, then made a few notes (before I got out of the car, lest the tide of family doings sweep it out to sea), and started work later that night. It's my habit to get a first draft, so that I don't lose the feeling, before I get into the research. Otherwise what I don't know overwhelms me. I spent the next few days obsessed with finding the voice and the turnaround for the book. Form was never a problem, because the line I was given brought its own structure (question led to question—"Who came before that?") and a certain playful exasperation at being hounded off the edge of the globe by a small child's questions.

Once I had a draft, I set to work in libraries and on the telephone, document-ing and double-checking what I had written. One thing that nagged me was the reference to goldenrod at the end. I hadn't seen any goldenrod at Blue Licks since it's gone by late October, but it just *sounded* right to me. Besides, I told myself, the plant grows all over Kentucky—everywhere but your basement—and it's the state flower; it's got to grow at Blue Licks too. So I let it stand. Then one day I was talking to someone at the park, and he wanted to know if I had put in anything about the goldenrod.

"What about it?" I asked.

"Well, this is a pretty famous place among botanists," he told me. "There's a kind of goldenrod found in a three-mile radius of Blue Licks that grows nowhere else in the world."

"Yes," I said, feeling again the shiver I'd felt on the trace, "I put that in."

Something put it in, made it feel right in relation to the whole. Seamus Heaney sheds light on this, too, when he says in the interview quoted earlier, "A poet has to find the language that makes the common, almost unconscious life vocal; he must be voice box for something that is in the land, the people."

You can't be a voice box for your own feelings and experiences, much less for those of your place, if you've accepted the teaching that your first speech was wrong. For if you abandon or ridicule your voiceplace, you forfeit a deep spiritual connection. As Bobbie Ann Mason said in a Kentucky Educational Television profile, "I was not able to write stories until I got over being ashamed of how my people talked."

"How [our] people talked" is the embrace of language that welcomed us into the world. It is nurture, humor, memory, vision. It is what we must get back to in order to know ourselves, the "first voice" that teaches us to speak.

JERRY BAUER

SHARYN
McCRUMB

Best known for her Appalachian novels and short fiction, Sharyn McCrumb (b. 1948) has a deep connection to the Appalachian South. Her great-grandfathers were circuit preachers in North Carolina's Smoky Mountains. Her grandfather was an eyewitness to the hanging of an elephant for murder in Erwin, Tennessee, back in 1916. Family tales and memories of Appalachia feed McCrumb's gift of storytelling, her love of the mountains, and her unending search for the truth about complex mountain culture. A resident of Montgomery County, Virginia, she is the author of thirteen novels, including the highly acclaimed Ballad series, *If Ever I Return, Pretty Peggy-O* (1990), *The Hangman's Beautiful Daughter* (1992), *She Walks These Hills* (1994), and *The Rosewood Casket* (1996), a series that weaves together the legends, natural wonders, and contemporary issues of Southern Appalachians. She has spoken or lectured at the Smithsonian Institution, Oxford University, the University of Bonn, the American Library of Berlin, the Antioch University Writers' Workshop, the Hindman Settlement School Appalachian Writers' Workshop, and the New Orleans Writers' Conference. She has won numerous awards for her fiction, including the *New York Times* Notable Book of the Year Award, the *Los Angeles Times* Notable Book of the Year Award, the Best Appalachian Novel Award, and every major award in crime fiction. McCrumb, whose novel *She Walks These Hills* spent five weeks on the *New York Times* best-seller list, is currently writing her fifth Ballad novel, *The Ballad of Frankie Silver,* the story of the first woman hanged for murder in North Carolina.

* * *

Keepers of the Legends

All around the water tank, waiting for a train,
A thousand miles away from home, sleeping in the rain . . .

When I was four, I thought that was the saddest story in the world. It was a Jimmie Rodgers tune, I later learned, but I only ever heard it sung a cappella by my father in our old Chevrolet on the five-hour drives to visit my grandparents in East Tennessee.

Who was the fellow in the song, I wondered, and how did he get stuck out there on the desolate Texas prairie all alone, so far from the mountains? He seemed to think he was going to make it home all right, but for the duration of the song, he was stranded, and I could never hear it without feeling the sting of tears.

I come from a race of storytellers.

My father's family—the Arrowoods and the McCourys—settled in the Smoky Mountains of western North Carolina in 1790, when the wilderness was still Indian country. They came from the north of England and from Scotland, and they seemed to want mountains, land, and as few neighbors as possible. The first of the McCourys to settle in America was my great-great-great-grandfather Malcolm McCourry, a Scot who was kidnapped as a child from the island of Islay in the Hebrides in 1750, and made to serve as a cabin boy on a sailing ship. He later became an attorney in Morristown, New Jersey, fought with the Chester Militia in the American Revolution, and finally settled in 1794 in what is now Mitchell County in western North Carolina. Another relative, an Arrowood killed in the Battle of Waynesville in May 1865, was the last man to die in the Civil War east of the Mississippi. Yet another "connection" (we are cousins-in-law through the Howell family) is the convicted murderess Frankie Silver, the subject of my next novel, *The Ballad of Frankie Silver*. Frances Stewart Silver (1813–33) was the first woman hanged for murder in the state of North Carolina. I did not discover the family tie that links us until I began the two years of research prior to writing the novel. I wasn't surprised, though. Since both our families had been in Mitchell County for more than two hundred years, and both produced large numbers of children to intermarry with other families, I knew the connection had to be there. These same bloodlines link both Frankie Silver and me to another Appalachian writer, Wilma Dykeman, and also to the famous bluegrass musician Del McCoury.

The namesake of my character Spencer Arrowood, my paternal grandfather, worked in the machine shop of the Clinchfield Railroad. He was present on that September day in 1916 at the railroad yard in Erwin, Tennessee, when a circus elephant called Mary was hanged for murder: she had killed her trainer in Kingsport. (I used this last story as a theme in *She Walks These Hills,* in which an elderly escaped convict is the object of a manhunt in the Cherokee National Forest. In the novel the radio disc jockey Hank the Yank reminds his listeners of that story as a prayer for mercy for the hunted fugitive.) I grew up listening to my father's tales of World War II in the Pacific and to older family stories of duels and escapades in Model A Fords. With such adventurers in my background, I grew up seeing the world as a wild and exciting place; the quiet tales of suburban angst so popular in modern fiction are Martian to me.

Two of my great-grandfathers were circuit preachers in the North Carolina mountains a hundred years ago, riding horseback over the ridges to preach in a different community each week. Perhaps they are an indication of our family's regard for books, our gift of storytelling and public speaking, and our love of the Appalachian Mountains, all traits that I acquired as a child.

I have said that my books are like Appalachian quilts. I take brightly colored scraps of legends, ballads, fragments of rural life, and local tragedy, and I piece them together into a complex whole that tells not only a story but also a deeper truth about the culture of the mountain South. It is from the family stories, the traditional music, and my own careful research of the history, folklore, and geography of the region that I gather the squares for these literary quilts.

Storytelling was an art form that I learned early on. When I was a little girl, my father would come in to tell me a bedtime story, which usually began with a phrase like, "Once there was a prince named Paris, whose father was Priam, the king of Troy . . ." Thus I got *The Iliad* in nightly installments, geared to the level of a four-year-old's understanding. I grew up in a swirl of tales: the classics retold; ballads or country songs, each having a melody but above all a *plot;* and family stories about Civil War soldiers, train wrecks, and lost silver mines.

My mother contributed stories of her father, sixteen-year-old John Burdette Taylor, a private in the Sixty-eighth North Carolina Rangers, whose Confederate regiment walked in rag-bound boots, following the railroad tracks from Virginia to Fort Fisher, site of a decisive North Carolina battle. All his life he would remember leaving footprints of blood in the snow as he marched. When John Taylor returned home to Carteret County in eastern North Carolina at the end of the war, his mother, who was recovering from typhoid, got up out of her sickbed to attend the welcome home party for her son. She died that night.

My father's family fund of Civil War stories involved great-great-uncles in western North Carolina who had discovered a silver mine or a valley of ginseng while roaming the hills, trying to escape conscription into one marauding army or the other. There were the two sides of the South embodied in my parents' oral histories: Mother's family represented the flatland South, steeped in its magnolia myths, replete with Gorham sterling silver and Wedgwood china; my father's kinfolks spoke for the Appalachian South, where the pioneer spirit took root. In their War Between the States, the Cause was somebody else's business, and the war was a deadly struggle between neighbors. I could not belong completely to either of these Souths because I am inextricably a part of both. This duality of my childhood, a sense of having a foot in two cultures, gave me that sense of "otherness" that one often finds in writers: the feeling of being an outsider, observing one's surroundings, and looking even at personal events at one remove.

So much conflict; so much drama; and two sides to everything. Stories, I learned, involved character, and drama, and they always centered on irrevocable events that mattered.

In addition to personal histories set in Appalachia, I was given a sampling of my father's taste in literature: the romantic adventure tales of H. Rider Haggard and Edgar Rice Burroughs, the frontier stories of Mark Twain and Bret Harte, and the sentimental surprise-ending works of Dickens and O. Henry. Add to that the poetry of Benét, Tennyson, Whittier, and Longfellow. It is no wonder that years later, when I was ready to be a published writer, I found that I had no aptitude for minimalism, despite studies in the contemporary trends in creative writing at my alma mater UNC–Chapel Hill and later at Virginia Tech, where I received my M.A. in English. I took all the courses in Victorian literature that the university offered, and it was there that I found my mentors.

My role model of a successful, important writer became Charles Dickens, not for his style but for his philosophy. Charles Dickens wrote best-sellers in order to change the world. Here's one example: In the mid-nineteenth century child labor laws in Britain were virtually nonexistent. Children worked twelve-hour days in factories, were maimed in coal mines, and died of lung disease in their teens from work as chimney sweeps. No one seemed to care. For decades ministers and social reformers wrote earnest pamphlets, reeling off the statistics of child mortality and calling for child-protection laws. These pamphlets were mostly read by people who already agreed with the author—other ministers and social reformers who were working on pamphlets of their own. And nobody did anything to help the children. Then Charles Dickens wrote a book. It was a novel about a little boy who suffered terribly in the workhouse: *David Copperfield.* Then came *Oliver Twist,* with its grim picture of a child's life on the street in the slums of London. Those books became best-sellers in Great Britain, and within two years of their publication *the child labor laws of England were changed.* The general public, who had never bothered to read the informative pamphlets, wept for a little boy who existed only in a novel and as an echo of the author's childhood. People became so outraged at the fate of these fictional children that they demanded laws protecting child workers. First Dickens had to make people care; then he could persuade them to act. This is what John Gardner later called "moral fiction," and I knew early on that I wanted my words to make a difference. Writing should do more than entertain.

Even the early "mystery" novels that I wrote reflect this sense of purpose, that a good book should have a message. The books featuring forensic anthropologist Elizabeth MacPherson have been described as "Jane Austen with an Attitude" for the way that they blend social issues into the plots. In each of the early novels, the murder is committed by someone who is trying to protect an assumed cultural identity—not for greed or revenge or any of the usual motives. Cultural identity, I learned from my dual-culture childhood, is optional. The point of these novels is not to reveal "whodunit" but to satirize a pretentious segment of society: in *Highland Laddie Gone,* for example, the Scottish wanna-bes at the Highland Games are lampooned. The last novel in that series, *If I'd Killed Him When I Met Him,* is a synchronically structured meditation on the dysfunctional nature of contemporary relationships: i.e., there is a war going on between men and women these days, and in this book Elizabeth McPherson becomes the war correspondent. These satirical novels reflect the culture of my mother's South, the mannered society where appearances and social position matter. The dark and troubled world of the Ballad novels is the other South, drawn on my father's Appalachian heritage.

The idea of being a writer took root early in my consciousness. When I was seven, I announced that I was going to be a writer—even though I had to ask my parents how to spell about every third word of my compositions. My first work was a poem called "The Gypsy's Ghost," written when I was in the second grade. It had the singsong rhyme of iambic octameter, and the most frightening thing about it to me now is the specter of seeing it in print, but it told a coherent ghost story in verse, and my parents seemed pleased with my efforts, so I persevered. I must have been nine when I heard the Irish song "Danny Boy" for the first time, and while I recognized the urgency and sadness in the song, I could not figure out where Danny was going, and why his father wasn't sure he'd ever see him again. Unable to get any satisfactory answers on these points from the lyrics, I invented a story to explain the situation in the song. It has to do with a changeling being reclaimed from his human foster parents by the Irish fairies, but it wasn't a bad effort for a nine-year-old's imagination. I still think it might be a good children's book.

This attempt to make sense of the inexplicable by making up my own "legend" is still an occasional source of inspiration for my work, most notably in the novel *If Ever I Return, Pretty Peggy-O,* which began as an attempt to answer the question "I wonder who lives in that house." *That house* is a stately white mansion set amid stately oaks on Highway 264 on the outskirts of Wilson, North Carolina.

My parents lived in Greenville, North Carolina, and practically the only way to reach Greenville from points west was to take Highway 264, which meant that I had been driving past that white mansion for nearly twenty years: home for weekends from UNC–Chapel Hill, back from my job as a newspaper reporter in Winston-Salem, and later back from the Virginia Blue Ridge, where my husband and I were attending graduate school at Virginia Tech.

In the spring of 1985 I was driving home by myself when I passed the big white house on Highway 264, and I said for at least the two-hundredth time: I wonder who lives in that house. I still don't know who really lives there; it isn't the sort of place that invites drop-in visits from inquisitive strangers. I decided to answer the question with my imagination. A woman lives in the house, I thought. She bought the house with her own money. She didn't marry to get the house, and she didn't inherit it. Who is she? A folksinger. She would have to have made a substantial amount of money to be able to buy the house, but in order to take up residence in a small southern town, her career would have to be over.

A character began to take shape. This folksinger had attended UNC–Chapel Hill in the sixties, as I had. She was still young-looking, a trim blonde woman in her early forties who had once been a minor celebrity in folk music, but her popularity waned with the change in musical trends, so now she has bought the white mansion in the small southern town, looking for a place to write new songs so that she can stage a musical comeback, probably in Nashville. She doesn't know anybody here, I thought.

I had loved folk music when I was in college, and I had grown up listening to my father's mixture of Ernest Tubb and Francis Child, so I began to consider what songs this folksinger character might have recorded. Since I was alone in the car, I could sing my selections as I drove along. After a couple of Peter, Paul, and Mary tunes, I happened to recall an old mountain ballad called "Little Margaret." I was reminded of it because I had heard Kentucky poet laureate Jim Wayne Miller sing it in a speech at Virginia Tech only a few weeks earlier. The song is a Child ballad. It is four centuries old, and it is a ghost story. Little Margaret sees her lover, William, ride by with his new bride, and she vows to go to his house to say farewell and then never to see him again. When she appears like a vision in the newlyweds' bedchamber that night, William realizes that he still loves her and goes to her father's house, asking to see her: *Is little Margaret in the house, or is she in the hall?* He receives a chilling reply: *Little Margaret's lying in her cold, black coffin with her face turned to the wall.*

I sang that verse a few times, because some instinct told me that the heart of my story was right there. The owner of the house is a folksinger. She has moved to a small town, where she doesn't know anybody, and one day she receives a post-card in the mail, with one line printed on the back: "*Is Little Margaret in the house,*

or is she in the hall?" The folksinger's name is Margaret! The line would terrify her with its implied threat, and she would take the message personally because her own name was in the line. Having sung the song many times in her career, she knows the next line: *Little Margaret's lying in her cold, black coffin with her face turned to the wall.* I pictured her calling the local sheriff in a panic, saying that someone is threatening her life, but the sheriff sees no threat in the line on the postcard. He tells her that the message is simply a prank. I thought, suppose something or someone close to her is violently destroyed that night. Then she will know that the threat was serious. Then all she can do is wait for the next postcard to come, as she and the sheriff try to find out who is stalking her.

As I drove toward my parents' house, I followed the thread of the plot, so that by the time I reached Greenville, I knew who lived in that house (which I had mentally relocated to East Tennessee), and I had the seeds of the first Ballad novel, *If Ever I Return, Pretty Peggy-O.* That hour of inspiration was followed by several years of hard work, researching the high school reunions of sixties' graduates, talking to Vietnam veterans, and interviewing law enforcement people, but the idea itself came from an old mountain song.

The theme of *If Ever I Return, Pretty Peggy-O* came from a more modern melody: the Doors's tune "Strange Days Have Tracked Us Down." I thought, suppose "strange days" tracked everybody down one summer in an East Tennessee village. For the baby boomers it is their twentieth high school reunion, forcing them to come to terms with their shortcomings; for the sheriff and his deputy, it is the memory of Vietnam, which haunts them both but for different reasons; and for Peggy Muryan, the once-famous folksinger, strange days track her down in the form of a stalker who still remembers her days of celebrity. For Appalachia itself, the "strange days" refer to the time when the traditional folkways began to be lost in the onslaught of the modern media culture. Child ballads gave way to the Top 40, quilts featured cartoon character designs, and the distinctiveness of the region began to erode as it was bombarded by outside influences. In each case "strange days" meant the sixties.

Music is a continuous wellspring of creativity for me. When I was writing the subsequent Appalachian Ballad novels, I would make a sound track for each book before I began the actual process of writing. The cassette tape, dubbed by me from the tracks of albums in my extensive collection, would contain songs that I felt were germane to the themes of the book, and sometimes a song that I thought one of the characters might listen to or a "theme song" for each of the main characters. Generally, the songs I use to focus my thinking do not appear in the novel itself; they are solely for my benefit, although I have thought of providing a "play list" in the epilogue to each book.

The taped sound track for *She Walks These Hills,* for example, is a mixture of bluegrass, Scottish folk songs, and modern country music. It begins with the Don Williams recording of "Good Old Boys Like Me," a song that captures the character of Sheriff Spencer Arrowood in a few well-chosen lines: *Those Williams boys, they still mean a lot to me: Hank and Tennessee.* A "good old boy" who is able to appreciate both Hank Williams and Tennessee Williams has a blend of urbanity and traditionalism that typifies the rural Tennessee sheriff I wanted to create. The music of Deputy Joe LeDonne is an acid rock tune from the sixties, "Break on Through to the Other Side." A Vietnam vet, LeDonne listens only to recordings made in the late sixties and early seventies: Otis Redding, the Grateful Dead, Kris Kristofferson, Janis Joplin. Other songs on my homemade album for *She Walks These Hills* include: "Jamie Raeburn," a Scots folk song about a convict forced to leave his homeland, the bluegrass standard "Fox on the Run" (both theme tunes for the novel's escaped convict Harm Sorley), as well as "Poor Wayfaring Stranger," "The Bounty Hunter" written and sung by North Carolina musician Mike Cross, and a selection of hammered dulcimer recordings of traditional Scottish and Irish melodies.

When the cassette tape is finished, I make one copy of it for my car and another one for my office. Then during the months that I am researching, before I write a word of the book itself, I play the car tape whenever I am driving so that I can absorb and internalize the sound and the themes of the novel to come. I suppose the music serves as both the means of directing my thoughts along the lines of motivation, characterization, and theme during the planning phase of the novel and later for the creation of mood when I am in my study actually working on the book.

The songs I listen to also provide the titles for the Ballad novels. *If Ever I Return, Pretty Peggy-O* is a line from the Joan Baez recording of "Fenario," a minor key variation of a Scots folk song alternately called "The Bonnie Streets of Fyvie-O"; a line from the chorus of Danny Dill's 1959 folk revival tune "The Long Black Veil" is the source of the title of *She Walks These Hills;* and *The Rosewood Casket* is named for a late-nineteenth-century song, most recently popularized by Dolly Parton, Emmy Lou Harris, and Linda Ronstadt on their album, *Trio.* As I write this essay the novel I am working on is entitled *The Ballad of Frankie Silver,* after a song attributed to the first woman hanged for murder in North Carolina (in fact, Frankie Silver did not write the song; she was almost certainly illiterate). I am also researching (still in the rather desultory fashion of one who is a long way from a plot) the Civil War in the Appalachian Mountains, where the conflict was intensely personal and there was no great Cause to illuminate the suffering. The song that I find myself listening to when I'm reading Appalachian Civil War material is the traditional tune "Rank Strangers"; surely that will be the title of the book, when I finally sit down to write it. I like the play on words, and the idea conveyed by the song that a civil war suddenly turns neighbors into strangers. The faux cowboy ballad "Ghost Riders in the Sky" is also on my Civil War soundtrack-in-progress. So far, I have no inkling as to why it's there.

I find that the more I write, the more fascinated I become with the idea of the past as prologue. I began the fourth Ballad novel, *The Rosewood Casket,* with a quote from Pinero: "I believe the future is simply the past entered through another gate." In order to make sense of the present, I look to incidents in the past, and I like to know where things came from so that I can understand how they came to be what they are today. This sense of inquiry led me to read books on such diverse subjects as the legends of the Cherokee, mountain botany and ornithology, and the natural history of Appalachia.

In *The Rosewood Casket,* I wanted to talk about the passing of the land from one group to another, as a preface to the modern story of farm families losing their land to the developers in today's Appalachia. The voice of Daniel Boone is central to the novel's message, a reminder that the land inherited by the farm families was once taken from the Cherokee and the Shawnee. The novel begins with Cherokee wise woman Nancy Ward, in the last spring of her life, as she realizes that her people are about to lose the land that she tried so hard to preserve for them. As a reminder of that transience of ownership, in a passage in chapter 1 of *The Rosewood Casket,* I trace the passing of the land even farther back—to a time at the end of the last Ice Age, twelve thousand years ago.

Appalachia was a very different place at the end of the Ice Age, when the first humans are believed to have arrived in the mountains. The climate of that far-off time was that of central Canada today, too cold to support the oaks and hickories of our modern forests. Appalachia then was a frozen land of spruce and fir trees, but it was home to a wonderful collection of creatures: mastodons, saber-toothed tigers, camels, horses, sloths the size of pickup trucks, and birds of prey with wingspans of twenty-five feet. The kingdom of ice that was Appalachia in 10,000 B.C. was their world, and they lost it to the first human settlers of the region, who hunted the beasts to extinction in only a few hundred years. Losing the land is an eternal process, I wanted to say. It seemed fitting to start with these early residents, as a reminder that even the Indians were once interlopers. The theme song for that book was "Will the Circle Be Unbroken?"

A scholarly publication on Appalachian geology provided me with one of the central themes of *She Walks These Hills,* a novel of intertwining journeys, past and present. An elderly convict escapes from the Northeast Correctional Center in Mountain City, Tennessee, and tries to make his way home through the same stretch of wilderness in which a Virginia Tech history professor is reenacting the eighteenth-century journey of a pioneer woman who escaped from captivity with the Shawnee. The climax of the novel is the convergence of all these epic journeys.

From a book by Dr. Kevin Dann, *Traces on the Appalachians: A History of*

Serpentine in America, I learned that the first journey was the journey made by the mountains themselves. A vein of a green mineral called serpentine forms its own subterranean "Appalachian Trail" along the mountains, stretching from north Georgia to the hills of Nova Scotia, where it seems to stop. This same vein of serpentine can be found in the mountains of western Ireland, where it again stretches north into Cornwall, Wales, Scotland, and the Orkneys, finally ending in the Arctic Circle. More than 250 million years ago (even before fish existed), the mountains of Appalachia and the mountains of Great Britain fit together like a jigsaw puzzle. Continental drift pulled them apart at the same time it formed the Atlantic Ocean. I thought this bit of geology was a wonderful metaphor for the journeys reflected in the book, and in a sociological way, it closed the circle: When our pioneer ancestors settled in the mountains because the land looked right, made them feel at home, they were right back in the same mountains they had left to come to America!

Because I do so much research for my novels, and because I like to include so many historical and scientific details in the narrative, people often ask me which comes first, the story or the research. I usually reply by quoting another favorite maxim of mine, one from Louis Pasteur, perhaps an unlikely source of inspiration for a southern novelist, but his advice is sound for many disciplines. Pasteur said, "Chance favors the prepared mind." Much of my reading is nonfiction, particularly natural history, anthropology, and the sciences. (Once my publisher sent me on a book tour with two other authors, and I nearly drove them crazy reading *The Coming Plague* for the entire tour, intoning ominous bits aloud to them when someone happened to cough.)

My reference shelves fill all the bookcases in my study, so that I have easy access to trail guides of the Cherokee National Park, field studies of birds and wildflowers, the poetry of Stephen Vincent Benét, *The Toe River Valley Heritage,* several hundred volumes of folklore of Britain, and a host of other arcane volumes that I do not trust libraries to have in stock.

When I am reading subjects that have nothing to do with the book-in-progress, I am ostensibly reading for pleasure and relaxation, but I am always alert for new ideas. There is no telling when a chance sentence or an unexpected topic will trigger an association or suggest a subject that can be put to use in one's work. I was reading a medical journal when I discovered Kosakov's syndrome, the form of brain damage that affected escaped convict Harm Sorley in *She Walks These Hills.* I chose to afflict the character with that mental disorder in order to have him stuck in the past; Harm became a twentieth-century version of Don Quixote, forever trapped in a better place and time than now.

Once I used an idea from folklore that I understood only intuitively, and then later found the confirmation in a volume on Celtic beliefs. The theme for the second Ballad novel, *The Hangman's Beautiful Daughter,* was the idea of being "betwixt and between," to be caught in a liminal state between life and death. I found that each of the issues in the novel—the polluted river, the stillborn child, the country singer forced into retirement, the old woman with the sight who talks to the dead, the hibernating groundhog, the young suicide who still contacts his grieving sister—involved someone or something lingering on the threshold between life and death, reaching both ways. My feeling that this theme was integral to the mountain culture was instinctive. After I completed the novel, I found the justification for this theme of liminality in a book discussing Celtic beliefs. In *Ravens and Black Rain: The Story of Highland Second Sight,* Scottish writer Elizabeth Sutherland says:

> Celtic mysteries occurred in twi-states between night and day, in dew that was neither rain nor river, in mistletoe that was not a plant or a tree, in the trance state that was neither sleep nor waking. The Christian sense of duality—good and bad, right and wrong, black and white, body and soul—was unknown to the Druid. The key to Celtic philosophy is the merging of dark and light, natural and supernatural, conscious and unconscious. The *sithean* themselves existed in this twi-state, beings who dwelled between one world and another, creatures who were neither men nor gods. [p. 26]

There it was. The liminality that I kept insisting belonged in the narrative of *The Hangman's Beautiful Daughter* was part of the worldview held by the ancestors of the mountain people for thousands of years. Although I hadn't been sure why I'd felt compelled to put the concept of liminality into the text, now the reason was clear. I was describing people of Scottish descent, keeping the old ways, and this "border" concept is central to their perception of life. The scene in the novel in which Nora Bonesteel gathers balm of Gilead plants for making medicine reflected this ancient philosophy. (But I wrote this passage *before* I read Sutherland's work. Is instinctive use of the correct cultural pattern Jungian, or the genius of the unconscious, or was I third from the left over the cauldron in act 1 of *Macbeth*?) Anyhow, here is the Celtic belief in liminality as expressed by Appalachian wise woman Nora Bonesteel in chapter 10 of *The Hangman's Beautiful Daughter:*

> When Nora was a girl, a few of the old women had claimed that balm of Gilead ought to be harvested at dawn or dusk, but these days she dispensed with that part of the ritual. Early mornings and evenings were colder than midday, and she was too old to brave a chill for the sake of rough magic. She understood the logic behind the stricture, though. There was a power in the borders of things: in the twilight hours that separated day from night; in rivers that divided lands; in the caves and wells that lay suspended between the earth and the underworld. The ancient holy days had been the divisions between summer and winter, and that border in time created a threshold for other things; that was why ghosts and

goblins were thought to roam on Halloween and Beltane. The mountains themselves were a border, Nora thought. They separated the placid coastal plain from
the flatlands to the west, and there was magic in them.

I read nonfiction incessantly, always trolling for some relevant thought or
fact that will add a grace note to the next story. I keep hardbound notebooks for
possible future novels, each one labeled with the working title. When I see an
article, a quotation, or a phrase that might pertain to the subject of this future book,
I copy it onto a blank page in the scrapbook. I have discovered through bitter
experience that it is much easier to stockpile things you may never use than it is to
try to track down an article or a reference several years after you've seen it, when
your memory of where it can be found is no longer reliable. The prepared mind
saves me much time and energy in the long run, and the background reading that
I have done has triggered associations and brought other facets of the story into
focus, giving my work a scope and texture that it would not otherwise have.

I read. I study. I interview people who are experts in the subject of the current
work. I have hiked the Appalachian Trail with a naturalist and explored country
music with Skeeter Davis. I research woodworking with a master dulcimer maker,
and I have sat in Tennessee's electric chair. I try to write interesting, compelling
stories because I think it is the duty of a fiction writer to entertain, *but* beyond the
reader's concern for the characters, I want there to be an overlay of significance
about the issues and the ambiguities that we face in Appalachia today. In my
novels I want there to be truth and an enrichment of the reader's understanding of
the mountains and their people. I have been known to warn folks not to read my
books with their brains in neutral. Dickens again: "Never be inducted to suppose
that I write merely to amuse or without an object." I have a mission.

Appalachia is still trying to live down the stereotypical "backwoods" view of
the region presented in the media. I think one of the best ways to combat this
negative portrayal is to educate the general reader about the real character of the
region, and particularly about the history and origins of Appalachia and its people,
both culturally and environmentally. Like Charles Dickens, I think that in order
to win hearts and minds, one must reach the greatest possible number of people,
and so I am pleased when my novels make the *New York Times* best-seller list,
because that means that millions of people have been exposed to my point of
view. Millions of people watched the *Dukes of Hazzard;* surely the opposite opinion deserves equal time. I am passing along the songs, the stories, and the love of
the land to people who did not have a chance to acquire such things from heritage
or residence. Perhaps my own theme song ought to be the one Joan Baez recorded
in an early album called *One Day at A Time:* "Carry It On."

Carry it on.

LLEWELLYN
McKERNAN

A transplanted Appalachian from Arkansas, Llewellyn McKernan (b. 1941) lives on a rural route in West Virginia and teaches part-time at Marshall University. She received a B.A. in English from Hendrix College, an M.A. in English from the University of Arkansas, and an M.A. in creative writing from Brown University. She is a poet and children's book writer, author of *Short and Simple Annals: Poems about Appalachia* (1983), *More Songs of Gladness* (1987), *Bird Alphabet* (1988), *Many Waters: Poems from West Virginia* (1993), *This Is the Day* (1994), and *This Is the Night* (1994). McKernan has received numerous grants and awards from various West Virginia arts agencies, as well as from *Artemis Magazine, Modus Operandi, Poets & Writers,* and the Chester H. Jones Foundation. Her work has appeared in *Appalachian Heritage, Appalachian Journal, Southern Poetry Review, Kenyon Review, Laurel Review, Grab-A-Nickel,* and *Now and Then,* as well as in many anthologies.

*   *   *

Letter from a Poet
in West Virginia

Dear Reader,

Caught off guard by the blues this afternoon, I recover by crooning a few notes on poetry in these words I write to you. Lonely, alone, I listen with an attentive ear to the sounds in the small mountain holler where I live. Will you listen, too—to the black walnuts that thud on my lawn, to the birdsong that threads the trees topping the hill behind my home (it slopes down to my sprawling brown house in a coat of many colors: green grass, white Queen Anne's lace, goldenrod, amethyst thistles—some of them in my herb garden).

Except for my study, where an air conditioner hums and computer keys play my finger tunes, all the rooms are silent. My husband is gone, working in his office at Marshall University, where he doubles as English professor and professional poet. Our daughter, Katie, has been gone—at first for five years as a Marshall University student in Huntington, and now even farther away as a schoolteacher in Charlotte, North Carolina.

But being alone is all right. I share my loneliness with you, the reader, as I've always shared my poetry. Even as a child, when I lived in the country in southern Arkansas—with no friends nearby and with family members that often seemed distant and reserved—thoughts and feelings bubbled inside me that I dared to put on paper by imagining a reader whose empathetic ear was eager to be filled with what I had to say.

Faith in such a reader is what gave me the courage to start on my writing journey, and finding many such readers in West Virginia (and other Appalachian states) has kept me writing and publishing poetry for almost twenty-five years. It was like finding family members who finally listened to me. That's what every writer needs, and I found it by living and working in West Virginia.

Sometimes these readers have provided financial support. For example, those at the West Virginia Humanities Council in 1983 who funded the printing and distribution of *Short and Simple Annals,* my first book of Appalachian poems (which made available to the region work I'd produced throughout the seventies). And those at the West Virginia Commission on the Arts who around the same time awarded me a literary fellowship whose monies meant a whole year spent just drafting poems and ideas for poems, ones that I worked on throughout the eighties (many of which appeared in literary magazines and *Many Waters,* my second book of Appalachian poems, published in 1993). I am profoundly grateful for these two decades of work, whose cornerstone was reader support on the state level.

Awards from other readers came at moments in my life when I was discouraged and needed hard evidence that my work had found an appreciative audience. Like those in the 1978 Tri-State Author's Council who named me one of their Regional Authors of the Year. Those at the Cabell County Library in Huntington who sponsored my successful 1984 application to Poets & Writers, a national organization that funds local readings. Those directing reading series who called to schedule my appearance throughout Appalachia—from Lexington, Kentucky, to Chapel Hill, North Carolina, to Highlander, Tennessee, to Richmond, Virginia. At these places and others audiences quenched my writer's thirst with the cup of kindness that took the small words of my poems and made them overflow with their kinship of feeling.

Those poetry audiences and a community of readers drawn from every rank and file of Appalachians in this state and others have kept me working hard throughout the long years of a trial-and-error poetic apprenticeship that continues to this day. Editors of regional journals, judges of contests for West Virginia writers, Civitan and Kiwanis citizens, senior citizens, North Central Women's Studies and University of Kentucky Women Writers' conferees, high school students from Buffalo and Winfield, West Virginia, residents at the Virginia Center for the Creative Arts, Hindman Appalachian workshoppers, Putnam County's Museum in the Community brownbag lunchers, Huntington's Renaissance Coffeehousers, those whose thoughtful critiques helped me write my poetry books, those who bought them—I thank you all.

Don't think I'm boasting by this long overview of my reading public. It's a mere drop compared to the stream of regional and national acclaim attained by the other supremely gifted writers in this book. No, it's only to show the extent of my gratitude. Without this affirmation feeding the writer in me and making her strong, she might have been swallowed up by the overwhelming pressures of her personal life: the ardent challenge of marriage, the tremendous job of raising a daughter, the intellectual hardships of teaching, the prolonged grief over losing a father, several episodes of clinical depression, and two operations for cancer. The irony, dear reader, is that though you kept me writing, I needed to express myself much more than you needed to hear what I had to say.

What did I have to say? Something not profound but heartfelt to which I think you responded in a heartfelt way. How were we able to meet on this plane? I believe it was possible because we had experiences common to our generation (me in Arkansas, you in Appalachia) that brought us together in the poems I garnered from that time, but in your place.

We both grew up when the United States was still mainly agricultural, and Arkansas and Appalachia were more rural than most places. Our families were extended ones, with parents, children, grandparents, and other kin living close by. Our environment was mostly a natural landscape with the stability of seasonal routines. We were taught a firm religious faith, a deep respect for education and the work ethic. But in the sixties, seventies, and even in the eighties (when I realized that I had lived in Appalachia longer than anywhere else on earth), this way of life, at first an endangered species, rapidly became extinct: killed by an increasingly secular and technological society where even immediate family members lived hundreds of miles from one another; where urban sprawl was reaching into remote woods and mountain hollers; where an indulgent hedonism and an ironclad God-is-dead-so-anything-goes attitude was destroying respect for religious and educational institutions.

I cannot help but think that the poems I wrote then, poems that came from my personal experience of that old-fashioned lifestyle, were triggered by my seeing how fast it was disappearing from a landscape and a people I had come to call home. And I think you wanted to read these poems because you, too, were feeling the loss of this lifestyle and the profound changes occurring all around us.

I am not implying that all the old ways were good and all the new ones bad— just different. That was the rub for me and the reader in whom the former ways of behavior and being were still powerfully at work. For me it was like going back to the old home place and finding it and the landscape razed. It was like standing there, gaping, and remembering: The sunlit breakfast nook, windowsills filled with green growing things. The piano in the living room, dark, upright, and always ready to be played. The tree outside my bedroom window tap-tapping the chinaberry tunes that lulled me to sleep. Of course, some rooms were too small and cramped for comfort, and the roof leaked in a few places, and part of the foundation hadn't been aligned properly with the earth. But the home place was beautiful even in its imperfections because it was joined to the mystery of my life as I had experienced it there and remembered it here. This perception is the basic theme running through all my poetry about Appalachia. A theme you as readers identify with because you have experienced it in your own lives.

What are these experiences? Here are a few examples.

In *Short and Simple Annals*, I celebrate in "Mother Milking" the purity and simplicity of that former lifestyle by symbolizing it as "that moment / in my childhood where nothing belongs but milk / filling the pail inch by inch / with its white froth / warm and sweet / as the breath of a baby." Yet that moment occurs because my mother has stepped through "the muck of the barn," faced a blacksnake, and settled down to what must have been at times a laborious morning chore. That pure, simple lifestyle was sustained by physical bravery, perseverance, and hard, dirty work.

In that same book I celebrate both the good and bad in the evangelical religion taught to me in rural Arkansas and to you in the Appalachian Bible Belt. In "Fresh from the Vine," a miracle occurs, and in "The Shaker," an ecstatic believer whirling in a divine dance at the front of a meetinghouse shakes off not only some excess flesh but also her sins, thus making room for Christ. Yet in "Mountain Magic," a fanatical fundamentalist imposes on her child a religious regime so harsh it's a miracle the girl survives. But she does—by God's grace. And tells us all about it.

In that same book and also in *Many Waters* are poems that celebrate the joy and sorrow in the intense bonds formed by close-knit extended families. In "Aunt Anna" and "The Strike," the love among family members is so strong that it prevails over deep trauma and death (so does knowledge over ignorance). In others like "The Hollow," "Love in the Mountains," and "Brief Encounter," love/hate bonds among kin stretch relationships to the breaking point. In "The Fast," the long central poem of *Many Waters,* a daughter struggles to recover from a father's violent emotional abuse and discovers pain persists but love of life triumphs.

In both these books I celebrate the Appalachian landscape by incorporating in poems its unique features, especially its creeks, rivers, and streams. I called my second book *Many Waters* simply because liquid images occurred so often—as subject, symbol, or natural detail.

And this afternoon the creek that rambles along the border of my front lawn, tumbling and talking to itself, is perhaps my happiest invention. Even when I leave my study to sit for a while on its rugged green banks, it returns me to my original theme. Just as it joins the Guyandotte that becomes the Ohio flowing into the Mississippi, so, too, my own small body of work—fluid, ever-changing (I have yet to write my best poem)—gets caught up in a larger stream of readers, riding on the crest of their every wave.

MELISSA MILLER

HEATHER
ROSS
MILLER

Born in 1939 in Albemarle, North Carolina, still her residence on major holidays and in summers, Heather Ross Miller spends the academic year in Lexington, Virginia, where she is professor of English at Washington and Lee University. She received both a B.A. and an M.F.A. from the University of North Carolina at Greensboro. Between 1984 and 1986 she served as director of the M.F.A. program in creative writing at the University of Arkansas. Miller is the author of seven works of fiction, *The Edge of the Woods* (1964), *Tenants of the House* (1966), *Gone a Hundred Miles* (1968), *A Spiritual Divorce and Other Stories* (1974), *Confessions of a Champeen Fire-Baton Twirler* (1976), *La jupe espagnol* (1990), and *In the Funny Papers* (1995), and five books of poetry, *The Wind Southerly* (1967), *Horse Horse, Tyger Tyger* (1973), *Adam's First Wife* (1983), *Hard Evidence* (1990), and *Friends & Assassins* (1993). She has been awarded three National Endowment for the Arts Fellowships, Woodrow Wilson and Danforth Fellowships, a doctor of letters degree from Methodist College, and the Alumni Achievement Award from the University of North Carolina at Greensboro. Miller has also received several nominations for Pushcart Prizes in both fiction and poetry and was named to the Distinguished Stories list in *Best American Stories 1993*. Currently she is advisory editor of *Shenandoah,* a role she has assumed for various literary magazines throughout her career.

* * *

A Natural History

It is hard for me to talk about writing, mine or anybody else's. I'd rather talk about stories and poems in the raw—the origins of all that energy and joy and anguish that percolate into what we call Life, or maybe Love—those things that come together and make a natural history. My life, my love, and my natural history now ramble over three mountain ranges, the Uwharries, the Appalachians, the Ozarks. The Uwharries, my birthplace, are part of the Oconee range, the oldest mountains in the East, worn to rolling hills thickly forested, with hard granite escarpments and clear water, old grapevines, old honeycombs, old home places. The place where I met and married Clyde Miller, a park ranger.

We lived in the park for a while, actually in the park rangers' barracks, making a quite cozy home place in the big pine-paneled kitchen. No other rangers lived there. Deer came up on the porch each morning. Owls swooped the long misty meadows. We took long hikes through the park and often saw no other people for hours. And I felt my life as cozy as the kitchen, as wild and uninhibited as the deer and the owls, and a good mixture of the tender and the unpredictable.

When we had a baby, though, we moved outside the park into an old farmhouse. But Clyde and I still made long expeditions into the park. And so he drove me one bitterly cold and sunny November morning deep into Morrow Mountain State Park along the labyrinth of fire trails carpeted then in brown pine needles and leaves. We had a three-month-old baby girl. She slept in my arms, a warm, breathy little bundle of pink wraps and a tasseled pink cap. On and on we drove until it seemed we actually parted the mountains with the blunt green nose of the park truck. They rose up over us—even they, the low Uwharries, I fancied, now given the energy and muscle of younger peaks. As young and as adventurous as we.

We were the only people left in the world. We had a bag of Fig Newtons in the truck, a heavy thermos of coffee, and the sudden thick isolation made this tame food taste sweeter, exotic, and more sustaining. Somewhere deep within the cuts and swales of the Uwharries, the baby still sleeping, we stopped. All around us rose old woods, pines and hickories and oaks, rich earth covered in leaves and cones, no sound except the truck popping and cooling, an occasional scampering of squirrels.

My husband wanted to show me farms and home places, barns and sheds, chimneys, habitations long established, then abandoned, most all of them, well before the park land was annexed. He pointed to the wooden steps, the stacked and chinked fireplaces, the old fences. He found it sad. These places had once held families, children, dogs and cats. He felt their absence.

I felt their presence, and the tenacity of survival out there in such loneliness, such impossible wilderness, no roads, no neighbors. Would I be able to manage so well? The baby shifted in my arms, sighed, and opened her eyes and fixed me with such a look of contentment that I felt encouraged.

Those people put themselves into the arms of the Uwharries and trusted, much as my baby trusted my arms, my lap, the pink coverlet wrapped around her, littered now with Fig Newton crumbs. It was a place of trusting. And trial. A place of cozy kitchens and unpredictable wildness. The thick hot fragrance of coffee lifted all around us, while the squirrels quarreled.

Can you live in such a place, my husband seemed to ask me? Can you love a park life, a life of woods and silence? I nodded. I smiled. The baby slept again. We drove on deeper, winding around the steep fire trail, catching glimpses of brilliant sky, then the dark shadows of the Uwharries closed over, then brilliance again, bright/dark, an almost intoxicating effect.

The mountains opened once more as we came to a long meadow banked on two sides, north and east, by a low stone wall, and stopped. "I want you to see this," Clyde said, and we got out of the truck.

Somebody gathered and piled the stones, fitted them so tightly they didn't require mortar or chink. And there they still held, a hundred, maybe two hundred years, still keeping the boundaries of the old field. "Look here," my husband took me to a slight rise in the meadow and hunkered down to part the red broom straw. "You can still see the furrows, the old corn rows." He rubbed a hand over the ground.

I felt as old and wise as Eve. And what was the Garden of Eden but an old farm place, a field bound by stones, the sounds of trees and squirrels in the background, and a glimpse of the Uwharries rising in all directions? A man and a woman and their baby girl. The endurance of all family.

A half dozen years later, this time with a little boy as well as a little girl, we again explored the old back trails of Morrow Mountain State Park. Since that cold brilliant November, we had been transferred to another park down east, a place of flat white sand, flashing cola-dark lakes, and swags of Spanish moss festooning the aromatic swamp junipers. A place as exotic and remote as the moon to us born and raised among mountains. But we brought our children back to enjoy our place of origin. Like pilgrims returning to shrines.

The season was humid and heavy, midsummer, the Uwharries lush in green leaf and flowering things. We came upon an enormous old hedge pulsing with honeybees. The hedge, once trimmed to follow the corners of some old farm porch and hug a now-fallen chimney, had spread and flourished to the size of a house itself. The hedge blossomed with honeybees, their wings buzzing like low thunder or maybe the tumbling of water over rocks. They worked over the hedge's white flowers, crawling and swarming and flying in and out, until the place seemed alive with honeybees. Until it seemed the whole moment could take flight.

A strong sweet smell wafted off the bees and the hedge, brushed over us, cooling our hot faces for a moment. It refreshed us beyond measure just to discover the bees in their old hedge, just to hear them, to catch the smell of their labors. It was a gift, I think, from the old Uwharries, from the vanished people who first built houses and established hedges. Under one branch of the hedge, our son found a tiny white seashell, chalky with age. A shell so far from the ocean. A hole neatly bored into one end. Some child's lost treasure.

Those were the Uwharries, the love and the life and the natural history that touched my own love and life, my stories and poems. A place of brilliant cold and heavy heat, old stone walls, a hedge full of honeybees, and a white seashell. They go together. They fuel the energy I need to write. They merge the cozy elements with the wilderness.

The Ozarks. My children grown. I traveled across three states and the Mississippi River to get to Fayetteville, Arkansas, and a position with the master of fine arts program in creative writing at the university. Just the other side of Little Rock, the Ouachitas rose and rose toward Oklahoma and the original badlands. Bonnie and Clyde held up a gas station in Fayetteville. Those old-timey gravity pumps with the glass bulbs. My son had his picture made beside one when he came out to visit.

I was separated by miles and miles from the people I loved. My husband was developing a new state park in the sand hills of North Carolina. My daughter was finishing college, my son halfway through. And I was trying myself out in this strange land, the Ozarks.

They get their name not from American Indians, as most people think, but from the original French explorers who identified a turning point or landmark as the place where the river bowed or made arcs, the *aux arcs,* quickly becoming Ozarks. Arkansas had many such curious place-names garbled from the French— Toad Suck, Smack Over, Hog Eye.

I settled on the side of Mt. Sequoyah in a small house with a cathedral ceiling and corner fireplace. Every day after class, I hiked around Mt. Sequoyah, up to the old Methodist meeting grounds on the very top, a spectacular view of Fayetteville all around. Fayetteville was burned three times in the Civil War, more than Atlanta. Families split apart, half their sons Union, the others Secesh. And the border wars, the bloody bushwhackers of Missouri, Kansas, Oklahoma, and Arkansas, were a scourge upon the land throughout the war and for years following.

But the old church meeting grounds, originally a place for brush arbor camps and revivals, brought some healing. People from the border states came to Mt. Sequoyah and tabernacled in the sight of the Lord. They prayed and sang, ate and shared and slept on top of the mountain. You could sense something of their energy and faith as you hiked around modern Skyline Drive built over the original road. The campgrounds now replaced by cottages with porches and TVs. The cooking fires, by central kitchens with stainless steel sinks and steam tables. But still something of that fierce need to heal and share remained. Maybe it was the old wild grapevines tangling in the trees. The exotic Osage oranges filling the ditches. Maybe the little red hoot-owl staring from his hollow.

Not too far from Mt. Sequoyah, the Confederate cemetery lay on another mountaintop. Men from all the bordering states, most of them no more than eighteen years old, slept together. The cemetery fanned out in sections charted Kansas, Missouri, Arkansas, Oklahoma, and so on. Some of these places were just territories during the Civil War, but designated here as definite states.

I first went there with a Fayetteville writer friend, Ellen Gilchrist. We drove up on a soft October evening, the leaves just turning, the sun still hanging in the western sky. We wandered among the graves and read the stones. Ellen said, "No wonder they were so wild. When they knew they'd die before they were eighteen."

We agreed we'd have been wild too, maybe, if we were young men in those days, kick up in people's faces, get drunk, have a good time. Then go off to die of gunshot or gangrene. We both had young sons and so agreed we hated war. We drove to downtown Fayetteville, back to the lights and cozy comfort of the 1980s.

Another writer friend, Marcella Thompson, seemed the epitome of mountain strength. Dressed like a lumberjack, alternately tough and tender, she wrote highly profitable Harlequin romances, taught sociology at the university, and with her third husband operated The Berry Patch, shipping blueberries all over the land. Marcella's family had come in covered wagons, the women walking along in poke bonnets, able to shoot as accurately as any of their men. They could do anything from making fine lace to doctoring a sick horse. They knew hog-butchering and embroidery. They could take anything that came.

Marcella did not butcher hogs or walk around in poke bonnets. But she knew the many sides of the Ozarks, the art and the hard labor, and stood ready to help anybody who needed her. She showed me Eureka Springs and Mount Ida, one a place of healing waters and the other a place of eerie crystals. The water at Eureka tasted like iron, sparkling out of the limestone cliffs, a faint green sheen to it. The crystals we dug out of the Mount Ida mud and then washed in oxalic acid. They emerged from the buckets brilliant as diamonds, possessing who knows what powers, soothing to your thumb, a delight to gaze upon.

Again, it all seemed to fit together, made love, life, a natural history. Marcella and I did not conquer any wilderness as her family women had. We enjoyed our modern conveniences, wrote our books, taught the young Arkansans to write theirs. But I fancied we had some of that old wisdom, that hard-edged surefootedness of those women who came to the Ozarks and lived and thrived. One of Marcella's grandmothers was called Cinderella, Marcella receiving the end of the name. This Ozark Cinderella did not marry a prince, but she went to square dances and cut a fancy step. She left behind quilts and coverlets, trunks full of clothes with tucks and appliqués, insertion and lace. The trunks were sturdy hard things, bound at the corners with leather and metal. It made sense.

Now I am back in the Appalachians, the Blue Ridge of Virginia, teaching at Washington and Lee University. The Appalachians, like the low rolling Uwharries, feel like home to me. They were the first tall peaks I ever encountered, the Smokies around Cherokee, Maggie Valley, the Quallah Reservation. I was maybe fifteen, a reckoning age, eager to be free of my parents, ready to make my own way in the world. Yet I had come there with them. They were taking part in a North Carolina Writers' Conference. My father had just published his novel, and he was caught up in the glamour of literary companions.

My mother and I trailed in the background, not sure what was actually going on, yet proud of my father's successes. We joined a tour group to pass the time, and our particular guide was Mr. Crow, a Cherokee man of few smiles. Mr. Crow took our group around the Quallah territory with a strange mixture of pride and anger. If he made a joke, we didn't know if we should laugh or give thanks.

Somewhere outside Cherokee, Mr. Crow stopped the tour, had us all get out of the van and crowd to a rushing clear spring banked in coral honeysuckle. "That's the Twins Spring," he said, standing beside it and folding his arms like a clichéd cigar-store Indian. "Anybody drinks outta this spring, has twins." And he gave a quick, rare grin that flickered through his hard face like a flash of lightning.

Most of the women giggled, some took a few sips, scooping the water with paper cups. My mother refused. But as they all stood around, chatting and fanning themselves in the August sun, I approached the spring, cautious lest there be mean snakes hiding under the honeysuckle. The steady bubbling water cascaded in a short modest fall from dark wet rocks, throwing a delicate spray in my face. I gazed at the water, trying to see where it came from, but all I could discern were the dark wet rocks. Then I saw a small pool farther back in the honeysuckle, and, forgetting the mean snakes, I lifted the vines, crept toward the pool.

The water was so deep and cold that it looked purple. I plunged both hands into the pool. The cold shock of it thrilled me through to the bone, and I lifted my hands and drank and drank. The cold purple stuff streamed through my fingers and down my T-shirt and over my jeans. Again I plunged both hands. Again I drank and drank.

I don't remember what happened next. If my mother, embarrassed more by my sodden appearance than my sudden belief in Mr. Crow's Cherokee legend, dragged me back to the van, and we all returned to the ugly little motel called Max's Indian Village, the cabins with a phony tepee front outlined in neon. Or if Mr. Crow discovered me, flashed another crooked little grin, and announced, "That girl gonna get her some twins!"

In any case, I grew up, married, had two children, no twins. But carried the taste and the promise of that purple water all my life and will never lose it. A silly thing. But my twins are somewhere. They have the tenacity of coral honeysuckle. The thrill of cold Appalachian springwater.

Mr. Crow also took us that day to see a Cherokee wood-carver named Waddy. Waddy stood over six feet into the hot afternoon, a shock of coarse gray hair adding to his height. He wanted to sell things to us, little wooden Indians, canoes, bears, and birds. He didn't say much, except "This'un costs five dollars."

Still sopping wet from the Twins Spring, I gawked at the edges of the group, then wandered around Waddy's yard, noticing a low porch railing that closed off one end. A shock of jet black hair, just like Waddy's gray hair, stuck up a little over the top railing. A little Indian baby stared back at me when I went over to peep. He had eyes as jet black as his thick hair, and a face as serious and blank as Mr. Crow's. No smiles. No gurgles. He stood there dressed only in a little white undershirt, no diaper, no shorts, his genitals bobbing free to the air and the mosquitoes. And he held in his little hands an open razor. I drew in my breath, blinked at the razor so close to the baby's genitals, his smooth belly. And all I could say was a soft, "Hey."

Then I stepped back. He had not made a move, uttered a sound, just stood there, maybe a year old, with his terrible razor, that old-fashioned kind that opens like a clam shell. And he never blinked.

But what business did I have feeling anxious? His people, his family women, had been there in those Appalachians centuries before mine. They knew things about survival and stamina I did not. They knew babies and smooth naked skin. They knew razors. Waddy out there selling wooden bears and canoes, maybe he knew this child held a razor, maybe it was ordinary, some ancient Cherokee ordeal. And what business was it of mine, a fifteen-year-old white girl, the closest she ever came to trial by ordeal being her initiation into the Scouts?

So I left the little Indian on the porch, making no sudden moves of my own, no white-girl noises, and I felt somehow he was okay. For all I knew, his mother, silent and dark, waited just inside the door, watching me, deeming me more a threat than the razor her baby held.

And so what do I make with this love, this life, this natural history? These three mountains, Uwharries, Ozarks, Appalachians? I have tried to put their survival and challenge into stories and poems, flavoring the writing with tenacity and purple water, hog-killing, honeybees, fine lace, gravestones, open razors in the hands of babies, and lost white shells. I have put in a man, a woman, and their two children. I have tried to say what it was like when they were together, bound in love and energy, establishing their home places. And I have tried to say what it was like when they were broken apart, separated by distance, alone in strange lands. And through it all runs the long backbone of the rising land, the high places, the mountains that challenge and either defeat or strengthen those who attempt them.

I want the stories, the poems, to be natural. I am a southern woman, and I write about the places that flavor me. I cannot help myself. I drank from the Twins Spring. I followed the man into the fire trails. I tested myself in the Ozarks, those long flat-topped but thickly wooded mountains. I am not finished writing. We are all naked babies with open razors in our hands.

ELAINE
FOWLER
PALENCIA

Elaine Palencia (b. 1946) grew up in Morehead, Kentucky, and Cookeville, Tennessee, but now lives in Champaign, Illinois. Her stories have appeared in *Crescent Review,* *Virginia Quarterly Review, Iowa Woman,* and other magazines, and several have been anthologized. A graduate of Vanderbilt University, Palencia is perhaps best known as the author of *Small Caucasian Woman,* a collection of interconnected short stories published in 1993. Set in a fictional eastern Kentucky town based on Morehead, the book features remarkable women like Shug Watson, Dreama, and Aunt Sadie. Her stories record the familiar Appalachian pattern of exile true of her own life, even including a stint living in Detroit, a place she calls "the ultimate city of exile for Briarhoppers." Her poetry chapbook about her son, *Taking the Train,* was released in 1997. She has received awards for her fiction and poetry from the Illinois Arts Council, *Iowa Woman, Willow Review, Appalachian Heritage,* and the American Association of University Women. In 1990 the Appalachian Writers' Association named her the recipient of the John Ehle Award for Short Fiction. Palencia is also the author of four mass-market novels, three written under the pseudonym of Laurel Blake, and was a finalist for the Golden Medallion Award of the Romance Writers of America.

*   *   *

Leaving Pre-Appalachia

In 1962, my parents and I moved from Morehead, in the Knobs region of eastern Kentucky, to Cookeville, Tennessee, on the edge of the Cumberland Plateau. As we drove away from the house I had grown up in, I sprawled in the back seat of our Chevy, my nose stuck in a mystery novel.

From the front seat, her voice trembling with emotion, my mother asked me, "Don't you want to take a last look at the house?"

Surly teenager that I was, I mumbled, "No," and kept on reading.

This was probably the moment that sealed my future as an Appalachian writer. Through writing, I have been looking back ever since, trying to recapture all that was left behind by the three of us that day, not to mention all that our wider family left behind on the long journey from the British Isles and, by stages, through the Appalachian mountain chain, always moving westward and reinventing ourselves.

Growing up in Morehead in the fifties, where my father taught at Morehead State College (now University) and my mother taught at the county high school, I had little sense of regional identity and would not even have known how to pronounce "Appalachia." Except for learning a few folk songs like "Barb'ry Allen" and eating fresh sorghum on white bread as part of some student teacher's unit on the pioneers, I do not recall receiving any sense of the region in school. We learned primarily what it was to be an American and, secondarily, what it was to be a Kentuckian. My first public recognition as a writer came from winning an essay contest in junior high school on "What the Kentucky Education Association's Legislative Program Means to Me" (as if it could have meant anything at all to a thirteen-year-old).

We read no Appalachian authors in school, but I heard of James Still and Jesse Stuart from my parents; and the first live creative writer I ever saw was an Appalachian poet. One day my mother pulled back the living room curtain and pointed to a man walking down our street.

"There goes Albert Stewart," she said. "He's a poet."

That summer Mr. Stewart was teaching at the college and renting the top floor of the house next to ours. He might be amused to know how often I secretly watched him pass by, amazed that such a magical beast as an author was living next to us. Later, when grown, I would read the books written by our neighbor, James McConkey, who left Morehead before we did, and I would be sustained in my wish to be a writer by the knowledge that an actual Morehead father and neighbor could not only be a writer but could publish stories set in that little town.

Overall, I think of myself as having grown up in "pre-Appalachia," that is, in a region without a shared consciousness of its uniqueness. Of course I can speak only for my own experience in this regard, and things are different there now, sometimes to an extreme. Recently, after having attended a cultural heritage festival in Morehead, which included a dulcimer-making demonstration, the elderly mother of a friend of mine remarked with some disgust, "Why, when I was growing up I never knew *anybody* who played a dulcimer, much less built one!"

But of course I was living and breathing the culture every day. The bedrock of my Appalachian writing is certainly my father's stories about growing up on farms in Cabell County, West Virginia, first on Spurlock Creek and then up Nine Mile Hollow. In his tales, the neighbors, our family, and the landscape take on mythic dimensions. As a trained historian and a collector of epics, he is particularly well suited to mold the stuff of everyday life into a heroic vision. But always there is the underlying theme of loss, which seems endemic to the Appalachian experience. To move ahead is to betray the past. To become educated is to become different. To better oneself can ultimately lead to exile and loss of self.

Furthermore, my father's stories, despite his prodigious memory, inevitably go back to a vanishing point, beyond which there are only tantalizing glimpses of an unrecorded past. One such story has at its center my grandfather's decision in the 1920s to pull down the "shackly" old three-story barn on his property and put up a sturdier structure. To build the stone foundation, he, my father, and my uncle Daryl hauled sandstone boulders from the pastures to the barn lot, where the rocks were expertly cut and dressed by an old English stonemason who lived farther up the hollow. The old mason died shortly after the barn was finished, and my grandmother used to say that the work on their barn killed him. Today, the house, barn, and outbuildings are all gone, but the stone foundation still stands on the lip of the hill; and I am left wondering why an English stonemason was living alone, in poverty, in the West Virginia hills. What is his story? Where history and memory fail, fiction can step in.

While I learned from my father all that was good about subsistence farming and life in an isolated Appalachian community, his sister, my late aunt Glenith, told a different tale—and told it with determination. The stories of those who leave are different from the stories of those who stay. And Aunt Glenith left, as fast as she could. My father and my aunt taught me two opposing but inseparable ways of being from Appalachia.

From an early age Aunt Glenith seems to have been ashamed of her upbringing and desperate to get "out of the last briar patch over the hill" and to the city.

Running away from home at eighteen, she married an older man she met while working in an amusement park and spent the rest of her life in a series of rented apartments in industrial cities in Ohio. She never stopped making fun of Briers and extolling how exciting it was to work in factories and go to nightclubs. Yet despite the fur coats and nice cars, she never managed to erase her Appalachian character, expressed in every colorful sentence she uttered ("Yeah, that's easy— about as easy as ramming butter up a wildcat's ass with a red-hot poker"), the food she cooked (fried rabbit, parched corn, fresh blackberry cake, apples fried in pork shoulder grease), her grit, her mordant sense of humor, and her suspicion of other people who got above their raising. She and my uncle Carl became the models for Dreama and Floyd McDonald in *Small Caucasian Woman,* as my grandfather and grandmother Fowler were the models for Talbot and Sarah Forrester.

If I had only *heard* the stories, I might never have been moved to write about them. But I *saw* them, too, played out before my eyes in visits to both sets of grandparents, whose way of life placed them firmly in a nearly bygone Appalachia. My Fowler grandparents lived in their clapboard-covered, two-story log house up Nine Mile Hollow until 1956, when Aunt Glenith took them to Middletown, Ohio. That farm is the ur-farm of my fiction. Whenever Appalachian exiles in my fiction yearn for a piece of mountainside they have left and lost, that is the farm I am writing about. Whenever characters choose to stay in the hills, that is the farm they stay on. Though someone else now owns that land, to my father and me it will never belong to any family but ours.

My Cochran grandparents, on my mother's side, farmed for many more years outside Etowah in the Tennessee Overhill country. I regret now that I didn't listen to their stories more closely, for they were yarn spinners, too. Invariably, when Grandpa Cochran would get cranked up about hauling lumber by mule team from Blue Ridge to Ellijay, Georgia, my grandmother would cry, "Oh, Boyd, stop telling them old tales!" Then, as soon as he subsided, she would launch into memories of her girlhood near Patrick, North Carolina. Often when I write, I think about her speech patterns, the songs she sang, and the poems she recited. A self-taught pianist, she loved to sing hymns and mountain ditties, and she insisted on her grandchildren being ready to perform in the manner she remembered from her one-room schooldays. She would exclaim at us, "What if you're called on for a recitation and don't have anything ready?"

Fortunately, in recent years my mother has written a number of essays that preserve anecdotes of her family. She has observed this difference between the Cotter side of her family, which she characterizes as "pure Appalachian," and the Cochran side, which she sees as more "southern": Although the rural lifestyles and values were essentially the same, the Appalachian folks were more resourceful, and the ways the two branches of the family defined themselves through stories were different, the southern relatives having more to say about the Civil War, for instance. On all sides of my family, men and women put in long hours of hard, physical labor, belying the stereotype of the lazy mountaineer. And they liked it. Aunt Glenith used to say, "If a Fowler don't have work, he'll make work."

From Cookeville I moved on to study at Vanderbilt University. There, at first inspired by the protracted afterglow of the Fugitive Poets, I majored in English literature. My time at Vanderbilt also moved me into a deepening sense of dislocation. Until then, rather than Appalachian, I would have characterized myself as southern, for I still had no idea of what being Appalachian meant. But the students, who appeared to be largely from the urban centers of the Mid and Deep South, by and large had a different sense of class, privilege, race relations, and heritage than mine. I suspected that they were *authentic* southerners. Who, then, was I?

Perhaps the real distinction that needs to be made is between the mountain South and the cotton South. I was surprised to find that among most Vanderbilt students there was not the same respect for, and faith in, a college education that I grew up with in Morehead, where so many of our friends and neighbors had come out of the hills expressly to attend Morehead State in order to become teachers. It took my father, the first of his family to go to college, eight years to get through Marshall University, working a quarter and going to school a quarter. In Morehead there was general reverence for teachers. At Vanderbilt, the acquiring of a good education was taken for granted by the wealthier student body. It would be years before I consciously understood all of this—I am still working out the subtleties—and years before I learned of the Vanderbilt connections of such writers as Mildred Haun, Jesse Stuart, James Still, and Jim Wayne Miller.

Perhaps Vanderbilt was typical of the times in having no female faculty in the English Department and few women writers listed on its syllabi. Of the fine writers who visited the campus in the four years we were there, neither my husband (also an English major) nor I recall a single woman among them. The year that Kingsley Amis taught there, he brought along his wife, Elizabeth Jane Howard. At a cocktail party, my then future husband asked Howard what she did.

"I'm a novelist," she said shortly.

"What kind of novels do you write?" he asked.

Ms. Howard looked down her nose at him and replied with deadly, British scorn, "Rather good ones, actually."

She was right, as I later found out by reading them. But I never would have known that by her nonpresence on campus.

But Vanderbilt was to train me in the method of literary analysis that would instruct my approach to writing. John Crowe Ransom and others had established the critical tradition of New Criticism there years before. Applying this explication de texte method to the work of Eliot, Stevens, Tate, Ransom himself, the Metaphysical Poets, Shakespeare, and anything else that came under the New Critical lens taught me to pay attention to every single element of a text and to demand that each particle enhance the whole. (Flaubert was the other important influence here.) With its emphasis on an unmediated relationship between the reader and the text, it seems to me that New Criticism must have arisen out of an essentially religious sensibility, specifically the Protestant stress on a personal relationship with God and the Bible. In such a practice, however, what one gets out of the text depends entirely on what one brings to it. Listening to Allen Tate stroll through an Auden poem, casually yet somehow rigorously bestowing meaning here and there, was to understand that Tate's ideal reader would not be a lay reader but a member of an intellectual, literary priesthood. My upbringing was considerably more egalitarian than that. And two things, I see now, that New Criticism did not particularly value, given its interest in structure and style, were story and emotion, which would come to be my main interests as a mature writer.

With only male writers and teachers as role models and having read relatively little work by women after childhood, I subconsciously felt that I did not have permission to write fiction and poetry. I wrote my first short story in Spanish (not in English) while spending a summer in Colombia in 1971, for my husband came from another mountain chain—the Andes. Writing in a different language seemed safer to me then and allowed me to be creative. But once I seriously began writing, I quickly switched to English and tried setting down reminiscences and short fiction set in Kentucky and Tennessee. Looking over my shoulder, though they may not be evident in my writing, were those male writers whose work I saw as essentially one lifelong book broken into individually published volumes—Faulkner, Joyce, Proust, Zola, García Marquez. I was interested in whole worlds, fiction that told the story not just of a person or of a group of people, but of an entire culture. Most important, they showed me how the regional can be universal.

The women I thought about when I wrote were not authors but rather women I had known in childhood. The actual women in my life have perhaps had the greatest influence on my work. My first published short story was about a friend of my mother's, a high-toned teacher from the Old South whose life in eastern Kentucky seemed a life of brave exile. I would tell stories of such women again and again, women ordinary on the outside but extraordinary on the inside; the kind of women who, as Faulkner once remarked about the entire gender, can't bear anything but pain, poverty, and tragedy.

After a year in Cologne, Germany, and five years in Boston, we moved to Detroit, where my husband began his teaching career. There, I consciously started to see myself as living in exile. I met relatives who had come to Detroit years before to work in industry. They seemed edgy and defensive about their way of life, extolling the virtues too highly, as my aunt Glenith did. One night during a family evening at our apartment in Inkster, my solemn great-uncle Herman smiled and his face was momentarily transformed into the face of my long-dead grand-mother. The connection back to her, though brief, was electric in its intensity. More and more, I felt the need to write my way back home.

We moved to central Illinois. Often when I left the house, I felt as if I had left my purse behind or had forgotten to put on a slip. There was a persistent sense that something was missing. One day I realized what it was: I missed having hills around me, watching over me, sheltering me, cutting the horizon down to a man-ageable size. Although the vast, flat fields of corn and soybeans have their own beauty, I missed living in a crowded and detailed natural environment. In a re-lated way, conversation in the Midwest was different from what I was used to. It was pared down, straightforward, and bereft of colloquialisms, similes, and the anecdotal approach to the simplest exchange, which I encountered whenever I talked with Kentucky friends. I began to wonder if the convoluted tales that people told back home weren't influenced by the winding roads and intricate scenery of the hills and mountains. There, in conversation as in travel, the shortest distance between two points is not only impossible, it is unthinkable. A couple of years ago, I rediscovered a friend from eastern Kentucky who is married to an Illinois native. Her husband noted that when they visit his family in Illinois, the talk is of the weather and world events. But when they go to eastern Kentucky, "all people talk about is people."

I have a theory that in order to be a writer you have to come from a small town, because only in a small community can one hone one's powers of observa-tion and participate in the full range of human experience in all its high drama and trivial variations. This small town, the laboratory of the future writer, can be an extended family or a religious community or a tightly knit profession or an ethnic neighborhood within a metropolis—just so long as it is a place where, intensely and without cease, "people talk about people."

But I was not living in my small town, and my Kentucky stories were going nowhere. After a reading I gave in Illinois, a professor came up to me and said, "I found only one flaw in your stories. Such people wouldn't be intelligent enough to say the things you have them say. They wouldn't be that clever."

"Thank you," I replied, "those particular characters are drawn from my fam-ily." Of course this was neither the first nor the last time I would encounter a low, smirking opinion of anything having to do with Appalachia.

Meanwhile, in order to earn money and to teach myself basic writing tech-niques, I had become the romance novelist Laurel Blake. I published four ro-mances, signed a contract to write three more, and subsequently broke that con-tract to get out of writing formula fiction. I had started writing in order to speak for characters whose stories would never be told unless I told them. Anybody could write the romance novels I was writing.

In 1985, I learned that the Appalachian Writers' Association was going to hold its annual meeting at Morehead State University, in conjunction with the Appalachian Celebration that takes place on campus every June. Garry Barker has written about the perils of being "gone too long" from one's hometown. I should have known this was true of me when my thirteen-year-old daughter, whom I decided to take with me, asked if we would be able to get good fruit to eat in eastern Kentucky.

At the conference I met Garry, Sharyn McCrumb, and other writers of the region. I listened to a lecture by Bill Best on the evils of school consolidation and on how little the school system in his day did to promote regional identity. At another session, George Brosi sketched the history of Appalachian literature. I heard a storyteller and listened to string bands. At the AWA banquet, I received first prize in the short fiction competition and listened to Harriette Arnow give what must have been one of her last speeches before her death. I had written a story about an Appalachian woman in Detroit, but I had never read *The Dollmaker*. I bought a copy of Jim Wayne Miller's *Dialogue with a Dead Man*. In the dorm, I read the work of other writers in *Appalachian Heritage* magazine and recognized my own themes, language, and settings in their stories. Like Molière's *Bourgeois Gentilhomme* discovering that he has been speaking prose all his life, back home in Morehead I discovered that I was writing Appalachian fiction and thus was part of a recognized literary tradition.

In the years since that turning point, I have tried to catch up with my literary heritage by building my own library of Appalachian literature and history. My childhood friend, Vanda Botts Manahan, now living in exile in Minnesota, has spent hours speculating with me about the region, its people, and the qualities of story and speech that are particular to it. I have learned from my father's genealogical research just how typical our ancestors are of the Appalachian stereotype— heavily Scotch, Irish, and Scotch-Irish with a tad of Native American, farmers and factory workers, craftspeople (weaving and blacksmithing), country preachers and teachers. No matter what else they did, they always seemed to be fooling with food, farming and canning. Nobody is famous, though they have rubbed shoulders with the famous, living next to Daniel Boone in the Yadkin Valley and fighting in the Revolutionary War, the Civil War, and the two World Wars. There is a persistent family rumor that at the westernmost edge of his surveying trip into the frontier as a young man, George Washington surveyed the terrain of the Nine Mile farm. Somebody has got to tell the stories of these people and places, or make them up. Almost nobody thought to write anything down, not even in the Bible. The sheer anonymity of my background calls out for a scribe.

When I was writing *Small Caucasian Woman,* one night I had a dream that I was standing on the hill of Hisarlik in Asia Minor, the site of ancient Troy. At my feet yawned one of the great, damaging trenches that Heinrich Schliemann cut through the mound in his search for the fabled city Homer described in *The Iliad.* In my dream, out of the layers made by the several Troys that were built one on top of the other over the course of centuries spilled the wealth of the Aegean— brilliantly colored silks, gold, jewels, painted amphorae, marble statues, the polished weaponry of heroes. My eye followed the cascading spoils down and down until it reached the bottom of the excavation. There, stretching down the length of the trench, lay the Main Street of Morehead. My fabled past. My source.

Well along in my writing career, I began to write and publish poetry. At first I wondered why my musings about my Appalachian heritage never took the form of poetry but only of stories. Then I realized that I could only approach the subjects of my poetry—subjects such as the struggles of our son, who has multiple disabilities—indirectly through metaphors. But I don't approach Appalachia through metaphors. For me, Appalachia *is* the metaphor.

I grew up on the edge of that metaphor. In fact, a poet friend of mine claims that Appalachia starts at the western border of Rowan County, of which Morehead is the county seat. Due to my family circumstances, it is highly unlikely that I will ever live in Appalachia again, although it is still the only place I call home. So these days I return there as to an archaeological site. I ask questions, write down snatches of overheard dialogue, take photographs, roam the streets like a ghost, poke around in the college library, buy local newspapers, visit the folk art museum, drive the country roads, talk to friends about how daily life there is changing, and rake up the past. Then I go back to Illinois and write about the Appalachia in my mind, which, as the years go by, has less and less to do with the actual places I have just visited and everything to do with the Appalachia, good and bad, in which I want to believe.

JAYNE
ANNE
PHILLIPS

Jayne Anne Phillips (b. 1952) is the author of two novels, *Shelter* (1994) and *Machine Dreams* (1984), and of two widely anthologized collections of stories, *Fast Lanes* (1987) and *Black Tickets* (1979). She is the recipient of a Guggenheim fellowship, two National Endowment for the Arts Fellowships, a Bunting Institute Fellowship, the Sue Kaufman Award (1980), an Academy Award in Literature (1997) from the American Academy and Institute of Arts and Letters, and a National Book Critics Circle Award nomination. Her work has appeared most recently in *Granta, Doubletake,* and the *Norton Anthology of Contemporary Fiction.* Phillips is currently writer-in-residence at Brandeis University.

*   *   *

Premature Burial

I'm ten years old in 1962 and my hometown is still pretty. It's a college town, the county seat, in north-central West Virginia. It seems more a college town than a coal town, though in fact it is both—home to a private Methodist college where Bible classes are required curriculum, home to a network of rural deep mines connected by two-lane roads. In fifteen years the mines will begin to close, give way to stripmining that will ruin the land even faster, fill the air with fine black dust that subtly changes the colors of the houses. The coal trucks will cease their circuitous routes and lumber right along Main Street, breaking the pavement, scattering coal dust and sick exhaust through downtown, past the grade schools, out toward Interstate 79, where they'll carry away what little the state has left. Stripminers aren't really miners; they're heavy-equipment operators from out of state, and the only local businessmen who survive will become their suppliers. Everything else will dry up, and the town will go down. But in 1962, there is no stripmining, no interstate highway, no fast-food chains or malls. Stores are owned by men whose fathers owned the stores, and restaurants are run by women in their fifties who have worked in the restaurants for thirty years. The town listens to the mine report before the national news, and the local radio station begins its broadcast on snow days with lists of shifts: *These shifts will work . . . Century No. 2 . . . Nitro . . . United Bethlehem . . . Hundred . . . Ludlow 1.* The miners are employed— paid well for compromising their lives. Every twenty years or so there's a cave-in or an explosion, men trapped, women camped out above ground to pray. Veteran miners are habitually short-winded, but most of them are smokers and the term "black lung" is not yet common usage. The streets of the town are clean and the teenage sons of the miners drive new pickups up and down Main Street on Saturday nights, conducting a kind of class warfare with the boys from town, who drive Mustang convertibles and date the most popular girls. Everyone goes to church on Sundays. There are the First and Central Methodists, Central and Southern Baptists, First and Second Presbyterians; past the city limits, out closer to the mines, are the Pentecostals and Holy Rollers. There's one large Catholic church, near the hospital run by nuns. In deference, the schools serve fish sticks every Friday. There are no Jews. There are three or four black families in the town and they're all related. Their children are well accepted by their same-sex peers but, funny thing, the teenagers don't date and no one even wonders about it. The larger world, the world that might question the social and economic drift of the town, just doesn't exist beyond the mountains and valleys and small skies. We see that world in *Life* magazine, on TV, and at the movies.

The movies are beautiful. There are two theaters. The Kanawha is the bigger one and sits at the bottom of Kanawha Hill, nicknamed "Quality Hill" in the twenties. The branches of hundred-year-old oaks and elms meet heavy-leaved over the wide street where the grandest houses have already been given over to fraternities and funeral homes. The Kanawha signals the edge of the tiny downtown, its giant "K" blinking alternating stripes of blue and violet neon. The lobby is art deco inside, not much of a lobby at all, just two big ascending corridors to the right and left on either side of the candy counter. The smaller Colonial is on Main Street next to the Dairy Queen. The old-fashioned marquee is lit by tinkly pink lights, the cave of its dim rococo interior papered in wavery pink and green scallops. The Colonial is popular with teenagers because it has a balcony, accessible from the lobby along a steep tunnel of twisting, carpeted stairs. Mr. Winkler, the wizened owner, takes tickets by the big double doors of the theater and won't let little kids up the balcony steps. We sneak up when his back is turned. Later, when we call our parents to pick us up, Mr. Winkler stands with us in the little office that smells of his cigars, hugging us, saying what good girls we are, stroking our chests through our cotton sweaters or bulky winter coats. He hugs us from behind while we dial numbers on the old black telephone. We jostle to evade his grasp but not one of us thinks of mentioning his embraces at home. We don't talk about anything that happens at the movies, so why would we talk about him? We talk about which clothes we want to wear or which TV shows we want to watch, and we watch a lot of TV because TV is still a sort of innocent miracle in regressive West Virginia time. It's as though we were living in the late forties rather than the early sixties. Most people have had TVs for only a few years. Often we watch TV as a family, Perry Como sitting on a stool and tapping a glass with a teaspoon: *Catch a falling star and put it in your pocket.* But kids go to the movies alone, dropped off at the door to meet our friends. We girls sit in groups of five or six across; we never know what exactly it is we're going to see until we sit down and watch, and the scary movies are delicious because we scream in unison and get right down on the floor, writhing and peering through our fingers. We're nine or ten years old, growing up together at the movies before we have to think about boys; only the dim buzz of parental struggle at home shadows the intensity of our own politics. We love Vincent Price in *The Last Man on Earth.* We are terrified when he walks down the steps of a big white public building that resembles the Lincoln Memorial, dodging the undead with his inimitable scowl. We cover our eyes, giggle nervously, hide in each other's arms. And we love *The Phantom of the Opera,* the great moment when he swings across the opera house on a vast crystal chandelier as the audience gapes, and his feat seems wholly believable in the world of this theater, where it is always dark and the dark is filled with sound, and the only reality is the colossal picture on the screen. In fact, this world seems more real to us in many ways, more the way life should be, than what we see in our town, in the county around the town, where in fact bad things happen. Despite crowded Main Street and employment in the mines, there is grinding, entrenched poverty, poverty that a pittance of monthly welfare checks does nothing to alleviate. We don't know much about it; it's a secret we take in by osmosis in Murphy's Five and Ten Cent Store on Saturdays, where we gather by the record rack to listen to 45s. We see the families standing inside where it's warm. The women have dead eyes and their children's hair is uncombed. Their skin is alabaster white, blue-veined, and they haven't been able to get clean. The kids are dirty in an old, dry way; they are dark between their fingers, and their wrists are cuffed with shadow. The delicate bracelets of lines on the backs of their wrists are etched with dirt, as though someone had taken a pen with a very fine point and traced each tiny cross and whorl. Their eyes are not dead. They look—what, exactly? They look startled. Their eyes are wide with apprehension. I look at them and wonder what they've seen; I know the world of the town is not what it seems. The movies are exactly what they seem, but the world is not like the movies.

My mother is a first-grade teacher in the town and tells me how some kids come in off the buses so hungry that she has to take them to the school lunchroom and find them something, anything, to eat before she tries to teach them. She collects odd mittens and gloves from neighbors and matches up same-size rights and lefts for the kids from the country, so at least their hands will be warm. Some of them are too proud to wear those mittens and their hands are chapped and mottled, almost mauve, when they finish the long bus ride to school in town. Every fall the churches donate warm clothes to the welfare office, but the clothes, if they show up on the kids at all, get dirtier and dirtier, and wear out before winter is over. My mother says the parents cash the welfare checks and drink the money. She says it's the mothers in Murphy's with the children waiting for the fathers to finish drinking at the bars. She says some of the mothers break down and take off, or they break down in a different way and go to the bars with the men. Then it's the older sisters waiting with the children, sisters who are not much older than me. Soon they'll quit school, if they haven't already, and be taken up by some man who probably already has a brood of kids. They'll live in a hollow like the one they grew up in, places with names like Mud Lick, Sago, Volga, a cluster of buildings around a coal tipple, the wood-frame houses fanning off, far apart, up dirt roads. Those roads are beautiful in summer, and the creeks are still full of catfish, but in winter the cold is brutal. The little houses are heated with coal stoves, easy enough to keep going, but someone might forget or not be home or be drunk. I hear my mother discuss this or that story with other women: *That poor baby got too cold to wake up—they were keeping it in a cardboard box on the floor* or *Mother of five, just sat down on her own subzero porch, couldn't take it anymore.*

I don't know how the women know these stories. I know my friends and I don't see the country kids at the movies. But I think about them in the dark, inevitably, as though they are ghosts mixed up in the light of the overwhelming image flickering over us. I fantasize a tall man in black like Vincent Price, evil enough to meet any evil, slitting the screen with a big knife, and letting those children in. He lets them into a world of velvet gowns and jewels and pink cravats and sparkling glasses, operas and great houses and British accents. Then I don't have to think about them anymore, and I can watch the movies, one after another, every Friday night and every Sunday afternoon.

I see Doris Day and James Bond and John Wayne but what I'll remember most from these years are the B-grade horror films of Roger Corman—not the creature films, but the opulent versions of Poe. The fog machine is always working overtime and the air is billowy with clouds. I'll realize later that Corman's luxuriantly gothic (and inexpensively produced) sets were the stuff of a girl-child's dreams, and I'll know too that I remember certain images because of my real life—not because the images changed me, but because they were haunting, inverted metaphors of things that were true, things too frightening to think about as a child. What about those houses with slanted porches up the dirt roads, the houses where women and babies freeze? What about my own family, how shaky things seem, how hard my capable mother seems to work at school, at home, coping always with my father's anger and resentment. What does it mean: *buried*? The frequent, gothic burials in Corman's films are relatively speedy events; here in our town, there's daily life—a long, slow process. There is no screaming, no hugging or group catharsis, for the observers or the participants. I suppose my friends and I are both, though at least we are town kids—we won't wake to find our mothers frozen on a broken-down porch. My brothers and I really are town kids, definitely, I tell myself. Though we live out a rural road, the road is paved and we're only a mile from the city limits. More important, my family is well thought of—my mother's people were wealthy once, owned a lumber mill, went broke in the Depression. My father's established and owned the non-Catholic hospital. Later he owned a concrete plant, but that is gone now. This winter my parents have had to cash in their children's savings bonds, and my father is working for the local Chevrolet dealership, selling used cars. Cars don't sell in the cold weather, my father tells me, and sometimes when we get home from school with my mother, my father is already there, frying potatoes for supper in the big iron skillet. He always drives us into town on Friday nights for the movies, which cost fifty cents. I occasionally pretend to have lost one of my quarters; he grimaces and looks pained, shakes his head, but it's only pretense. He digs into his pocket for another coin, chuckling. Lately I realize the ritual has gained importance for him, and I remember to do it each time. Tonight he drops us off at the Kanawha to see something called *The Premature Burial.* When I read the title on the marquee I think maybe the film has to do with babies born too soon, but when I see the poster in the lobby I realize I'm on familiar ground. My friends buy popcorn but I purchase a Sugar Daddy, a rectangular caramel sucker on a stick that I can warm to the shape of my mouth and taste throughout the previews and well into the feature itself. My friends have names like Susie, Kathy, Janie, Joanie, names that are just not serious, and we all settle in, pretending to be what we're supposed to be, and then the lights go down.

Corman characterizes *Premature Burial* as one of his less successful efforts. It may have been a formulaic low point in his career, but, seeing it twenty-five years later, I think it must have been great fun to make. I'd always remembered Vincent Price in the role of Guy Carrell, scion of a dwindling Victorian family, rattling around with his drab sister and assorted servants in a mansion on the foggy moors. But it's actually Ray Milland, who doesn't steal the film as Price would have. He leaves that to the female leads, who do suitably restrained but campy versions of the spinster sister, Kate, and the love interest, "sweet, beautiful, gentle Emily." Milland is distanced, rather vague, obsessed with the idea that his father had catalepsy and was buried alive. He's certain he's inherited the illness and will meet the same fate. We girls take it all in, slouched down with our knees propped up on the seats in front of us. We first see Milland dressed in black top hat and cape, grave robbing at night in a cemetery with doctor colleagues. They are decidedly unlike our fathers, standing there in their evening clothes as Sweeny and Mole, the whistling grave diggers, unearth a casket in a hole below them. They are rich men watching poor men work, but they all look so funny in their formal attire as dirt flies around them that we snicker into our hands. Music swells as the lid of the casket is wrested off and slammed into the face of the viewer, its inside streaked with blood. We stop snickering. Close-up of a shrunken corpse that does in fact resemble a fetus, its hands upraised like knobby, foreshortened limbs. The grave diggers continue to whistle the excellent, beautifully timbred version of "Molly Malone" that will haunt Milland throughout the movie. It has already occurred to me that my own father is haunted, but I don't yet know why. I've observed that some of my friends' fathers hold the power in the family matrix as my own father does not. Even so, they seem disgruntled; they don't converse much with their daughters. When we see Emily, a daughter herself in the film, her auburn hair is upswept and her snowy cleavage is concealed in a hooded velvet cape. She is driven in her carriage to the mansion of the suffering Milland, who's decided not to marry her because his imperfect genes forecast disaster. I immediately think he is referring to the children of their union rather than to the hardship of his own demise, and I think of the man who lives in the house next to the town jail, just across the parking lot from the theater. He's a grown-up man with the mind of a boy; my mother has told me he's a mongoloid, which reminds me of the country of Mongolia, and he does look Oriental, ancient, with his jowls and his wrinkled, down-sliding face. Doglike, he sits at the window staring toward the traffic on Kanawha Street, his face pressed to the glass. I've never seen him outside and I've never seen his mother, but she couldn't be anything like the glamorous Emily, who pronounces herself unafraid of disaster. Maybe she is more like the drab sister, Kate, who is clearly the villain—wrenlike, embittered, dressed always in black, her little mouth clamped into a straight, disapproving line. But the drab, dark sister turns out to be the honorable one; Emily is after the house and the money and is typically, underhandedly feminine: she's hired the grave diggers to whistle the song and appear at second-story windows. She's "set her cap," as my mother would say, for the handsome, sincere Dr. Miles Archer. Miles has invented a tabletop contraption with cords and clamps, the better to observe the contractions of electrically stimulated frogs, but his real interest is the human mind. They are all here for the wedding—not the frogs, of course, but the good doctors and all the other elegant guests—and so is the noisiest lightning storm on record, with claps of foreshadowing thunder drowning out the vows. At the reception in the great hall, Emily goes to the piano in her wedding gown to play "Molly Malone," whose strains precipitate Guy's swoon into a sleep of dread.

Now Guy lies in funereal repose on his baronial bed. It resembles my mother's high, antique beds, but when my mother feels dreadful, she lies still on the narrow couch in the living room, and my father is not home. She has a blinding headache and can't open her eyes. She lies with her arms straight down at her sides and directs me to press down on her forehead with both hands, press down, hard, harder, don't stop. In the moments when my muscles begin to ache and I have to rest my arms, she groans, so I start again, pressing on her forehead, pressing as hard as I can. I am thinking about my mother while I watch the movie, her form supine in the house on the rural road, her smooth forehead just the size of my two hands, and I see Guy awaken with a plan. The quality of my attention changes. Soon Emily summons the helpful Miles to view the mausoleum Guy has designed to curb his fear. It's a sort of Greek Revival–style temple with all sorts of built-in devices. Guy himself narrates its wonders and demonstrates with obvious pride: there is a tasseled cord to pull which activates a sliding door in the stone wall; a coffin whose lid is fitted with tools, whose push button instantly pops the top and sides apart. There is a bell to pull for help from the house. One may have to wait—there are books, periodicals, food and drink, and a gramophone to provide the soothing effects of music. If help doesn't come (or no one cares to answer), a gate automatically opens in the wall. A pull cord drops a rope ladder to a door in the roof. Then there is the dynamite in a gold box ("a recent invention by a Swed-ish chemist called Nobel"). If all else fails, there is poison in a silver chalice. After-ward, Emily takes Guy walking in the fog and dark, where he hears the grave diggers whistling and runs through thorns and brush in a panicky search to find some physical presence responsible for the sound. The tune gets louder and faster like an ether dream. Guy faints alone on the moors and has a nightmare. He wakes up in his coffin but the button doesn't work and the tools are gone. He cries out noiselessly in the eerie blue light of the box, finally upsets the coffin with his struggling and breaks it open. The food, of course, is spongy with mold. The velvet rope has rotted and the escape gate is jammed; the rope ladder falls from the ceiling in strands. A tarantula crawls over the box of dynamite, which crumbles to dust in Guy's hands. Rats scramble everywhere. He pulls the chalice from its cob-webbed crevice and begins to drink, and the worms in the cup tumble right into our faces. Girls to the right and left of me have their faces in my neck, but I'm staring straight into the image. Here is a movie about a foiled escape, and I am already plotting mine. I must succeed, not fail; the escape is not only mine, it is hers—my mother's—because I am her and she is me, and my escape will be her escape, the only escape she will ever have. I am plotting our escape, not by think-ing or planning, it's too soon for that, but by looking, watching, perceiving even the smallest useful detail, and remembering—what? Everything, everything that matters. This is love. This is who and what I will be.

But Emily's love is false. She convinces Guy to blow up the mausoleum, scares him into a cataleptic seizure, watches him buried (in a coffin with a window, no less). Secretly, though, her heartless father has him immediately dug up as a re-search specimen. Freed, he goes on a bit of a rampage and does away with all the villains. He actually buries Emily alive in his own grave and is holding Miles off admirably when Kate, the honorable sister, puts him out of his misery with one quick, clean shot.

There is no clean shot in life. There is Kanawha Street, shimmering with rain and darkness when we walk out of the lighted theater. And there is my father's big white Ford, floating like a boat on the rain-slicked blacktop, wipers clacking, motor idling, the headlights sending two long beams through the dark. I see rain falling in the light he makes, and the oily puddles at my feet are faceted with color.

The honorable sister in my family is me. I'm the only sister—for years, I think I have no choice. But no, actually I choose to be honorable. I'm the one my mother will confide in as she exits the marriage in careful stages, moving us to a house in town, moving her bedroom to the basement of that house, asking my father to leave the year the children are all off to college. She has a graduate degree now and a demanding job in administration. For some years we live parallel lives, living alone with our dogs, doing our work, except I move at least once a year, establish a number of intense relationships, experiment in every way. My mother wishes I'd encounter a Dr. Miles Archer, but I'm moving too fast, I take no prisoners, sabotage any rescue. When I'm thirty, I buy my own house. Shortly after, I'm the one holding my mother's hands in the radiologist's office when he clips the X-rays to light boards and touches the white spots with his pointer. "Here," he says, "and here, and here, and here." We try one thing after another: radiation first, then stoic acceptance, then, when I'm pregnant with my first child, chemotherapy. She has to leave home in a wheelchair, move in with me on the East Coast. My son is born, and the drugs help her for a while, then they fail. Now we are really terrified—there's no putting it off. I begin to understand what premature burial means, I begin to understand about foiled escapes, and anguish. When my mother dies in her room at my house, I'm the one who is with her, and my husband is there, and so is the young black woman who helps us at night. She's from an isolated place, like me, where there is warmth and lush vegetation and wrenching poverty, where there are town kids and country kids and just one or two theaters. She tells me, in her lilting island patois, that we've all done well.

But my mother's death is not like death in the movies. My husband, who is, in fact, a doctor, tells me later she wasn't there when it happened, but I know she was, trapped inside. I know how it will all stay with me, nothing buried, nothing even out of sight. For years, I'll find myself staring right into the image that changed my life.

At the cemetery I stay alone while the cremation takes place. It is a raw November day, banked, melting snow, very misty and foggy. I sit by a half-frozen pond in my raincoat while smoke ascends from the crematorium chimney. This is the oldest section of the cemetery; the stones are Victorian and dramatic. It's so foggy that I can't see the road beyond the wrought-iron fence, only dimly hear the sluicing sound of passing traffic. I have patterned my adult life on escape and redemption, escape being flight, movement, self-reliance, redemption being the circle back, the writing, the saving of a version of events that is emotionally real, that can't ever recede or be lost. Escape is no longer possible; I no longer believe in escape, and there is too much at stake now to simply rely on myself. It's as though I hold my child in my arms and move in an inexorable spiral toward the eye of life and death. When I was a child and watched someone else's dreams at the movies, the stories were shadow plays. *You and I were very close once. You stood aside and let them bury me alive. I shall not bury you; that sorry task I shall leave to the earth, and the darkness, and the terrible pounding of your own heart. Stay where you are, Miles, this has nothing to do with you. My beautiful, treacherous, perfidious love . . . She's dead. Thank God.* There are no shadows in this white day. The smoke of my mother's transformation is dark as it meets the air, climbing in curls, but the color lightens, drifts, disintegrates in the fog, completely taken up.

RITA
SIMS
QUILLEN

Born in 1954 in Hiltons, Virginia, the fifth generation to be born in that place, Rita Sims Quillen is the oldest of four children. When she was thirteen, she almost got the part of Mick in the film version of *The Heart Is a Lonely Hunter*. She married her high school sweetheart at nineteen, graduated from a local community college at the age of twenty-three, and then transferred to East Tennessee State University, where she majored in English/education and minored in business. While an undergraduate, Quillen won first place in the Virginia Highlands Writing Contest (essay division) and published two stories in small magazines. She received the Outstanding English Student Award from ETSU in 1980. Her M.A. thesis, *Looking for Native Ground: Contemporary Appalachian Poetry,* was published in 1989. Quillen, also author of an elaborate bibliography of modern and contemporary mountain poetry that was published in *Appalachian Journal* in 1985, is fast being viewed as an authority on mountain literature. A chapbook of her poetry, *October Dusk,* was published in 1987. A new full-length book, *Counting the Sums* (1995), contains a collection of her most recent poetry. Since 1987, Rita has taught in the English Department at Northeast State Technical Community College. She is an associate professor and received the Outstanding Faculty Award in 1992. Quillen currently lives in Weber City, Virginia, a small town about five miles from Hiltons, with her husband, Gary Mac Quillen, and two children.

*   *   *

Counting the Sums

I must tell them someday
when they are old enough for memory
about the family of twelve
huddled in a creaking cabin
cracked feet oozing
on splintered floors,
show them the photo album
my father by a '52 Ford
his foot propped on the bumper
with the confidence
only the baby boy
in a clan of doting sisters
could ever know,
my mother in a red coat
the hat with fur trim
beaming at the camera
with the smile of a survivor
the strong one
in a house of weakness.
A counting of all their sums
requires the telling
of day after day in two rooms
with four kids and an ironing board
$20 in a drawer
two weeks to payday
the mouth-drying grief
of a busted radiator,
a day of stinging sweat
in a heat-dancing field
coal grit
in the back of the throat.
                    —*Counting the Sums*

"We are all the sums we have not counted," Thomas Wolfe wrote, "and every moment is a window on all time." In my writing, I attempt to count my life's sums, revisiting the mystery of particular moments. I am positive that I would have become a writer regardless of my life's circumstances, but I am also sure that had I lived somewhere else, had I been grown in other soil, I would have been a different writer. The time and place of my birth is crucial to understanding some things about my material and my viewpoint.

Like many of the writers in this volume, I am part of the reaction to what I call the "cultural pressure cooker" of Appalachia. As I discussed in my book *Looking for Native Ground,* the Deep South earlier in this century and the Southern Appalachian region today represent rural communities with distinct cultural traditions and values that are being challenged and shaped by rapid industrialization, commercialization, and mass media. Allen Tate, one of the Southern Agrarians, or Vanderbilt "Fugitives" as they were called, pointed out what happens when there is such a "crossing of the ways." He notes in his essay "The Profession of Letters in the South" that there has always been an intense literary reaction, no matter what culture or what era. "It [the cultural clash] has made possible the curious burst of intelligence, . . . not unlike, on an infinitesimal scale, the outburst of poetic genius at the end of the sixteenth century when commercial England had already begun to crush feudal England" (p. 768). As part of a place and culture under the intense pressure of change, I felt the strong urge to record, to capture, to preserve every word, every experience, every image I could before it was too late.

I live by my senses and my instincts, and this time and place called Appalachia is fertile ground for someone like me. There are so many powerful images, from my childhood in particular, in a world so different. I remember cakewalks with fiddle music, revival meetings, and molasses stir-offs where neighbors came together to help each other. I can still see my grandmother administering stitches to her quilt, the black round perfection of my mother's apple-butter kettle, bubbling over the fire. I remember many gardens, lush symmetry in vegetation, the black mud and hay smell of the barn.

There are negative memories, too. I remember how poor some of my schoolmates were. I remember white, dusty, bare feet contrasting sharply with the black, oiled wooden floors of the elementary school. The dark and stink of the outhouse behind my parents' first home is still with me. I can see the dust boiling into the air, back when all roads were dirt, coating everything inside and out. I remember country stores with nickel Cokes and candy in cases.

But until sixth grade, I didn't know the rest of the world was any different from my own, that we were "hillbillies" that were to be pitied and laughed at. That's when the folks that worked at the Kingsport Press in Kingsport, Tennessee, went on strike. It was a very emotional issue in the area, and I remember arguments and some shoving among the kids at school over it. The strike went on for a long time and attracted a great deal of attention. Eventually, a newspaper writer from up North came down and wrote a book about the whole affair. The *Kingsport Times News,* our family's daily glimpse at the world, reprinted the writings of this journalist as a service to its readers.

I was only in sixth grade, but this fellow's view of the area just didn't match mine. His version read like the funny papers' version of mountain life. He claimed that the press was staffed by the local "mountaineers," as he called them, who mostly sat around on their porches chewing tobacco, picking their teeth, and drinking moonshine, waiting for someone to come by and yell, "The Press is hirin'!" I got out my pen and paper and fired off a letter to the *Times.* I told the newspaper that they ought to have more sense than to publish some visiting Yankee man's distorted view of things. I was very proud of the letter because I used big words and fancy syntax. I signed it: "Rita Sims, Sixth Grade—Hilton Elementary School."

This was the beginning of my revelations about the difficult issue of cultural identity and self-concept. Years later, my supervising teacher for my undergraduate teaching practicum informed me that I would have to get a tape recorder and practice until I lost my mountain dialect (advice I continue to defy). "No one is going to take you seriously," she explained coolly, "as long as you talk the way you do." I had straight A grades, was named Outstanding Graduate in English at ETSU, and had already published numerous poems, stories, and articles. But still, as I have since learned, a hick is a hick is a hick.

My sense of identity as a person and a writer continued to evolve throughout my twenties as I looked at the world through all sorts of filters. Like many other mountain communities, my Scott County, Virginia, home became a haven for all the disillusioned refugees from the upper and middle class of my generation who started popping up like mayapples all along the ridge tops of Appalachia during the 1970s. Armed with their *Whole Earth Catalogs* and copies of *Walden,* they invaded in hordes to live the pure and simple life among the poor. Of course, they wanted to improve and help us poor folks. (They evidently skipped the part of Thoreau's essays about do-gooders and other kinds of natural pestilence.)

I came into their company primarily because of the music of the area. I grew up listening to mountain music and secretly loving it. I spent a great deal of time in the home of Janette Carter, daughter of A.P. and Sara Carter, and I was a musician and singer myself. For a time, these idealistic and refreshingly nonmaterialistic people enchanted me, and we met on an almost spiritual plane through our passion for the old mountain songs. But over time I began to realize the implications of some of their actions and ideas. I saw that they looked down on mountain people, even as they tried to emulate them, because mountain people held conservative views, ate white bread and bologna, used fertilizer in their gardens, and held down dirty, regular, time-clock jobs instead of being farmers or grant-supported artists. I became the disillusioned refugee.

But there was nowhere to turn, really. Among educated and enlightened mountain people, there was a self-loathing and uncertainty that was just as harmful. In many mountain towns, like Pikeville, Kentucky, there was a "Hillbilly Days" parade where people portray unflattering cartoon images of themselves. Writers like Pinckney Benedict from West Virginia depict Appalachia as a world full of people who do violent and/or stupid things for no good reason. I've been told that the *Arts Journal* in Asheville published a review of my poetry one time that dismissed my writing as "too Appalachian." I would have much preferred the reviewer say it was bad poetry than to suggest that there was something inherently negative about regional writing. It is hard to imagine the same journal calling Marilou Awiakta "too Cherokee" or a D.C. periodical sniffing that some Howard University poet was "too black." My point is that when your culture and history are misunderstood and often devalued and ridiculed from not only those outside it but also *inside,* then the "cultural pressure cooker" is even more intense.

So I've been particularly grateful to have a "family" in the writing community, complete with the annual family reunion. I first discovered them while in college. As a student struggling to put myself through Mountain Empire Community College in Wise County, Virginia, I devoted much of my time to writing horrible poetry while studying the great poets of the past—Donne, Yeats, Whitman. But at the urging of one of my professors, I discovered a body of work created by real, breathing people who lived fairly close by. I'll never forget sitting in the college library reading poems by Fred Chappell and Jim Wayne Miller for the first time. I could smell the honeysuckle and loamy creekbanks. I felt as if I had stepped out of the woods into an old abandoned homestead with the silent house, barn, and garden patch on every page. Here were poets, men of learning, who also knew my world.

I soon found out that Jim Wayne Miller, along with Harriette Arnow, James Still, Barbara Smith, Richard Day, Richard Hague, and others, gathered at a place called the Hindman Settlement School for a writers' workshop every August. This was in 1981. With great excitement and trepidation, I sent in my registration forms, packed my old Toyota, and set out across Pound Gap in absolute terror. I could never have dreamed how this trip would change my life.

I spent the first twenty-four hours with the sound of blood rushing through my ears, certain that someone would discover my pretense and banish me from this holy community of writers. At first everyone was very friendly and kind to me, but I still had those conferences with the workshop leaders to dread. When I walked into the dining hall to meet with Jim Wayne Miller, I had a nightmarish vision of being dismissed by someone I admired, of being told by word or body language that I was wasting time and didn't belong here.

Instead, I found myself in shock, unable to believe how carefully, how thoughtfully Jim Wayne had read my poems. He smiled and told me, "Meeting you and discovering your work will be a highlight of this week for me." With those generous words of encouragement a long friendship began. Jim has continually helped me find publication opportunities, including locating a home for the chapbook *October Dusk* in 1987. His encouragement and advice entitle him to significant credit for my second book, *Looking for Native Ground: Contemporary Appalachian Poetry,* which contains a critical essay about his work. He is the founder and CEO of the Jim Wayne Miller Correspondence School of Plain Living, High Thinking, and Pure Poetry who has been a friend and mentor to dozens of writers. Jim Wayne, along with the other writers mentioned earlier as well as writers I have met and learned from over many summers at Hindman such as Jeff Daniel Marion, George Ella Lyon, Al Stewart, Robert Morgan, Lee Smith, and Jo Carson, has helped shape the direction of my writing and its purpose by holding a light to follow, like an old lantern out on the front porch beckoning me home.

So I do have a tribe that I belong to, but they are with me only in spirit most of the time. I live and think and feel and write alone, as everyone ultimately must. I will persist in writing because it is the only way to get some peace, the only antidote to the mostly-manic-occasionally-depressive kind of mind I have. The white page is the safety valve on the bubbling steam plant of words and images fogging up my brain.

Writing is also my ultimate connection with others. The irony of that forever amazes me. The most solitary of activities leads to the most public of lives, and while society as a whole may not value poetry, individuals reading your words under their bedside lamps will feel transported to a kind of intimacy that weeks of ordinary interaction cannot supplant.

As with most writers, I think my writing is an attempt to affront death. My poems are a record of a life well-spent, of love, of ideas that matter. It is a record of my life and the lives of others I've cared about. I want my children and grandchildren to know me and remember me—and what I lived for. They need to understand that the feminine is the everyday grit and grind of living; the rhythms of a woman's day are the heartbeat of life itself. Women must write poetry to record their lives, praise them, and preserve their legacy.

I will work to find my voice and my vision in solitude on a trail blazed by others. The stereotypes of Appalachia and its people loom at my shoulder and demand constant vigilance if I am to be honest. The constraints of being a woman who chose to be a wife and mother and writer must be acknowledged and accepted. It has become apparent to me that affirmation will never come from anywhere outside myself—not from my neighbors, not from the media, the literary establishment, or the academy. The person who will validate my experiences and affirm my worth as a person and a writer is me. I know who I am, where I came from, and where I'm going.

Though I now live differently than I did as a little girl, I still know how the fiddle music should sound, what the kettle of apple butter means, what the garden can grow. And I know what it feels like to be a woman doing womanly things. I will remember and write it all down until I leave this earth, and the next white page, to someone else.

JEAN
RITCHIE

From Viper, Kentucky, near the mouth of Little Elkhorn Branch, Jean Ritchie (b. 1922) is the youngest of fourteen children. Her father, Balis Ritchie, a descendant of Scottish farmers, taught her how to play the dulcimer in 1927. Ritchie moved to Port Washington, New York, in 1955, where she still resides, although she spends many months each year "at home" in Kentucky. Her discography includes recordings over five decades, most recently *Kentucky Christmas, Old & New* (1994) and *Mountain Born* (1995). Known not only as a performer of folk songs and a distinguished dulcimer player but also as a poet and prose writer, Ritchie published her first book in 1955, the now classic *Singing Family of the Cumberlands,* a book that has been continuously in print for over forty years. Her other books—*The Dulcimer Book* (1963), *Celebration of Life* (1971), and *The Dulcimer People* (1974)—have been invaluable resources for musicians, Appalachian scholars, and general readers across the nation. Her book *Folk Songs of the Southern Appalachians* (1965) was reissued in 1997. Ritchie has won numerous awards and honors, including the University of Kentucky Founders' Day Award, an honorary doctor of letters from the University of Kentucky (1983), an honorary doctor of arts from Berea College (1991), and the 1984 Milner Award from the Kentucky Arts Council as Outstanding Kentucky Artist of the Year. In 1986, Ritchie Family Week was declared, and she accepted proclamations from the city of Lexington, the state of Kentucky, and the U.S. Congress, together with a capitol flag and a letter from the president, honoring Jean Ritchie and her family's contribution to music. Ritchie has been a guest teacher at the University of California, Santa Cruz, and California State University in Fresno. She led 180,000 people in singing "Amazing Grace" for Pope John Paul II in Washington, D.C., was featured in Bill Moyers's PBS documentary *Amazing Grace* and is the subject of *Mountain Born: The Jean Ritchie Story,* produced by Kentucky Educational Television in 1996.

*   *   *

The Song about the Story—
The Story behind the Song

I was born into my big family, the fourteenth and last child, at the end of 1922. All my life I have heard us called "The Singing Ritchies." What not all folk know is that we were just as much a family of storytellers as singers. Well, songs *are* stories in a way—at least the old ballads, "Barbry Ellen," "Lord Thomas and Fair Ellender," "The House Carpenter." Songs like that. And singing them of a summer evening on our little porch, settled down in a ring of listening hills and accompanying branch-waters, would always call back all those long-gone grands and greats who had sung them before us.

Then, sooner or later, the memories would call forth a story—a tale not to be sung but told, with much laughing, and joining in, maybe a tear or two—and life would stretch broader for a while as older generations lived again.

One such a time comes plain to my mind. We were not on the porch but in our kitchen, and it was midday, not evening, once when Uncle Jason Ritchie was visiting us. He was the oldest living family member then and a master for remembering. We were all talking and laughing around the long table after dinner (our main meal, taken around noontime), lingering too long to suit Dad, whose mind was on the cornfield.

"Too much triflin around now, younguns. The Floyd Field's a-waitin to be hoed out o' the first weeds."

Mom flustered, "Ah, now Balis! Jason hain't here but about once or twice a year, and he's a-thertnin to leave fore dark. Let the corn go till to'marr."

Jason was about as deaf as Dad was, not hearing a thing they said, and he hummed a little and tipped his chair back, commenced singing out on an old love song. We quieted. His eyes shut after the first verse or so, and we knew he was seeing and hearing the sweethearts talking back and forth as his big swoopy voice wrapped itself around the story.

Awake, awake, ye drowsy sleeper!
How can you lay and slumber so
When your truelove is a-goin to leave you,
Never to return anymore?

How can you slumber on your pillow
When your truelove must stand and wait?
And must I go and wear the willow,
In sorrow mourning for your sake?

O Molly dear, go ask your father
If you my bride, my bride can be,
And then return and quickly tell me
And I no more will trouble thee.

O no, I cannot ask my father;
He's a-lyin on his bed of rest,
And in his hands a silver dagger
To pierce the one that I love the best.

Down in yon valley there grows a green yarrow.
I wish that yarrow was shot through my breast—
It would end my grief, it would end my sorrow,
And set my troubled heart at rest.

His voice held the last word awhile, then let the note drop down to the next octave, putting a period on the song, letting folks know it was over (my dad's explanation of it). We all were still for a minute or two, coming back to ourselves. Jason hemmed and cleared his throat.

"Hmmm . . . well now. Hain't thought on that'n for years . . . you know, don't you, Balis, that they called that a raftsman's song? Ay, I know hit's a love song— just a short part of a long ballad with the main action verses dropped out over the years. But the tune, ay, that's one a feller could holler out on, where't swings up high on that third line? Drown out the river. . . . Yeah, hit'd be a-roarin, when they took the rafts down. A puny tune'd be no-account. Couldn't hear y'rself sing, y'know."

And that started a long tall-tale-telling session about life that was really adventurous—the golden days of the middle and late 1800s when nearly everybody had plenty of timber, and all they had to do to get cash money was to cut down as many trees as they wanted to, raft the logs together, and wait for the spring floods to float them down to Jackson and Frankfort and the hungry lumber markets.

Now, the North Fork of the Kentucky River is full of shoals and narrows (or "narrs," as the older folk said) and is hardly more than a good-sized swimming hole in many places, where even a girl can throw a rock across easy. I couldn't see how a big raft made of all those logs could possibly make that trip, flood or no flood. Uncle Jason smiled tolerantly.

"Wy child, when that little river's got a right-enough roll of spring rain in 'er she makes one of the sweetest highways you ever traveled over. Yes sir, deep and smooth. And allus a-singin. Allus a-singin."

"Well," Mom remembered, "sometimes you'd have to build a dam, to get started. If it rained too much you couldn't go your trip cause then that river'd go roarin wild, be so swift you couldn't keep yr raft frm crashin into the banks at the bends."

"Shore. Hit was a dangerous undertakin, anyway, any time," Dad added his bit. "Whoever took a raft down had to have someone on'er that knew that river like a book, knew ever narr and shoal."

Uncle Jason chuckled. "Balis, do you and Abbie remember Newt Smith? Now there was a raftsman. They tell a tale on him—must be so cause it sounds just like him.

"First raft he ever run, floated her down to Jackson, purty nigh all the timber he had in her. Sold it all bout as soon's he got there, got three hundred dollars all t'once. Back then, if they didn't have someone meet 'em with a horse they'd walk back, so, Newt he started walkin.

"One night he couldn't find a hotel and he stopped at a house on the road, and the folks said he could stay all night. They went to eat supper and the old woman commenced saying they wasn't much to eat—you know how some women will go-on thataway and the table it just loaded down. Newt he went fillin up his plate, and motioned fr her to stop talkin. 'That's all right,' he says, says, 'I know how y' feel,' says, 'I used t' be a pore man myself.'"

Dad couldn't wait for us all to stop laughing, nor himself. He gasped, "Newt Smith—Yes—Newt! Yea, Newt 'uz a master feller, all right. They say one time he had to take his timber all the way to Frankfort. He was right dazzle-eyed at the city sights, but he aimed to behave proper; gazed at the Capitol and all the other big buildings and swore Nance 'n the chillern'd never believe his telling about them. And . . . he'd walk down the street, a-bowin out his back, takin off his hat, sayin howdy-do to every one passed by, same's if he 'uz home here.

"Old man Jim—Jim Squirrelly—'uz with him and he said purty soon they come to one of them there cigar store Indians, and Newt spoke to him, too, and took off his hat. After they'd gone on a little piece, said Newt peeped back at the old Indian, said right gruff, 'Now whut 'uz that, the Washington Monumint?'"

Jason took another turn. "They told too on Ben Brown a purty good'n. That's Boney Ben, y'know. Now he never could read nor write—never knew one letter in the alphabet but he'd allus let on like he 'uz smart. On one of them trips he picked up a newspaper on the hotel porch and they found him settin in the rockin chair, lookin at the paper upside down. They asked him fr fun, says, 'What's in the news today, Boney?' They 'uz a picture of a boat on the page and he looked hard at it for a minute, said, 'Ay, nothin much . . . I see here where they've turned a ship right bottom-uppards.'"

Mom's gentle voice came out of the laughing. "City people in Frankfort used to make fun of the men come down the river, laughed at their mountain ways, as they say, but one time the river men got the best of them.

"There 'uz a crowd of raftsmen there stayin at the same hotel next the river, and they'd just come in from their trip down and they must've been purty near starved I guess . . . Come in to the big supper table and the hotel people got to watchin 'em eat. Didn't have much manners you know—they 'uz hungry and just themselves there, so they all j'st crammed-in ever which way, and hollered and joked each other—carried on like men will together.

"Well the hotel people sent out in the town to their friends said, 'We got a bunch of hill men off the river today and you ought to see them eat . . . come over and watch at breakfast in the mornin.'

"Well some of the men got wind of that and they made it up to give them city folks a real show. Got up next mornin, put on the nicest clothes they had, shaved and washed themselves nice and clean, slicked down their hair. Bell rung and they walked in, took their chairs just as quiet and slow and all smiled and nodded, said good-mornin to one another. Then they begun to pass things, and say please and thank you kindly. One man they said even got up rolled up his sleeves and went round the table servin the bacon, a-waitin on the others . . . said them people gathered in to watch were the wust took ever was . . . said they didn't know what to think . . . "

That was one tale-telling session, and hardly a day passed that there weren't several of them. My sister Mallie (fourth from the top) had a hair-raising story called "Little Dog Toby and the Hobby-Ahs" that she had learned from Granny Katty, and Granny herself, whenever she stayed with us, would sit before the fire on a cold winter's night and recollect old h'ant tales for us—true stories handed down in the family, some even of h'ants she herself had seen. How scared we'd be, and how we believed her! Well, she *was* the first charter member of the Clear Creek Old Regular Baptist, and now she wouldn't lie, would she?

Then Dad and Mom, Uncle Jason, all the older sisters, the neighbors, all knew the old legends and fairy stories from their old folks. "Tigs and Tags and Long Leather Bags, and All My Gold and Silver" was one of them, and there were dozens.

Time passed, and my life was pretty much the same until I finished high school and went away to college. The old tales and songs began to seem old-fashioned and I soon put them all in the far-back of my mind. I never disowned my Appalachian Mountain heritage, but for a time I tried very hard to be a very modern member of society. At the University of Kentucky I joined the glee club, tried to learn to read music and get my voice trained. Neither took, but I learned about many kinds of music and literature, pushing the old traditional lore farther and farther back.

What to do with my life? I considered being a missionary but decided I wasn't religious enough, or not along the required lines, at least. A new subject was being offered at UK—social work. Since I wanted to "help people," and I was rather embarrassed with organized religion, I decided that social work was the way for me and became the first enrollee in the new course and its first graduate in 1946.

In 1947, very much the educated young woman of the Modern Age (I thought), I accepted a job in New York City with the Henry Street Settlement. The staff was in residence, living in rooms on the third floor of the programs building.

The idea was that I would work in New York long enough to get some experience in the field, then return with my vast knowledge to Hazard, Kentucky, and Set Up Something . . . at that time, the only thing there resembling social work was welfare.

My new job at the Settlement was recreation work with seven-, eight-, and nine-year-old girls in an after-school program. I was thrown in cold with the children. The first afternoon, about twenty-five little girls from New York's Lower East Side came screaming and scrapping into the meeting room and they were going to stay there, *with me,* for two hours!

All my training seemed suddenly useless—how to quiet this group down to tell a story, have a discussion, play a game? Not knowing what else to do, I sat down in the middle of the room and got out my dulcimer, brought from home, borrowed from Dad. The girls all crowded around, waiting to touch, strum the strings.

I said to the nearest ones, "You won't be able to hear the music unless everyone is quiet."

Four girls whirled on the others, shouting and pushing them into a sitting position, holding them down.

"Dummies! Listen to the lady! She's gonna play that thing!"

Sliding the noter along the strings, sounding chords with the goose-feather pick, I thought frantically, then lit into "Goin to Boston" and "Over the River, Charlie." They giggled and clapped along, scuffling their feet. At the end I was able to yell before their noise started.

"That's a singing game from where I live in Kentucky. It's like a dance!"

"Show us! Show us!" And I was off for my two-year stay at the Settlement. I was wearing a Kentucky Wildcat shirt with a big semicircular "Kentucky" logo, so from that day, that was my name, Kentucky.

What would I have done without the old family games, songs, and stories?

They helped me over all the hard parts, with the children, with the teen girls (The Vic Damone Club!), with the old men and women who had their gatherings and seasonal celebrations there. Visitors touring the Settlement heard the music, and I began to get invited to sing at parties, schools, and small social clubs in the neighborhood. On Saturday nights, we had community square dances, and I often performed at intermission. One night I shared that time with a storyteller named John Henry Falk. After our performance, he asked me to dance.

"You know, you ought to meet Alan Lomax. I know he'd love to record you for the Library of Congress."

Within a week, I was singing ballads for Alan in a small office at Decca Records where he then worked. Days passed, weeks, and I was still singing ballads, telling about the family. He was so impressed with the size of my family repertoire that he decided that it should be published. For months we made the rounds of New York–based publishers, but none was interested. Finally, a telephone call came from the Oxford University Press, and they didn't say no—they even made an offer.

"Miss Ritchie, you must realize that, in the first place, you are an Unknown, and in the second place, music reproduction is quite expensive—and you want to publish over three hundred songs! For these reasons, we cannot publish the book in its present form. However, we do very much like your written introductions, and we would suggest that you expand these stories, tell of your own growing up a part of a large Kentucky mountain family. Include a few songs if you like along the way, to help the story, and we'll publish."

I was stunned. I called Alan, barely able to speak. "Oxford likes my *writing!* They'll graciously *allow* a few songs if I'll only write a book!"

It took me two years, but the "research" was the most fun. Visiting all the older members of the clan. How the old tales and songs poured out—often a dozen different versions of the same story—and what glorious parties we had! I met folks I had hardly known, and some extremely shy ones came out of their shells and told the best tales of all.

I'm really not a dedicated writer, and the several books to follow *Singing Family of the Cumberlands* have been song collections and dulcimer lore, for the most part. Someday I'll write another book, for real, but it has been a great joy to have *Singing Family* so well accepted—used in schools at all levels, translated into many languages including Braille, read aloud over the air, used as research on Appalachia for novels (for example, *Christy*), inspiring thousands of letters from people all over the world. It has been continuously in print since its publication in 1955, and is currently published by the University Press of Kentucky.

Throughout the forty years since that first publication, other roads have had to be explored—some people know me as a writer, others as a folksinger and dulcimer player, still others (in many countries) as a collector of folklore—and all these roads have come from Appalachia. In private life, too, the old ways, sayings, songs, family, have directed the rocking of my children, the feeding of my family, the furnishing of my home. The last verse of our favorite clan-gathering song, "Twilight A'Stealing," says it best:

> *Voices of loved ones, songs of the past*
> *Still linger round me while life shall last,*
> *Cheering my pathway while here I roam*
> *Seeking my faroff home.*

BETTIE
SELLERS

Bettie Sellers (b. 1926) is a resident of Young Harris, Georgia, and was Georgia Author of the Year in Poetry for 1979, 1982, and 1989. She holds an M.A. from the University of Georgia and an honorary doctor of literature degree from La Grange College, her undergraduate alma mater. Sellers was the Goolsby Professor of English at Young Harris College until her 1996 retirement after thirty-one years of service. She is currently teaching and serving as an officer in the Institute for Continuing Learning at Young Harris College. Sellers is the author of seven books of poetry, including *Westward from Bald Mountain* (1974), *Spring Onions and Cornbread* (1978), *Morning of the Red-Tailed Hawk* (1981), *Liza's Monday and Other Poems* (1986), and *Wild Ginger* (1989). She has been named Poet of the Year by American Pen Women for *The Morning of the Red-Tailed Hawk* and has received numerous awards, including the Caroline Wyatt Memorial Award, the R.G. Beyer Award, and the John Ransome Lewis Award. She also is author of *The Bitter Berry: The Life of Byron Herbert Reece* (1992) and scriptwriter of a documentary film based on that book, a film that won the Judges Award at the Sinking Creek Film Festival as well as a Georgia Emmy. Her poems and essays have appeared in *Georgia Review, Appalachian Heritage, Green River Review, Chattahoochee Review,* and *Arizona Quarterly,* as well as anthologies such as *An Introduction to Poetry, Appalachia Inside Out,* and *Women in Literature.*

*   *   *

Westward from Bald Mountain

Seven miles as the crow flies, more than twenty as the road winds, the Young Harris Valley lies westward from Enotah Bald, the highest mountain in north Georgia, while Choestoe and Nacoochee Valleys are just over the ridge not far away. If you stand on almost any mountainside, you can see the tower on Bald rising against the sky or veiled in the blue haze that gives these mountains their name, the Blue Ridge. Pine and oaks, poplar golden in fall, joe-pye weed and wild honeysuckle hide the deer and rabbit, nests of the cardinal and rufous-sided towhee. At night you may hear the eerie call of the screech owl or the womanlike scream of bobcat or even the larger cat the old-timers call the "painter."

Winter comes with a cold northwest wind, a time of hickory-fragrant wood fires, crisp apples to munch, and moments to reflect on the changing of the seasons. Here there are four very definite atmospheres for a writer to ponder, to know that as surely as winter comes with snow, spring will send new colors crawling up the mountainsides until the slopes that surround the valleys are a gentle mounding of evergreens interspersed with the more subtle shades that are the oak and sourwood trees.

I have seen the turning of the seasons in these valleys, felt the coming of spring in the red furrows of newly plowed earth in the creek bottoms. My ears have heard the rich stories that tie me to the past, the oral tradition that is the stuff of poetry and fiction, the source for telling and retelling for all of the generations that we can remember.

In August of 1965, I came with my family to the Young Harris Valley as to a fabled land. I was coming home to a place where I had never lived, the mysterious and wonderful past from my maternal grandmother's days as a child in the Nacoochee Valley nearby. Her father, the Reverend Robert Alexander Seale, had been a circuit-riding Methodist preacher in the surrounding hills. After preaching for some years in the mountains, Great-grandfather was sent by the church to a parish near Macon, Georgia, where my grandmother lived until she traveled by train in 1889 to attend Young Harris College, a small Methodist mission project then only three years old.

When my husband and I came to teach at the college, I found that Corn Creek, winding through the valley, ran rich with the tale of how my young grandmother, with her fellow students Mary and Violet, had gone strolling of a Sunday afternoon, not knowing that the "forbidden" boys were sneaking along behind. As the young gentlemen jumped from behind a laurel thicket shouting "Boo!" the girls, startled, fell backward in the cold water, and as Grandmother would tell it, "just purely ruined" their best Sunday frocks and hats.

This and so many other tales had been told to a little girl, her namesake, in Grandmother's back garden, a garden fragrant with ragged robins and larkspur near the sundial that pointed to that elusive thing, the passing of the days. The garden was in Griffin, the town where my grandparents settled when my mother was about grown. After my birth in Tampa, Florida, my own parents had bought a farm in middle Georgia near Griffin. Here Dad could not only express his country heart but also commute into town to work for my grandfather in a cotton brokerage office. And here I could enjoy my favorite days of childhood, to come in the three miles from the farm to the Griffin house on Taylor Street with a flower garden and electric lights and big bathtubs of hot water and a grandmother who thought that her namesake was a very special child.

How little did I know when I came to her fabulous land in 1965, I would decide that I must be a writer and I must write about her and that place. True, the place had changed: the old wooden dorm with the bell tower was long gone, and the white frame church had tipped over during a particularly fervent repentance sermon by evangelist Tom Coke Hughes. But the creek remained and flowed merrily at the foot of Sunset Ridge where we would build our permanent home. And it was surely the same laurels and rhododendrons, chickadees and cardinals that had so enriched Grandmother's world—and which she had painted while a student at Young Harris. As a curious wandering child, I found stacks of those paintings stored in the dim and dusty carriage house up behind her house on Taylor Street. One, a mother duck and ducklings with cattails, now hangs in my den.

It was January of 1946, when I was nineteen, that I first saw the valley with my own eyes. Just before Christmas, a young grad student at the University of Georgia had asked me to marry him with these exact words: "Bettie, will you marry me and go to Young Harris?" Sight unseen, I said "Yes." As soon as we could arrange it, we visited this place that seemed so important to him. We took the local bus from Atlanta to Cleveland and over the frightening mountain road to Helen, Hiawassee, and on to Young Harris. I wasn't sure that weekend whether it was the bitter cold of January or the terror I had felt on my first-ever ride over high mountains that gripped me, but I could see that this was very important to my young love. As a young man, he had dropped out of school and later had come to Young Harris for the rest of high school and two years of college. This place and these people had become the nearest thing Ezra had to call "home." And his idea was that he must give back all that had been given to him.

It would be another twenty years or so before his dream could come true and we would move to Young Harris, but that dream surrounded our marriage like a beckoning hand for our years in Athens and more years at La Grange College where I began my education to teach.

Ezra's stories about Young Harris, its people and the surrounding country-side, joined my reminiscences of my grandmother, adding to the fund of knowl-edge and lore I would later bring to my writing when I finally took up residence. Joined to all of this was the important fact that my husband had lived in the working gang house at the college while the would-be writer Byron Herbert Reece also resided there. In fact, Ezra's collection of books that he brought into our house contained the first of Byron's books of poetry, *Ballad of the Bones,* and some-time soon after that he brought me up one weekend to stay at the college and to visit Reece in his home. This was yet another tie being woven that would not bear fruit until we took up residence in Young Harris.

The years between our move to Young Harris and the publication of my first book, *Westward from Bald Mountain,* were filled with adjustments—to life at the college, to my first teaching job, to the problems of combining a job with a family (one child only, five years old). I had never written with any serious intent—except for those requirements that are a part of every college degree. I had, of course, taken a course in creative writing and produced a few "well wrought" sonnets that sounded just like those of every other English major, but it would take some years in Young Harris before my own voice began to sing.

It was in that first book, *Westward from Bald Mountain,* that I first wrote particularly from the experience of living high above the valley overlooking the campus of Young Harris. The opening poem, "Shadows on the Wind," traces my sensibilities back from the present through the tales of Grandmother to the even earlier settlers, to the Creek and Cherokee "fishing the Hiawassee and Chatuge / hunting Salali the squirrel / and Awanita, the young deer in the pine woods." They had, indeed, "left stone footprints on Trackrock / and arrowheads in my garden soil." This early book reflects my becoming aware of the complex nature of life in the valleys and on the mountain. From my window on the ridge overlook-ing Young Harris, I saw the rabbits dancing, the maples splashing red across the slopes; I felt the sad spirit of the Cherokee, found his potsherds among zinnias and petunias, and came to understand why he called this "the enchanted valley."

I came to know the people and hear their stories. There was Mr. Billy Cantrell, brilliant science teacher, who in his retirement came to live back in the wilderness by Big Bald Creek and subsisted on rice and chicken gizzards, cooked once a week on his old wood stove. I couldn't bring myself to share the odious concoction, but many a time did I sit by his fire and listen to his tall tales about life in the moun-tains when he was young.

But Mr. Billy was not just an armchair storyteller; sometimes his memory leapt up at the most unexpected times and in the most unexpected places. One day I had a flat tire just outside the town and Mr. Billy pulled up behind and stopped. He offered to change my tire, but I was reluctant since he must have been eighty and looked like a puff of south wind would blow him away. No, he absolutely must put on my spare. As he hunkered down, taking off those things that hold the wheel on, he looked up at me and said with high seriousness: "Bettie, what do you think about the relative merits of the longbow and the crossbow in the Battle of Crecy?" Now, that was conversation! Of such as Mr. Billy is the legend of the pioneer made, and it proved to be grist for the writer's mill.

I remember that on one of the first times we came up to sample the valley, we met Professor Lovick Adams on the bench by Leon's General Store. After a few words of greeting and catching up with his former student, he invited us to accompany him on a rattlesnake hunt near his cabin, not far up Big Bald from Mr. Billy's. It is with some trepidation that I can still see myself, the girl from outside, standing on the end of a long pole prying up the big rock that covered a nest of many writhing and deadly snakes. In short, I was scared to death—and that day learned some of the facts of nature that keep me ever wary as I now mow or dig in my yard. In the many years from then until his death at almost one hundred years, Professor Adams filled in my sense of the past with many a tale told on the porch of the old white house on the corner by the campus. Lovick Adams was the oral historian of the valley and knew every thunderstruck oak and pine that marked a property line in Towns County. I miss his beautiful garden of dahlias the most; I could watch him working in the garden as I taught my classes in the Rich Building and, in that first small book of mine, they live on:

Old man, I watch you
across the greening valley;
your spring planting feeds
my soul with scarlet dahlias.
I shall mourn them when you die.

I am sure that my fellow feeling for these hills comes in part from having grown up on a farm in middle Georgia. Only there, for instance, and here on the ridge has it been dark enough for me to enjoy the wide expanse of night sky bright with Orion and the Big Dipper. So close is the feeling of these two spots that many readers have assumed that *Spring Onions and Cornbread,* my second book, is part and parcel of my writing about my life in Young Harris. The language of a transplanted mountaineer is, of necessity, somewhat different from that of one born here. The rural way of life, though, is much the same, and it has been easy for me to think that I truly do belong.

Rural scenes and the kinds of people who live and work there are much the same no matter where they lie geographically. There is everywhere life and death, in Byron Reece's two novels or in my poems remembering my eight-year-old brother George laid out in his white linen suit so different from the overalls I was accustomed to seeing. Poems remember "that first taste of winter's meat" and the time the family gathered at Uncle Harry's when Aunt Cora baked six kinds of pie and the black ants got in the pie safe overnight. What a commotion that was! And Cora, like Grandmother and all the other women in the family, made quilts with the same patterns as those made by the women of the hills. My "Quiltin' Bee" names "Texas Star" and "Step around the Mountain" with scraps from "Mama's meetin' dress" and squares from other garments that were a mystery to me. "Who wore those brightly patterned scraps / my fingers do not know?"

As I write, these women come back to life again, and, as always, it is Grandmother who is telling the best tales. It might be the one where her father is off preaching in the hills, somewhere in the circuit of his many small churches, and Great-grandmother Rebecca is left alone to guard home and children. There is a mighty squawking from the nearby chicken run one night, and she takes the shotgun from its pegs and aims out the window at everything and nothing. One more squawk, then silence, and whatever varmint was after her hens has been scared off. But that is not the end of the story or even the best part, so Grandmother will say in her best laughing voice. Why just the next Sunday, when the Reverend Mr. Seale has finished his favorite sermon, Rebecca notices that one of the parishioners is limping most mightily. Asked about his limp, he makes up some unconvincing tale about a mishap in the barnyard, but Rebecca knows better. She looks at the liar knowingly, all the time wearing her "usual Sunday smile." And my very own grandmother, looking back across so many years, will smile and travel for a moment in a silent tribute to a mother who, except for the tales, is now only a portrait that hangs on the wall in the dining room of my youngest daughter's house. And thereby also hangs another tale.

It was Grandmother who taught me the fine art of people watching, a necessary adjunct to the art of writing. While it would have been rude and unsociable to have peered into the windows of her neighbors' houses, it was perfectly acceptable that we should watch whatever scenes emerged on the yards and sidewalks and make our several surmises as to how old Mrs. Ingram was getting on these days by who came and went through her verandahed front door. And we could see who visited whom up and down Taylor Street as the soft murmur of afternoon conversations floated across Mrs. Ingram's rose garden or Mrs. Williams's peonies pink and white in late spring.

When the green wicker rockers on the front porch had palled, it was not in Grandmother's book of what ladies did to go walking downtown and stand on a corner watching life go by, but she could and would drive me there and park near her favorite dry goods store and sit for a while. This method of people watching broadened our scope from the immediate neighborhood to the wider world outside and has stood me in good stead in many a locality from a bench on the campus to an airport in Nairobi, Kenya. Just think of all the places where you might have to wait and might enliven the time by imagining the lives of the people who pass. Of such are much poetry and fiction made.

One of the problems in writing about the past is the ephemeral nature of the memory. I never am sure just what part of what I remember is my own and what part has been told to me (heaven forbid that there be a part that I have purely made up). A large part of the joy of having a family is the stories that are told, and in the way of good storytellers, embroidered around the edges in the telling. I don't think I remember the day I insisted that the visiting bishop come with me down to the pen to see a new litter of baby pigs. But my mother could still blush with embarrassment as she described this reverend friend of Great-grandfather Seale's and his uneasiness about his neatly pressed black trousers in the mud of the barnyard. And it was Grandmother who would take such delight in embellishing her tale of how once I removed all my clothes and washed them under the faucet in the front yard—right on Taylor Street where all the neighbors could see. It was her way of encouraging me into more modesty than I generally possessed. Grandmother, bless her heart, spent much time and effort trying to make the proverbial silk purse out of this natural-born sow's ear.

Could it have been Grandmother's tales of her father and his sermons that contributed to the fact that I have seen visions here in the valley? One came, between sleeping and waking perhaps, in the wee hours of a January morning in 1981 to be what was really the beginning urge of the book *Liza's Monday and Other Poems.* A strange and disturbing one, the dream or vision had Satan passing through this valley on his way into an exile. Stopping by Corn Creek down the mountain from my house, he put his evil touch on the beautiful valley before flying on to Hell. Somehow that dream led me to thinking about what life must have been like for the women living in the isolation and hardship of this pioneer land in the early part of the nineteenth century. Mostly narrative poems, the collection sketches various women, no different from the wife Mary in Reece's *Better a Dinner of Herbs,* caught in situations of homesickness and pain, grief and nameless despair, as in the title poem, where Liza, distrait with some unnameable inner fear, climbing Double Knob,

Raked inside by gales howling bleak
as northern winds around the cabin whine,
she does not feel the laurel tug her dress,

the briars pricking dark red beads that shine
on bare arms . . .

or Sheba, lonely in her widowhood, watching her handsome neighbor passing

. . . by each day to climb the slope
of Cedar Ridge, cut logs to build a barn
near where the trail that crosses Unicoi
turns west through Brasstown Gap.

When I began to write *Liza's Monday,* bits and pieces of Grandmother's stories joined hands with others that I had heard to make enough material out of which to create a small host of women characters who might have lived in this same valley even before Grandmother came in 1889. What fun and what a challenge it was to visualize where each woman must have lived, what blossoms she could smell, what birds she scattered breadcrumbs to. For I took my personal observations of the valley and created settings as real as I could make them to house my largely imaginary women. I had peopled the valley with the full gamut of fears and hopes that are common to women here and in the many isolated valleys that wind northward from Blood Mountain all the way to Maine. There is even a sequence told in the sharp tongue of the local gossip Ellie who sees her neighbors "warts and all." She speaks with some indignation in the opening poem, "Mary's Apples":.

. . . Just because she came here first,
she thinks that every spoonful of earth
from Double Knob to Raven Cliffs was made
for her benefit! You'd think that line
from the thunderstruck oak to Corn Creek
was drawed by Moses with a golden stick
to keep the rest of us from crossing
to the upper gap . . .

While the women in *Liza's Monday* reflect Grandmother's tales and those of others, each in some way reflects my own experiences of learning to live on the far side of the mountains from the little farm in middle Georgia.

I must not forget the debt I owe to the others who have written so movingly of the mountain valleys near my home. As I began to write poems with serious intent, I also became interested in another project—writing articles and essays about the life and works of Byron Herbert Reece, the writer I first met through Ezra. Reece died on the Young Harris campus in 1958. His four volumes of poetry and two novels had been well received by the critics in the forties and early fifties but had been out of print for some years. In Reece I had found a fellow being whose feelings and thoughts were so like my own. He too loved the land and its people, the creeks dancing over rocks as they meandered down the mountainsides into the lowlands. He too was steeped in the Bible Belt faith that Great-grandfather had preached before the turn of the century. That sense of sin and retribution, the possibilities of repentance and redemption permeate both of his novels, *Better a Dinner of Herbs* and *The Hawk and the Sun.* In so many ways, Reece and I, though not quite of an age, were coming from the same place in our feelings for the land, the family, and the religion of our forebears. By studying Reece's life and works, I was further steeping myself in the place he expressed so great a tie with in a few short untitled lines that I found in an old copy of *The Progressive Farmer:*

These hills contain me as a field, a stone,
    Yet I contain them also; when I fare
Beyond their borders and am all alone
    I need but think of them to see them there,
Each hill, each hollow, each familiar place
As clearly imaged as a loved one's face.

I also feel the influence of *The Mountains within Me,* written by the present governor of Georgia, Zell Miller, born and raised in my valley with family ties going back to the days when his grandfathers coexisted with the Cherokee, as had Reece's. Both family groups had been among the earliest white settlers to come westward from Unicoi Gap and Bald Mountain. Governor Miller's book gave me something of the history of that period, bits of folklore and language patterns, in short, a look into the old ways practiced in the area. And, again, I found that both men's ways and tales, though removed by space from parts of my past by many miles, were not so different from the tales and ways I remembered from childhood and the farm. I could even match some of their stories of the Indians since there had been a Creek village where Shoal Creek met Flint River near my father's house. So, in writing about my mother in *Morning of the Red-Tailed Hawk,* I would picture her "where she had scratched up arrowheads for us / and told such tales that Creeks were lurking / behind every pine and oak for all our summers."

What a rich heritage we all have had—Grandmother, Ezra, Zell Miller, Reece, and I. And although not "born and bred in the briar patch" like Byron Reece and Zell Miller, I have come by many a road to a deep appreciation for the complexities of life in the valleys westward from Bald Mountain. It is the cry of the bobcat at night, his pawprints in the first snow of the winter, and the yellow of poplar on a fall hillside. It is the soft sad murmur of the Cherokee down by Corn Creek, and the echoing of the sounds of that early farmer urging his mule through the bottom-lands by Wolf Creek. It is long acquaintance with all of this that continues to tie me ever closer to this place, this small part of the earth that I write about with love in *Wild Ginger:*

> When September's quarter moon tips down
> toward Sunset Rock cool and distant at dusk,
> the mountains darken blue in solid shapes
> quieting the valley for the coming of the night.
> Crickets scratch in the grass, a catbird whines.
> The dome fills up with darkness, reveals
> the Dippers, great and small. My eyes
> trace the distance to the farthest star—
> but the mountain holds my feet in place.

MARY
LEE
SETTLE

The founder of the PEN-Faulkner Award, Mary Lee Settle (b. 1918) grew up in Charleston, West Virginia, and attended Sweet Briar College. She enlisted in World War II as an aircraft woman in the RAF, an experience she recounts in *All the Brave Promises* (1966). After the war, she returned to New York City, working briefly as an assistant editor at *Harper's* before deciding to devote herself to writing. She is best known as the author of the Beulah Quintet, five novels that trace America's roots from Cromwellian England to twentieth-century West Virgina. *O Beulah Land* (1956), the first novel of the quintet to be written but the second in the story's chronology, reflects the many years she spent researching the history of her West Virginia roots in the British Museum. *Blood Tie* (1977), a novel set in Turkey, where Settle lived from 1972 to 1974, won the National Book Award for fiction in 1978. In 1989 she returned to Turkey, telling this story in *Turkish Reflections: A Biography of a Place* (1991). Settle's most recent fiction includes *Celebration* (1986), *Charley Bland* (1989), and *Choices* (1995). She has taught creative writing at Bard College, the Iowa Writers' Workshop, and the University of Virginia. Her numerous awards in addition to the National Book Award include Guggenheim Fellowships, a Merrill Foundation Award, the Janet Heidinger Kafka Prize in fiction by an American woman for *The Killing Ground* (1983), and the Lillian Smith Award for *Choices*. She currently lives in Charlottesville with her husband, columnist and historian William Littleton Tazewell. The first volume of her memoir, *Addie,* will be published by the University of South Carolina Press as a part of the Mary Lee Settle Collection.

*   *   *

The Search for the Beulah Quintet

In 1953, I began a third novel—*O Beulah Land*—before the first two had been published. It grew from a questioned image. A man hit a stranger in a drunk tank on a hot, summer night in a small town in the Alleghenies. The image was modern. "Why?" was the question about one act of violence that would draw me away from the present—how far back I had no idea then. I began to learn a past and a language. I found fears, dreams, and hatreds that once had reason, frozen into prejudice. I began to see people at the time of these reasons, these hopes, these illusions. I found not only what was happening but what they thought was happening, a change and flow of belief that reflected the time as a mirror. The search would grow into a quintet I never intended. It would take twenty-eight years to finish. The five volumes cover over three hundred years.

O Beulah Land begins with the image of a woman stripped down to survival, lost and mindless with fear, moving toward the east through the Endless Mountains, now called the Alleghenies. Her name is Hannah Bridewell. The time is 1754. She glimpses and remembers a small valley, the first sight of Beulah. Hunger for land of one's own, safe from exile, is the guiding force of the time. The land would be always a little farther west, a little out of reach, over the next mountain, down the next river.

I did not have the luxury of looking back on the years of *O Beulah Land* from the present with all the arrogance and future knowledge of a past time. That is the privilege of historians. I had to become contemporary, think as they thought, fear what they had feared, use their own language with its yet unchanged meanings, face a blank and fearful future. I had to forget what I already knew.

I was living in England, far, I thought, from the place and time I sought. I was wrong. I went to the British Museum, and there, all around the walls, in the huge catalogues that had been kept so carefully for so long, I found an Aladdin's cave of memory. The eighteenth-century *Gentlemen's Magazine* was in the shelves near my favorite seat in the great round reading room. I began with that. In the back of each issue were the book reviews. They were my first source, long-forgotten books about the new, feared, fascinating land of Virginia, which was a generic name for a wild place beyond a terrifying sea. They were all there, still in the stacks—the books about battles, about discoveries, about laws, about captivities, told by the people who had experienced them, in their time and in their language.

Our memories are long. We are the children of our grandparents' childhoods, their memories of their parents and grandparents, what they have cleaned, deleted, forgotten, denied. But nothing in my own historic memory seemed to reach into the mid-eighteenth century. To inform my book I had to create an eighteenth-century past of my own. I read for ten months without taking a note, let the past become a present, let it fall beyond intelligence into reliving, which is true sensuous recall, where dreams come from with all their fears and future hopes of things long past.

Then, one night, I dreamed that I was building a log cabin in a clearing in the woods. It had to be at least four feet high so that I could claim occupancy and get my deed for the land by paying a quitrent to the colonial government. I still remember the smell of buckskins long worn, the wind in trees gashed by my axe to claim tomahawk rights, the gaunt, naked trees that had been girdled so that they would die and be easier to clear for planting. Memory had entered dream and I was ready to write.

I began to find everything I needed, there and in England—American brown bears at the zoo, a puma, Tower muskets at the ancient arsenal, the Tower of London. An ex-guardsman who was one of the librarians at the British Museum taught me the order of drill of the guards' regiments that had not changed since the eighteenth century, whispering commands as we stood in the corridor between the North Library, where some of the rarest books in the world are kept, and the reading room, porting arms with imaginary muskets that were higher than our heads.

I measured how much I could see across a wild unknown river by pacing the Roman façade of the museum. I found out how to call a hog from a Shakespeare scholar in the North Library, reading first folios at the great leather-covered table across from me. He was so surprised at my question that he lifted his head as if he were still in Iowa, and called, "Sooeey!" across the silent company of scholars and people staying warm in one of the coldest winters in England who read, wrote, and slept all around us.

I took a bus to the New Forest, what is left of the royal hunting forest of the Saxon kings, and found more huge virgin trees than there are in all of the modern surviving forests of what once was the wilderness of Virginia.

I was taken into the storage vaults below the British Museum, and there were Indian artifacts that had come from the valley that I would call Beulah. In the corner of the vaulted cave were two tea chests full of what I thought were furs. There were stretched circles of leather painted with designs. I lifted one of them and found that the leather circle was attached to a long hank of blond hair. I had found the scalps of our own ancestors.

A review in *Gentlemen's Magazine* led me to the story of an engineer attached to Braddock's army who had been captured while building the Braddock Road (now route 40 through Virginia and Pennsylvania). He was a prisoner in Fort Duquesne. He was there when the battle took place a few miles upstream from the fort. After the battle a French soldier brought him a book found on a body. It was *Russell's Seven Sermons*. I went to the catalogue, heaved it out, and found the entry that I had learned to expect, the early 1750s edition. The only secondary reference I used was a reprint of primary documents that covered the true events, long misted over by contemporary self-protecting excuses and our own romantic illusions about Braddock's defeat at Fort Duquesne, a battle fought in the wrong place and at the wrong time of day, a real battle where everybody was late.

One day I came on a painting in the Tate Gallery and began to cry, and I think of it now, of all it tells, however covered by legend, of the sadness of having to leave home. It was called *The Last View of England*. The sad faces of a young couple and their small baby, standing on the deck of an immigrant ship, haunt me, and should haunt us all—not intrepid pioneers, but poor young people leaving home forever for a strange place of hope and fear.

One evening I found the title and the impassioned theme of my book. I had brought back to London from a visit to my family in West Virginia a recording of old hymns sung by Burl Ives. I listened to the hymn "O Beulah Land" for the first time.

> *O Beulah Land, sweet Beulah Land,*
> *As on the highest mount I stand,*
> *I look away across the sea,*
> *Where mansions are prepared for me,*
> *And view the shining glory shore,*
> *My heaven, my home for evermore.*

I still stand in that room in England, and still hear that hunger for a land hoped for, fought over, and never quite found—what we think of as the American dream, lost, defiled, complicated and used by the cynical, and still so deeply sought by the rest of us—to own your own home, shrunk from a claim in the great woods to a lot in a suburb, a place nobody can make you leave.

Over and over it happened. I stumbled over, walked into, sought out, found my book *O Beulah Land,* beginning with Hannah, lost in the Endless Mountains, and ending with the last colonial year before the American Revolution.

ANNE
SHELBY

Anne Shelby (b. 1948) is a native of eastern Kentucky and now lives on a farm in Clay County, Kentucky. Shelby, who has a B.A. and an M.A. in English, has published five books for children: *We Keep a Store* (1990), *Potluck* (1991), *What to Do about Pollution* (1993), *Homeplace* (1995), and *The Someday House* (1996). Her poems, essays, and short fiction have appeared in journals including *Appalachian Heritage, Appalachian Journal, Now and Then, Mountain Review,* and *Pine Mountain Sand & Gravel.* She has developed a play based on the work of Kentucky writer and AIDS activist Belinda Mason, and her play for voices, *Storehouse,* was selected for production by West Virginia Public Radio. Shelby has taught on the creative writing faculties of the Kentucky Governor's School for the Arts, the School for the Creative and Performing Arts in Lexington, the University of Kentucky Gifted Student Program, the Kentucky Arts Council's Artist-in-Residence Program, and the Appalachian Writers' Workshop at Hindman Settlement School. A storyteller as well as a writer, she collects and performs Appalachian folktales.

*　　*　　*

Piddlin'

More clearly than yesterday, I remember a summer afternoon over forty years ago. I was, perhaps, seven. We lived in Jackson County, Kentucky, in McKee, the county seat (population 100), a town that had, it seemed to me then, exactly what it needed with nothing extra left over. There was one bank, one grocery store, one five-and-dime, a restaurant, a filling station, two funeral homes, and half a dozen churches. Throw a rock from the courthouse steps, you could hit about anything in McKee.

The town lay in a flat narrow valley between two ridges. On one ridge sat the high school, where my father taught agriculture; my mother, English. The hillside opposite was dotted with small frame houses, and we lived in one, near the top of the hill. In our yard, my father put up a swing set for my sister and me, and this particular summer afternoon I spent swinging, as high and as long as I wanted to—for some reason nobody came out that day to warn me about children being killed turning their swing sets over—and looking out on the treetops and roof-tops of the town, on women and children and men and dogs on the courthouse lawn, on a world that seemed to make perfect sense. And so I sang, as long and as loud as I wanted to:

> *I love my rooster*
> *My rooster loves me*
> *I'll cherish my rooster*
> *In a greenberry tree*

The song, the swing, the summer air, my mother and sister inside the house—for a moment were all one motion, one feeling. I had never been so content. I have not been since.

Songs, music seemed to me then as natural and certain a thing as rocks in the creek.

Most of my relatives did not have indoor plumbing. They did have big stacks of 78 rpm records—the Carter Family, Mainer's Mountaineers, Fiddlin' John and Moonshine Kate—and windup Victrolas that filled the house with music so loud you had to go out in the yard to listen to it.

Uncles Arnold and James picked guitar. Aaron played harmonica. Don sang in a gospel quartet. Myrna and Glenna harmonized, washing the supper dishes.

Mother sang in the kitchen, too, while she cooked, "I'll Fly Away" and "Somewhere Listening" accompanied by the sizzle of grease, the clatter of pot lids.

> *When the Savior calls I will answer*
> *When He calls for me I will hear*
> *When the Savior calls I will answer*
> *I'll be somewhere listening for my name*

Dad sang Hank Williams and Ernest Tubb. Uncle Millard preferred cowboy songs—"Streets of Laredo," anything by the Sons of the Pioneers. At one grandmother's house there was an old organ, where great-aunts wept while singing sentimental songs, pumping vigorously on the foot pedals. My grandfather, usually stern-faced and dignified, sometimes erupted unexpectedly:

> *Get out of the way, Old Dan Tucker*
> *You're too late to get your supper*
> *Supper's over, breakfast cookin'*
> *Old Dan Tucker, stand there lookin'*

Decades after his death, neighbors still talk about how that man could whistle. You could hear him, they say, on "Little Birdie," all the way from the lower field clear up to the Road Run Gap. He'd once played for Saturday night dances but traded his banjo for a mantel clock when he joined the church. I imagine the time went by a little slower after that.

We sang on the porch, in the car, and at family reunions, songs from church, records, the radio, and TV. And when we sang up all the songs we knew, we made up our own—sad songs, mostly, but we had fun singing them, about dying cowboys, lost love, and the hope of heaven.

I don't think my family was particularly unusual in this way. I remember talent shows in the high school gym and at the county fair. And one of the highest forms of praise, right up there with "He'll do anything in the world for you" and "She's not a bit stuck up" was "She has got the purtiest voice," "He can hear a tune one time and play it. Never had a lesson in his life."

Music flowed out the windows, summer evenings, of the Pentecostal Church down the road, and pulled me from the playhouse and the TV show *Your Hit Parade* to stand on the flat rock steps and listen. We had "special music" Sunday mornings at the Gray Hawk Baptist Church, and when it was time for congregational singing, the small wooden churchhouse—no pads on the pews, no carpet on the floor—rang with "I Am Resolved," "Standing on the Promises," "Leaning on the Everlasting Arms."

> *I am resolved no longer to linger*
> *Charmed by the world's delights*

Things that are higher, things that are nobler
These have allured my sight

Before I could read, I knew those songs by heart. Then one Sunday, looking at my mother's hymnbook, I suddenly recognized the words. I got lost, though, when the words seemed not to match the singing anymore. She took my hand— I can still feel her cool fingers—and pointed to the words as the congregation sang, verse and chorus, verse and chorus, till I caught on. I looked up at her and smiled. I could read.

Music still seems to me as present and as necessary as air. I've never understood, in fact, some people's objections to musicals, to the notion that, baling hay or standing on a street corner in the rain, somebody might burst out singing. I'm surprised it doesn't happen rather more often in real life. And as someone who learned to read out of a hymnbook, music and writing are to me not distant relatives in the family of the arts, but close akin, double first cousins.

Unlike some of my own cousins, I don't have perfect pitch. I can't play the guitar or piano by ear. I try to write that way.

There were, in addition to music, other art forms in that small country place. I remember plays, at church and at school, and while they might not have been well reviewed, had they been reviewed at all, they were lively productions that attracted large and enthusiastic audiences.

Dance was perhaps the most neglected of the arts, being associated with elitism on one hand and sin on the other. I can report, however, that my aunt Mildred delighted nieces, puzzled pups, and scattered chickens dancing the Charleston on the porch.

Many people I knew worked in the visual arts, though they didn't call it that. They called it "piddlin'."

As a boy, my father's brother James wanted only crayons for Christmas. Later, if he couldn't afford canvas, he painted on the window shades. Pull down the ring with the crocheted cover, and there was a mountain lake, a snow-covered cabin, a tree full of birds. Aaron went into the hills and brought back pieces of wood he "just liked the looks of." Under his hands they were transformed into vases, tables, twisted abstract sculptures. Jack set up a woodworking shop in an old storehouse in McKee, fashioning doll furniture from scraps of walnut he salvaged from the lumber yard. "I just can't stand to see good walnut go to waste," he said.

The aunts piddled, too, creating room-size displays of antique furniture, dolls, and dishes they collected, drying wildflowers to arrange under glass. My mother's mother—and hers—pieced so many quilt tops they died before they got them all quilted. Mother finished them, then made her own quilts from patterns she drew herself. She painted, too, barns and cardinals in acrylics, and made bolder patterns of line and color in the yard, in the medium of marigolds, petunias, and scarlet sage.

Nobody I knew claimed to be an artist—or a philosopher—but as much a part of the air we breathed as Saturday soup beans or a bubby bush in the yard were abstract questions, posed earnestly and often, which entered our experience through the church or arose from a heightened awareness of death, which was as close and as real as the family graveyard.

How can we know God's will in our lives? Are we free, or are our lives predestined in some way? How can we tell the right from the wrong action? What is our duty to others? Will all sins be forgiven, come the end of time? Will we know one another, on the other side?

I've never found convincing answers, but the questions have stayed with me, and any occupation that does not include them has seemed frivolous somehow.

There were books, too, which we regarded with great respect, if not actual attention. Our greatest reader was perhaps my grandmother Pearlie who, after raising nine children and burying her husband, lived by herself in a little house across the creek that War on Poverty photographers would have taken pictures of if they'd found out about it and that we all unselfconsciously called "the shack." There she proceeded to catch up on some thirty years of reading. For me, while kick-the-can and hoopey-hide with the cousins had their pleasures, so too did slipping off to Mamaw's shack, to sit for a while in her gentle presence and leaf through old copies of *The Saturday Evening Post*.

There were books, but the language that seeped into my bones did not come from them.

My father's family, his eight brothers and sisters and their children, gathered most evenings at the home place at Gray Hawk. In warm weather while the children played in the yard, the men pitched horseshoes or drew a ring for marbles. The women, supper over, sat on the porch with glasses of iced tea. Winter nights were for playing rook, making fudge, tending the fire, and telling tales.

Well, you know what Granddad Cornett said before he died. He was bad off, very low, they did not expect him to live through the night. Talking out of his head, craziest stuff ever was. They was all gathered around the deathbed there, and Kermit bent over him, real quiet, whispered to him, said, "Dad, can you hear me? Do you know who I am?" Granddad never moved, just answered, said, "What's the matter, Kermit? Don't you know who you are?"

Weekends we crossed the county line from Jackson into Clay, clouds of white gravel dust billowing behind the car, to visit my mother's side of the family. There were no cousins at that end of the road, but there was a store, a tiny country store my grandparents kept, full of pop, candy, plug tobacco, nails, flies, and talk, including spirited debates on the subjects of politics, hunting dogs, and who was the laziest man in the county.

I knew a feller too lazy to breathe. Set down under a tree one day, leaned up against it, said, "Breath, you can come and go as you please. I've pushed and pulled all I'm a-goin' to."

Sunday afternoons in summer, the store spilled over into the yard—there being no real distinction between customers and company—and we sat on benches under the apple tree or lay on pallets in its shade. Men whittled, women fanned, and talk flowed like Teges Creek, a little slower here, a little faster there, pooling quiet for a spell, then cascading in laughter like water over a falls.

Shade and Dewey Fox, Marthie and Orthie, Morris and Tildy Allen, my parents and grandparents, aunts and uncles—these were my first and most important literary influences. I spent my childhood among people who laughed and cried rather often, who wrote songs, laboriously drawing the notes on homemade staff paper, who worried about predestination and could not stand to see good walnut go to waste. They showed me, humbly and without ever talking about it, the necessity of such activities. I can't do much with walnut. I piddle with words.

I meant to tell the truth, but now I see that I have created a fiction, not by what I said, but what I didn't say. I left out what a family of the fifties we were, how we went to the beach and the lake for summer vacations, to Lexington and Louisville on shopping trips, how we longed for a brick ranch house with a big picture window and shiny new appliances. I have left out the parts that were not very artistic, and I have left out the parts that hurt.

Another thing I did not tell. My father and mother and sister and I moved away from Jackson County when I was eight, leaving the cousins and grandparents and aunts and uncles, leaving the world I have described, and lived in a series of other places, and never went back, except for brief visits, for holidays, funerals, and family reunions.

Forty years later I find myself writing books for children eight and younger. Only when they are finished, I see how they recall parts of that lost world—the store, the home place, the potluck supper—a small and singing world that seemed, for a time, to make perfect sense.

Little birdie little birdie
Come and sing to me your song
Got a short time to stay here
And a long time to be gone

ED MONTALVO

BETSY
SHOLL

Betsy Sholl (b. 1945) grew up on the New Jersey shore. She was educated at Bucknell University, the University of Rochester, where she was a Woodrow Wilson Fellow, and Vermont College. She lived in Big Stone Gap, Virginia, from 1976 to 1983, writing and working as a freelance teacher. While in Virginia she was associated with Christ Hill, a residential community that served people in need of housing and other forms of support. She has published five books of poetry: *Changing Faces* (1974), *Appalachian Winter* (1978), *Rooms Overhead* (1986), *The Red Line* (1992), selected in 1991 for the Associated Writing Programs Series, and *Don't Explain* (1997). Her poems have appeared in *Beloit Poetry Journal, Field, Massachusetts Review, Indiana Review, Ploughshares,* and *West Branch,* among others, and in anthologies such as *Letters to America: Contemporary American Poetry on Race.* She is the recipient of a National Endowment for the Arts Fellowship and a Maine State Writers' Grant. Sholl lives with her family in Portland, Maine, and teaches at the University of Southern Maine and in the Vermont College M.F.A. program. For the last ten years she has served on the board of directors for the Wayside Evening Soup Kitchen.

*   *   *

Big Stone Gap

In 1976 I moved from Boston, Massachusetts, to Big Stone Gap, Virginia, with my husband and two young children. We lived in Big Stone for seven years, most of them in a double-wide trailer on Clinch Haven Farm in Powell Valley, one of the most beautiful places I've ever seen. Though I don't often write about those years directly, they remain germinal for me in many ways, having an almost elemental quality to them and having effected elemental changes in me. When I think of those years four things come to mind: the astonishing beauty of that valley, the cultural awareness I gained, my abiding sense of exile, and the spiritual rebirth those elements combined to spark. Earth, air, water, fire—those primary substances embody my experience as a transplant with much to learn.

Where I came from—first, the New Jersey coast of my childhood—was a prototypical landscape for me, with the exhilaration of its salt smells, waves, rubble line, stark beaches and dunes, always a sense of being on the world's edge. Then in my adult years, the city of Boston took over that role. In the crowds of people waiting for the subway, waves of strollers crossing the Common at dusk, the daily press of others, there was a vastness beyond myself, a largesse suggesting the mysteries of existence. Why not see humans as a form of magnificent wildlife, full of beauty and danger and otherness, I used to argue when people first urged me to appreciate the Appalachian countryside.

At the time we moved, I had recently published my first book and was teaching creative writing at MIT. Leaving those connections, I was forlorn. I missed sunlight on brick, brake lights on rain-slick streets, the arc of bridges over the river, the sudden wind tunnels of certain narrow streets, and always the little human scenarios on the train. I missed people who sounded and looked like me, countercultural crossbreeds, semi-intellectual, artsy, social activist types. The new isolation frightened me, and my new cultural otherness infuriated me. At that same time my stepfather had retired from banking and moved to Florida, where he would sometimes stand in bank lobbies like a greeter, trying to strike up a conversation. It exasperated and humiliated my mother. But I understood how he felt. My identity, my ability to talk and be understood, to have my allusions tracked, my assumptions shared, to have work and an identity in the world—it was all dissolving. Eventually I would come to appreciate this small peacetime version of what losing a war must be like, discovering just how frail one's security really is.

It's the loss of a kind of innocence that needs losing, an innocence that turns sour and myopic if held on to. And it hurts like hell, being stripped, shaken.

But the land was beautiful. It was like entering a picture book—morning fogs, fields full of spiderwebs, paw-paws, grasshoppers, bluebirds, big old moon faces rising over the mountain. That land never lost its beauty, its own kind of otherness and mystery. If urban life is inherently self-conscious, in Big Stone there were whole days, evenings, late afternoons of pure, unself-conscious joy, walking the fields with my children, sitting among the fireflies at night, watching lightning across the valley. Indigo buntings, blackberries, wildflowers from March to November along the side of the road, free—this was all new. There were the mines too—not in our town, but all around—deep mines in the town of Appalachia next door, stripmines flanking the road up the mountain to Norton and Wise. The combination of destruction and romance connected to the mines is still beyond my understanding. The exploitation by owners and managers, the bravado of the miners, black lung, fast money, the courage it takes to go down there day after day, the fear of the mines closing up—when I think of earth, certainly I see the tipple lit up at night like a skyscraper, and those dark tunnels underground I never entered, open mouths seductive and terrifying, surrounded by Keep Out and Hazard signs.

One of my most powerful earth-lessons occurred out of another kind of darkness, the loss of a friend, a man we had become close to almost as soon as we arrived. He was our age, from the town of Appalachia, but had lived in Berkeley and San Francisco for several years, so he helped cross the cultural gaps for us. He understood our adjustments and trusted us with his own difficulties. Almost a year to the day of our arrival, while we were visiting family in Cleveland, Ohio, our friend killed himself. He was already buried by the time our long weekend was over. It was a devastating experience—to have no closure, to have known the depth of his trouble and been so unable to change a thing. That death still haunts me. But one morning driving along the narrow farm road, I stopped to look across the fields. Goldenrod formed a kind of apron around a distant barn; the fog was gathered into one long tongue stretched midway across the valley; there were clusters of ironweed and joe-pye; and thousands of spiderwebs filled the valley like the secret gears of the world briefly visible. For maybe the first time in my life I understood that beauty existed outside and independent of what I was feeling. The world was there, in all its loveliness and pain, utterly separate and bigger than I was. Maybe one should learn that in grammar school. But I learned it mourning for my lost friend, on Clinch Haven Road. The earth became primary and elemental, not just a projection of my own state of mind.

Maybe culture can be compared to air—unnoticed until one moves outside of it. Things I had assumed were fact suddenly appeared to be cultural prejudices. What I assumed was essential now seemed to be learned—northern arrogance, speed, and abruptness, for instance, or my assumption that skepticism was synonymous with education. Of course I saw cultural elements in Big Stone that people took for truth—the role of women, for example, or the undercurrent of fatalism. And there was always the way people would apologize for using the word "Yankee" as if it were a curse, when up north that word sold cars, furniture, food, magazines. I gained a visceral understanding of how culture forms values, reinforcing some, discouraging others. I saw the difference between people who had never left the culture and those who had journeyed away and returned. I saw too how a culture can provide people with the means for growth and change.

A friend on welfare would often share her resources with others, whose checks came in at different times of the month. No one could possibly have enough goods to survive singly, so each shared goods and swapped services. Whoever had a check come in first would disseminate coveted resources to the others, knowing reciprocation would come when needed. I burn with impatience when people who have never seen such a community in action stereotype welfare recipients. But I wanted to tell a different story about my friend. She was living with her three children after leaving an abusive marriage, and one month she spent her precious resources on a velvet painting of the Last Supper. When another woman scolded her because her daughters had holes in their shoes, my friend answered that when she went to church on Sunday everyone would see that her children needed shoes and someone would offer them hand-me-downs. But, she swelled to her full height, who would look at her girls and see that they needed art?

At first, when I moved to Big Stone, I thought I had lost culture—lost the art museum I passed on the train every day, lost poetry readings, concerts. I had fancied myself rather well-read in current fiction, sniffing out from friends the newest novels. The loss of that possibility became the gain of another kind of culture. I started reading to fill in gaps—St. Augustine and Abigail Adams. A librarian had stocked the shelves with several then-new feminist literary critics. Flannery O'Connor's letters were recently out. I had a *War and Peace* winter, an *Anna Karenina* spring, a *Brothers Karamozov* fall. So during those years, it seems we traded speed for depth, in some ways becoming more profoundly aware of our culture than we'd ever been.

Air, I might add, suggests wind, and we had the most wonderful windstorms. Dog food bowls and lawn chairs would clatter down the road. Rags that had long been soaked and dried and resoaked in the fields would rise up. Shingles flew, windows rattled in their casings. We'd wake up the children and dance in the yard like wild little Rumpelstiltskins, glad to be battered and blown, relieved of our delusive solidity.

Water reminds me of what I continued to miss during those years—the waters of longing, ever-shifting streams of loss, my sense of exile. Anyone who grows up in a strong landscape probably never stops yearning for it. That's why my neighbors had to leave Cincinnati and come back to the mountains. "The green gets in your eyes," one told me. I missed water, that feeling of being on an edge, being able to see the sky go all the way down to the ground. Red suns and orange moons—always invisible behind the mountains. And the sense of belonging. I was often affectionately tolerated and even more often just plain accepted for whoever or whatever I was. But there were gaps. I was less circumspect and domestic than most of the women I knew in town. I was less conservative and more mouthy. Having to rely on my own drive and sense of purpose, it was easy to doubt myself as a writer.

What a relief to make trips to Lexington or meet up with other writers at readings in Johnson City or Bristol, or at Clinch Valley College. The larger community of Appalachian writers was always remarkably open and generous to me. George Ella Lyon, Jane Wilson Joyce, Jim Wayne Miller, Fred Chappell, Jo Carson, Dick Peake, the Appalshop folks, and many others—I am deeply grateful to them. When we got together it was a wonderful, joyous occasion.

But on a daily basis, I worked alone, and writers who work in isolation often suffer from self-indulgence. Most of us need others to challenge us, to point out where we are not applying artistry to our passions, submitting our own personal needs to the requirements of the form. Not having that sort of challenge on a regular basis, I often slipped into being precious, or clever, or whimsical. While the upbeat fantasy is that writing alone takes one to truer depths, in fact one is just as likely to avoid them, or sink in their turbulence. Without the clatter of activity, the interaction and neon flash of urban life, I slowed down. Elements of my character and upbringing that I'd avoided for years started to swamp me. This is probably a necessary part of any artist's growth, but when one's in the middle of it, the experience is raw and turbulent. And art requires distance, at least some detachment from the raw murk of confusion. We have to be able to step back, to choose what to emphasize or understate, to squint and see new patterns or slants. Occasionally, everything lined up—external trigger, inner response, formal insight—and something new and fresh emerged. But often the combination of landscape and isolation led me into writing poems that were essentially nostalgic, looking back toward childhood, because I didn't know how to take on a more adult voice.

What was a kid from New Jersey, a city girl, doing in the middle of nature? I was clueless to know how to write about it. My poetry had almost always been social—cityscapes and human interactions, semisurreal political observations, or at least monologues in which some kind of dramatic action was implied. Suddenly I spent whole days alone, seeing no one for the hours my children were in school. It should have been glorious—hours to write—but it weighed heavily on me, as if I'd lost my source. Certainly there were social problems I was actively involved in—a food pantry, a safe home. But being an outsider in the culture, I didn't feel the inner authority to take on those subjects. It was partly a matter of needing a tone or voice, a legitimate stance from which to speak. Such elements require confidence, a sense of engagement as well as distance. That's where I was shaky, so my growth as a writer during these years was largely subterranean, an interior growth that would come out later. We were often told that turn-of-the-century coal magnates had hoped to make Big Stone Gap the Pittsburgh of the South but failed because they couldn't find a cheap means of transporting the coal out of the mountains. That was how I felt sometimes—all the wealth of inner growth and experience, but how to get it out, how to give it shape?

Perhaps it was my own weakness, that I couldn't persist till I found a way to learn what I didn't know. At any rate, while my experience deepened during those years, I'm not sure the poems did, or my ambition for my poems. Still, any growth I've experienced since that time has occurred only because those years prepared me, gave me a sense of depth, an emotional life in three dimensions, rather than the shallow, propped-up feelings I experienced in the city.

I still don't know what to do with the gorgeous landscapes I can close my eyes and almost reenter. Some of them have made their way into poems—about my friend's death, about the almost self-annihilating beauty in those valleys and hills. The huge stands of redbud and indigo buntings appear. So do the snarling dogs waiting to gouge my legs if I jogged into their domain. And I jogged every day on that farm road, so each dip and rise, each turn and shift from field to stand of trees, is still imprinted on my mind—the rusty autumn colors slowly moving down the mountain, leaving the peaks like doused matches; the spring green and white slowly moving up; the wild apple trees nobody seemed to care if I pillaged; the gossamer strands of ballooning spiders; woods the cows had foraged so there was no scrub, just trunk straight down to the ground. And those winter mornings where everything was misted—white frost on the ground, white streak of fog across the valley, white breath of the cows, steam rising from the bales of hay— maybe it isn't necessary to write about it all. Maybe it's enough to have witnessed such beauty, to have been moved and changed by it. Maybe if it needs to be recorded it will press itself forward to my mind. The images are abiding. Poems come when those images marry some dramatic situation or conflict or a particular passionate inquiry. Lately, I've noticed that as I think more about beauty, about that which is larger and more mysterious than human understanding, these images start to enter poems.

Fire. Baptism by fire, wheels and tongues of fire, the Holy Spirit, the Bible Belt. Probably the greatest gift my years in Appalachia gave me was in terms of reentering my own religious tradition after years of alienation. I had spent a fair amount of time reading in other religions, so I could glimpse the beauty of Judaism or Zen Buddhism as a tourist, an outsider, looking through the window. But Christianity for me was mired up in childhood rules, right-wing pronouncements, restrictive piety, sappy cultural kitsch, and the ever-present left-wing critique of its tolerance (if not downright promotion) of imperialism. And yet my only chance of being an insider, not an observer but a participant, was through my own tradition. What better place than the Bible Belt to wrestle with these angels? Everybody we knew, it seemed, was saved or had backslid or was wrestling with the whole business of conversion and what it meant. We attended a Methodist church that was lively—almost wild—but also led by a very balanced and spiritually shrewd man, convinced that God was loving, infinitely patient, infinitely smarter than humans, and willing to let us trip on our own wires. That church community was a place where cultures met and made room for each other, where people let go of prejudices and defenses. If I had put down every church I'd ever entered—not all that many, actually—this one seemed to be doing what a church should. We took friends from MIT, and years later they were still quoting lines from those sermons. The minister's gift was in preaching to the parts of us that were vulnerable, fearful—the child, the arrogant jerk secretly miserable and sick of her own jerkiness.

Probably I would never have had the patience or the humility to go through the spiritual fires if I had stayed in Boston. It would have been too easy to keep reading little essays on Zen or Hasidism and sighing appreciatively about those strange mysterious worlds like very foreign cultures I know I'll never visit. But exile—even self-imposed, domestic exile—has a way of breaking the spirit just enough to show cracks where something not-self, something huge and other and mysterious can be glimpsed. Husks get burned off, the ego is downsized. My humanized, culturally controlled world cracked open just enough so I could find a place in the tradition I thought I had outgrown. Maybe a kind of mini-exile is also the artist's condition, at least in terms of the need to step back and observe, then reflect on what we've seen. Maybe an artist is also like those folks who leave their culture for a time, gain a new perspective, then return. If there's a sadness to that, there is also a benefit. If we're limited in some ways, we're made free in others.

In a turn-of-the-century folk study, Emma Bell Miles said that the dominant groups in Appalachian culture were the young men and the old women. I've thought about this many times. The power of young men may be obvious. But those old women, now they were something else. They'd been through hard times, raised their families, kept their homes together, survived, and in old age they had *power*. They were fierce and fearless in speaking their minds, focusing on truth, compassion, order. Nobody intimidated them. The older women I knew often called each other by their last names, as if they'd earned their stripes and were no longer defined by roles or relationships. They could laugh at themselves. They could look at you with piercing eyes and know what was on your mind, and if it wasn't good, Honey, they'd set you straight. Talk about role models. As I get older and start to admit I might actually get *old,* these women are my guides. They even make age seem desirable, fruitful—a possibility American culture rarely embodies.

Probably anything one says about a culture can be challenged. People are complex, contradictory. I was an outsider, so how much did I really see? What I thought I saw was an incredible testimony to human character. People had their secrets, but they were also more used to living in the open. It was a small town and everybody knew their business, so they made peace with that, they allowed themselves to season into a sense of character, individuality. At least that's how it seemed sometimes. Other times it felt almost the opposite, as if living close to generations of family led people to suppress their disruptive feelings and individuality, led to a kind of compliant attitude. Maybe I don't have to make up my mind, maybe both views, and even more, are part of the complex identity. I only know that the people with whom I spent those seven years live with me still, in the way they met adversity, the way they cared for each other, valued their stories and culture, combined practicality and mysticism. They will always be bigger than I can define, they will haunt me and call me back, remind me of all I don't know and all I do, my instructors in how to love both the visible and invisible world.

DON LEWIS

BENNIE
LEE
SINCLAIR

Resident of Cleveland, South Carolina, and poet laureate of the state, Bennie Lee Sinclair (b. 1939) is a Phi Beta Kappa graduate of Furman University and the ninth-generation descendant of settlers of the state's mountainous "Dark Corner." Her first volume, *Little Chicago Suite* (1971), was introduced by Mark Strand and very quickly became known in poetry circles. Her second volume of poetry, *The Arrowhead Scholar* (1978), received the Winthrop College Excellence in Writing Award. *Lord of Springs* appeared in 1990 and won a Pulitzer Prize nomination. And in 1992 she published *The Endangered: New and Selected Poems*. Sinclair is the author of a mystery called *The Lynching* (1992) that relies heavily on her memory of the last lynching in South Carolina—a lynching that occurred in her hometown when she was nine years old. Poems, stories, and essays by Sinclair have appeared in journals including *North American Review, Foxfire, San Jose Studies, Poet Lore,* and *South Carolina Review.* She has also written a short story chapbook and two regional histories and received the Appalachian Writers' Association Book of the Year Award. Sinclair lives on a 135-acre wildlife and wild plant sanctuary in the mountains above Cleveland with her husband, Don Lewis.

*   *   *

Appalachian Loaves and Fishes

I came into life part of a mountain family whose landscape, culture, and people were my own. But before I was five, my parents' separation closed this world to me.

At nineteen I reentered it when I married Don Lewis and we began our pilgrimage of the hills. Now I am fifty-seven and have come to know this world with special intimacy. Its influences on my life and work I consider to be gifts of biblical proportions, my Appalachian loaves and fishes. Why?

My father was born on a mountaintop between Fruitland and Bearwallow, North Carolina, in 1912. My great-uncle John told that, as a boy, he watched the Cherokee doctor ride up to the house with a large satchel thrown over the saddle. "There's a baby in that satchel," my great-grandmother Lizzie Sinclair told him. "The doctor has come to deliver it."

My father, Waldo Graham—"Graham"—Sinclair was born later that March morning, safely delivered.

My mother, Bennie Lee Ward, entered life a seeming great distance away, though it was only sixty miles, in a modern hospital in the South Carolina foothills town of Greenville. Her mother, Pernecy—"Necy"—a grieving young widow, named the baby "Bennie," after its father, Ben Ward, who had died six weeks earlier of swine flu, aged twenty-six. A half-century later Necy recalled that birth of her only child when spring peepers chanted forlornly, "Ben! Ben! Ben!" It was the first day of spring, 1917.

My father, Graham, grew up at the top of the Blue Ridge escarpment, in a remote region of high mountains, deep forests, and small farms. Mother was raised at the bottom of the escarpment, in a growing metropolis. Necy drove her own car. The first time my father visited Greenville, in 1921, he and his parents, brothers and sisters, rode down from the hills in a "bow frame" covered wagon. His mother, Effie, had hitched up the horses. The family moved to Greenville in the first years of the Great Depression, when farming failed.

An unlikely match, my parents met in early 1933, when Daddy went to work in a small grocery. Perhaps the only thing they had in common was striking good looks, but that was enough. When Mother came to the store to buy meat, she was charmed by the newcomer's tightly curled, widow's-peaked, blue-black hair and pale blue eyes. He was in awe of this ninety-pound, petulant socialite with wren-brown curls and tiny waist. When she got home, she found he had written her a love note on the butcher paper. She was fifteen, he twenty-two. Against both families' objections, they soon married. My brother, Waldo Graham Jr., "Buster," was born that December.

When I came along six years later, my parents and brother had been living for some time with Necy and her second husband, Ocron Jones. Necy and Ocron had married in June 1929, when he was a very wealthy man. Mother was given finery, the run of a palatial house, and even a chauffeur. By the end of that histori-cally dreadful year, Ocron was bankrupt, but not before Mother had developed a taste for riches and importance never again to be satisfied. Daddy had been raised austerely and disdained wealth and status. This was only one of many differences between them.

For my first four years, I had the best of both their worlds. The house we shared with Necy and Ocron was a roomy, graceful brick home with arched porches and French doors. Our furnishings, left over from wealthier days, included fine antiques and art.

Necy kept our large yard beautiful with flowers, plentiful with vegetables and fruit. Daddy raised cages full of quail, pheasants, and rabbits and, in big tubs, grew huge tomato plants taller than he was. In those days people still raised live-stock at the edge of town, and we had chickens—prize Rhode Island Reds and Dominiques—and each year a hog and a steer to be slaughtered. Buster and I had dogs and cats, and Daddy brought home any wild thing he could catch for us, which included a large snapping turtle, mallard ducks, and a very tame squirrel.

Necy taught me gardening, sewing, cooking, preserving, and homemaking. Mother enjoyed the Greenville social life of afternoon teas and bridge parties, often taking me with her on these genteel rounds. Wearing hats and white gloves, we visited grand houses where grand dames held court. My favorite was a grouchy, very old lady whose very old parrot squawked on a perch at her shoulder. It was the most irascible-looking creature I ever saw and probably the only animal from my childhood I did not try to pet or pick up. This way of life, and most of the old houses, passed on at the end of World War II.

There was a strict formality to Mother's life, a necessary punctuality, and an all-absorbing concern for what other people thought. Daddy, other than getting to work on time, preferred to move in a casual drift of days and seasons. Evenings after work or on weekends, he often took me adventuring. I wonder now why Mother permitted it, as we usually came in quite late. It may be that she thought my presence would be proof to preying women that he was spoken for. My parents were each quite jealous of the other. But the only instructions she gave me were to tell her if Daddy drank beer. I knew what beer looked like, it was amber-colored, came in tall bottles, and Daddy never drank it. He drank "bootleg"—colorless fire, "white lightning." We'd leave home and drive to the Dixie Grill, the closest honky-tonk, pass through the large diner section, down a few steps to a long room where a beautiful garnet and silver jukebox throbbed with music. There were women in sequined dresses, dyed hair, and heavy makeup who made much over Daddy and me. He would sit and talk for a while, take a few swigs from somebody's bottle, and on we'd go.

Late into the night, we'd wander up and down the Blue Ridge escarpment, back and forth across the eastern Continental Divide. He drove a 1940 Ford with the shotgun window out. He had draped a heavy black cloth across it, and I stood or sat or slept beside it. I loved to put my face against it and feel the cool dark air. It flapped and made a whistling sound. I thought there was a strange black bird perched on the outside mirror.

Daddy's mother, Effie, was from the "Dark Corner," the South Carolina side of the escarpment in northern Greenville County, a notoriously remote and law-less region. It was rife with bootlegging, off-limits to outsiders, and Daddy loved to go there. Effie's people, Bartons and McKinneys, were original settlers from the 1700s, and we were some kin to everyone. Besides, Daddy had his charm, har-monica, and tow-haired little girl to help gain entry.

One evening, when we were at a bootlegger's house near Little Chicago, Daddy was drinking and making music with the grown-ups while I was supposed to play with the other children. But they were older and rough, and I hid behind the front door, flung open to exchange body heat for cool air. I woke later to find everyone searching frantically for me.

On the way home from these rounds, instead of a lullaby, Daddy would sing such a rollicking version of "Froggie Went a Courtin'" that I giggled myself to sleep.

Our good times together were coming to an end. One evening, before my fifth birthday, my parents and I went riding, and soon Daddy and Mother began arguing. In those days the road across Paris Mountain, at Greenville's outskirts, curved around a steep cliff. In a rage, Daddy pulled off and dragged Mother to the edge. When they came back, she was too shaken to speak. Whatever had passed between them was terrible and final, and Daddy left home and our lives soon after, taking my Appalachian heritage with him. Mother's world, at least our cor-ner of Greenville, was more influenced by South Carolina midland and lowland culture than by Appalachian.

In late 1957 I met Don Lewis, a handsome ex-Marine also enrolled as a freshman at Furman University. This too was love at first sight, though luckily our similari-ties far outweighed our differences. Our growing-up years had been marred by illness and our parents' divorces. But what worked against us also worked for us. We were penniless, as were our families. We had no option but to turn to a simple way of life if we struck out on our own, which we did, marrying in 1958.

My father, now an invalid, lived in the nearby town of Greer with his second wife, Della Mae. She was an Atkins from Little Chicago who still owned her home place there, a fifty-acre, run-down farm I had once visited with Daddy and Buster about the time Daddy left. I remembered that long-ago Sunday vividly. Daddy had held a rifle and taught me to shoot, a mountain-Zen method of sight, concentrate, squeeze that works well yet. He caught a bumblebee and held it in his palm. I waded in the creek with a flock of children, was mesmerized by the fact that the old farmhouse, where people still lived, had a hole in the back room floor big enough for me to crawl through. Now, as a wedding present, Della Mae and Daddy gave us two acres on the backside of that farm. They might have given us the moon, for it seemed that glorious. Ours was mostly cutover timberland, with a snatch of field, and surrounding us, though we did not own it, a seemingly unending stretch of woods and fields to explore. "Little Chicago," a crossroads that had gotten its name during Prohibition, when there was a shoot-out between bootleggers there at the same time as one in "Big Chicago," was a mile or so distant. It consisted of two old general stores, a barbershop, and a small café. Our land was a half-mile back from the nearest dirt road, which wound on to an old gristmill then in operation. The miller, Harve, sat his days out in a wheelbarrow propped thronewise against the outside entrance.

We had no driveway to our land, and so we hauled in by hand the rough sawmill lumber Don used to build our twenty-by-twelve-foot cabin. There was also no electricity, telephone, or running water, as was the case for several years, insuring our isolation, which we came to cherish.

While still at Furman, we each had work scholarships—Don as biology lab instructor, I as literary magazine editor—and held outside part-time jobs. Don also had the GI Bill, which first made his coming to Furman possible. Summers we worked as "gourmet" pickers of peaches and grapes, selecting table-ready fruit, especially the sweet, white, exquisitely bruisable Georgia Belle peach, for the housewives and chefs who did their early shopping at the Farmers' Market. Dozens of black peach pickers worked around us, having a good laugh at our "pickiness." The women wore long dresses, and both men and women wrapped their heads in bright bandanas against the sweat and flies. We all wore heavy shoes and socks, pants rolled down to cover them against the yellow jackets swarming on fallen fruit, as well as to protect our feet from the "jungle rot" one got from wading in wet grass all day. In addition, we sold produce from our own garden at the Farmers' Market or to restaurants. Don did freelance work as a photographer and I as a journalist. Sometimes we combined our talents and did articles together.

We both had lived with grandparents who taught us the "from scratch" method of doing or growing almost anything. We raised much of what we ate, kept goats for milk, and bartered for what we could not grow. Most of our earned income went toward tuition, books, or gas to go to and fro.

It was an idyllic time. The woods came right to the cabin door, and so did the animals. Baby crows perched on the roof during flight training. My kitchen had a glass wall. Daily the foxes who denned in a dirt bank at the edge of the field trotted by on their way down to the creek. A tribe of baby snipe, almost never seen, walked past, the babies' heads tilted back as if to allow for their long, long beaks. A six-foot-long blacksnake fell out of the top of a pine and lay stunned. Red-tailed hawks nested not ten yards out back. Don added a sleeping porch, and on moonlit nights, the animal traffic was worth staying awake for: possums, foxes, and raccoons feasted on the persimmons that fell beside the front door. One snowy evening, a pony and two pigs wandered by.

A screech owl fell down the chimney into the fire. Don scooped it out, a singed and sooty mite, but, amazingly, uninjured. It spent the day in a cloth-covered cage, getting itself cleaned up, and, come dusk, flew back into the twilight.

From the cabin it was a fifteen-minute drive to enter the mountains proper. We drove a Scout and explored the Dark Corner roads across Hogback and Glassy. In summer we showered under Skyuka Falls. We picnicked and camped across the Blue Ridge, in Georgia, South Carolina, North Carolina, Tennessee, Virginia, and West Virginia. We learned how the subtle character of the mountains and their people changed from state to state, range to range.

We drove the Blue Ridge Parkway from end to end many times, collecting memories: of climbing the mountain to Ellijay, Georgia, in icy weather and composing a song about it along the way; of having a bear pull our pup tent over on us in Shenandoah; of sleeping out on the edge of an apple orchard in West Virginia, where deer leapt and trotted around us all night; of attending a square dance in Sodom, North Carolina, with only local folk thirty years ago—only a few of our Appalachian adventures.

Don became a professional potter in 1961, following our graduation and a summer of study with Bauhaus master potter Marguerite Wildenhain in California, the first time—except for trips to Florida and Charleston—that I had traveled out of sight of our mountains. I was acutely homesick.

I had been writing, and publishing, since first grade, but now that I had finally finished college and was ready to be a writer, I found myself at a stage of development no one had warned me of: I knew how to handle words fairly competently but as yet had nothing worthwhile to say. It was an astounding discovery, and very depressing. I kept on practicing but did not send things out for a long time.

For the next ten years, we earned our living through Don's pottery. A whole new face of Appalachia was making itself familiar to me, that of the artist and craftsman. Don was accepted into the Southern Highland Handcraft Guild, and its fairs at Gatlinburg and Asheville, as well as the Plum Nelly Clothesline Art Show in Georgia, became part of our yearly itinerary and income. We met and became friends with legendary figures, visited them at their homes at remote ridges and hollows, heard firsthand the stories of their lives, their work, their tall tales, and their songs. Some of these people—Going Back and Mary Chiltoskey and the late Shadrack Mace and his daughter Pauline Keith—were so classically representative of the Appalachians that photographs and drawings of them are still widely used. Pauline, who looked the stereotypical dream of a mountain woman, thin and madonna-esque, with her long hair twisted in a simple bun, shy around strangers, could, if she knew and liked you, "talk up a storm." I've found that the stereotypical mountain person doesn't exist. It is true that we are reticent around outsiders—who, after all, have not always "done right by us."

During this period, there were sadnesses in my life that made our happiness at Little Chicago all the more to be cherished. In 1960 my father died. My dreams of getting to know him, of making up for lost time, were never to be realized, as, over the past several years, he had been crippled, physically and mentally, by a series of strokes caused by diabetic complications. At death he was still remarkably handsome, and, to my dismay, a number of people took pictures of him in his coffin.

For the first time in years I tried my hand at poetry, trying to write an elegy for him, but my attempts seemed too mediocre to pursue.

The winter of 1966–67 Buster spent with Mother and Necy. He was getting over a divorce, and depressed. The ancient sites of the Keowee and Toxaway Indian villages were being flooded for a nuclear dam, and he and Don and I decided to spend a day or two each week helping to salvage what we could. This, too, was an idyllic time, when we three wandered the doomed wilderness together and became close friends. But in June of that year Buster suffered a brain aneurysm and died five days later in Asheville. He was thirty-three.

Effie's three-greats grandmother had been Sallie Wilson, a North Carolina Cherokee. Della Mae's grandmother had been a Crowe from the reservation. Daddy's uncle Wade Sinclair had kept the Baptist Mission there, riding on horseback to preach at the scattered churches (as in *The Education of Little Tree*), and later founded the newspaper at Robbinsville. Daddy had many friends on the reservation, including an old man whom he called a "wizard," who lived in a shack built on stilts back near Big Witch. My favorite snapshot was of Daddy with the old Cherokee and his bear sitting on the porch. It was natural that Buster, "The Arrowhead Scholar," should come to love Indian lore.

*   *   *

In the late 1960s, my writing, thought, and experiences began to come together. My father's and my brother's deaths had propelled me toward poetry, and when I read that a young poet named Mark Strand was visiting Converse College, I took a few poems and sat in on his workshop. The poems the students had written for Mark were "silly," and he was not in a good mood when I came up afterward and asked him to read my work. But he read, read again, and his face brightened. He separated a couple and said emphatically, "These are *real* poems!" He particularly liked "Sidney" and "The Evangelist." He had the galleys with him of his now classic anthology, *Contemporary American Poetry since 1941,* and spent an hour or so going over some of the tenets of good contemporary verse with me. It was the encouragement and direction I needed. In hindsight, it's interesting that the future poet laureate of the United States took time to give encouragement to the future poet laureate of South Carolina. But at that moment, it was simply a very tired, upcoming poet affirming the efforts of an unsure fledgling.

My mentor/teacher Alfred Reid, a Furman University professor, had published a story of mine in the *South Carolina Review,* which he had recently founded. My first poems were published in a new "little" magazine from the Georgia mountains called *Foxfire.* I corresponded with Al Stewart, who also printed my work, and I became an advisory editor of the recently inaugurated *Appalachian Heritage.* Without realizing it, I was establishing an identity as an Appalachian writer and becoming part of an exciting revival and continuance of Appalachian letters.

When I gathered the poems for my first collection, I realized they would not have been written if Don and I had not lived at Little Chicago. My life and my work were, and are, inseparable—not necessarily autobiographical, but inseparable. The Drummer Press first brought out *Little Chicago Suite,* with an introduction by Mark Strand, in 1971. Drummer also published a book by Jim Wayne Miller in their effort to promote promising young poets. During the seventies and early eighties, there followed the most public years of my career. I did poetry readings and workshops, including such exciting (to me) places as Notre Dame, and traveled a great deal in and out of Appalachia. It was not long before I realized that like craftspeople and authors Bernice Stevens and Alice Zimmerman, I wanted my *work* to be recognized but not myself. I didn't want to be known as a celebrity, or a personality, which is something else entirely.

In 1976 we moved into the mountains proper, to a 135-acre tract of old hardwood forest, with two streams and innumerable springs. Don's dream was to own our own watershed, which we do (he is the "Lord of Springs" in the title poem of that book); mine to have stately white pine and hemlock, which we do.

We designated our place a wildlife and wild plant sanctuary, so that the deer, bear, raccoon, wild turkey, and myriad other animals and plants have at least this to help them survive. We have a number of endangered species, fauna, and flora, including the rare and lovely Oconee Bell.

That year I attended "An Appalachian Symposium" held at Appalachian State University in honor of Cratis Williams, which was a landmark event for me and a stellar occasion for everyone who participated or attended.

I had not thought of Appalachian studies as a field but simply gathered what of it came my way. But suddenly, in two days' time, I heard papers by premier scholars and writers that expounded and expanded a dozen different aspects of our region's landscape, people, and culture—much of it customs or ways that I had experienced but taken for granted. It was a small conference and papers were given in full to a rapt audience. I particularly remember those by Wilma Dykeman, Loyal Jones, and one by Chester Young on Appalachian Old Christmas. I had celebrated Old Christmas at my "Little Great-Grandmother" Lizzie Sinclair's snow-covered home above Fruitland, North Carolina, in January of 1942, when I was going on three. This tiny lady (4 feet, 11 inches), born a few days before the end of the Civil War, still had only a few streaks of gray in her red hair as she sat primly and read the Christmas story to us from her much-used Bible. I also remembered the evening as the last time I had been together with all of Daddy's family. He and his three brothers had enlisted shortly after, though Daddy was sent home from the Navy when it was discovered he had diabetes. Now I learned that I had enjoyed a rare and unique Appalachian holiday.

Jean Ritchie gave a concert for our group, where I sat beside Doc Watson. One paper about the Parham family's music, by Joan Moser, also struck home. Don and I had stopped by the Parhams' once to pick up a friend, a banjo picker. The music from within was tempting, but I had been hearing this music since childhood, and we were in a hurry. Now I realized, through a scholar's articulation, that I had, again, been privy to a special and private treat outsiders seldom witnessed. The intense excellence of the papers, as well as the care of presentation and critical and informative discussion following, set for me a new standard. I woke to the knowledge that my window on Appalachia had to be shared.

In addition, I made new friends. After an exhilarating day, a few writers, including Jim Wayne Miller, decided to make the short drive to downtown Boone for pizza. But it was later than we thought, and the place was closed. On down the Blue Ridge escarpment we drove, in and out of the mist, to the more populous foothill towns, only to find it was now Sunday morning and everything closed. A loiterer told us of an all-night pizza parlor somewhere back up in the ridges, and back up the escarpment we went, on what had now become a do-or-die quest.

The fact is, we were all having such a zany good time we didn't want to give it up. Jim Wayne held forth, challenging us to match wit and memory as we recited, told tales, talked until dawn drove us back, pizzaless. I learned then that five or six uninterrupted hours with Jim Wayne was never quite enough.

My grandmother Necy taught me "a lady is a lady to everyone"—an early instruction in egalitarianism—and Wilma Dykeman impressed me not only as a fine writer and scholar but also in the courtesy, interest, and care with which she regarded everyone she met.

I came home from that symposium an enlightened person. There, and at the early Appalachian Studies Conferences, which grew out of the symposium, and at the Appalachian Writers' Association, which grew out of that, I made new and lasting friends whose quick minds made a reading or a paper or a workshop an exciting challenge. I found Sharyn McCrumb's candor energizing, her drive invigorating.

One Appalachian Writers' Association conference was especially memorable. It was held at Morehead State University, and I went a few days early to do readings. One morning someone summoned me excitedly to the president's office. There I met naturalist/poet Clyde Kessler, who had spied scarlet tanagers nesting on the president's window ledge. The bemused president did not seem too upset by the interruption. A poem about Clyde later became the title poem for my most recent book, *The Endangered.*

I also met one of my idols that week—Harriette Arnow—who was AWA's keynote speaker. *The Dollmaker,* I hope, has saved many of us from leaving our Appalachia—or whatever our true homeland is in this world—with its incredibly sad account of displacement. But it is so much more than that, a true masterpiece. I don't know what I expected Harriette Arnow to be like, but certainly not as tiny or irascible as she was. I think that I sat by her at the speaker's table by default, she having reduced her host to a sputtering displacement of his own. Of another well-known writer she commented, "I think I made Miss ___ angry. Tough!" I was to ease into her good graces quite unintentionally. Morehead is famous for its apple dumplings, but when the carts full of dessert were rolled out, there were only a few dumplings, which were wheeled to the back of the room. When I saw that Ms. Arnow was looking hungrily after the vanishing treats, I gathered courage, bolted down to the floor, and retrieved two dumplings for us. Throughout the rest of the evening I could hear her inquiring, "Who *is* that nice young lady who got me my apple dumpling?"

But I've been talking mostly about the good memories, which affect the quality of my work, or the quality of behavior I strive for. It is the bad memories, the painful experiences, the losses that nevertheless shape us. Perhaps that is what a true shape-changer is—one who can adapt and flourish through the hardest that life offers—

beginning as a bird, light and airy and singing, and ending as a bear, heavy and hunted, but feasting on berries, nevertheless.

Neither my mother nor father were able to pursue their dreams once they were apart. Mother began to drink when I was eight. One evening I walked into her room and there sat my mother, but it was as if another person looked out at me. The change that the merest amount of alcohol created in her was appalling. At the same time, it exacerbated a deep-rooted mental disorder that I sensed in her but was not old enough to comprehend. Her best years had been her young-mother years, when Daddy was still with us.

In the mid-forties Mother went to work at the Greenville County Court-house, an old and lovely building on Main Street, as a clerk in the Mesne Convey-ance Office, recording property transactions in precise and beautiful cursive. She was much liked by the lawyers and judges, many of whom were our cousins, but being a working mother was difficult in those days, and she pined for her loss of social status. Divorce had only recently been made legal in South Carolina, and separation was considered a social stigma. But the stories she brought home from the courthouse are still fodder for me, as in my novel, *The Lynching*.

Her mental illness, later diagnosed tentatively as manic-depressive with schizo-phrenic tendencies, followed no simple pattern. She had always been given to fabrication, but gradually her half-truths became lies or delusions that had devas-tating effects involving others. Tidbits of her craziness flashed through our daily lives. Finally, she became psychotic and was institutionalized. One day I went to visit and found her in a straitjacket within a wire-mesh-covered bed, looking frail and harmless as an angel, though I knew better. I agonized for years over the fact I had not been able to help her that day and finally, when we were having a very good and, I thought, lucid moment, mentioned it to her. She looked at me, her eyes wide with amazement. "Oh, that's all right!" she said. "As soon as you and the nurse left, I flew out the window!"

In a strange way, the sad life experiences, the tragic ones, are loaves and fishes also, for they truly do build character, as well as wisdom for writing.

In 1993 my life was saved by a kidney transplant from a young woman from the Georgia hills who died tragically. Certainly, hers was a gift of biblical propor-tions, and one I feel I must live up to, in my writing and my life.

Because of these loaves and fishes, I am never lacking for subject matter. My ghosts implore me to tell their stories, write their elegies: a lifetime's work.

BARBARA
SMITH

Barbara Smith (b. 1929) was raised in Wisconsin but "came home" to West Virginia in 1960. She served for over twenty years as chair of the Division of Humanities and for over thirty years as professor of literature and writing at Alderson-Broaddus College in Philippi, West Virginia. Smith has published over two hundred poems, short stories, and journal articles, plus four books of nonfiction. *Six Miles Out,* her award-winning novel about Cedarcrest, a retirement home, was published in 1981. She has been active in social and political arenas throughout her life, most recently in the establishment of hospice care for a three-county area of West Virginia and in her work as a fellow with the Medical Ethics Committee under the auspices of the West Virginia Humanities Council and the West Virginia Network of Ethics Committees. In 1993 Smith won the Dennie C. Plattner/Appalachian Heritage Award for Excellence in Writing of Fiction and was a Pushcart Prize nominee. She describes herself as a music and art fancier and a "sports nut."

*   *   *

Inside Discoveries

The word "eureka" may belong to Archimedes, but the sensation doesn't. He shares that with his physicist buddies, his oil painting relatives, and all serious writers. It comes with the creator-inventor-explorer territory, with the discovery of gravity, the brand-new shade of cerulean blue, the absolutely perfect ending to a story. And it comes with the discovery of who you are. The sound of it may be a chorus of hosannas or it may be a declaration of independence or it may be a whimper.

Eureka will feel different, too, sometimes as smooth and cool as frozen yogurt, sometimes as slick and brassy as a slide trombone. Sometimes fuzzy and treacherous as larva. Sometimes it's as sucky as quicksand. Or all of the above, depending upon the nature of the discovery or how the light falls.

Take writing. It's a bronze moment when your laptop is open on a hand-hewn picnic table at Buckhorn Lake and the breeze is whispering sweet nothings and you've just eaten a nice, firm banana and a bunch of seedless grapes and the words are tumbling out of your fingertips like a team of cheerleaders in a glitzy routine. Or you're in the New York City Public Library and you're surrounded by a hundred thousand book voices speaking directly to your ballpoint pen. Or Jaromir Jagr has just scored on another hat trick. Or you've just taken a sip of fresh coffee from a thick china mug in a truck stop on a back road outside of Harmon, West Virginia, and you hear a deep-mine voice declare, "I'm telling you, Merlin, we just gotta do something about them damned zebras."

Those are eurekas if you're a writer, and the consequence comes, if you're lucky, loud and clear and of its own free will. Given half a chance, that laser probe will turn itself into a short story or a poem or at least an article for the local newspaper.

Unfortunately, it's just as likely that the beam will be broken before it really penetrates. The phone rings or you have to do the taxes. Or it's time to head for the bus stop. Or it's your mother-in-law's birthday. Or there's a chapter to read before class. Groceries if you're ever going to eat again. Grass to mow. Beds to change. A root canal.

Or, an experience all too common to any left-brainer: every month or so you burst into the dimly lit living room exclaiming, "It's great! It's a masterpiece! Best thing I've ever written! Read it!" And your would-be audience, completely committed to a repeat broadcast of *America's Funniest Home Videos,* mutters, "How nice. Put it on the table, will you?" Sure. As you fold the laundry and cram it into overstuffed drawers, you give up trying to patch the latest of many holes in your balloon. You settle for whatever.

Fortunately, some eurekas last a lifetime. Like this one. My father had been bugging me for over a year: "You really should read the family history." But my aunt in Oregon had the only copy. Dad had read it on a visit out there during the previous summer. His demand finally took root in my skull, and I realized that the story would make a great birthday present for him. By then the patriarch, he could send copies to members of our very small family. So I called my aunt, and she sent it registered mail, and I typed the seventy-six pages.

And there it was. My paternal grandfather several generations back had been a governor of West Virginia. His brother had been the first dean of the ag school at WVU, and it was his handwriting I was reading. My name—Barbara—had come from a branch of the Philip Barbour family (as in Barbour County). This sizable eureka was reinforced a few months later when, strolling through the archives at the Science and Culture Center in Charleston, I looked up and saw a portrait of my father's sister. Well, not really—the woman in the picture was the wife of that governor of West Virginia—but she was a virtual clone of my aunt Amytis.

The magnitude of this discovery becomes clear when I add that my father and aunt were born and raised in Kansas City, Missouri. I was born and raised in Wisconsin. In 1960 my husband and infant daughter and I moved overnight from New York (Manhattan) to Philippi, West Virginia. We came because we both wanted to teach in a church-related liberal arts college away from the city streets where the cats used the parkside sandboxes to "litter." We knew virtually nothing about West Virginia and absolutely nothing about its governors. This was not a matter, though, of relocating. It was a matter of *locating*.

Some discoveries and connections, on the other hand, must *grow* into permanence, like that "sense of place" we Appalachians talk about or that friendship with a miner's wife or a workshop buddy. Some of these character-changers come as eavesdroppings that etch themselves into the brain: "You tell your daddy he don't have to worry—that woman can't have no more babies." Some become your internal landscape, like the riffles in the Upper Middle Fork River on a laurel-shaded July afternoon.

Thanks to my father's family history, my words and I are permanently planted in the people and places of Appalachia. I spent one life-changing summer interviewing coal miners' wives, for instance, thirty-nine women who became a key to my existence. That manuscript had been commissioned and the book did get finished, but two weeks before the publication date, the publisher declared bankruptcy. Several of the interviews—chapters of the book—have been published in such journals as *Goldenseal* and *Down Home,* but the rest of the stories are still in the box, and the publisher never returned all the photos of the women. Yes, I'd like someday to see the whole book in print, but the real reward lay in meeting those women and hearing their stories. Those interviews and many others since then have provided material for other pieces of fiction and nonfiction.

I have also gone every year to the Appalachian Writers' Workshop in Hindman, Kentucky, where I met one of those soon-to-become lifelong friends, Jolene Morgan Boyer, a native of eastern Kentucky who has led me to and sent me material enough for four or five writers. It was she who took me one day to where she was born, and it was near there that I saw a man being kept in a cage on his mother's front porch. He haunted me for ten years, as did his mother, whom I named Sophronia when I made them the focal characters of a novel that I finished last winter.

There is, in fact, no end to the stories I could tell about the workshops and the people at Hindman. I can't name all the names—there are so many who have given so much to so many! But there is one—Al Stewart—whom many of us look to as patron saint. Founder of the Appalachian Writers' Workshop, he was also the founder and twelve-year editor of *Appalachian Heritage*. His everlasting arms have supported many of us, and it was he who encouraged me to turn a short story called "Cattleman" into a novel that was published in 1981—*Six Miles Out*. "Cattleman" is at the heart of that book, a book set, like the caged-man story, in West Virginia.

Between major adventures in Hindman and coal towns and at lakes hidden high in the mountains, beside rivers carving their way down through the valleys to China, there have been weekly workshops and occasional conferences, acceptances from friends and rejections from editors, interactions with other writers and interferences from other departments. There have been births of babies and deaths of parents, Elizabethan banquets and ramp dinners. Piano recitals and the Pirates and the Penguins. An antique rocking chair purchased from a roadside stand. Carnival glass in a neighbor's garage. The sight of Hyakutake over the local softball field.

And under and around and above it all there has been the writing. The great bulk of mine has been in response to someone's need—a hospice wanting a feature article written about a client, an editor asking for a book review or an introduction, the Czechoslovak Baptist Convention of the U.S.A. and Canada needing a children's page or the editing of a translated article, a friend asking for help with a eulogy for another friend's funeral, a Christmas play for the church.

And every once in a while has come a shining moment, that propulsion, that sense of eureka that is the artist-writer's intravenous injection. That infusion keeps us breathing. The blood continues to flow, and we keep writing. All of which is to say, again, that some bright moments are as permanent as the compulsion to write. From my own revelations and self-revelations have come all kinds of relationships with the people and places of West Virginia, Kentucky, Tennessee—Appalachia. And from those relationships come poems and stories and journal articles—and some inkling of who I think I am.

LEE
SMITH

Lee Smith was born in 1944 in Grundy, Virginia, and is currently professor of English at North Carolina State University. She is the author of numerous works of fiction, including *The Last Day the Dogbushes Bloomed* (1968), *Something in the Wind* (1971), *Fancy Strut* (1973), *Black Mountain Breakdown* (1981), *Cakewalk* (1981), *Oral History* (1983), *Family Linen* (1985), *Fair and Tender Ladies* (1988), *Me and My Baby View the Eclipse* (1990), *The Devil's Dream* (1992), *Saving Grace* (1995), *Christmas Letters* (1996), and *News of the Spirit* (1997). *Oral History* (1983), her ambitious story about four generations of the Cantrell family of Hoot Owl Holler in the Virginia mountains, treats Appalachian language, legend, and character with richness and complexity and has influenced the writing of other authors in the region. Also, her stories and articles have appeared in various periodicals and anthologies such as the *Southern Review, Redbook,* and the *New York Times.* Smith has won numerous awards and accolades, including two O. Henry Awards (1979 and 1981), the John Dos Passos Award, the Weatherford Award for Appalachian Literature, the Sir Walter Raleigh Award in 1983 for *Oral History* and in 1989 for *Fair and Tender Ladies,* a Lyndhurst Grant, the Robert Penn Warren Prize for Fiction, and the Lila Wallace–Reader's Digest Award.

* * *

Terrain of the Heart

Although I don't usually write autobiographical fiction, my main character in a recent short story sounded suspiciously like the girl I used to be: "More than anything else in the world, I wanted to be a writer. I didn't want to learn to write, of course. I just wanted to be a writer, and I often pictured myself poised at the foggy edge of a cliff someplace in the south of France, wearing a cape, drawing furiously on a long cigarette, hollow-cheeked and haunted. I had been romantically dedicated to the grand idea of 'being a writer' ever since I could remember."

I started telling stories as soon as I could talk—true stories and made-up stories, too. My father was fond of saying that I would climb a tree to tell a lie rather than stand on the ground to tell the truth. In fact, in the mountains of southwestern Virginia where I grew up, a lie was often called a story, and well do I remember being shaken until my teeth rattled with the stern admonition, "Don't you tell me no story, now!"

But he was hardly one to talk. Both my mama and my father were natural storytellers themselves. My mamma, a home ec teacher from the Eastern Shore of Virginia, was one of those southern women who can—and did—make a story out of thin air, out of anything—a trip to the drugstore, something somebody said to her in church. My father liked to drink a little and recite Kipling out loud. He came from right there, from a big mountain family of storytelling Democrats who would sit on the porch and place twenty-five-dollar bets on which bird would fly first off a telephone wire. They were all big talkers.

So my parents might say, as they did later, that they wished I would just stop all that writing stuff and marry a surgeon, which is what a daughter really ought to do, of course, but the fact is that they were so loving that they gave me the confidence, and the permission, early on, to do just about anything I wanted to do.

And so I read. I read everything I could get my hands on. My book choices proceeded alphabetically: the B's, for instance, included Hamilton Basso, the Brontës. I did not read casually, or for mere entertainment, or for information. What I wanted was to feel all wild and trembly and intensely alive, an effect always produced by *The Secret Garden*, which I read at least twenty times. Other books affecting me strongly were *Little Women*, especially the part where Beth dies, and *Gone with the Wind*, especially the part where Melanie dies. I hoped for a wasting disease, such as leukemia, to test my mettle. I also loved *Marjorie Morningstar, A Tree Grows in Brooklyn, Heidi,* and books like *Dear and Glorious*

Physician. I remember that after I read *Raintree County* I had to go to bed for a day or two, to sort it all out. Luckily I often had pneumonia as a child, and got to stay in bed a lot anyway, which gave me time to read and make up stories in my head.

I wrote my first book on my mother's stationery when I was nine. It featured as main characters my two favorite people at that time: Adlai Stevenson and Jane Russell. The plot was that they went west together in a covered wagon, and once there they became—inexplicably—Mormons. Even at that age, I was fixed upon glamour and flight, two themes I returned to again and again as I wrote my way through high school, fueled by my voracious reading.

At Hollins College, I wrote about stewardesses living in Hawaii, about evil twins, executives, alternative universes. I ignored my teachers' instructions to write what you know. I didn't know what they meant. I didn't know what I knew. I certainly didn't intend to write anything about Grundy, Virginia.

But then Louis Rubin, my teacher, had us read the stories of Eudora Welty, and a light went on in my head. I abandoned my stewardesses, setting my feet on more familiar ground, telling simpler stories about childhood, though I was never able, somehow, to set the stories in those mountains I came from.

I guess I had done this once when I was young, now that I think about it. My best friend Martha Sue Owens and I had published a laboriously copied-out neighborhood newspaper named *The Small Review* in which we published newsworthy local events such as the following, from a 1954 issue: "Lee Smith and Martha Sue Owens went shopping at Kings Department Store in Bristol, Tennessee, to buy their school clothes. Lee Smith got to look at her feet through a machine to see if her shoes fit." And then the controversial editorial entitled "George McGuire Is Too Grumpy" for which I had to go and apologize to the neighbor across the street. Oh, yes, and a poem by me comparing life, capitalized, to a candle flame.

But I never *really* understood that the mountains could be a place for fiction until I encountered James Still—all by myself, pursuing the S's in the Hollins College library.

Here I found the beautiful and heartbreaking novel *River of Earth,* a kind of Appalachian *Grapes of Wrath* chronicling the Baldridge family's desperate struggle to survive when the mines close and the crops fail, familiar occurrences in Appalachian life. Theirs is a constant odyssey, always looking for something better someplace else—a better job, a better place to live, a promised land. As the mother says, "Forever moving yon and back, setting down nowhere for good and all, searching for God knows what. . . . Where air we expecting to draw up to?"

At the end of the novel, I was astonished to read that the family was heading for—of all places!—Grundy. "'I was born to dig coal,' Father said. 'Somewheres

they's a mine working. . . . I been hearing of a new mine farther than the head o'
Kentucky River, on yon side Pound Gap. Grundy, its name is.'"

I read this passage over and over. I simply could not believe that Grundy was
in a novel! In print! Published! Then I finished reading *River of Earth* and burst
into tears. Never had I been so moved by a book. In fact it didn't seem like a book
at all. *River of Earth* was as real to me as the chair I sat on, as the hollers I'd grown
up among.

Suddenly, lots of the things in my life occurred to me for the first time as
stories: my mother and my aunts sitting on the porch talking endlessly about
whether one of them had colitis or not; Hardware Breeding, who married his
wife, Beulah, four times; how my uncle Curt taught my daddy to drink good
liquor; how I got saved at the tent revival; John Hardin's hanging in the courthouse square; how Petey Chaney rode the flood.

I started to write these stories down. Twenty-five years later, I'm still at it. And
it's a funny thing: Though I have spent most of my working life in universities,
though I live in Chapel Hill and eat pasta and drive a Toyota, the stories that
present themselves to me as worth the telling are most often those somehow connected to that place and those people. The mountains that used to imprison me
have become my chosen stalking ground.

This is the place where James Still lives yet, in an old log house on a little
eastern Kentucky farm between Wolfpen Creek and Deadmare Branch. Still was
born in Alabama in 1906; went to Lincoln Memorial University in Cumberland
Gap, Tennessee, and then to Vanderbilt; and came to Knott County, Kentucky, in
1932 to "keep school" at the forks of Troublesome Creek. After six years, as he
likes to tell it, he "retired" and turned to reading and writing full-time. As one of
his neighbors said, "He's left a good job and come over in here and sot down."

Last summer he told me he had read an average of three hours a day, every
day, for over fifty years. His poetry and fiction have been widely published and
praised; his *Wolfpen Notebooks* came out in 1991 from the University Press of
Kentucky. In the preface to that fine collection of sayings and notes he has made
over all these years, Still says:

Appalachia is that somewhat mythical region with no known borders. If such an
area exists in terms of geography, such a domain as has shaped the lives and
endeavors of men and women from pioneer days to the present and given them
an independence and an outlook and a vision such as is often attributed to them,
I trust to be understood for imagining the heart of it to be in the hills of Eastern
Kentucky where I have lived and feel at home and where I have exercised as much
freedom and peace as the world allows.

This is an enviable life, to live in the terrain of one's heart. Most writers don't—can't—do this. Most of us are always searching, through our work and in our lives: for meaning, for love, for home.

Writing is about these things. And as writers, we cannot choose our truest material. But sometimes we are lucky enough to find it.

JANE
STUART

Resident of Greenup, Kentucky, Jane Stuart (b. 1942) graduated with a B.A. from Case Western Reserve University and a Ph.D. in Italian from Indiana University. Within the past few years several of her translations from Eugenio Montale's *La Bufera e Altro* have been published in *Oasis, Tampa Review,* and *Mother Tongues.* She is the author of numerous books of poetry, including *A Year's Harvest* (1957), *Eyes of the Mole* (1967), *White Barn* (1973), *The Wren and Other Poems* (1993), *Passage into Time* (1994), and *Cherokee Lullaby* (1995). She has also published several novels—*Yellowhawk* (1973), *Passerman's Hollow* (1974), and *Land of the Fox* (1975)—as well as the short story collection *Gideon's Children* (1976). *Transparencies,* her book of remembrances about her father, Jesse Stuart, was published in 1985. Recent work has appeared in *Poet's Challenge, Poetic Eloquence, Medusa's Hairdo, Pegasus,* and *Reflect.* One of her stories was just reprinted in the annual edition of *White River Quarterly.* She is listed with Poets & Writers, the British Library, and the International Biographical Center in Cambridge, England, and is a member of both the Kentucky State Poetry Society (KSPS) and the Academy of American Poets. In 1992 she won the KSPS grand prix for "From Winter Meditations" and in 1995, the *Poetry Forum* chapbook contest for *Moon over Miami.* Stuart is currently serving as regional director for the eastern district of KSPS.

* * *

This House and This World

I have found a world at home. Even when I traveled to other places, I wanted to remember things and bring them home with me. It's the eloquence of home that overwhelms me, and that I write about.

One evening long ago my father borrowed my watercolors, went out on a walk, and began painting. All my life I have tried to sketch and draw, but what I found I really could do was recall that evening—recall that evening with words, not paint. I still see the trees, his trees, and the moon.

Later I listened to people talk and absorbed words this way. When I went to school, I found myself searching to understand things that were taught to me as concepts, things I was told to read and explain. I think that I wanted to say something more, even then, and so I began constructing small odes, with words that fascinated me.

From the beginning I used words mainly to recall and understand the world I knew, the world that was close. Because I have always been able to name the moments and things of this world—of my world—that have meant something to me (and see them even more clearly as I age), I write about them every chance I get. For in them is my life, the world, the universe.

My dolls are still upstairs in the trunk. It's all right to narrow in and have a small world that may look no bigger than a dollhouse to someone else.

This is a family home I write about. The house, which was once a log cabin, is over a hundred years old. In fact, it is nearly 150 years old. It's covered with shingles and has four fireplaces; the flues and chimneys, when seen from outside in the backyard, remind me a little of the characters that "pop up" from the roof in Dylan Thomas's *Under Milkwood*.

Nestled in a valley are the house and outside rooms, with a creek running underneath. Behind us is Shinglemill Hollow, and across the road and near a salt block for the deer is what I used to call Breadloaf Hill. Split-rail fences run up and down the road, the fields are filled with hay that is cut and baled for cattle, and although I have added a satellite dish—we are modern—squirrels still run over the roof at night. Two years ago the wind blew part of a chestnut tree down, but three chestnut trees still stand on the hill behind the well.

There are ten rooms in the house with books in eight of them and three workrooms outside. My parents lived here. And now my grandson visits. My father worked in the kitchen, then the study or the workroom, then upstairs, then out-side. Sometimes he went to the ridge and worked at what was later known as Op's Cabin in his book *The Good Spirit of Laurel Ridge.*

The house is full of pictures, poems, and illustrations from my father's books. There is a beautiful print, *The Betrothal of Robert Burns and Highland Mary,* and a handwritten poem by Robert Burns given to my father on *This Is Your Life.* (I flew to California with an aunt and uncle to see my father recognized on this pro-gram.) My mother decorated the walls with baskets, made handmade rugs, and chose white ruffled curtains for the windows. In one bedroom are lace curtains from Belgium; I was with my mother when she purchased them. In the attic room is a quilt on a bed that once stood in my grandparents' home.

I prefer the comfort and stories of this home to an outside world. My study, desk, music, and small library of essential books are all I need. I work in a room next to a window where I have hung, outside, a bird feeder in a fir tree. I have had a typewriter for eight years now and am not happy when away from the simple machine that has adjusted to my hands and the pressure of my fingers.

I let the outside world crisscross with this more quiet one now and then. I sometimes borrow or buy books that are recommended to me. The *Princeton Encyclopedia of Poetry and Poetics* has been helpful; I have almost "memorized" Miller Williams's "Patterns of Poetry."

What I like best is working in this room while looking out the window. I some-times see deer in the yard and across the road at the salt block. At night, when I can no longer watch, the cat sits in the window and takes my place; I leave the radio on for her in the kitchen and she stands guard until morning.

Out that window are memories and objects that sustain me, and that sustain my writing. When I was a little girl my parents took me to New England to see the writers' homes. I loved Louisa May Alcott's house, and after seeing the win-dow where she had scratched her name with a diamond, I remember wanting to stay home and be a writer. I have learned the importance of returning home to our houses; of putting the world away so that we can see what we are and what we have become. I have learned the importance of windows. In my poem "Walnut Tree," I talk about this, talk about my return home to W-Hollow in Greenup, Kentucky:

Could you lend me five, I'm going home
into the land of foxes and lost thyme
where leaves are green
and lostness at my side.
The river has run dry.

The little home I carry with me
is the chalice you have offered.
Sweet forget-me-nots are dancing
on my face . . .

I have seen the world. I have traveled to Balbek and known deserts, sand, mountains, oases, rivers, and cities. I hold a master's degree in Greek and Latin and have earned a Ph.D. in Italian literature and written a dissertation about the love motif in the poetry of Eugenio Montale. I have studied Dante and Petrarch and translated verse. But I never really understood Dante until I took him home. "Cities are memory," I wrote in "Phoenicia." "Only sand remains, bees and scorching heat; / the blue of ocean repeats what never was." At home the day is full of more hours and things to be done than in a world that was once city and "strada facendo."

Out the window I see myself as a child again, drawing a little red wagon behind me. My sons later found that wagon, which was stored away. Now I have a grandchild and am thinking of taking out this wagon and painting it, again, bright red. The wagon appears in a prose piece called "Wildflowers" and jumpstarts my memory: "When I was a little girl my father and I both had little red wagons. We pulled them up and down the hills. He showed me how to curry the calves Ginger and Pepper. I had my own brush. I helped my mother hang clothes on the line, handing her clothespins and we hung the curtains together when she had ironed them."

I have studied myth, but only now am beginning to understand its place in my art and in my life. I taught Greek and Roman mythology but always suspected those fabled creatures who lived, danced, sang, or spoke were really only the subjects of real men's dreams. Myth, I came to learn, was just a way of trying to understand through religion and philosophy the things that we are searching for. Myth is what's outside my window in W-Hollow. Myth is trying to describe the tree, and to remember it.

There is an apple tree here on the hill in W-Hollow with apples that fall in the "well yard," as it is called. Down the road a way an old tree rests in the crevice between two sloping hills, and deer sleep in this opening and eat the apples from the old trees. In the yard where once there was a garden there is also a tree with small apples that can be gathered for cooking or left for the deer and for the groundhogs that live under the house and come out in the spring with their young.

My children have grown up but they can remain small with me at home. I can remember and laugh about when my younger son announced that he was going to grade school and when my older son hid in a tree so no one would see him. The image of my son in a tree stays at home when I write, even though my children are older and free now.

Looking into time is not impossible.
Simple things bring beauty,
softness and satisfaction;
the country line dance, words and trees
and stars that linger when
no stars are there. ["Forgetting Gemstones"]

Sometimes dreams mix with the visions outside my window. The garden swing I put in "Lithograph" was there. Or was it? I don't remember now, but I know I dreamed of having a swing like one I later saw on cards I bought and sent to people. So the dream, in some way, *is* part of my past.

Filled with beauty still, the unread picture
rests in its frame. Greens and myrtle hues,
an unwed limb, a branch of phlox, forsythia
are all blended in the little garden.

A swing relaxes underneath dark clouds,
a child sits at the mirror that is water
and an old, old gate swinging in the wind
is made of starch.

Rain is coming, stones are laughter,
the daffodils are singing.
Gently now a dove speaks of tomorrow
and all is gray.

I have noticed how powerful my attraction is to the objects of this world. Sometimes my words even form themselves into the things they describe or represent. Cats stretch across the lines and flowers show a hint of petal. Recently, in a poem for my grandson called "Joshua," I found myself shaping a flower basket, to give him something he could touch.

One soft morning reaches arms to sky;
earth is singing.
April gathers lemon clouds while stars
fill distant horizons.
You and I reach through a wilderness of hours
finding summer white
as chrysanthemums
in a silver
bowl
on a table leaning into sky.

> Time then is ours, one soft morning
>   dazzling us with song.

My attraction to music is just as strong—there is a piano here, there is a pump organ, I have a dulcimer, and there are records, tapes, and now CDs. I don't know exactly how the music enters in. I do not think I always have an "ear" for poetry. So music hasn't helped that way. Sometimes I do read my work aloud and catch an off-line or one in which the meter does not sound out quite right, but I don't like to pad or add a word just so a poem "sounds right." Rather than play music, I listen to it. I think this helps with my word selection, meter, and tone. But music, most of all, is memory.

> Two steps into the wilderness
> and I am coming back to you
>   so distant and aware
> of what I am now, once was
> And here we are in amber moments
> as fiddle touches chair . . . ["Fiddle in the Night"]

Music is the tune my past is set to. It is all fiddle touching chair.

If music is the tune to my past, the seasons are the backdrop. My favorite season has always been autumn when the leaves turn and colors crackle in the wind. I like the fresh, cool mornings that keep summer's mist and the memory of rain. I like winter because the snow reminds me of being a child, warm and cared for inside the house, looking through windows. As a child I touched the same window I look through now and with my fingers wrote my first words on that cold pane. I have dreamed of sitting by the fire, remembering embers, the soft glow of blue flames, and the smell of pinecones dusted with cinnamon.

When spring comes, you wake to violets and dandelion, the knowledge that warm sunlight will fill the creeks and trees across the road, and on the hill will soon be a patchwork of every shade of green. I long for whippoorwill then and think of fireflies that will come with summer, until summer itself finally arrives.

> A red fox leaps the sun,
> leaves turn into wind
> and night falls in shawls of indigo.
> Summer has piled the grass
> with baskets of oranges and flowers.
> The silk wings of butterflies beat on;
> Earth sleeps, the wind is rising. ["Summer"]

Of course Death is the final season for all of us, for poet and farmer and city dweller alike. But words have knit together life, time, places, faces, mystery, and always the memory of honeysuckle on a warm summer night. And the season of Death is diminished by that. My poem "Hurricane" is about this, I guess. There are brown leaves, ashes, reflections that encompass years gone by, the sun "break-ing like eggs," and the rain I have always loved. Death is a familiar item to a poet and writer, but the fable is perhaps silver which speaks, and there is, I hope, the serenity of someone drawing the seven of clubs so that we come home . . . to deer, the split-rail fence, and somehow always Dante.

Brown leaves have entered time.
Reflections fall to ashes, yesterday is nothing
but burnt moments and the caravan
is moving east, rifles and mirrors,
hanging curtains and feet moving
against the window. The dream is a
child's face, the woman is
all chain and mystery.
Against the horizon the sun breaks like eggs
and rain falls into ditches.
Sawdust is in the corridor and death is everywhere,
tears and no regrets—
Silver speaks, someone draws the seven
of clubs and we return
to our destiny of deer, the split-rail fence and
Dante.

ANDREW B. WEINBERGER

MEREDITH SUE WILLIS

Born in 1946 in Clarksburg, the county seat of Harrison County, West Virginia, and now living in South Orange, New Jersey, Meredith Sue Willis was recently honored for her significant contribution to letters at the Fourteenth Annual Literary Festival sponsored by Emory & Henry College. Her maternal grandfather, Carl Meredith, a coal miner, was an eyewitness to the great Monongah mine disaster of 1907, and her maternal grandmother, Pearl Barnhardt Meredith, was a sometime midwife in the mining camps of Marion and Harrison Counties. The Willis grandparents were store-keepers who followed store managerial positions with Consolidation Coal all over the Appalachian mountains. She grew up in an atmosphere of storytelling, preaching, and radio melodramas and published her first story at fifteen. She has won grants from the National Endowment for the Arts and the New Jersey State Council on the Arts, among other awards. Willis has several works of fiction including *A Space Apart* (1979), *Higher Ground* (1981), *Only Great Changes* (1985), *Quilt Pieces* (with Jane Wilson Joyce, 1991), *In the Mountains of America* (1994), *The Secret Super Powers of Marco* (1994), and *Marco's Monster* (1996). She is also an acknowledged authority on the teaching of writing, having published books with Teachers & Writers Collaborative in New York, including *Personal Fiction Writing* (1984), *Blazing Pencils* (1990), and *Deep Revision* (1993). Her books are used in writing classrooms throughout the nation.

*   *   *

An Inquiry into Who
My Grandmother Really Was

Soon after I moved into his apartment on the Lower East Side of Manhattan, my boyfriend, Andy—now my husband—started a grueling medical internship. He was on at the hospital every third night, and when he came home, he slept. I was working on a master of fine arts degree and trying to write a novel. At the end of that same summer of 1970, a friend of Andy's came to stay with us. This friend had dropped out of medical school and was trying to get himself back on track. Once he arrived, though, he sat around our apartment oozing depression, obviously lonely, clearly in trouble—suicidal, although we didn't realize it yet—and without any compunction about interrupting my writing.

Nothing in my life has ever made me angrier than the particular lack of respect I perceived at that period when people didn't take my writing seriously. I was largely unpublished, and my ego was so fragile that the slightest rejection sent me sheering into a tailspin. When our houseguest walked into the room where I was trying to write, sat on the extra chair, and said he was looking forward to the day my book got published so he could buy it for his wife, I practically screamed: "For your wife! For your wife! Do you think I write JUST for women?"

He was no fool. He said, "Oh, of course *I* want to read it too, I was just thinking, that way, I'd buy the book—it would be a gift for her—but I could read it too—"

I don't know if he was just talking his way out of trouble, or maybe actually fantasizing that somehow my book would help him reconnect with his wife, who was living in another state. Most likely he was merely making conversation to hear another human voice. He was a very damaged young man. Within a few months, he moved back into the medical school dorms, collected a supply of sleeping pills, and took his own life.

I felt guilty, as did Andy and all his other friends. Could we have done more? Had my pushing him away been the straw that broke the camel's back? I had been raised to be good in the First Baptist Church of Shinnston, West Virginia. I wanted to be loving to people around me—but I also wanted to write. There seemed to be a great abyss between Good Woman and Great Writer. I thought there might be a contradiction between being a woman and being a writer at all.

Part of my plan was to live in New York City. Part of my plan was to be nonnurturing, even ruthless and hard. Hadn't I refused to cook for our unhappy guest? Hadn't I willed myself to be *not just* a woman writer and certainly *not just* a regional writer? Nor was it a fantasy to think that regional, racial, and gender-identified artists are devalued in our culture. All the jokes and attacks about so-called political correctness seem to me part of a rear-guard action against the insistent voices of ignored people. It has long been assumed that women write for women, while men write for Man. That women's writing at its best is charming chamber music (think of how Jane Austen is typically praised), while men create great word symphonies (think of the literary stature of Henry James, a fine writer but surely a miniaturist). It is an unfortunate truism of children's publishing that books with male protagonists can be sold to an audience of boys and girls, but books with female protagonists have to be incredibly special for a boy to identify enough with the character to read it. It is also a truism of our culture that regional people and people of minority groups write for Their Own Kind.

And yet, for all my determination to be universal, the portion of my work during the 1970s that seemed richest and most promising centered on a little West Virginia girl's moral dilemma over being baptized when she wasn't sure she could remain good. The question of goodness—of propriety and rule-following as distinguished from honesty and integrity—has always engaged me. I approached these themes through writing about a specific, local act, which was this child's baptism: a northern West Virginia Baptist baptism of a believer, not an infant, by immersion, not sprinkling; indoors in a metal baptistery, not out-of-doors in a river.

I am grateful that some doggedly honest part of me stuck with this material, insisted on writing what honestly gripped me. Art only works when it is authentic. It can be political or personal, tightly structured or open-ended, didactic or romantically individual; it can be naturalistic, expressionistic, abstract, or some combination of all these, but it is a hollow exercise if it isn't authentic to the artist's experience.

My novel with the little girl's baptism in it, *A Space Apart,* received validation from the larger culture. It was published several years after completion, in 1979, by Charles Scribner's Sons, the New York publisher with the sterling backlist of Faulkner and Hemingway and other such cigar-and-whiskey icons of masculine narrative art. I sometimes wonder now if the editor acquired my novel for its universality or for some exotic charm she found in it. It is a passionate book, written with sufficiently mature craft, but its world was created from the vivid afterimages of childhood perception. I was writing out of a West Virginian experience, but I had very little historical or sociological knowledge of my region. My literary education had included the reading of English, European, and some Asian literature. My education in political and economic issues came from practical experience as an antipoverty worker in an urban setting and through struggles over the Vietnam War. But what I knew about Appalachia was personal and emotional. I wrote out of memory and imagination and did not feel the need for other knowledge.

I probably imagined vaguely that publishing *A Space Apart* would separate me even more from Appalachia. I expected to join a New York literary world of books, intellectual discourse, and famous writers. Like much of life, what actually transpired was not what I expected. I continued to live in New York, and I certainly had writer friends and a New York City life, but it centered on my work with Teachers & Writers Collaborative, a still active artists-in-education organization. The writers I knew were interested in transforming society via the public schools.

My second surprise was that Appalachia reclaimed me. Scribner's arranged West Virginia publicity tours for me in 1979 and again in 1981. To my delight, my writing and I were news. How many natives of New York or New Jersey or San Francisco get to go on the Noon News in their state's capital when they have a book published? I did—in Charleston, West Virginia. It's true that the interviewer referred to my book as the "one with the blue cover" and had never read it. During commercial breaks, he pumped me for connections to broadcasting in New York, but I didn't care. I was having a great time. I was on television! People from home were proud of me.

Of more lasting impact were the librarians and West Virginia writers I met. They invited me to give workshops and introduced me to Appalachian literature. I had not known, growing up in the 1950s, that we had writers, let alone a literature. I began tentatively to read books like *The Dollmaker* and a little of Mary Lee Settle's work and Davis Grubb's. I read some of the checkered history of King Coal and attended my first Harrison County West Virginia Italian Heritage Festival and discovered the complex ethnic history of my home state.

Enthusiastically, if a little nostalgically, I approached the Appalachia that had preceded me: the coal camps and company towns of Harrison and Marion County, West Virginia, where my parents had grown up, and the hollows of southwestern Virginia where my grandmother operated a general store. I recalled how, as a very young child, I had been aware of Wise County, Virginia, as my first real Place. The southwestern counties of Virginia are almost as separate in culture and history from the Old Dominion State as the politically distinct state of West Virginia. To me, though, as a child, what was important was my awareness of this Place as different from Home. Wise County, Virginia, had a character of its own. It had smells, speech patterns, landscapes, and folkways that were intensely, interestingly different to me.

A mythic version of that place, southwestern Virginia, is the setting for my very first published story, written around 1961, when I was fifteen. In that story,

"Billy and the Bridge," a family lives in isolation up on a mountain, and the son has a preternatural fear of the bridge they have to cross in order to get to town and the rest of the world. I wrote another story called "Irita Mullins," also about a young person who lives in isolation on a mountaintop and faces a life-and-death dilemma. In both of these stories I displaced a lot of psychological baggage about breaking free onto a setting made up of equal parts of memory and stereotypes of Appalachian life that I had picked up from popular culture.

Those early stories, psychologically acute but stereotypical in their portrayal of Appalachia, were written in the early 1960s. I was an adult when I began *A Space Apart* ten years later. By that time, although I was far more sensitive to the damage that stereotypes do, I still knew little historically about the Appalachian region. After the publication of *A Space Apart* in 1979 and *Higher Ground* in 1981, however, when my new friends in West Virginia began my Appalachian education, I began to draft some stories using the new material I was searching out. These stories, written throughout the 1980s and the first half of the 1990s, were collected in my 1994 book, *In the Mountains of America.*

The emotional heart of this book was my real-life grandmother Mae Glass Willis, the storekeeper. I envisioned her as a widow in her mid-fifties, arms crossed over her chest, wearing an apron and housedress, hair still brown and tied in a bun at the nape of her neck, standing in her store on Middle Fork at Bold Camp, up the road from Pound, Virginia, over the mountain from Wise. She sold Pepsi and lunchmeat to the coal truck drivers who pulled their behemoths up to her door at midday. In winter, she carried coal from the shed, stoked up her Warm Morning stove. In my memory, her beds have feather bolsters and quilts of her own piecing. On her screened back porch are pecks and bushels of tomatoes and potatoes and apples and sometimes government surplus cheese that her customers used to give her in lieu of cash. She seems, in my imagination, as much a part of that place as the steep mountain drops, the vegetation crowding every ditch, and the whining songs from the Free Will Baptist Church across the creek.

This image of my grandmother became the point at which I could tap into my roots and write about the Appalachian region. She was the one with the earthy humor, who had seen me at ten in my new yellow nylon nightgown and said, "Well look at that, you're getting titties!" She joked about how country men like their women big because "they keep you warm in the winter and shady in the summer," and she told how, when she was a girl, no one took baths in winter. You just washed "as far as possible," and when spring came, then you washed "Possible" too.

In "My Boy Elroy," first published in 1983, I played with the stories she used to tell and honed my own storytelling skills. At her kitchen table, in the rooms where she lived in back of the store, *she* told stories. From the moment we arrived after the ten hours of snake-coil roads from West Virginia into Virginia, even as she put out pie for a snack before supper, even while my mother put the baby to sleep, Nannie would release her narratives. She seemed to need to tell my father the entire story of everything that had happened to her since our last visit.

Some years after that story was published, Professor Jack Wills of Fairmont State College in Fairmont, West Virginia, wrote a paper about "My Boy Elroy" and Flannery O'Connor's classic of evil and grace, "A Good Man Is Hard to Find." Professor Wills made me aware of something I had missed in my own story that led me to another look at my real-life grandmother. I knew that my story was partly a literary response to O'Connor and partly about storytelling, but Professor Wills also called attention to the fictional grandmother's attitudes toward some of her poor neighbors. He called her "sympathetic but socially pretentious."

This observation set me back a little. It was a side of my grandmothers (both real-life and fictional) that I had never noticed. To my mind, both grandmothers were earthy and plucky, a little proud, but not snobbish. Yet the grandmother in the story does have an attitude toward the poor Possett family that is unattractive at best, and I could, in retrospect, remember similar attitudes in my real-life grandmother. I think I had created the Possett family to deserve revulsion—to be immutably, even mythically, ugly and stupid. They were throwbacks to the stereotypical Mullins family in my adolescent story "Irita Mullins." But Professor Wills suggested that the social position of the Possett family in my story had a sociohistorical context, and that my grandmother's pretensions might too.

I had a hint of what might lie behind my fictional Possetts very recently, on a 1995 reading tour—my first visit to Wise County, Virginia, in nearly thirty years. During that visit, I began to read about a somewhat mysterious, or at least little-documented, subgroup of Appalachians known as the Melungeons. They were often despised and isolated and may have been unconscious models for the Possett family. More interesting to me and possible future writing projects is that I also suspect that the Willises (the family my grandmother married into) may, like many families in that part of the world, have Melungeon roots. ("Not me!" said my father when I broached this idea. "And even if *you* turn out to be a Melungeon, I'm not! That Melungeon stuff skips a generation!")

My grandmother wasn't very interested in sociohistorical contexts. She didn't discuss ethnic identity and cultural diversity. How people behaved and what they accomplished were her measures. And according to my father, she would not have been flattered by my portrait of her in "My Boy Elroy." My father said of the story, "Well, it's good, but I'm just as glad Mother didn't live to read it." I was hurt, because I had thought of the story as a monument to her—my first story written in light of my new interest in my region and my roots. I asked my father what was wrong with the story, and he repeated that it was a good story, but just not how she saw herself.

That conversation and the later remarks of Professor Wills fueled my efforts to remember other sides of my grandmother. My writing may have needed a grandmother with her hair parted in the middle and gathered back in a bun, but my real-life grandmother had her hair cut, permed, and set professionally. I might have wanted a homespun linsey-woolsey grandma, but my real-life Nannie had a wardrobe of dresses made of jersey and lawn with elegant little prints, polka dots, and tiny florals. These dresses had self-belts and decorative buttons, and she wore them with hats, pumps, stockings, and gloves. They were the church dresses of women of her age and generation, women who liked their maturity, whose ideas of beauty and propriety were closely blended.

I think my grandmother, and other women of her generation—the ones who had enough money to buy false teeth when theirs fell out—liked being older. And, yes, I think they recognized the advantages of widowhood as well. When my grandmother was young, she had to follow my grandfather wherever Consolidation Coal Company sent him. She fired up the inefficient stoves the company provided and baked biscuits every morning and washed clothes and babies' diapers by hand. As a widow, she could eat cold cereal and toast for breakfast or have a slice of leftover pie for supper.

Only after the book publication of my Appalachian short stories did my father give me a vital piece of missing information. "You know," he said one day, "Mother never wanted to leave West Virginia." It seems that it was his father who wanted to go south, back to Virginia. I was stunned: I had been so taken with my vision of her, even with the emendation of the ladylike dresses, that this was hard to believe. She hadn't wanted to go run the store and listen to the country people tell stories? She had preferred the gentility of the small-town ladies of northern West Virginia to storytelling in the hollows of southwestern Virginia? Didn't she want to be my mountain granny?

No, she didn't. She went south in 1948 because Papa Willis wanted to own a store. He wanted to go back to Bold Camp, where they had lived when they first married, where he had taught school and briefly owned a small store, where my own father was born. My grandfather, the company's man for thirty years, wanted a business of his own, back in the mountains where he had been a young man full of hope. But within two years of the move, he was dead, and she was left alone in four cheaply built rooms behind the store. She had running water, but it was so hard with minerals that you had to collect rainwater to do the wash.

Other things came back to me, and I thought about her at Bold Camp in the 1950s when she was running the store and I was a little girl visiting her. There was Evening in Paris cologne on her vanity. She had the first electric blanket I ever encountered. She subscribed to the Reader's Digest Condensed Books. Her two-tone Pontiac, cream and burnt orange, stayed in the garage except for Sundays when she put on stockings and heels, gloves and a hat, and went out for dinner with Fletcher Baker.

Fletcher was her boyfriend. She had known him from the first time she lived at Bold Camp. In fact, he and his wife stood up for her and Papa Willis at their wedding. He lived on Baker Mountain with his sons and their families and drove an unregistered four-wheel-drive Jeep. A kindly man, good-humored and good-hearted, he came courting in a gray suit and bow tie, and I believe my grandmother stayed at Bold Camp at least partly because of him. They courted; he was her "friend-boy"; they traveled together down to Tennessee to visit my aunt and my grandmother's sister. He shoveled coal for her, she cooked an occasional meal for him. But she never came close to marrying him. I don't think this was snobbishness. True, she described him as "just an old farmer" but said it coquettishly, as if being an old farmer were a sign of cleverness or virility. Having him as an escort and boyfriend was part of her freedom. Having another husband would have been the opposite.

Here is an outline of my grandmother's life: born in a tiny farming community in Virginia where everyone knew everyone and everyone was related. Her cousins and her future husband's siblings and cousins filled the schoolroom and church. A cousin ran the post office. An uncle taught the school. When she was six years old, her father ran away with the hired girl to Arkansas. Everyone knew this. Her adult sister sided with her mother; her brothers said their mother drove him to it. Her mother married a widower named Creed McPherson whose kids went to the same country school as my grandmother and her future sister-in-law.

She went away to a finishing school for half a year. At eighteen, she married my grandfather and started following his jobs to Bold Camp, Virginia; Jenkins and Burdine, Kentucky; Coeburn, Virginia; Owings, West Virginia. After years in company housing, they finally rented a house in Shinnston, a town with a high school and a bank and a restaurant and a yellow brick First Baptist Church with stained glass windows next door to a red brick First Methodist Church, also with stained glass windows. A streetcar line led south to the county seat and north to the county seat of the next county, where there was a teacher's college. I imagine that it must have felt expansive and substantial to her, living in north-central West Virginia. I imagine the refinement we make fun of today—the white gloves and scrutinizing eyes of the dowagers—was not restrictive to her but instructive. Fine distinctions added an aesthetic dimension to her life. She was happy to stay in Shinnston where she called the ladies Mrs. Burnett and Mrs. Hardesty, and they called her Mrs. Willis. Where there were big hills and farms at the end of the town streets, and mines over the hill. Where the frame houses in town had porches and swings and front yards with flowers and backyards with vegetables.

But she did what was called for, uprooted herself once more and followed

Papa Willis back to the high hollows of Bold Camp in southwestern Virginia, to the small, roughly built country store. Why did she stay after he died, barely two years later? Perhaps she wanted to make a living so she wouldn't be dependent on her children who were just starting families. She may also have been tired of moving, or faithful to Papa Willis's dream of independence and entrepreneurship. Maybe she was too proud to retrace her steps, or maybe she believed in the American adage that you can't go home but must always forge ahead. At some point, her attachment to Fletcher was part of it. She may also have been proud to discover that her skills in housewifery transferred to storekeeping. Possibly (she was known to be tight with her money) there was simply too much "on the books"—debts owed by customers. In the end, I think, however much she may have preferred the gentility and community of ladies in Shinnston, she also liked the particular freedom and status of being a widow storekeeper in the mountains. I think she was at home in those sharply ridged, beautiful southwestern Virginia mountains, that she found a place there. She was welcomed, she was admitted. She filled a need for her neighbors for manufactured goods and a place to congregate.

What most interests me now about her life is what I left out of the stories she inspired. My grandmother was, in the end, neither an exile from gentility nor some mythmaker's mountain granny—not even mine. She was from the mountains, and she returned to the mountains, but the terms were her own. She was a storekeeper. She was a woman who subscribed to book clubs and made loans to her children. She owned a two-tone Pontiac and was proud of her slim, nyloned ankles. Her high heels and pocketbooks matched, and she hired a local boy to fly her in his private plane to her granddaughter's high school graduation.

She was, with all her complexities and contradictions, an Appalachian woman of the twentieth century.

Works Cited

Lisa Alther: Border States

Kennedy, N. Brent, with Robyn Vaughan Kennedy. *The Melungeons: The Resurrection of a Proud People: An Untold Story of Ethnic Cleansing in America.* Macon, Ga.: Mercer Univ. Press, 1994.

O'Connor, Flannery. *Mystery and Manners.* New York: Farrar, Straus, and Giroux, 1961.

Sherman, Sarah Way. *Sarah Orne Jewett: An American Persephone.* Hanover, N.H.: Univ. Press of New England, 1989.

Maggie Anderson: The Mountains Dark and Close around Me

Anderson, Maggie. Introduction to *Hill Daughter: New and Selected Poems,* by Louise McNeill. Pittsburgh: Univ. of Pittsburgh Press, 1991.

Doty, Mark. *Atlantis.* New York: HarperCollins, 1995.

McNeill, Louise. *The Milkweed Ladies.* Pittsburgh: Univ. of Pittsburgh Press, 1988.

Rukeyser, Muriel. *The Life of Poetry.* 1949. Reprint, Ashfield, Mass.: Paris Press, 1996.

Thoreau, H.D. *H.D. Thoreau: A Writer's Journal.* Selected and edited by Laurence Stapleton. 1855. Reprint, New York: Dover, 1960.

Marilou Awiakta: Sound

Awiakta, Marilou. *Abiding Appalachia: Where Mountain and Atom Meet.* Memphis: St. Luke's Press, 1978. Reprint, Bell Buckle, Tenn.: Iris Press, 1995.

———. *Selu: Seeking the Corn-Mother's Wisdom.* Golden, Colo.: Fulcrum, 1993.

Kathryn Stripling Byer: Deep Water

Byer, Kathryn Stripling. *Alma.* Cullowhee, N.C.: Phoenix, 1983.

Chappell, Fred. *Farewell, I'm Bound to Leave You.* New York: Picador USA, 1996.

Mathis, Linda. "Darling of My Heart." *Nomad* (Western Carolina University Art and Literary Magazine), 1982.

Miles, Emma Bell. *The Spirit of the Mountains.* 1905. Reprint, Knoxville: Univ. of Tennessee Press, 1975.

Milosz, Czeslaw. *Selected Poems.* New York: Ecco, 1980.

Smith, Lee. *Oral History.* New York: G.P. Putnam's, 1983.

Lou V.P. Crabtree: Paradise in Price Hollow

Crabtree, Lou. *Sweet Hollow.* Baton Rouge: Louisiana State Univ. Press, 1984.

doris diosa davenport: All This, and Honeysuckles Too

Brown, Edward K., II. "An Interview with Ntozake Shange." *Poets & Writers* 21, no. 3 (May/June 1993).

Hilda Downer: Mutant in Bandana

Eliot, T.S. "Tradition and the Individual Talent." In *The Sacred Wood: Essays on Poetry and Criticism.* London: Methuen, 1920.

Wilma Dykeman: "The Past Is Never Dead. It's Not Even Past."

Faulkner, William. *Requiem for a Nun.* New York: Random House, 1951.

Sidney Saylor Farr: Women Born to Be Strong

Farr, Sidney Saylor. *Headwaters.* Blacksburg, Va.: Pocahontas, 1995.

Gail Godwin: Uncle Orphy

Godwin, Gail. *A Mother and Two Daughters.* New York: Viking, 1982.

Terrell, Bob. "A Testimony to Good Living." *Asheville Citizen,* 21 October 1977.

Ellesa Clay High: The Standing People

High, Ellesa Clay. *Past Titan Rock: Journey into an Appalachian Valley.* Lexington: Univ. Press of Kentucky, 1984.

Lisa Koger: Writing in the Smokehouse

Carr, Virginia Spencer. *The Lonely Hunter: A Biography of Carson McCullers.* New York: Doubleday, 1975.

Solotaroff, Ted. "Writing in the Cold." In *Pushcart Prize XI,* edited by Bill Henderson. New York: Penguin, 1987.

George Ella Lyon: Voiceplace

Coleman, Mary Joan. *Take One Blood Red Rose.* Cambridge, Mass.: West End Press, 1978.

Howard, Lee. *The Last Unmined Vein.* Washington, D.C.: Anemone Press, 1980.

Lyon, George Ella. *Come a Tide.* New York: Orchard Books, 1990.

———. *Mountain.* Hartford, Conn.: Andrew Mountain Press, 1983.

———. *Who Came Down That Road?* New York: Orchard Books, 1992.

Mason, Bobbie Ann. "Signature by Bobbie Ann Mason." Kentucky Educational Television, first aired April 23, 1996.

Whitman, Walt. "Song of Myself." In *Leaves of Grass.* 1855. Reprint, New York: Doubleday, 1940.

Sharyn McCrumb: Keepers of the Legends

Dann, Kevin. *Traces on the Appalachians: A History of Serpentine in America.* New Brunswick, N.J.: Rutgers Univ. Press, 1988.

McCrumb, Sharyn. *The Hangman's Beautiful Daughter.* New York: Scribner, 1992.

———. *If Ever I Return, Pretty Peggy-O.* New York: Scribner, 1990.

———. *The Rosewood Casket.* New York: Dutton, 1996.

———. *She Walks These Hills.* New York: Scribner, 1994.

Pasteur, Louis. Address given on the inauguration of the Faculty of Science, University of Lille, France, Dec. 7, 1854.

Pinero, Arthur Wing. *The Second Mrs. Tanqueray.* Boston: W.H. Baker, 1894.

Sutherland, Elizabeth. *Ravens and Black Rain: The Story of Highland Second Sight.* London: Constable, 1985.

LLEWELLYN MCKERNAN: Letter from a Poet in West Virginia

McKernan, Llewellyn. *Short and Simple Annals: Poems about Appalachia.* Huntington, W. Va.: West Virginia Humanities Council, 1983.

ELAINE FOWLER PALENCIA: Leaving Pre-Appalachia

Barker, Garry. "Gone Too Long." *Appalachian Heritage* 21, no. 4 (fall 1993).

RITA SIMS QUILLEN: Counting the Sums

Quillen, Rita. *Counting the Sums.* Abingdon, Va.: Sow's Ear Press, 1995.

Tate, Allen. "The Profession of Letters in the South." In *The Literature of the South,* edited by Thomas Daniel Young and Floyd C. Watkins. Glenview, Ill.: Scott, Foresman, 1968.

Wolfe, Thomas. *Look Homeward, Angel.* New York: Scribner, 1929.

JEAN RITCHIE: The Song about the Story—The Story behind the Song

Ritchie, Jean. "Drowsy Sleeper." In *Singing Family of the Cumberlands.* Oxford: Oxford Univ. Press, 1955. Reprint, Lexington: Univ. Press of Kentucky, 1988.

———. *Folk Songs of the Southern Appalachians.* New York: Oak Publications, 1965. Second ed., Lexington: Univ. Press of Kentucky, 1997.

Unseld, B.C. "Twilight A'Stealing." Music by A.S. Kieffer. From *The Practical Music Reader.* Dayton, Va.: Ruebush-Kieffer, 1904.

BETTIE SELLERS: Westward from Bald Mountain

Reece, Byron Herbert. Untitled. In "Country Voices," by Russell Lord. *Progressive Farmer* 61, no. 6 (June 1945).

Sellers, Bettie. *Liza's Monday and Other Poems.* Boone, N.C.: Appalachian Consortium Press, 1986.

———. *Morning of the Red-Tailed Hawk.* University Center, Mich.: Green River Press, 1981.

———. *Spring Onions and Cornbread.* Gretna, La.: Pelican, 1978.

———. *Westward from Bald Mountain.* Privately published, 1974.

———. *Wild Ginger.* Atlanta: Morning Glory Ink, 1989.

LEE SMITH: Terrain of the Heart

Still, James. *River of Earth.* New York: Viking Press, 1940. Reprint, Lexington: Univ. Press of Kentucky, 1978.

———. *The Wolfpen Notebooks.* Lexington: Univ. Press of Kentucky, 1991.

JANE STUART: This House and This World

Stuart, Jane. "Fiddle in the Night." *Block's Poetry Collection* 5 (summer 1995).

———. "Lithograph." *Muse Odyssey Orbital News* 11 (April/May 1994).

———. *Moon over Miami* [chapbook]. Erie, Penn.: Poetry Forum Press, 1995.

MEREDITH SUE WILLIS: An Inquiry into Who My Grandmother Really Was

Wills, Jack C. "Meredith Sue Willis's 'My Boy Elroy': 'A Good Man Is Hard to Find' with a Difference." Paper presented at the spring meeting of the West Virginia College English Teachers, April 3, 1993.